Documenting the
Software
Development Process

Related Books

ISBN	AUTHOR	TITLE
0-07-157788-2	Dixon	*Winning with CASE: Managing Modern Software Development*
0-07-040235-3	Marca	*SADT: Structured Analysis and Design Technique*
0-07-032813-7	Jones	*Applied Software Measurement: Assuring Productivity and Quality*
0-07-044119-7	Musa	*Software Reliability*
0-07-157879-X	Sodhi	*Software Requirements Analysis and Specification*
0-07-042632-5	Modell	*A Professional's Guide to Systems Analysis*
0-07-055663-6	Schulmeyer	*Zero Defect Software*
0-07-002603-3	Ayer/Patrinostro	*Software Configuration Management: Identification, Accounting, Control, and Management*

Documenting the Software Development Process

A Handbook of Structured Techniques

Steve Ayer

Frank Patrinostro

McGraw-Hill, Inc.

New York St. Louis San Francisco Auckland Bogotá
Caracas Lisbon London Madrid Mexico Milan
Montreal New Delhi Paris San Juan São Paulo
Singapore Sydney Tokyo Toronto

Library of Congress Catalog Card Number 91-44934

1 2 3 4 5 6 7 8 9 0   DOC/DOC   9 8 7 6 5 4 3 2

ISBN   0-07-002604-1

The sponsoring editor for this book was Jerry Papke, the editing supervisor was Joseph Bertuna, and the production supervisor was Suzanne W. Babeuf.

Printed and bound by R.R. Donnelley & Sons Company.

Contents

Chapter 3. Software Development Analysis Documentation 101

Preface

The successful implementation of information systems is contingent on three factors: people, technology, and procedures. Organizations which effectively blend these elements are rare enough that we read about them in our trade journals. Managers often point to the lack of qualified personnel or the lack of money to acquire new technologies as the causes for delays or failed development efforts. However, even when new personnel or technologies are acquired, they find themselves unprepared to implement the technologies or to adequately integrate the new skills.

This book addresses the procedures which can both enable an organization to maximize the existing human and technical resources, and position itself for the integration of new technologies. We focus on the documentation aspect of systems development because it defines measurable completion points within the systems development process. With a predefined deliverable, we can estimate the time to create it, and measure our performance against that estimate.

Predefined deliverables are established within the context of a systems development methodology. Many analysts and programmers reject out of hand the forced structure of a methodology. These same people, however, are demanding better tools with which to do their jobs. Key among these tools are the CASE technologies. Organizations which have implemented these technologies have found, however, that they are unsuccessful without first enforcing a standard development methodology. Some of the integrated CASE tools, in fact, enforce a development methodology in order to use them.

The document structures and methods presented in this book can be adopted as presented. However, our intent in presenting these structures is to provide a model and a starting point from which an organization can customize the document structures and the methodology to fit their needs. We have included alternatives for each of the documents presented and a chapter on integrating a systems development methodology with CASE. We recommend a JAD-like approach to customizing the methodology and defining the detailed deliverables suitable to your environment. This approach has the advantages of bringing ownership of the methodology to the people who will use it, and of fitting the methodology to the environment.

Acknowledgments

The numerous people and companies we have worked with in system development and documentation projects have all contributed to the ideas presented in this book.

In addition, the many people who participated in seminar programs which we presented helped to flesh out the concepts. We would specifically like to thank Dr. Kenneth Bonnet for his efforts in using these concepts to create an automated systems documentation package based on these ideas. We would also like to thank Jerry Papke, senior editor at Tab/McGraw Hill for his work in making this book a reality.

Steve Ayer
Frank Patrinostro

Chapter 1
Introduction

Integrated systems documentation theory, of course, has been in existence for more than three decades. During this period, systems development managers have become increasingly aware that a computer system cannot be completely effective unless it is adequately documented and that *it should be documented as the system is being developed, not retrospectively.* Unfortunately, many analysts and programmers who regard documentation as a necessary evil have been slow to accept the integrated concept of development and documentation as a way of life. These individuals, however, tend to be naive and inexperienced in managerial skills such as record keeping, which is essentially the function of documentation.

In recent years, systems development methods have undergone dramatic changes with the emergence of *computer-aided software engineering (CASE)* tools and a growing acceptance of structured concepts of systems planning and development. Because documentation is the essential deliverable product of the systems development process, it is only fitting that a book be written that correlates a systems development methodology with the functions performed by documentalists in preparing task and phase end-documentation.

We will begin the dissertation by defining four terms that are referred to throughout this book: *systems development methodology (SDM), tasks deliverable, phase end-document,* and *document item.* Simply stated, a *systems development methodology (SDM)* is defined as the process of breaking the work to be performed into manageable phases, tasks, and task steps. A *task deliverable* is the record of accomplishment that describes the result of each task performed during the phase development of a computer system. An *end-document* is the vehicle of communication that cumulates and arranges the task deliverables of each phase for presentation (in either manual or electronic form) to a particular audience. Here the work of a technical writer usually comes into play. *Document item* is defined as either the aggregation of the elements that comprise a specific deliverable document or the subset of a phase end-document (e.g., section, subsection, paragraph, etc.). The identification of each document item is a prerequisite to the application of software configuration management, a subject dealt with by the authors in a separate work.

This book presents a structured approach to systems development and views the creation of documentation as a combined effort of systems planners, analysts, programmers, and technical writers.

1

1.1 FORWARD PLANNING

The development of automated data processing systems cannot be allowed to result from chance or the enthusiasm of users and systems developers. Unless forward planning is done, and unless project requests can be evaluated against established criteria, the goals of the systems development effort will probably not be realized.

Forward planning involves first determining protocols for systems development and management, and then creating documents that clearly define policy, methods, standards, and procedures to guide the systems development process. These documents, properly disseminated, can serve as a system of checks and balances for the information and opinions that are generated in the course of the software development effort.

The planning function should direct the gathering of information and the performance of tasks for each phase of the software development life cycle – from project initiation through implementation and maintenance. Chapter 2 examines a variety of planning and management documents and suggests techniques for their editorial preparation. The documentation orientation of forward planning is illustrated in Figure 1-1.

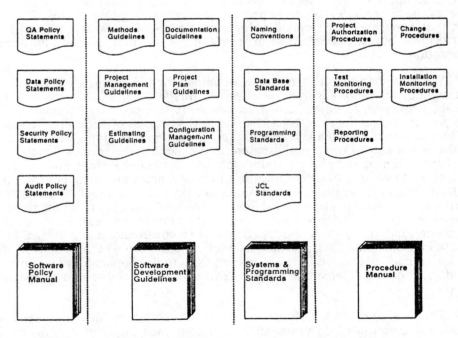

Figure 1-1. Documentation Orientation of Forward Planning

1.2 SYSTEMS DEVELOPMENT METHODOLOGY

A *systems development methodology* (*SDM*) is a set of mutually supportive and integrated guidelines organized into a series of chronological phases that make up the development cycle of a computer system. A well-organized SDM should provide step-by-step descriptions of the tasks to be performed for each phase and should identify the end-items that are deliverable to the project file.

The documentation orientation of an SDM should be viewed at two levels: *task documentation*, which provides a record of accomplishment through which progress can be measured, and *phase documentation*, which synthesizes and reorganizes the task documents for presentation to a particular audience. The SDM may be expanded upon by developing a handbook that provides a general guide for determining the content arrangement of the various document types that must be produced during the development life cycle (see 1.3, *Documentation Standards*).

Numerous SDM packages are available commercially, and hundreds of companies have chosen to develop their own methodologies for development and documentation in-house. Almost all these methodologies, commercial and home-grown, are structured with definable life cycle phases and end-of-phase documents that are generated as by-products of each activity. Some methodologies provide work planning checklists and structures for recording task results. Others provide hard-copy form structures. Still others present screen formats that can be used by documentalists to record tasks results. The more comprehensive methodologies include documentation guidelines that describe the precise nature of the content of phase end-documents that must be produced. A study of these methodologies, however, will quickly reveal an inconsistency in the breakdown and timing of life cycle phases. For example, one methodology may refer to a *feasibility study,* while another may call the same *assessment analysis*. Regardless of these differences, all methodologies essentially provide step-by-step procedures for the performance of

- *Analysis tasks* aimed at determining the feasibility and establishing the functional requirements of a proposed system
- *Design tasks* aimed at establishing specifications for systems development
- *Programming and testing functions* required for program design, coding, and debugging and
- *Implementation tasks* required to place the system in an operable mode

1.2.1 Life Cycle Phases

Although the breakdown and terminology of life cycle phases differ from methodology to methodology, there has been at least partial agreement that the phased development of a computer system should revolve around four traditional concepts of science and engineering: *study, design, program,* and *implement.* The phased approach to systems development presented in this book breaks the four basic functions into nine phases to form the basic system life cycle as illustrated in Figure 1-2. Each phase is a self-contained component of the systems development process.

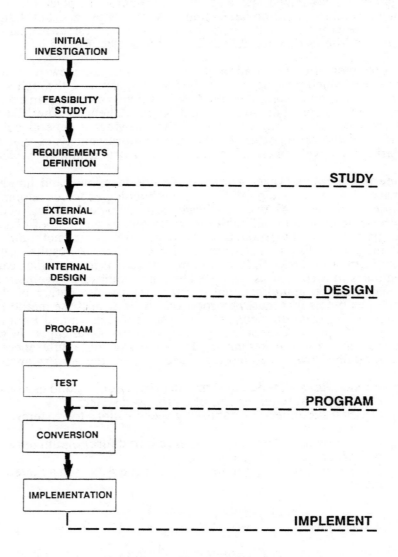

Figure 1-2. Life Cycle Phases

The primary tasks for each phase of the system life cycle are outlined on the following pages.

Phase 1. Initial Investigation Task Guidelines

The *initial investigation* phase centers around six primary tasks as noted below. Each task consists of a functional group of activities that may be assigned to specific members within the project team.

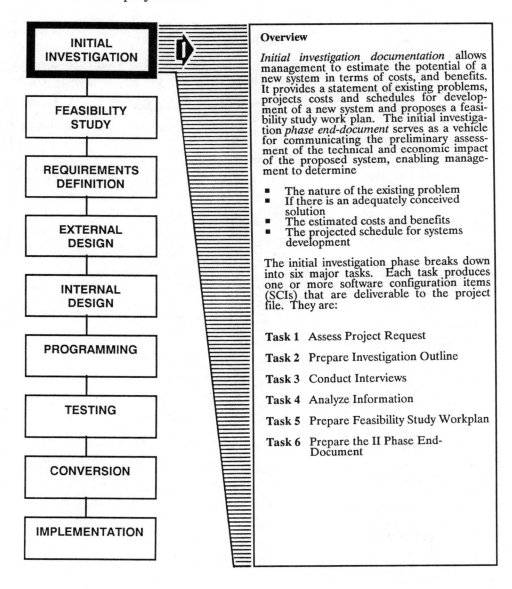

Overview

Initial investigation documentation allows management to estimate the potential of a new system in terms of costs, and benefits. It provides a statement of existing problems, projects costs and schedules for development of a new system and proposes a feasibility study work plan. The initial investigation *phase end-document* serves as a vehicle for communicating the preliminary assessment of the technical and economic impact of the proposed system, enabling management to determine

- The nature of the existing problem
- If there is an adequately conceived solution
- The estimated costs and benefits
- The projected schedule for systems development

The initial investigation phase breaks down into six major tasks. Each task produces one or more software configuration items (SCIs) that are deliverable to the project file. They are:

Task 1 Assess Project Request

Task 2 Prepare Investigation Outline

Task 3 Conduct Interviews

Task 4 Analyze Information

Task 5 Prepare Feasibility Study Workplan

Task 6 Prepare the II Phase End-Document

Phase 2. Feasibility Study Task Guidelines

The *feasibility study* phase centers around seven primary tasks as noted below. Each task consists of a functional group of activities that may be assigned to specific members within the project team.

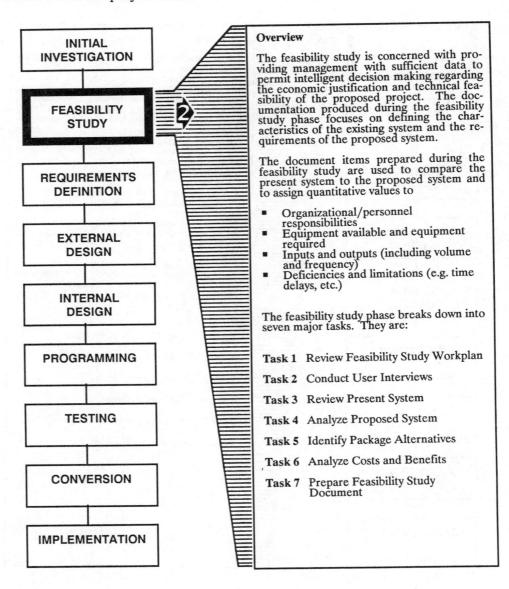

INITIAL INVESTIGATION

FEASIBILITY STUDY

REQUIREMENTS DEFINITION

EXTERNAL DESIGN

INTERNAL DESIGN

PROGRAMMING

TESTING

CONVERSION

IMPLEMENTATION

Overview

The feasibility study is concerned with providing management with sufficient data to permit intelligent decision making regarding the economic justification and technical feasibility of the proposed project. The documentation produced during the feasibility study phase focuses on defining the characteristics of the existing system and the requirements of the proposed system.

The document items prepared during the feasibility study are used to compare the present system to the proposed system and to assign quantitative values to

- Organizational/personnel responsibilities
- Equipment available and equipment required
- Inputs and outputs (including volume and frequency)
- Deficiencies and limitations (e.g. time delays, etc.)

The feasibility study phase breaks down into seven major tasks. They are:

Task 1 Review Feasibility Study Workplan

Task 2 Conduct User Interviews

Task 3 Review Present System

Task 4 Analyze Proposed System

Task 5 Identify Package Alternatives

Task 6 Analyze Costs and Benefits

Task 7 Prepare Feasibility Study Document

Phase 3. Requirements Definition Task Guidelines

The *requirements definition* phase centers around nine primary tasks as noted below. Each task consists of a functional group of activities that may be assigned to specific members within the project team.

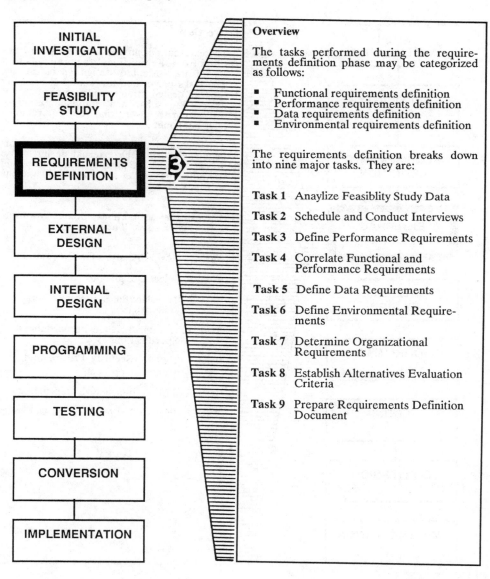

INITIAL
INVESTIGATION

FEASIBILITY
STUDY

REQUIREMENTS
DEFINITION

EXTERNAL
DESIGN

INTERNAL
DESIGN

PROGRAMMING

TESTING

CONVERSION

IMPLEMENTATION

Overview

The tasks performed during the requirements definition phase may be categorized as follows:

- Functional requirements definition
- Performance requirements definition
- Data requirements definition
- Environmental requirements definition

The requirements definition breaks down into nine major tasks. They are:

Task 1 Anaylize Feasiblity Study Data

Task 2 Schedule and Conduct Interviews

Task 3 Define Performance Requirements

Task 4 Correlate Functional and Performance Requirements

Task 5 Define Data Requirements

Task 6 Define Environmental Requirements

Task 7 Determine Organizational Requirements

Task 8 Establish Alternatives Evaluation Criteria

Task 9 Prepare Requirements Definition Document

Phase 4. External Design Task Guidelines

The *external design* phase centers around seven primary tasks as noted below. Each task consists of a functional group of activities that may be assigned to specific members within the project team.

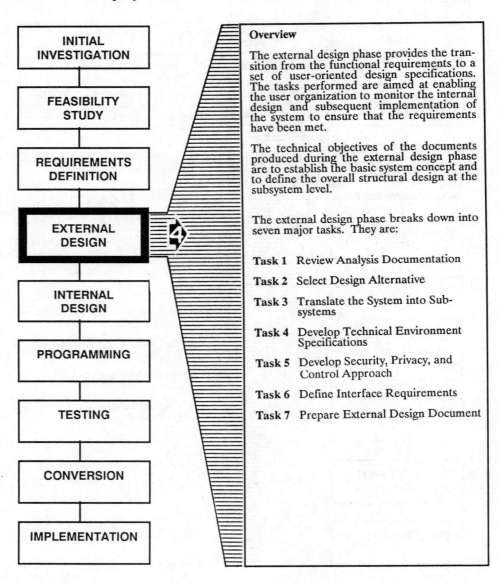

Overview

The external design phase provides the transition from the functional requirements to a set of user-oriented design specifications. The tasks performed are aimed at enabling the user organization to monitor the internal design and subsequent implementation of the system to ensure that the requirements have been met.

The technical objectives of the documents produced during the external design phase are to establish the basic system concept and to define the overall structural design at the subsystem level.

The external design phase breaks down into seven major tasks. They are:

Task 1 Review Analysis Documentation

Task 2 Select Design Alternative

Task 3 Translate the System into Subsystems

Task 4 Develop Technical Environment Specifications

Task 5 Develop Security, Privacy, and Control Approach

Task 6 Define Interface Requirements

Task 7 Prepare External Design Document

The flowchart shows the following phases:
INITIAL INVESTIGATION
FEASIBILITY STUDY
REQUIREMENTS DEFINITION
EXTERNAL DESIGN
INTERNAL DESIGN
PROGRAMMING
TESTING
CONVERSION
IMPLEMENTATION

Phase 5. Internal Design Task Guidelines

The *internal design* phase centers around nine primary tasks as noted below. Each task consists of a functional group of activities that may be assigned to specific members within the project team.

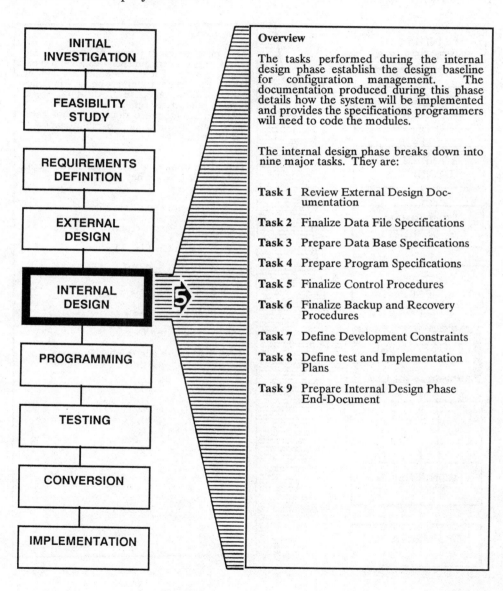

INITIAL INVESTIGATION

FEASIBILITY STUDY

REQUIREMENTS DEFINITION

EXTERNAL DESIGN

INTERNAL DESIGN

PROGRAMMING

TESTING

CONVERSION

IMPLEMENTATION

Overview

The tasks performed during the internal design phase establish the design baseline for configuration management. The documentation produced during this phase details how the system will be implemented and provides the specifications programmers will need to code the modules.

The internal design phase breaks down into nine major tasks. They are:

Task 1 Review External Design Documentation

Task 2 Finalize Data File Specifications

Task 3 Prepare Data Base Specifications

Task 4 Prepare Program Specifications

Task 5 Finalize Control Procedures

Task 6 Finalize Backup and Recovery Procedures

Task 7 Define Development Constraints

Task 8 Define test and Implementation Plans

Task 9 Prepare Internal Design Phase End-Document

Phase 6. Programming Task Guidelines

The *programming* phase centers around eight primary tasks as noted below. Each task consists of a functional group of activities that may be assigned to specific members within the project team.

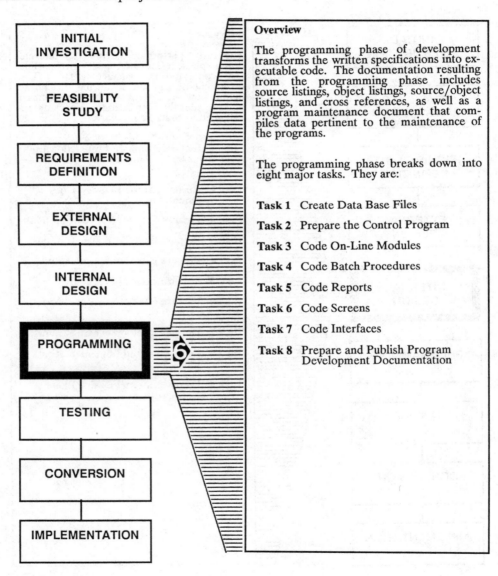

INITIAL INVESTIGATION

FEASIBILITY STUDY

REQUIREMENTS DEFINITION

EXTERNAL DESIGN

INTERNAL DESIGN

PROGRAMMING

TESTING

CONVERSION

IMPLEMENTATION

Overview

The programming phase of development transforms the written specifications into executable code. The documentation resulting from the programming phase includes source listings, object listings, source/object listings, and cross references, as well as a program maintenance document that compiles data pertinent to the maintenance of the programs.

The programming phase breaks down into eight major tasks. They are:

Task 1 Create Data Base Files

Task 2 Prepare the Control Program

Task 3 Code On-Line Modules

Task 4 Code Batch Procedures

Task 5 Code Reports

Task 6 Code Screens

Task 7 Code Interfaces

Task 8 Prepare and Publish Program Development Documentation

Phase 7. Testing Task Guidelines

The *testing* phase centers around seven primary tasks as noted below. Each task consists of a functional group of activities that may be assigned to specific members within the project team.

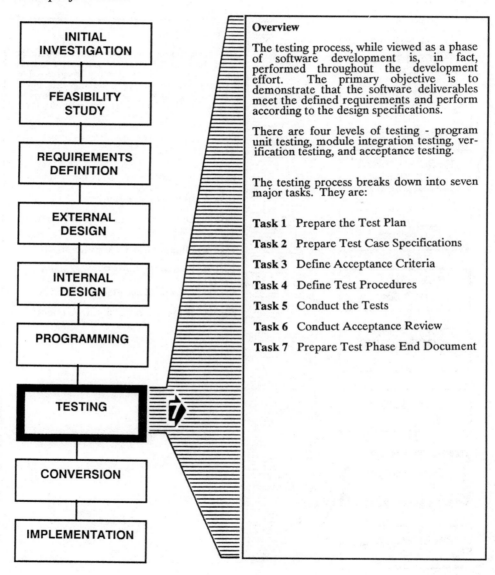

Overview

The testing process, while viewed as a phase of software development is, in fact, performed throughout the development effort.   The primary objective is to demonstrate that the software deliverables meet the defined requirements and perform according to the design specifications.

There are four levels of testing - program unit testing, module integration testing, verification testing, and acceptance testing.

The testing process breaks down into seven major tasks. They are:

Task 1 Prepare the Test Plan

Task 2 Prepare Test Case Specifications

Task 3 Define Acceptance Criteria

Task 4 Define Test Procedures

Task 5 Conduct the Tests

Task 6 Conduct Acceptance Review

Task 7 Prepare Test Phase End Document

Phase 8. Conversion Task Guidelines

The *conversion* phase centers around seven primary tasks as noted below. Each task consists of a functional group of activities that may be assigned to specific members within the project team.

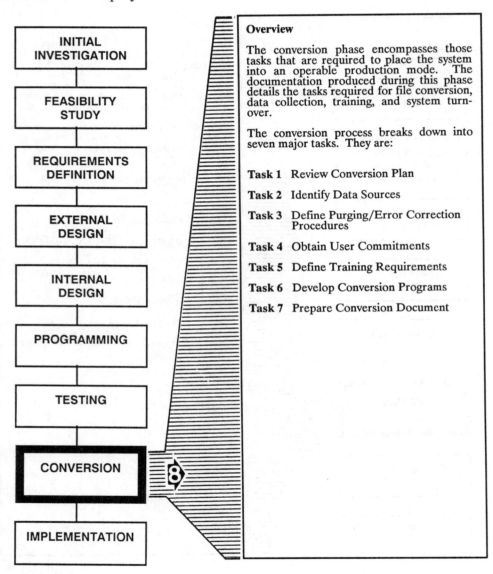

Overview

The conversion phase encompasses those tasks that are required to place the system into an operable production mode. The documentation produced during this phase details the tasks required for file conversion, data collection, training, and system turnover.

The conversion process breaks down into seven major tasks. They are:

Task 1 Review Conversion Plan

Task 2 Identify Data Sources

Task 3 Define Purging/Error Correction Procedures

Task 4 Obtain User Commitments

Task 5 Define Training Requirements

Task 6 Develop Conversion Programs

Task 7 Prepare Conversion Document

Phase 9. Implementation Task Guidelines

The *implementation* phase places the system into operation. It includes finalizing and distributing user and operations documentation, placing the appropriate files into production, and initiating the system operation.

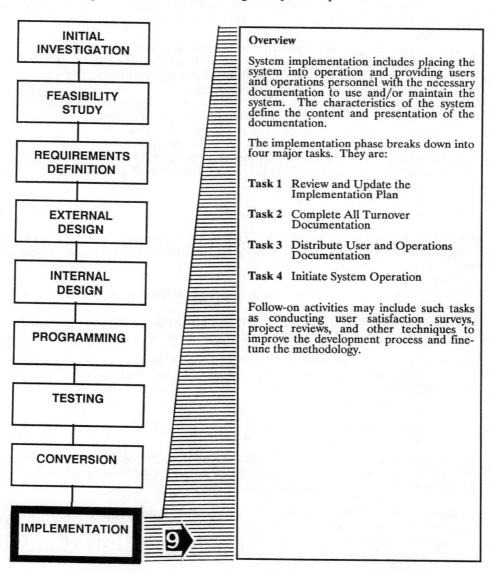

INITIAL INVESTIGATION

FEASIBILITY STUDY

REQUIREMENTS DEFINITION

EXTERNAL DESIGN

INTERNAL DESIGN

PROGRAMMING

TESTING

CONVERSION

IMPLEMENTATION

9

Overview

System implementation includes placing the system into operation and providing users and operations personnel with the necessary documentation to use and/or maintain the system. The characteristics of the system define the content and presentation of the documentation.

The implementation phase breaks down into four major tasks. They are:

Task 1 Review and Update the Implementation Plan

Task 2 Complete All Turnover Documentation

Task 3 Distribute User and Operations Documentation

Task 4 Initiate System Operation

Follow-on activities may include such tasks as conducting user satisfaction surveys, project reviews, and other techniques to improve the development process and fine-tune the methodology.

1.3 DOCUMENTATION STANDARDS

The effective development and implementation of a documentation system is contingent, to a great extent, on the establishment of sound documentation standards. Documentation standards should be established that specify the document items that should result from each task, identify the phase end-documents to be produced, and define the content of each document. The objectives of such standards are

- To provide project managers with documents to review at significant development milestones so that they can determine if the functional requirements are being met and whether the project warrants the continued expenditure of financial resources
- To record the results of tasks performed during a particular phase of development in a manner that allows coordination of later development and use/modification of the system
- To ensure that documentation managers and technical writers have a guide to follow in preparing computer systems documentation
- To provide for uniformity of the format and content of presentation

1.3.1 The Documentation Manager

The primary role of the documentation manager in document planning is to ensure that a documentation plan is developed for each systems development project that defines

- Which document types should be produced and their appropriate level of detail
- The dates that these documents must be delivered
- The quality assurance procedures to be followed

The documentation manager is also responsible for conducting periodic reviews to ensure that all documents are being prepared in accordance with established standards and schedules.

1.3.2 The Technical Writer

The responsibility for preparing a systems development document rests with the technical writer. The writer of any one of the document types discussed in this book must ensure that he/she has an understanding of

- The relationship between the various document types produced during the systems development life cycle
- The overall content requirement of the document to be prepared
- The audience for whom the document is intended

The collection of data relevant to the preparation of a particular document type requires that the writer have sufficient business and technical experience to gather quantifiable information. He or she must apply value judgments in order to determine the applicability of the information to the content specifications prescribed by established documentation standards.

1.3.3 Review and Maintenance

The logical step to ensure accuracy and completeness in a particular systems document is to subject that document to a formal management review prior to publication. The reviewers must answer the following questions:

> Did the writer interpret the information correctly?
> Is the presentation complete and accurate?
> Does the document convey the information it was intended to convey?

Document reviews may be conducted at various stages during the development process (i.e., periodic, milestone, phase, etc.). Additionally, the publications manager should provide continuous surveillance to ensure that the documentation process is accomplished in accord with guidelines and standards for documentation preparation and control.

1.3.4 Timeliness

The preparation of documentation within time and cost constraints requires an effective time management scheme. Delays in delivering required documentation can translate directly into delays in project completion.

The preparation of documentation is often identified as a function separate from the systems development process. This gives the erroneous impression that the work of the documentalist does not begin until the development activities are completed. In fact, documentation should be considered an ongoing function of the development process, whereby the results of the tasks performed are recorded as the system is being developed, not retrospectively. It should be recognized by all personnel involved in the development effort that documentation is an integral part of their job function.

1.3.5 Redundancy

Documentation standards for content development of systems documents often show a certain amount of redundancy. For example, introductory material may be included with each document type to provide a frame of reference as to how to use the document. Such information is generally included to provide stand-alone documents with a minimum amount of need for cross reference. Redundancy is also apparent insofar as most document types specify that a description of inputs and outputs, a program summary, and the like, be included. The actual information included for each of these items in the various document types, however, is different. The information is intended to be read by different audiences and must, therefore, be written in the terminology appropriate to each audience.

1.3.6 Security and Controls

Controlling the dissemination of systems documentation is another prime consideration in document planning. Each of the document types produced during the system life cycle should provide information that explains any security requirements that may exist. When applicable, the limitations and restrictions pertaining to certain documentation should be explained. The procedures for gaining access to controlled documentation that is not included in a specific document should be detailed; and when applicable, the controlled sources of documentation should be identified and cross-referenced.

1.3.7 Management Options

In chapter 7 we examine various management options for document preparation. These options are summarized in the following paragraphs.

Determination of Document Types. All of the document types discussed in this handbook may not be needed on a particular project. The determination of which document types should be produced is generally the responsibility of the project manager. The level of complexity of the system to be documented is generally the essential determinant. Basic factors for determining project complexity include the following:

- The level of originality required
- The degree of generality
- The span of operation (e.g., local, worldwide, etc.)
- The complexity of the equipment (single computer, routine processing, extended peripheral system, etc.)
- Programming tools and utilities available
- Systems development methodology
- The number and experience of both user and MIS personnel
- Development costs
- Criticality of the system
- Average response time to program changes
- Average response time to data inputs
- Programming languages
- Concurrent software development

Based on the complexity rating determined by the project manager, the types of documentation to be produced are then defined and scheduled for production.

Sizing of Document Types. Each of the content alternatives outlined in this book may be used to prepare documents that range from a few to several hundred pages in length. The magnitude and complexity of the project to be documented will determine the overall size. The level of detail to be included in each document should be determined by the documentation manager in consultation with the project manager. Another factor to be considered in determining document size is the environment in which the system will operate. As a general rule, each section within a given document type bears a relationship to the other sections of that document in its percentage of volume.

Combining or Splitting Document Types. It may be necessary in some operational environments to combine two or more document types into a single volume. Conversely, it is sometimes appropriate to split the contents of a specific document type to produce several different manuals. For example, an internal design document may include a program specification section, or the program specifications may be published in a separate volume. The primary factors governing decisions relative to combining or splitting a specific document type are the size of the document and the needs of the document audiences.

Divisions, Headings, and Numbering. Each of the content alternatives presented in a documentation standards manual should establish requirements and guidelines for

- Division of systems manuals into parts, sections, subsections, and paragraphs
- Numbering of these divisions
- Selection of titles, headings, and sub-headings for the various sub-divisions

Systems manuals are organized into divisions and subdivisions to make the information easy to understand, find, and correlate with the systems development process. The usual divisions of a systems manual are:

Front matter
Parts
- Chapters
- Sections
- Paragraphs
- Illustrations/tables and charts
- Subparagraphs
Appendixes
Glossary
Index

As a general rule, there should be at least two of each division used. For example, if there is a Part I, there should be a Part II; if there is a Chapter 1, there should be a Chapter 2; if there is a Section 1, there should be a Section 2, etc.

Preparation of Documents. The document items that record the results of tasks performed during the development cycle of a computer system are generally intended as deliverables to a project file. The decision as to whether to accumulate these documents and publish them as a compilation of phase documentation must be made by the appropriate managers. Since the requirements for documentation vary widely depending on the management techniques employed by both the MIS and user groups for whom the documentation is intended, the decision to produce formal documents will vary. For example, when the user group is also the development group, the approach to serving audience communications needs will be entirely different than when these two groups function as separate entities.

Graphic Presentation. Schematic and functional diagrams sometimes play a critical role in documenting an application system. Properly drawn and organized, these diagrams help the systems designers and programmers do the job more quickly and more efficiently by making the data easier to locate, understand, and use. Thus, the planning of a documentation system requires the following actions on the part of those responsible for documentation preparation:

- The determination of where flowcharts, tables, action diagrams, etc., are needed
- The selection of the proper form of presentation
- The establishment of standards for the -preparation and presentation of graphic representations

The Narrative Approach. A common approach to document preparation is the narrative outline approach. This approach uses a free-form text narrative based on a standard outline. When the narrative approach is used, various aspects of text preparation must be considered during the document planning process. Some of the salient principles which are especially important are summarized below.

Preparation for writing. The technical writer must first analyze the writing task, collect source material, and organize the information collected to coincide with a standard outline.

Determining user reading levels. A systems manual can be effective only if it uses words and ideas the reader understands. Unfamiliar terms and abbreviations may be necessary at times for precision and clarity, but they must be thoroughly explained.

Development of text. Text in a narrative approach to documentation must be carefully prepared so as to be as easy as possible to read and understand. Each paragraph must be limited to a single idea; sentences to a single thought; and words to those which are short and familiar.

The Forms Approach. A second approach to document preparation that must be considered in planning a documentation project is the forms approach. This approach revolves around the use of prestructured forms for all components and items of documentation. Each form is intended for use in a specific section or subsection of a particular document type. The forms cover a wide range of systems development functions and can be formatted to present all types of documentation (e.g., descriptive narratives, flowcharts, table content descriptions, logic and algorithms, layouts and facsimiles, screen displays, etc.). Instructions may accompany each form to assist the technical writer in preparing phase documents.

The forms approach to documentation has many advantages. They provide for uniformity of format and consistency of content throughout the system development cycle. The predetermined tables of contents can serve as automatic *checklists* of the documentation to be included in a particular document type. They provide a measure of control for ensuring the completeness of required documentation. Clerical and support staff can be used to prepare phase end-documents, thus relieving programmers and analysts from the burden of end-document preparation. Moreover, documentation can be prepared concurrently with the systems development effort, not retrospectively.

The On-Line Approach. Both the narrative approach and the forms approach summarized in the preceding paragraphs may be adapted to an on-line approach to documentation. Numerous word and text processing systems are available to facilitate adapting the narrative approach to documentation to an on-line system. Packages such as Page Maker, Interleaf, DCF, and Ventura Publisher have broad capabilities for document formatting, text editing, page composition, and graphics design. In combination with laser printer technologies, these and other software tools can produce near-typeset-quality output and page mechanicals that can be used for conventional printing of systems manuals.

In adapting the forms approach, specific considerations may include the development of a menu-driven documentation system that enables the technical writer to call up screen structures that can be used for document preparation. For example, a main menu may be designed that shows all of the document types that correlate with a specific project. The technical writer could select from the main menu the specific document to be prepared. On command, a primary task menu could be displayed. This menu, in turn, could identify the content structure for the selected document type. On selection of the applicable menu item, a subtask menu could be called up which lists the sections and subsections of the document and which enables the writer to call up a screen format that can be used for on-line document preparation. As a final step, a print option can allow the recorded data to be output in a hard-copy form. Of course, the documentation prepared in electronic form can also be presented electronically. The user documentation, for instance, may be included as context sensitive help screens within the application being documented. This requires that the documentation be incorporated as part of the system design. Context sensitive help screens are increasingly being used in on-line systems to facilitate access to system documentation.

1.4 USING MENUS AND SCREENS

In this chapter we shall present an overview of a menu-driven methodology that provides screen structures for recording task results and preparing task deliverables. The cumulation of task deliverables resulting from this process may be used to prepare phase end-documents that range from a few to several hundred pages in length. The size, of course, will depend on the magnitude and complexity of the project, the opinion of the project manager as to what level of detail should be included, and other factors. Instructions for performing the tasks and subtasks that comprise the SDM are arranged to facilitate *branching.* The methodological approach may be viewed as the branching of a tree. The tree has a *trunk* (the Phase Selection Menu), *large branches* (the Primary Task Menus), *smaller branches* (the Subtask Menus), perhaps *smaller branches still* (Information/Instruction Screens), and *leaves* (screen formats to record the task results). The end-item deliverables prescribed by the methodology may be correlated with the *fruit* of the tree. Most of the tasks and subtasks prescribed can be accomplished in four "jumps" or less - from the *Phase Selection Menu* to the *Primary Task Menu* to the *Subtask Menu* to the *Task Record Screen.* The process is described and illustrated below.

1.4.1 The Phase Selection Menu

The system begins with the Phase Selection Menu. The menu shows the SDM life cycle phases and provides for selecting the desired phase.

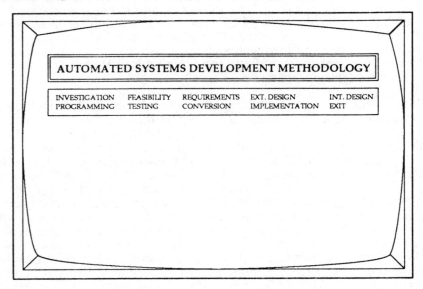

In addition to the phase selections, the menu provides an Exit option for returning to DOS.

1.4.2 The Primary Task Menu

After the appropriate life cycle phase has been selected, the display switches to the Primary Task Menu which shows all the tasks that comprise the selected phase.

Example:

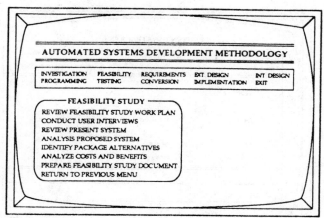

1.4.3 The Subtask Menu

The menu path from the *Primary Task Menu* then takes the user to a *Subtask Menu* which lists the task steps and provides options for selection.

Example:

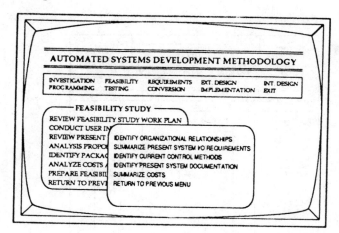

In some instances, the options on the *Subtask Menu* will lead to a *Sub-Subtask Menu* which further breaks down the task steps to be performed.

1.4.4 The Task Record Screen

After completing the work to be performed for a given task or subtask, the user calls up the prescribed *Task Record Screen* to record the task results.

Example:

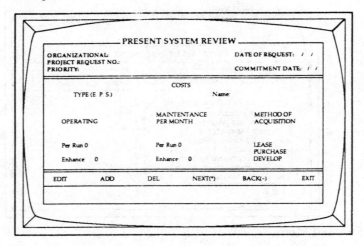

1.4.5 Printing the Task Record

A print option is provided to print the task records on computer-generated structured forms that correlate with the data on the task record screens.

Example:

Company Name/Logo	SYSTEM NAME FEASIBILITY STUDY		PAGE: REL. DATE: REV. DATE:				
Section 1.0 – PRESENT SYSTEM REVIEW							
1.11 COST							
EQUIPMENT/SOFTWARE	OPERATING		MAINTENANCE PER MO.		METHOD OF ACQUISITION		
	PER RUN	PER MONTH	ROUTINE	ENHANCEMENT	LEASED	PURCHASE	DEV'PT
EQUIPMENT System 34 Disk Drive	$ 50	$ 500	$ 1000 100				
SOFTWARE DB Security MUSM 1			500 500				
STORAGE DISK–DYSAM MAG. TAPES			150 150				

1.4.6 Instruction/Information Screens

The automated documentation system includes a variety of screens that provide special instructions or information that relate to a specific task or task step. Examples of these screens are shown below.

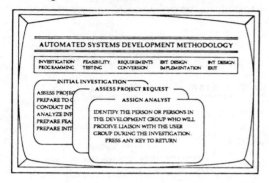

Administrative Task Instructions

This category of screens provides instructions for performing *administrative* tasks that are essential to carrying out the tasks and task steps prescribed by the SDM.

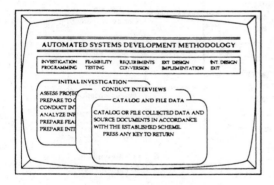

Project Control Instructions

This category of screens provides instructions for performing *project control functions* prescribed by the SDM that do not require a document deliverable.

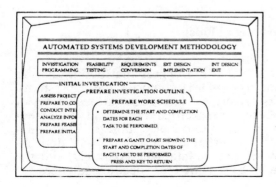

Manual Task Instructions

This category of screens provides instructions and information related to the preparation of physical end-items prescribed by the SDM that must be generated manually.

1.5 THE DOCUMENTATION DATA BASE

An *automated documentation system* may be defined as a set of input and output subsystems which communicate with each other via a data base to provide user and development personnel with documentation needed at all levels of the system development process. Figure 1-3 depicts the subsystem model for the automated documentation system proposed in this book.

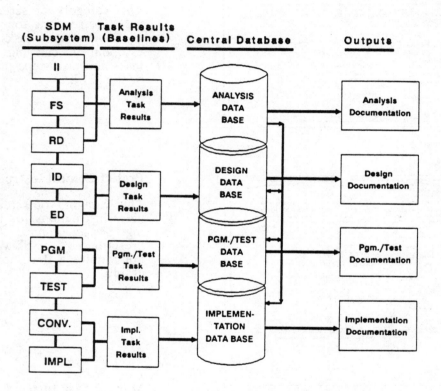

Figure 1-3. Subsystem Model

In reviewing the above model, we can see that the phases that define the life cycle of the systems development methodology (SDM) comprise the subsystems. The composite of task results from the tasks performed during the various phases of the development effort form the analysis, design, program and test, and implementation baselines. The central data base is subdivided into major subsets. These subsets are analysis data base, design data base, program and test data base, and implementation data base. The four data bases are maintained separately, and the data are manipulated to produce document types intended for specific audiences.

1.5.1 Data Base Management System

A key element in the design of data bases for an automated documentation system is, of course, the selection of a *data base management system* (*DBMS*). The DBMS software that specifies how data may be structured controls all access to the data. In this model, a DBMS is required that facilitates both a functional and a hierarchical integration of the subsystem data bases. Functional integration will allow one subsystem to share data in its data base with another subsystem (e.g., the subsystem concerned with the preparation of test procedures may draw data from the subsystem data base concerned with the preparation of requirements definition documents). Hierarchical integration will permit the same records and/or data elements to be used at more than one level in the development process (e.g., details of screen data elements required for programming may be sorted and synthesized to prepare summary data element listings for project management).

1.5.2 Subsystem Files

As previously indicated, each phase of the SDM is defined as a file. Each data base consists of two or more files. The task results of a particular task or a task step are assembled into a record. Each record is comprised of data elements. All of the records resulting from the series of tasks performed during a specific phase of the system life cycle constitute a file. The aggregate of the files for a given project comprise the project repository. Although each subsystem is structrured in a manner compatible to generating a particular type of document, a high degree of interaction exists between the subsystems and the central data base subsets. Some of the tasks performed during the requirements definition phase, for example, are amplified during the external design phase. In this event, data may be drawn from one data base, entered into another data base, and recycled to generate updated documentation. Thus, the data relevant to a given task may be passed from one data base to another. In fact, many of the data entered into the program and test data base are drawn from data that reside in the analysis and design data bases. Virtually all of the data in the implementation data base are drawn from data that reside in the other data bases.

The following paragraphs identify the files associated with each subsystem and the records contained within each file.

Analysis Task Results Data Base. The files and records resulting from the analysis activities are stored within the analysis data base. The files which comprise the analysis data base are

- Initial investigation documentation file
- Feasibility study documentation file
- Requirements definition documentation file

The three data bases jointly form the functional baseline for configuration management. Table 1-1 shows the records contained in each of these files.

Table 1-1. Analysis File Records

Data Base File	File Records
Initial Investigation	Problem and Need Statement Preliminary Costs Analysis Target Schedules Present System Review Proposed System Requirements Applications Package Review Economic Evaluation
Feasibility Study	Present System Schematic Organizational/Personnel Responsibilities Equipment Requirements List of Programs List of Inputs List of Outputs Data Base/File Summary Summary of Controls Documentation Index Cost Index Proposed System Schematic Statement of Objectives Summary of Improvements ▪ New Capabilities ▪ Upgrading Existing Capabilities Summary of Impacts ▪ Equipment Impacts ▪ Organizational Impacts ▪ Operational Impacts ▪ Development Impacts Assumptions and Constraints List of Available Packages Benefit Statement Cost Report
Requirements Definition	Statement of Baseline Purpose Project References Terms and Abbreviations Security and Privacy Accuracy and Validity Requirements Timing Requirements Failure Contingencies Fallback Contingencies Restart Contingencies

Table 1-1. **Analysis File Records** (*continued*)

Data Base File	File Records

Requirements Definition (*continued*)	Equipment Requirements
	Support Software Requirements
	Interface Requirements
	Security and Privacy
	Control Requirements
	Data Descriptions
	  ▪ Static System Data
	  ▪ Dynamic Input Data
	  ▪ Dynamic Output Data

1.5.3 Design Documentation Data Base

The files and records resulting from the design activities are stored within the design data base. The files which comprise the design data base are

- External design documentation file
- Internal design documentation file

    Table 1-2 shows the records contained in each of these files.

Table 1-2. **Design File Records**

Data Base File	File Records

External Design	Statement of Purpose
	Project References
	Application Package/Chosen
	  Alternative
	Terms and Abbreviations
	System Schematic
	System Functions
	System Input Data/Source Documents
	System Input Data/Record/
	  Transaction Content
	System Input Data/Table Content
	System Input Data/File Content
	System Input Data/Input from Other
	  Systems
	Processing Logic/Input Processing

Table 1-2. Design File Records (*continued*)

Data Base File	File Records
External Design (*continued*)	Processing Logic/Data Base/File Processing Processing Logic/History File Processing Processing Logic/Table Processing Processing Logic/Output Processing Output Descriptions/Document Forms Output Descriptions/Screen Formats Security and Privacy Controls Hardware Considerations Software Considerations Performance Criteria/Acceptance Response Time Performance Criteria/System Up Time Window Backup Considerations Hardware Interfaces Software Interfaces
Internal Design	Purpose of the Internal Design Project References Index of Programs Index of Files Index of Outputs Terms and Abbreviations Input Document Formats Input Screen Formats Output Document Formats Output Screen Formats Data Base Specifications/ Summary Data Base Specifications/ Labeling and Tagging Conventions Data Base Specifications/Data Base Organization Data Base Specifications/Special Instructions Data Base Specifications/File Layouts Data Base Specifications/Table Layouts Data Base Specifications/Record Layouts Program Specifications/Support Software Environment

Table 1-2. Design File Records (*continued*)

Data Base File	File Records

Internal Design (*continued*)	Program Specifications/Interfaces
	Program Specifications/Storage
	  Requirements
	Program Specifications/Program
	  Design/Detail Summary
	Program Specifications/Program
	  Design/Logic Flow
	Program Specifications/Program
	  Design/Initialization/Sign On
	Program Specifications/Program
	  Design/Operator Messages
	Program Specifications/Program
	  Design/User Messages
	Program Specifications/Program
	  Design/Job Setup
	I/O Controls
	User Controls
	Data Base/File Controls
	Access Controls
	Error Controls
	Audit Trails
	Backup Procedures
	File Retention Procedures
	Restart Procedures
	Constraints/Operating Time Window
	Constraints/Hardware
	Constraints/Software
	Constraints/Communications
	Test Plans
	Implementation Plans
	Maintenance Plans
	Documentation Plans

1.5.4 Program and Test Documentation Data Base

The files and records resulting from the program and test are stored within the program and test data base. The files which comprise the program and test data base are:

- Program performance specification documentation file
- Program design specification documentation file

- Program description documentation file
- Program package documentation file
- Test plan documentation file
- Test procedure documentation file
- Test report documentation file

Table 1-3 shows the records contained in each of these files.

Table 1-3. Program and Test File Records

Data Base File	File Records
Program Performance Specifications	Purpose Scope Reference Program Description Peripheral Equipment Descriptions Input/Output Utilization Interface Block Diagram Interface Program Interfaces Function N/Inputs Function N/Processing Function N/Outputs Function N/Special Requirements Test Requirements Acceptance Test Requirements
Program Design Specifications	Purpose Scope References Function Allocation/Input Functions Function Allocation/Output Functions Storage Allocation Processing Allocation Functional Flow Diagram Programming Guidelines Peer Review Procedures Period Review Procedures Technical Review Procedures Configuration Audit Procedures
Program Description	Purpose Scope References Subprogram Detailed Description Subprogram Data Design/Arrays

Table 1-3. Program and Test File Records (*continued*)

Data Base File	File Records
Program Performance Specifications	Subprogram Data Design/Variables Subprogram Data Design/Constants Subprogram Data Design/Flags Subprogram Data Design/Indexes Subprogram Data Design/Common Data Base References Input Formats Output Formats Library Subroutines Conditions for Initiation Subprogram Limitations Interfacing Description
Program Package	Purpose Scope References Source Program Object Program Source Listing Source/Object Listing Cross-Reference Listing Record Layouts Data Dictionary Subprogram References Subprogram Flowcharts

Test Plan	Purpose
	Scope
	References
	Unit Test/Task Responsibility Checklist
	Unit Test/Monitoring Methods
	Unit Test/Test Software Requirements
	Unit Test/Schedule
	Unit Test/Test Environment
	   Requirements
	Unit Test/Test Cases
	Module Integration Test/Task
	   Responsibility Checklist
	Module Integration Test/Monitoring
	   Methods
	Module Integration Test/Test Software
	   Requirements
	Module Integration Test/Schedule

Table 1-3. **Program and Test File Records** (*continued*)

Data Base File	File Records
Test Plan (*continued*)	Module Integration Test/Test Environment Requirements Module Integration Test/Test Cases Verification Test/Task Responsibility Checklist Verification Test/Monitoring Methods Verification Test/Test Software Requirements Verification Test/Schedule Verification Test/Test Environment Requirements Verification Test/Test Cases Acceptance Test Specifications
Test Procedures	Purpose Scope References Unit Test Procedures/Test Case No. N Module Integration Test Procedures/Test Case No. N Verification Test Procedures/Test Case No. N Acceptance Test Procedures/Test Case No. N
Test Report	Purpose Scope References Unit Test Report/Test Analysis Unit Test Report/Test Summary Module Integration Test Report/Test Analysis Module Integration Test Report/Test Summary Verification Test Report/Test Analysis Verification Test Report/Test Summary Acceptance Test Report/Test Analysis Acceptance Test Report/Test Summary Recommendations

1.5.5 Implementation Documentation Data Base

The files and records resulting from the implementation activities are stored within the implementation data base. The files which comprise the implementation test data base are

- Conversion documentation file
- User guide documentation file
- Operations guide documentation file

Table 1-4 shows the records contained in each of these files.

Table 1-4. Implementation File Records

Data Base File	File Records
Conversion	Conversion Plan Update Conversion Plan Checklist Conversion Requirements/Resources Conversion Requirements/Organization Conversion Requirements/Hardware File Conversion/Creating New Files File Conversion/Updating Existing Files Training Requirements/EDP Personnel Training Requirements/User Personnel System Turnover/Task/Schedule Summary
Batch System User Guide	Purpose of the User Guide Terms and Abbreviations System Application General Description of Inputs, Outputs, and Processing Logic I/O Requirements/Screens I/O Requirements/Input Documents I/O Requirements/Reports
On-Line System User Guide	Purpose of the User Guide Project References Terms and Abbreviations System Application System Operation System Configuration System Performance

Table 1-4. Implementation File Records (continued)

Data Base File	File Records
On-Line System User Guide (*continued*)	I/O Requirements/Terminal Operation I/O Requirements/Sign-off Procedures I/O Requirements/Security Procedures I/O Requirements/Menus Query Procedures/Scenarios Query Procedures/Miscellaneous Inquiry Query Procedures/Miscellaneous Inquiry Screen Query Procedures/Codes Query Procedures/Update Menu Query Procedures/Update Function
Operations Guide	Purpose of the Operations Guide Project References Terms and Abbreviations System Application System Schematic Program Index File Index Security and Privacy Run Descriptions/Job Setup Run Descriptions/Job Step Instructions Run Descriptions/Job Outputs/Output Descriptions Run Descriptions/Job Outputs/Output Distribution Run Descriptions/Job Halts and Messages Run Descriptions/Aborts and Restart Procedures Backup and Recovery Procedures/System Backup Backup and Recovery Procedures/File Retention

1.5.6 Data Base Interrelationships

The model in Figure 1-3 shows that all the data entered into the system emanate from the tasks and task steps prescribed by the SDM for each phase of the systems development effort. We also see that certain subsystems (phases of the methodology) are connected by a flow of data into a common data base. For example, the data resulting from the tasks performed during the initial investigation, feasibility study, and requirements definition phases are entered into the analysis data base. In turn, these data are manipulated to produce the required analysis documentation. Likewise, the data resulting from tasks performed during the external design and internal design phases are entered into the design data base and the data, in turn, manipulated to produce design documentation.

Although each subsystem and each data base are structured in a manner compatible to generating a particular type of document, a high degree of interaction exists between the subsystems and the central data base subsets. Some of the tasks performed during the requirements definition phase, for example, are amplified during the external design phase. In this event, data may be drawn from the analysis data base, entered into the design data base along with new data, and recycled to generate updated documentation. Thus, the data relevant to a given task may be passed from one data base to another. In fact, many of the data entered into the program and test data base are drawn from data that reside in the analysis and design data bases. Virtually all of the data in the implementation data base are drawn from data that reside in the other data bases.

Chapter 2
Software Development Planning and Management Documents

Planning in a data processing environment involves devising a method for achieving the overall systems development objective. *Management* is the process by which the tasks and subtasks that comprise the life cycle phases of a systems development effort are controlled and directed. *Documents* that establish protocols for systems planning and management provide the primary means of communications between upper-level and functional managers responsible for the development and implementation of a computer system. This chapter examines a variety of planning and management documents and suggests techniques for their editorial preparation. It covers the preparation of policy statements, methods guidelines, systems and programming standards, and operating procedures as depicted in Figure 2-1.

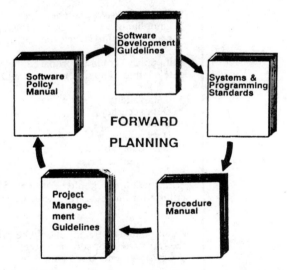

Figure 2-1. Planning and Management Manuals

Software policy establishes the framework for the software development process. *Software development guidelines* are necessary to ensure that the policy objectives can be met through strategic planning. *Systems development standards* establish design limitations and the measure for control. *Procedures* explain what has to be done, by whom, and when it must be done.

2.1 SOFTWARE DEVELOPMENT POLICY

The purpose of policy is not to achieve absolute uniformity of action, but rather to guide those responsible for developing a software product in making decisions that coincide with company objectives. Policy statements may be grouped as shown in Table 2-1.

Table 2-1. Types of Policy Statements

CLASSIFICATION	PURPOSE AND OBJECTIVE
QA Policies	QA policy should be established to ensure the development and delivery of acceptable software products. Policy statements should support ■ *Preliminary design* activities related to program scheduling, requirements definition, and test plan development ■ *Detailed design* activities related to monitoring design functions and verification and acceptance test procedures ■ *Program development* activities related to monitoring compliance with design specifications, test procedures, and to structured coding standards
Data Policies	Data policy should be prepared that provides a basis for data control. The statements should address ■ Data validity ■ Data accuracy ■ Data timeliness ■ Data reliability ■ Data compatibility ■ Data completeness
Security Policies	Security policies should be prepared that establish the criteria for implementing software and hardware security
Audit Policies	Audit policy statements should be prepared to establish the framework for software acceptance reviews. The policy statements should address ■ Functional audits required to verify that the software performance complies with the established requirements ■ Physical audits conducted to ensure the adequacy, completeness, and accuracy of the technical documentation

The writing and publishing of software development policy statements are prerequisites to ensure a consistent and controllable approach to software development. Policy statements should be written that state the general goal of the organization, define what constitutes an acceptable software product, provide direction of the software development program toward a specific objective, set forth requirements that take the place of opinion, and ensure that the software development effort is aligned with the company's long-range goals.

Each software policy statement should be drawn up in a formal manner and approved at the highest level of the data processing organization. By doing this, each step of the software development process can be directed toward a specific policy point. The cumulation of policy statements should then be published in a *Software Development Policy Manual* that is made available to everyone concerned with the development of a software product. All policy statements should be classified and indexed to allow for quick reference of the manual contents. The classification designation should remain constant from revision to revision.

2.1.1 Constructing a Policy Statement

There are, of course, numerous variations to formatting a written policy statement, but the following areas of policy concern should be incorporated in some way in the published document:

- *Organizational scope* that defines which organizations are affected by the policy

- *Subject scope* that states the specific areas of concern covered by the written statement

- *Responsibility* that identifies which individuals or what organizational entities are responsible for implementing and for enforcing the policy

- *Definition statement* that clarifies any terminology used in expressing the policy

- *Reference statement* that identifies published documents and other authorities that relate to the stated policy

The authors of this book suggest that each policy statement be written in six parts, titled and numbered as follows:

      1.0 Policy
      2.0 Authority and Applicability
      3.0 Responsibility
      4.0 General Requirements
      5.0 Definitions
      6.0 References

If a systems development effort is to serve the organization's needs, it must correlate with policy established at the highest possible level. It must be remembered, however, that although software policies are generally issued at top management levels, it is the people at the functional levels that must make the policies work. Therefore policy statements should be written at their level of understanding and must provide answers to questions such as

What functions and operations are subject to this policy?
Who is responsible for carrying out the policy?
How does the stated policy integrate with other protocols for systems planning and development?
Are all the terms used in the policy statement clearly defined?

Software developers often tend to gloss over these questions by stating in abstract terms that the new software product will provide profitable returns or improved services. But, in order for a software development effort to coincide with the organization's goals and objectives, policy must be written in a structured manner that provides direction to the system developers. Using the suggested content arrangement, the policy writer should consider the following:

The statement of *Policy* (1.0) should be expressed in a direct and concise manner, preferably in a single sentence.

The statement of *Authority and Applicability* (2.0) should define the authority under which the policy is issued and provide a clear, concise abstract of the coverage of the organizational activities to which the policy applies.

The statement of *Responsibility* (3.0) should clearly define who shall be responsible for carrying out the various provisions set forth in the written policy statement. If different people are responsible for enforcing the policy, the statement should be precise in identifying the specific responsibilities of each person or group.

The statement of *General Requirements* (4.0) should provide instructions for implementing the policy.

The statement of *Definitions* (5.0) should contain terms or acronyms which may be unfamiliar to the reader or which may be subject to interpretation.

The *Reference Statement* (6.0) should reference standards, procedures, vendor materials, and other documents that may relate to the implementation of the policy.

A policy statement should be drawn up in a formal fashion and approved by the highest level of the company. By doing this, there will be complete agreement on what constitutes an acceptable software product and on what must be determined about a software development proposal in order to accept or reject it. The format described in the preceding paragraphs is illustrated in the following example.

Example:

SUBJECT: Systems Development Methodology

1.0 POLICY
All major new development projects and enhancements to existing systems will be carried out utilizing the specific methodology defined in this policy statement.

2.0 SCOPE
The systems development methodology (SDM) applies to all MIS functions and operations. The methodology applies to both segmented and one-time project development and installation of $25,000 or more in expenditures from all sources during a single fiscal year. It is applicable to projects utilizing packages and/or in-house systems development.

3.0 RESPONSIBILITY
MIS and business systems development directors shall be responsible for carrying out the provisions of this policy.

4.0 GENERAL REQUIREMENTS
The company dependence on effective systems places a great deal of responsibility on MIS management at all levels. The systems development methodology (SDM) defined by this policy is a guide and tool designed to improve systems development productivity and quality. A phased systems development has been designed in order to achieve a manageable process. MIS management must, however, combine these technical methods with business awareness and sound judgment to ensure that systems developed are technical successes but, more importantly, bottom-line contributors.

5.0 DEFINITIONS
Major MIS Systems. Major MIS systems are defined as any system which requires development or enhancement costs exceeding $50,000 (U.S. dollars) from all sources.

Enhancements. Enhancements are defined as any additions, changes, or deletions to an existing system or as the addition of new systems capabilities which require in excess of $25,000 but less than $50,000 from all sources.

Systems Development Methodology (SDM). Systems development methodology (SDM) is the process designed to systematically segment and phase the management and development life cycle of systems and their enhancements.

6.0 REFERENCES
MIS Procedures Manual
Systems Development Methodology

All policy statements should be classified, indexed, and included in a *Software Development Policy Manual* that is made available to everyone concerned with a software development project. The classification designation must remain constant from revision to revision.

2.1.2 Software Development Policy Manual Content Arrangement

The content of a *Software Development Policy Manual* may be arranged as follows:

> Cover
> Policy Improvement Proposal
> Authority and Applicability
> Foreword
> Contents Page
> Introduction
> Policy Statements
> - Classification Group 1
> - Classification Group 2

The text on the *cover* should include the security classification, procedure identification, date of approval, title of the policy, and a statement as to how a copy of the manual may be acquired.

Example:

```
COMPANY PRIVATE          POL. MANUAL 036
                         1 JAN 91




              SOFTWARE DEVELOPMENT
              POLICY MANUAL







              ADDITIONAL COPIES OF THIS
              DOCUMENT MAY BE ACQUIRED
              FROM THE MIS LIBRARIAN
```

A *Policy Improvement Proposal* form should be included as the first page following the cover. The form should provide for the name of the organization and address of submitter, the identification of the policy for which changes are recommended, a statement of recommended changes, and the reason for recommending the changes.

Example:

POLICY IMPROVEMENT PROPOSAL	
The purpose of this form is to solicit beneficial comments which will help top management better understand the impact of the policy and which may assist management in policy improvement. Complete the form and send to CORPORATE POLICY COMMITTEE, Office of the President.	
NAME & ADDRESS OF ORGANIZATION	POLICY NO.
	POLICY TITLE:
RECOMMENDATIONS FOR IMPROVING POLICY	
SUBMITTED BY	TELEPHONE NO.
	DATE:

The second page following the cover should define the authority under which the *Software Development Policy Manual* is issued. It should also denote the organizational activities to which they the policy statements contained in the manual apply.

Example:

The policies contained in this manual are issued under the authority of the corporate president.

The organizational activities to which these policies apply include all activities that pertain to software development that are coordinated at various management levels by the following:

    Companywide Policies
        V.P./Corporate Planning
        V.P./Management Information Systems
        V.P./Quality Assurance

    Divisional Policies
        V.P./Systems and Procedures

    Departmental Policies
        Director Information Systems

A *foreword* shall be prepared to explain the reasons for, or purpose of the manual or give background information in the case of a revised manual. The foreword may also include a brief resume of the development history or a statement of reason for a particular format or sequence in the presentation of policy statements. The foreword should appear on the third page following the cover.

Example:

FOREWORD

The objective of these policies is to establish the criteria around which all software development activities must revolve.

Recommendations to improve any of the policy statements contained herein are solicited. Such recommendations must be submitted on the *Policy Improvement Proposal* form included as the first page of this manual and forwarded to:

> Policy Development Group
> Office of the President
> Any Company
> Any Town, USA

Additional copies of this part of the *Corporate Planning and Development Manual* may be requested from the corporate librarian.

The single word *CONTENTS* in capital letters shall head the contents page. The policy statements contained in the manual should be listed in index number sequence.

Example:

CONTENTS

Index
No.

Section 1. Companywide Policies

Section 2. Divisional Policies

Section 3. Departmental Policies

The *introduction* to the *Software Development Policy Manual* should include statements that explain the sectional breakdown of the contents and the nature of the policies contained in the manual. The introduction may also include general statements pertaining to the importance of corporate policy in a software development environment and considerations for policy enforcement.

Example:
_____

INTRODUCTION

This manual includes policies that impact the activities pertaining to software development at three levels of management control:

- Companywide
- Divisional
- Departmental

Section 1 contains all policies applicable to companywide activities related to software development. It includes policies concerned with development methodologies, documentation, estimating, and quality assurance.

Section 2 presents policies that impact divisional activities. It covers software development budgeting, project initiation, and configuration management.

Section 3 includes all policies that are enforceable at the departmental level that relate to project management.

The remainder of the *Software Development Policy Manual* should contain all the policies in indexed sequence.

2.2 METHODOLOGIES

Having defined the criteria for software development in a series of published policy statements, we can turn our attention to writing methods guidelines through which the policies can be implemented. The editorial structure of a published methodology should define the elements (or phases) of the methodology, delineate the precise tasks that must be performed for each element, and clearly identify the end-item deliverables. All the methodologies that establish protocols for structured systems development should be in place before the first project meeting is held, the first line of code generated, or the first item of documentation produced.

The alternatives in adopting methodologies are to purchase vendor-supplied packages or to develop the methodologies in-house. The major constraint in either case is usually economic. The purchase price of vendor-supplied methodology packages ranges from $10,000 to $250,000. The development of a home-grown methodology can be equally costly without careful planning and proper guidelines to guide the methodology development process.

Four types of methodologies needed to support a structured software development environment are shown in Table 2-2. Each of these methodology types is further described in this chapter.

Table 2-2. Methodologies

TYPE	PURPOSE AND OBJECTIVE
Systems Development Methodology	The systems development methodology (SDM) should describe how the life cycle breaks down into phases, specify the tasks and tasks steps to be performed during each phase, and identify the items deliverable to the project file.
Data Base Development Methodology	The data base development methodology (DBDM) should break the data base development process into prescribed phases. The following areas of data base concern should be considered: *functional analysis*; *data analysis*; *data base design*; *physical creation and conversion*; *integration*; and *operations and maintenance*.
Cost Estimating Methodology	The cost-estimating methodology (CEM) should establish procedures for estimating costs related to: ■ The *work breakdown structure* (i.e., person-hour and cost requirements related to the performance of each SDM and DBDM task) ■ *Application attributes* (i.e., costs related to project size and complexity, reliability requirements, interface requirements, program language requirements; etc.) ■ *Environment attributes* (costs related to MIS procedures, scheduling, life cycle methods, utility software, application package acquisition, etc.) ■ *Project team attributes* (i.e., costs related to project team size, skill level, familiarity, experience, staffing constraints, etc.) ■ *Training support requirements* (costs of travel, tuitions, lodging, etc.)
Project Management Methodology	The project management methodology (PMM) should present procedures for project plan development; monitoring and recording project progress; evaluating the progress of the development activity; initiating and evaluating change requests; implementing approved changes; and entering data in the project file.

A fifth methodology deemed essential to structured control of the software development process is *configuration management*. A detailed configuration management methodology is presented in a separate work entitled *Software Configuration Management: Identification, Accounting, Control, & Management* written by the authors of this book and published by McGraw-Hill.

2.2.1 Systems Development Methodology (SDM)

The structure of a *systems development methodology (SDM)* must define the life cycle phases, the tasks to be performed, and the end-item deliverables. The content organization of an SDM may be as follows:

> Section 1 Introduction
> Section 2 Life Cycle Phases
> Section 3 Tasks/Task Steps
> Section 4 Deliverables

Section 1, *Introduction,* should state the objectives and purposes of the SDM, define the project scope to which the methodology applies, and explain how the methodology is organized.

Example:
___

1.0 INTRODUCTION

Objectives and Purpose
The systems development methodology (SDM) complements and supplements the Policy Manual. It is intended to:
> (a) Define the tasks to be performed in a software development project
> (b) Specify the deliverable product of each task step

Scope
All systems development projects, without regard to their size or level of managerial control, must adhere to these guidelines.

How This Methodology Is Organized
The methodology is divided into three parts:

Part 1, *Methods Guidelines*, explains how the system life cycle is divided into manageable phases. It prescribes the tasks and task steps for each phase and identifies the items that are deliverable to the project file.

Part 2, *Documentation Guidelines*, provides a general guide for technical writers who are responsible for developing the content of systems manuals.

Part 3, *Estimating Guidelines*, defines procedures for estimating person-hour and cost requirements related to the performance of each development task; estimating costs related to project size and complexity, reliability requirements, interface requirements, and program language requirements; estimating costs related to MIS procedures, scheduling, life cycle methods, utility software, applications package acquisition, etc.; costs related to project team size, skill level, familiarity, experience, and staffing constraints; costs of computer time, graphics support, clerical support, reproduction, and other development support; and costs of meetings, travel, off-site training support, etc.

Section 2, *Life Cycle Phases,* should identify the life cycle phases of the systems development methodology and briefly describe the purpose of each phase. The phase structure presented in the following example is used throughout this book.

Example:
_____

2.0 LIFE CYCLE PHASES

The life cycle phases of a software development project are:

Initial Investigation Phase. This phase of software development shall start with a detailed review of the project request. If the request calls for a major enhancement to an existing system or the development of a complete new system, an analyst may be assigned to conduct an initial investigation. The results of this effort shall be a problem and need statement, cost projection statement, target schedules, and a feasibility study work plan.

Feasibility Study Phase. The objective of this study is to provide management with the predictable results of implementing the proposed project. The document items that must be delivered to the project file include present system documentation, equipment requirements, system requirements, and a statement of costs.

Requirements Definition Phase. The objective of this phase is to transform the user needs described in the initial investigation and feasibility study documents into specific requirements. The documentation items to be delivered to the project file include performance requirements, environment requirements, and data requirements.

External Design Phase. These specifications determine what must be done to bring the system into being and what will be achieved by installing it. The document items that must be delivered to the project file are system/subsystem specifications and security and control specifications.

Internal Design Phase. During this phase of development, the external design specifications are transformed into detail specifications that describe the program logic, input formats and processing, output formats, and processing and backup procedures.

Program Development Phase. During this phase, the program specifications developed during the internal design phase are translated into executable code. The items to be delivered include the program files, physical data bases, program descriptions, and file descriptions.

Section 3, *Tasks/Task Steps,* should itemize the tasks and task steps that are to be completed during each phase of the development process. These tasks and task steps may be presented in the form of checklists that present the activities to be performed in sequential order. A narrative description of each task and task step may be provided to enhance the checklist.

Example:

3.0 TASKS/TASK STEPS

Initial Investigation Task Checklist

The tasks to be performed during the initial investigation phase of software development follow.

( ) Review Project Request
( ) Prepare Initial Investigation Work Planning Checklist
( ) Conduct Interviews
( ) Analyze Collected Information
( ) Make Recommendations
( ) Prepare Feasibility Study Work Plan
( ) Prepare Initial Investigation Report

Feasibility Study Task Checklist

The tasks to be performed during the feasibility study phase of software development follow.

( ) Review Feasibility Study Work Plan
( ) Conduct User Interviews
( ) Review Present System
( ) Analyze Proposed System
( ) Identify Package Alternatives
( ) Analyze Costs and Benefits
( ) Prepare Feasibility Document

Requirements Definition Task Checklist

The tasks to be performed during the requirements definition phase of software development follow.

( ) Review Project File
( ) Conduct Interviews
( ) Define Performance Requirements
( ) Define Data Requirements
( ) Define Environment Requirements
( ) Define Organizational Requirements
( ) Select Package Alternative
( ) Prepare Requirements Definition Document

Section 4, *Deliverables,* should provide a checklist of the deliverable items that result from the tasks and task steps performed during each phase of the software development life cycle. The guidelines may include references to forms or screen formats that are used to record the results of tasks.

Example:

4.0 DELIVERABLES

Initial Investigation Deliverable Checklist

The deliverables resulting from the tasks and task steps performed during the initial investigation phase of development are as follows:

( ) An activated *Project Request*
( ) Analyst Work Assignment
( ) Initial Investigation Work Planning Checklist
( ) Work Schedule
( ) Project File and Index
( ) Interview Questionnaire
( ) Interview Responses
( ) Interview Summaries
( ) Supporting Data and Documents
( ) Updated Problem and Need Statement
( ) Key Inputs and Outputs
( ) Data Flow Diagrams
( ) Organization Charts
( ) Budget Constraint Statements
( ) Cost and Time Estimates
( ) Recommendations
( ) Feasibility Study Work Plan
( ) Initial Investigation Phase End Report

Feasibility Study Deliverable Checklist

The deliverables resulting from the tasks and task steps performed during the feasibility study phase of development are as follows:

( ) User Organization Chart
( ) Job Descriptions
( ) Questionnaires
( ) Interview Worksheets
( ) Interview Schedules
( ) Interview Summaries
( ) Proposed System Schematic
( ) Summary of New Capabilities
( ) Summary of Upgrades
( ) Summary of Impacts
( ) Future Operating Cost Worksheets
( ) Current Operating Cost Worksheets
( ) Return on Investment Worksheets
( ) Economic Evaluation Summaries

2.2.2 Data Base Development Methodology (DBDM)

The creation of a data base should first begin by defining a method to aid the development process. The content of a *data base development methodology (DBDM)* may be organized as follows:

> Section 1 Introduction
> Section 2 Functional Analysis
> Section 3 Data Analysis
> Section 4 Data Base Design
> Section 5 Physical Creation and Conversion
> Section 6 Integration
> Section 7 Operations and Maintenance

Section 1, *Introduction*, is organized in a manner similar to that shown for the systems development methodology. It should state the objectives and purposes of the DBDM, define the areas over which the methodology applies, and explain how the methodology is organized.

Example:

1.0 INTRODUCTION

Objectives and Purpose
The data base development methodology (DBDM) complements and supplements the systems development methodology. It is intended to:

    (a) Define the tasks to be performed in the design and development of a computer-based data base

    (b) Specify the deliverable product of each task step

Scope
All new data base development and any structural modifications to existing data base systems, without regard to their size or level of managerial control, must adhere to these guidelines. The primary user of this document is expected to be the data base analysts, administrators, and the systems analysts.

How This Methodology Is Organized
The methodology is divided into six phases, correlating to the sequential tasks performed in data base development:

Functional Analysis, explains the process of functional definition and process identification within the system.

Data Analysis, explains the process of functional decomposition and data accumulation to define the relationships between data elements.

Data Base Design, provides guidance for logical and physical data base design, schema and subschema design, integrity and security.

Physical Creation, defines the activities to be performed in generating and populating the data base.

Section 2, *Functional Analysis*, presents the tasks and task steps aimed at data base development associated with the analysis phase activities specified in the systems development methodology. The presentation should correlate the tasks to be performed with the activities of the business analyst as specified in the SDM. The deliverable items from these activities will be incorporated in the phase end-deliverable (initial investigation document, feasibility study document, or requirements definition document) prepared by the project leader. The complexity of the tasks will be determined as much by the size of the project as by the tools available to the data base analyst. Organizations with CASE reengineering and data dictionary or repository tools will, of course, want to incorporate the use of those tools as part of the DBDM.

Example:

2.0 FUNCTIONAL ANALYSIS

Functional analysis is a top-down process aimed at establishing the structural requirements of a data base before detailed elements of the data base design are defined. The data base administration activities during the initial investigation, feasibility study, and requirements definition activities are primarily in support of the business systems analyst. The specific tasks during each phase of development are

- *Initial Investigation Tasks*
  Plan investigation.
  Define project scope.
  Define business functions.
  Identify data types and volumes associated with the current and proposed functional flows.

- *Feasibility Study Tasks*
  Review existing systems, both manual and *data base management system* (DBMS)-based.
  Review current procedures (both manual and DBMS-related).
  Define computer system limitations.

- *Requirements Definition Phase Tasks*
  Define business function requirements (frequency, volumes, and timeliness of data access).
  Define procedural requirements (data security, entry, update, deletion authorizations, etc.).
  Define technical requirements (hardware, network, file storage, etc.).
  Define environment requirements (platform, DBMS, methods of access, etc.).

Deliverables from the data base developer include data dictionary definitions for the key inputs and outputs of the proposed system, estimates of time for logical and physical data modeling, and hardware and software requirements to support the proposed data base development.

Section 3, *Data Analysis*, identifies the tasks and task steps of the data base analyst during the time the business analyst performs the external design activities specified by the systems development methodology.

Example:

3.0 DATA ANALYSIS

Data analysis is a bottom-up process aimed at analyzing the products of the application system for which the data bases must be designed. The goal of the data analysis is to examine the products and, through a step-by-step process, convert the data into a model that shows how the data in the system interact.

The specific tasks associated with this activity are

- *Perform Functional Decomposition*. This process involves creating decomposition diagrams and defining specific data elements associated with each business process.
- *Accumulate Data*. This involves creating or updating the data dictionary to incorporate all of the data elements defined in the functional decomposition.
- *Data Relationship Diagramming*. The relationships between data elements are defined and linked to the processes in which they are used.
- *Data Model Generation*. The complete data entity relationship is documented and formatted for presentation in the external design.

Section 4, *Data Base Design*, details the tasks and task steps the data base analyst must perform to create the data base design. It provides the methods for creation of both logical and physical data base design. The activities of this phase correlate with the internal design activities of the SDM.

Example:

4.0 DATA BASE DESIGN

The outputs of the functional analysis and data analysis processes establish the framework for data base design. The data base design phase itself breaks down into four subphases:

- Schema design
- Subschema design
- Integrity and security design
- Operation and maintenance design

The results of these processes are the logical and physical data base designs to feed the physical creation of the data base. The documentation of these designs is incorporated in the repository and maintained for following phases of development.

Section 5, *Physical Creation and Conversion*, presents the tasks and task steps for creating the physical data base, converting the data to load into the data base, creating required indexes, and loading the required data. These activities occur concurrently with the program development phase of the systems development methodology.

Example:

5.0 PHYSICAL CREATION AND CONVERSION

When the data base design is completed, the physical data base must be created in conformance with the design specifications of the previous phase. The procedures, of course, are particular to the DBMS selected and the nature of the systems accessing the data. Once the data base files are created, the data must be loaded and any conversion routines run. The specific tasks associated with this phase are:

- Create data bases
- Create indexes
- Convert data
- Load data
- Implement data security procedures
- Initiate backup and recovery procedures

Section 6, *Integration*, identifies the tasks and task steps to integrate the data base into the applications and/or query programs needing the data. This phase corresponds to the test phase of the systems development methodology.

Example:

6.0 INTEGRATION

During the integration phase, two sets of applications may run concurrently. Updates performed on production files must be transferred to the test environment and the results compared to ensure the accuracy and validity of the processing and data handling.

The specific tasks to be performed during the Integration phase are:

- Team creation
- Integration testing
- Results comparisons

Upon completion of the integration phase, the data base system will have been validated and is ready to be placed into production. The documented test results are placed in the project file for future reference.

Section 7, *Operation and Maintenance*, defines the tasks and task steps to place the data base system into a production mode of operation and to maintain the system in that state.

Example:

7.0 OPERATION AND MAINTENANCE

This phase breaks down into two subphases: operation and maintenance. Once the data base environment has been tested, it is placed into production and is maintained to ensure acceptable levels of performance.

The tasks involved in this phase are:

- Shutdown of old system
- Initiation of production operation
- Index maintenance
- Data base file maintenance
- Modification of design (when required)
- Implementation of modifications (when required)

2.2.3 Cost-Estimating Methodology (CEM)

Having defined the software and data base development methods and tasks, we see that the next major function associated with software planning is the establishment of a *cost-estimating methodology* (*CEM*). This involves decomposing the work to be performed into manageable tasks, analyzing the development efforts required, identifying risks, anticipating production and schedule problems, and identifying support resources. The cost-estimating methodology illustrated in this in this book involves four basic steps:

Step 1. Identify the tasks and task steps to be performed for each phase of development.

Step 2. Estimate the total units (e.g., labor-hours, computer time, documents, etc.) each task will involve.

Step 3. Correlate the estimated units to predetermined unit costs.

Step 4. Adjust the estimates based on factors that may affect the estimated costs.

Conceptually, the methodology presented here is simple and straight forward. It involved only two worksheets: a *Phased Development Estimating* form and an *Adjustment Factor* form. These documents are supported by tables of adjustment factors relative to requirements, product, process, and resource factors. Without a careful analysis of these factors, it is practically impossible to estimate a software development project with any degree of accuracy.

The Phased Development Estimating form should be designed to identify the tasks to be performed. The form should allow space to enter the standard units for estimating. This may be in measures of hours, output records, interviews, and so on. To assist the estimator, standards for the minimum, average, and maximum should be pre-printed on the form. The standards should represent the judgment of experienced individuals based on historical records. An example of a Phased Development Estimating worksheet is shown below.

Example:

PHASED DEVELOPMENT ESTIMATING									
Phase: REQUIREMENTS DEFINITION			**PROJECT NO.** MIS-1201		**PROJECT NAME** Inventory				
Prepared by:			Date:						
Approved by:			Date						
1	REVIEW PROJECT FILE								
2	CONDUCT INTERVIEWS								
2.1	Identify Individuals								
2.2	Schedule Interviews								
2.3	Conduct Interviews								
3	DEFINE PERFORMANCE REQ.								
3.1	Define Accuracy Req.								
3.2	Define Timing Req.								
3.3	Define Contingency Req.								
3.4	Define Interface Req.								
4	Amplify Functional Req.								
5	DEFINE DATA REQ.								
5.1	Define Input Req.								
5.2	Define Output Req.								
5.3	Define Data Base Req.								
6	DEFINE ENVIRONMENT REQ.								
6.1	Define Hardware Req.								
6.2	Define Software Req.								

The Adjustment Factor form should list those factors that may affect the number of units/hours that may be involved. It should provide space to assign a value to each factor and to make adjustments to the estimates on the Phased Development Estimating form. An example of an Adjustment Factor form is shown in the example that follows.

Example:

ADJUSTMENT FACTOR				
Project Name:			Request No:	
Prepared By	Name	Approved		Date
ADJUSTMENT FACTORS			+	o
REQUIREMENTS FACTORS				
1. Clarity of Specifications				
2. Stability of Specifications				
PRODUCT FACTORS				
1. Software Size				
2. Difficulty				
3. Reliability Requirement				
4. External Interfaces				
5. Language Requirement				
6. Documentation Requirement				
PROCESS FACTORS				
1. Management Structure				
2. Management Controls				
3. Development Methodology				
4. Available Tools				
5. Available Packages				
RESOURCE FACTORS				
1. Staff Availability				
2. Staff Experience				
3. Hardware Available				

The values entered on the Adjustment Factor form may be based on the estimator's first-hand experience, or they may be taken from an *adjustment table*. To assist in weighing impact factors, we may prepare an *adjustment table* that assigns values to each variable. The published values serve primarily as guidelines and should not be considered a substitute for first-hand experience. The estimator, using the latest information on hand, should never feel obliged to use each factor or, in fact, any of the values stated in the table.

Example:

REQUIREMENTS FACTORS	PRODUCT FACTORS
Quality of Specifications 0 = Well Specified 1 = Too Detailed 2 = Insufficiently Detailed	**Software Size** 0 = Formal Sizing Guidelines Exist 1 = Informal Sizing Guidelines Used 2 = No Sizing Guidelines Used

Stability of Specifications
0 = Formal Change Procedures
    Exist
1 = Informal Change Procedures
    Exist
2 = No Change Procedures Exist
	Difficulty
	0 = Applications/Utility Software
	    Involved
	1 = Non-Real-Time Application
	    Required
	2 = Real-Time Application Required

PROCESS FACTORS	**RESOURCE FACTORS**
Development Methods 0 = Formal Methodology Used 1 = Informal Methodology Used 2 = No Methodology Used	**Staffing Level** 0 = Existing Staff Adequate 1 = Staff Must Be Retrained 2 = Additional Staff Required

Tools
0 = Compilers etc. Available
1 = Compilers etc. Must Be
    Acquired
2 = Test Tools Must Be Developed
	Experience of People
	0 = Experience with Specific
	    application
	1 = Experience with General
	    Application
	2 = Staff Inexperienced with
	    Application

Available Software
0 = All Software on Hand
1 = Existing Software Must
    Be Modified
2 = New Software Must Be
    Acquired	

The guidelines that relate to *requirements factors* must consider the task-oriented specifications prescribed by the software development and documentation methodologies. They should also reflect any constraints that must be imposed to ensure the stability of these specifications. Since the design detail of any software project is subject to change, special guidelines may have to be written and published to cope with this situation. Without the framework of a systems development methodology that clearly defines the requirements to be satisfied by a proposed system, there is no reliable way to estimate the costs involved in developing a computer system. To ensure that the estimating process is carried on in a manner that considers all of the requirements prescribed by the systems methodology, guidelines for analyzing requirements factors should be prepared and made available to the project estimators.

Example:

REQUIREMENTS ADJUSTMENT FACTORS

Two factors associated with the specification of requirements can impact the estimate of cost.

The first factor is the *quality of the requirements specification.* A clearly specified project will be much easier to develop than a sketchily specified one, because the clearer the specification, the more likely the design will meet the requirements. Of course, too much detail in the specification can result in too much limitation in the design parameters, making the development of the system much more difficult. Adjustment factors for quality of specification are

Well-defined specification − no adjustment

Overly detailed specification − .1 increase

Poorly defined requirements specification − .2 increase

The second factor is the *stability of the requirements specification.* Clearly, designing a system to a moving target will significantly increase the time to complete as well as the risk of not completing at all. Two key factors should be examined in making the estimate of stability:

1. Is there a formal change control mechanism established?
    Yes − No adjustment, informal procedure − .1 increase, No procedure − .2 increase

2. How many people are responsible for specifying requirements?
    One person − no adjustment, 2-5 people − .1 increase, 6 or more − .2 increase

The guidelines pertaining to *product factors* should focus on the characteristics of the software deliverables. The guidelines should be aimed at assisting the estimator in an analysis of the deliverable code and documentation in terms of size, complexity, reliability requirements, interface requirements, program language requirements, and documentation requirements.

Example:

PRODUCT FACTORS

There are six *product factors* that must be considered by the estimator when estimating a software project.

1. *Sizing Cost Factors.* The sizing considerations include the cost of both deliverable and nondeliverable software and the impact of size increases on the interfaces and the number of people required to develop the system.

2. *Complexity.* Cost can be greatly affected by the complexity and the scope of difficulty involved in some software applications. The estimator must be keenly aware that some types of applications require more time and consequently cost more to implement.

3. *Reliability.* The greater the reliability required from the system, the higher the cost to ensure that reliability. Factors that influence these costs are testing requirements, failure contingency planning, redundant checking, and monitoring functions added to the design.

4. *Interfaces.* The cost considerations relating to interface requirements must be carefully analyzed by the estimator. Peer-to-peer communications requirements, special-purpose device interfaces, and complex software interfaces all create additional design considerations, adding to system costs.

5. *Program Language Requirements.* The use of fourth-generation languages, applications generators, and similar tools can save considerable time in the development process. Conversely, assembly programming can take 10 times as long to generate a single function. Therefore, the estimator should carefully consider the cost of the language required in developing the system.

6. *Documentation Requirements.* The creation and maintenance of the system and user documentation can significantly impact the cost of development. Factors associated with estimating documentation costs include
   - Document types required
   - Level of content in each document
   - Method of preparation (manual, automated, etc.)
   - Quantity of published documents required

The guidelines that relate to *process factors* are concerned with an analysis of the management structure and the methods used in a software development effort. They reflect factors pertaining to management information processing procedures, scheduling procedures, technical support requirements, life cycle methodology, utility software, available applications packages, and data base parameters.

Example:

PROCESS FACTORS

There are five *process factors* that must be considered by the estimator when estimating the software development project. They are:

1. *Product Management and Control.* To effectively estimate a software project, the cost estimator must consider the various support units that comprise the management structures. Input for cost estimating must be derived from management and control areas responsible for applications development, data base development, data center operation, network installation and maintenance, and documentation development.

2. *Life Cycle Methodology.* The impact of the methodology used for software development must be analyzed. Although structured methodologies may require a major investment to establish, software projects developed in a structured environment are easier to manage and therefore generally cost less over the development cycle. Additionally, when CASE tools are in place, the structure of the methodology is a requisite for satisfactory results.

3. *Utility Software.* The cost estimator must determine what utility software is presently available and what utilities must be purchased or developed to accomplish the prescribed tasks. Utility software that should be considered include

   - Data base management software
   - Text/image management software
   - Front-end CASE diagramming tools
   - Reengineering tools
   - Testing tools

4. *Available Application Packages.* The acquisition and customization of off-the-shelf software may significantly impact the cost of implementing a new software system. The cost estimator must consider the cost of revalidating modified software when it is interfaced with existing software.

5. *Data Base Parameters.* The cost of data base development and installation must be considered in the software development cost estimate. Factors include DBMS, storage requirements, etc.

The guidelines pertaining to *resource factors* should relate costs of development associated with staff and hardware resources to be applied to the effort. The guidelines should identify impacts relating to the number of personnel, levels of experience required, variations in productivity, adequacy of computing resources, and time requirements.

Example:

RESOURCE FACTORS

There are four *resource factors* that must be considered by the estimator when projecting costs for a software development project. They are:

1. *Number of People Required*. The relation of cost to staff size is not a direct multiplier of rate times number of people. The time required for communications among team members and between the team and management expands as the size of the team grows. Specific types of communications that come into play as the project team grows include staff meetings, progress reports, letters, and other memoranda.

2. *Staff Experience*. The cost estimator must consider the various levels of experience that may be required for a particular software development effort. Experience factors may include
   - Years of experience
   - Familiarity with the type of application
   - Programming language skills
   - Special education and training

3. *Productivity*. Cost estimators must be able to analyze the variations in productivity within the development organization. Historical records that show the productivity levels of each individual assigned to the project would be beneficial. However, since such records do not exist in most organizations, the cost estimator must work closely with the project managers in evaluating productivity factors.

4. *Adequacy of Computing Resources*. The impact of available computing resources on schedules must be evaluated by the cost estimator. If additional hardware is required this requirement must be specified during the requirements definition phase. The cost of the hardware thus becomes an automatic cost factor. Specific areas of concern related to computing resources include

   - The requirement for computer time increases during the development cycle
   - Availability of computing resources during shift
   - The relationship between turnaround time and test costs

2.2.4 Project Management Methodology (PMM)

Successful project management in the data processing organization derives from the ability to achieve the project objective by developing or meeting the desired specifications − on time, within budget, at the desired level of performance, and with the resources provided. This is best accomplished by establishing a sound *project management methodology (PMM)* for planning, organizing, coordinating, monitoring, supervising, and managing a systems development effort.

Through application of a PMM, the thought processes from different individuals can be brought together to make a whole, visible, working project that satisfies the needs and desires of users. Those needs and desires are the project objectives. Thus, the function of project management is essential to ensure that the users' needs are thoroughly defined and properly communicated to the designers; a project plan is laid out that accurately defines the resources required; the designers prepare functional specifications that are understood and agreed to by the user; the designer transforms the functional specifications into computer design specifications that are thoroughly understood by the programmers and analysts; the programmers write efficient code that meets all specifications, is thoroughly tested, and is properly documented; user documentation is prepared and training conducted so that all user personnel understand the operation of the system; and implementation goes according to plan with no major glitches.

A breakdown or failure in realizing any one of the above can cause nightmares for the project manager. Risks can be greatly minimized through proper training of project personnel, strong project management leadership, and a PMM that breaks the project management process into definable areas of management responsibility.

One cannot discuss project management today without considering the methods, skills, and disciplines of *computer-aided software engineering (CASE)*. Therefore, in defining a PMM, the use of available project management CASE tools should be given consideration. Although project management CASE technology has been emerging for several years and a number of very sophisticated tools are available today, the technology is still in its infancy. Various CASE tools designed to facilitate project scheduling, resource leveling, and project status are available, however, very few of these tools have been integrated into a CASE-based systems development methodology.

The contents of a project management methodology should be arranged in accordance with five basic functional elements of software project management:

> Section 1 Planning
> Section 2 Project Control
> Section 3 Evaluation
> Section 4 Change Control
> Section 5 Project File Maintenance

Section 1, *Planning*, should correlate with the systems development and cost-estimating methodologies previously discussed in this chapter. The PMM may, however, expand upon these documents by establishing milestones for project management and procedures for staffing, estimating, working with subcontractors, and preparing a project plan. The planning methodology should identify the tasks and task steps required for each project phase as indicated in the following chart.

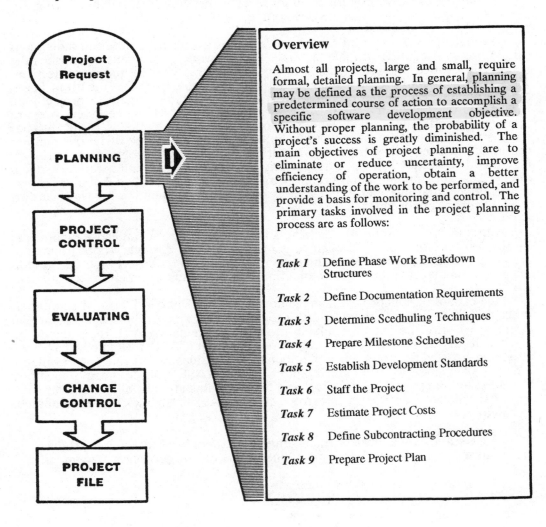

Overview

Almost all projects, large and small, require formal, detailed planning. In general, planning may be defined as the process of establishing a predetermined course of action to accomplish a specific software development objective. Without proper planning, the probability of a project's success is greatly diminished. The main objectives of project planning are to eliminate or reduce uncertainty, improve efficiency of operation, obtain a better understanding of the work to be performed, and provide a basis for monitoring and control. The primary tasks involved in the project planning process are as follows:

Task 1   Define Phase Work Breakdown Structures

Task 2   Define Documentation Requirements

Task 3   Determine Scedhuling Techniques

Task 4   Prepare Milestone Schedules

Task 5   Establish Development Standards

Task 6   Staff the Project

Task 7   Estimate Project Costs

Task 8   Define Subcontracting Procedures

Task 9   Prepare Project Plan

Section 2, *Project Control,* should provide guidance for *starting a project, tracking and reporting,* and *reviewing project progress.* The guidelines for starting a project should be aimed at establishing protocols for reviewing and approving the project plan and obtaining formal sign-offs related to the committed costs and committed dates. The guidelines for tracking and reporting should explain the functions of weekly time reports, work completion reports, computer usage reports, and incident reports. The guidelines for reporting progress should demonstrate the use of bar (Gantt) charts and graphics as a means for exhibiting or plotting progress. The guidelines for reviewing project progress should provide guidance for conducting peer, periodic, milestone, and phase reviews and for preparing reports that document the findings and recommendations of the review teams. The chart below summarizes the task orientation of the project control element of a PMM.

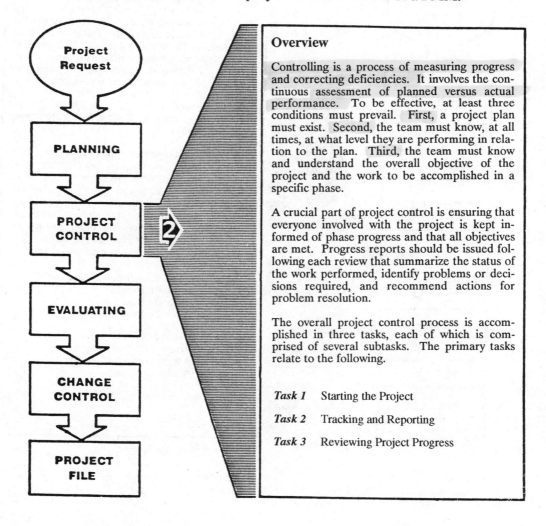

Project Request

PLANNING

PROJECT CONTROL

EVALUATING

CHANGE CONTROL

PROJECT FILE

Overview

Controlling is a process of measuring progress and correcting deficiencies. It involves the continuous assessment of planned versus actual performance. To be effective, at least three conditions must prevail. First, a project plan must exist. Second, the team must know, at all times, at what level they are performing in relation to the plan. Third, the team must know and understand the overall objective of the project and the work to be accomplished in a specific phase.

A crucial part of project control is ensuring that everyone involved with the project is kept informed of phase progress and that all objectives are met. Progress reports should be issued following each review that summarize the status of the work performed, identify problems or decisions required, and recommend actions for problem resolution.

The overall project control process is accomplished in three tasks, each of which is comprised of several subtasks. The primary tasks relate to the following.

Task 1   Starting the Project

Task 2   Tracking and Reporting

Task 3   Reviewing Project Progress

Section 3, *Evaluating,* should define procedures for evaluating both the product and the project. It should provide guidelines for performing a *cost/benefit analysis* and a *risk analysis.* The cost/benefit analysis methodology should establish guidelines for identifying and assessing tangible and intangible benefits, evaluating development and recurring costs, and assessing the value of the project to the organization. The risk analysis guidelines should define procedures for analyzing both product risks and project risks. The chart below summarizes the task orientation of the evaluation element of a PMM.

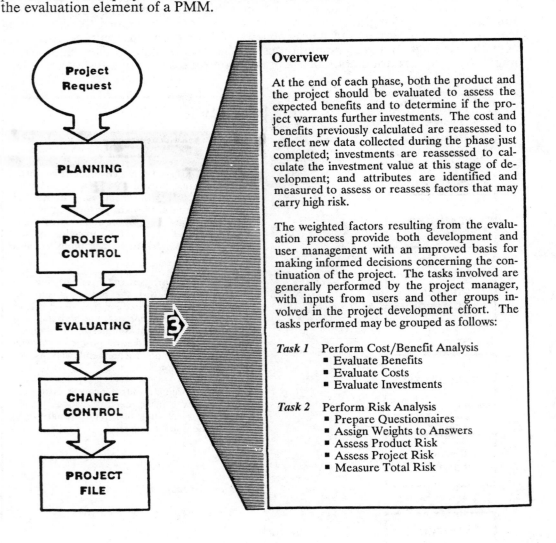

Overview

At the end of each phase, both the product and the project should be evaluated to assess the expected benefits and to determine if the project warrants further investments. The cost and benefits previously calculated are reassessed to reflect new data collected during the phase just completed; investments are reassessed to calculate the investment value at this stage of development; and attributes are identified and measured to assess or reassess factors that may carry high risk.

The weighted factors resulting from the evaluation process provide both development and user management with an improved basis for making informed decisions concerning the continuation of the project. The tasks involved are generally performed by the project manager, with inputs from users and other groups involved in the project development effort. The tasks performed may be grouped as follows:

Task 1 Perform Cost/Benefit Analysis
- Evaluate Benefits
- Evaluate Costs
- Evaluate Investments

Task 2 Perform Risk Analysis
- Prepare Questionnaires
- Assign Weights to Answers
- Assess Product Risk
- Assess Project Risk
- Measure Total Risk

Section 4, *Change Control,* should establish guidelines for controlling changes to baselines that are made during the development cycle. It should provide guidance for defining change initiation, technical assessment, business assessment, management approval, test tracking, and installation tracking policies. It should also include guidelines for establishing procedures for initiating change and for processing change. The following chart summarizes the task orientation of the change control element of project management concern.

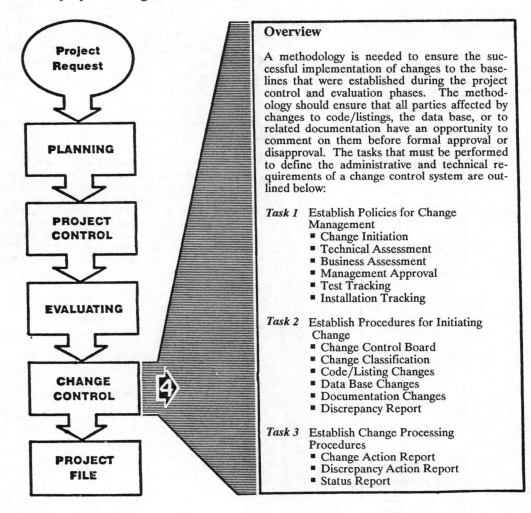

Overview

A methodology is needed to ensure the successful implementation of changes to the baselines that were established during the project control and evaluation phases. The methodology should ensure that all parties affected by changes to code/listings, the data base, or to related documentation have an opportunity to comment on them before formal approval or disapproval. The tasks that must be performed to define the administrative and technical requirements of a change control system are outlined below:

Task 1 Establish Policies for Change Management
- Change Initiation
- Technical Assessment
- Business Assessment
- Management Approval
- Test Tracking
- Installation Tracking

Task 2 Establish Procedures for Initiating Change
- Change Control Board
- Change Classification
- Code/Listing Changes
- Data Base Changes
- Documentation Changes
- Discrepancy Report

Task 3 Establish Change Processing Procedures
- Change Action Report
- Discrepancy Action Report
- Status Report

The flowchart on the left shows:
Project Request → PLANNING → PROJECT CONTROL → EVALUATING → CHANGE CONTROL → PROJECT FILE

Section 5, *Project File Maintenance,* should provide guidelines for defining the *acquisitions, cataloging, organization, circulation,* and *disposition* functions relative to the maintenance of a project file. The acquisition guidelines should consider both the acquisition of internally generated documents and, the acquisition of documents from outside sources. The cataloging guidelines should focus on procedures for descriptive cataloging, classifying project file items, and preparing indexes to enable the user to locate important items registered in the project file. The organization guidelines should discuss the various devices and filing methods required to accommodate the variety of media to be entered into the project file. The circulation control guidelines should explain the functions of an authorized patron file, title file, in-circulation file, and hold file. The disposition guidelines should provide alternatives for continued maintenance of the project file when the project is completed. The following chart summarizes the task orientation of the project file element of project management.

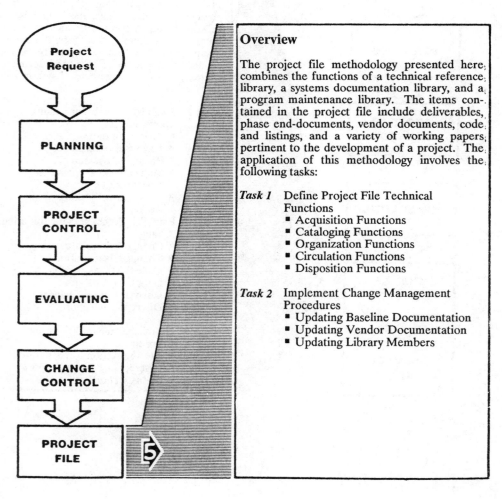

Overview

The project file methodology presented here combines the functions of a technical reference library, a systems documentation library, and a program maintenance library. The items contained in the project file include deliverables, phase end-documents, vendor documents, code and listings, and a variety of working papers pertinent to the development of a project. The application of this methodology involves the following tasks:

Task 1 Define Project File Technical Functions
- Acquisition Functions
- Cataloging Functions
- Organization Functions
- Circulation Functions
- Disposition Functions

Task 2 Implement Change Management Procedures
- Updating Baseline Documentation
- Updating Vendor Documentation
- Updating Library Members

Project Request → PLANNING → PROJECT CONTROL → EVALUATING → CHANGE CONTROL → PROJECT FILE

2.3 DOCUMENTATION GUIDELINES

Guidelines for preparing documents that coincide with the methodologies discussed in Section 2.2 are important for efficient production and control. The guidelines, once established, should be supported by policy, issued at the top management level of the data processing organization. A suggested arrangement of a documentation guidelines presentation follows:

> Section 1 Management Options
> Section 2 Format and Style
> Section 3 Documentation Standards
> Section 4 Management Review Guidelines
> Section 5 Change Control Guidelines

Section 1, *Management Options,* should include options for sizing document types, combining or splitting document types, organizing manuals into divisions and subdivisions, and document presentation (graphic presentation, narrative approach, forms approach, on-line approach, etc.).

Example:
_____

MANAGEMENT OPTIONS

Determination of Document Types
Not all of the document types discussed in this book may be needed on a particular project. The determination of which document types should be produced is generally the responsibility of the project manager. The level of complexity of the automated data system (ADS) to be documented is generally the essential determinant. Based on the complexity rating determined by the project manager, the types of documentation to be produced are then defined and scheduled for production.

Sizing of Document Types
Each of the content alternatives outlined in these documentation guidelines may be used to prepare documents that range from a few to several hundred pages in length. The magnitude and complexity of the project to be documented will determine the overall size. The level of detail to be included in each document should be determined by the documentation manager in consultation with the project manager. Another factor to be considered in determining document size is the environment in which the ADS will operate.

Combining or Splitting Document Types
It may be necessary, in some operational environments, to combine two or more document types into a single volume. Conversely, it is sometimes appropriate to split the contents of a specific document type to produce several different manuals. For example, an internal design document may include a program specification section, or the program specifications may be published in a separate volume.

Section 2, *Format and Style*, should stress the need for standardization. It should prescribe standards for dividing manuals into parts, chapters, sections, and sub-sections; numbering of these divisions; organizing user procedures and supporting information; illustration and table development; and the placement, capitalization, and style requirements for various subdivisions of the manual.

Example:

FORMAT AND STYLE GUIDE

2.1 SCOPE

This chapter contains guidelines and criteria to assist technical writers in defining the format and style requirements of an automated data system (ADS) manual. It suggests standards for

- Dividing an ADS manual into parts, chapters, sections, and subsections
- Numbering of these divisions
- Organizing user procedures and supporting information
- Illustration and table development
- The placement, capitalization, and style requirements for various subdivisions of the manual

2.2 DIVISIONS

As noted in Chapter 1, ADS manuals are generally organized in divisions and subdivisions to make the information easy to understand, find, and correlate with the system objectives. The usual organizational divisions and subdivisions are

Front matter
Parts
- Chapters
- Sections
- Subsections
- Paragraphs
- Subparagraphs
- Illustrations/tables and graphs
Appendixes
Glossary
Index

2.2.1 Front Matter

The front matter of an ADS manual generally consists of the following:

Cover
Sign-off sheet
Revision control form
Change control grid
Foreword/preface
Table of contents

Section 3, *Documentation Standards*, should define the standards for each of the technical documents that may be produced during the system development life cycle. A narrative of the table of contents should be included within each standard.

<u>*Example:*</u>

Summary guidelines for developing the content of an ID document are provided on the following pages.

3.0 GENERAL

This section should provide a summary description of the purpose of the ID document, a listing of publications, and an explanation of terms and abbreviations unique to the ID document.

3.1 Purpose of the ID Document
This subsection should describe the purpose, background, and intent of the ID document.

3.2 Project References
This subsection should provide a brief summary of the references applicable to the development of the project. Include

- The reference or catalog number for the item referenced
- The title of the item referenced
- The source or author of the item referenced
- The classification status of the item referenced

3.3 Index of Programs
This subsection should provide an index of programs used in the system. At least the following information should be provided:

- The program number
- The language in which the program is written
- The commonly used program name
- The procedure name
- A list of all input and output files that relate to the program.

3.4 Index of Files
This subsection should provide an index of files used by the new system and information about file structure and use. At least the following information should be provided:

- File label
- Program file name
- File organization (i.e., sequential, random, direct, etc.)
- Record length
- Record key/starting position
- Record key/length
- Record key/name
- Access mode

Section 4, *Management Review Guidelines,* should define procedures for conducting *technical reviews* that measure the technical accuracy of the document and *editorial reviews* that focus on ensuring that the format and style of presentation comply with established standards. The procedures should define when reviews should be conducted (periodic, milestone, phase, etc.) and explain how reviews are classified (e.g., checkpoint reviews, draft reviews, approval for production reviews, etc.). After each review, a report should be prepared to provide a formal record of the findings and recommendations. The guidelines should identify the organizations and individuals responsible for conducting document reviews and should provide instructions for marking review copies, conducting review meetings, and concurrence and sign-off.

Example:

4.1 CLASSIFICATION OF REVIEWS

Document reviews may be classified as *technical reviews* or *editorial reviews*. A technical review measures the technical accuracy of the document. An editorial review focuses on ensuring that the format and style of presentation comply with established standards. Reviews can also be classified by when they are held. Three types of reviews fall in this classification: *checkpoint reviews*, *draft reviews*, and *approval for production reviews*.

Checkpoint reviews are used to assess the status of the documentation effort after the completion of a particular chapter, section, or subsection. Not all projects may require checkpoint reviews. For large projects, however, checkpoint reviews can be critical in ensuring that manuals are being prepared in compliance with the requirements set forth in the documentation plan.

Draft reviews are conducted to ensure the technical integrity of the documentation and the consistency of the editorial format and style. In some instances both technical reviews and editorial reviews are conducted by the same review team. In larger projects, however, draft documents are reviewed by two separate review teams: a technical review team and an editorial review team.

Since most ADS manuals are published as accumulations of phase documentation, these reviews generally coincide with overall project phase reviews that are conducted to evaluate the phase outputs and assess the project status. Once approved, the ADS manual establishes a baseline for configuration management and control.

Approval-for-production reviews are comprehensive reviews generally conducted by the project manager, selected team members, and cognizant users. These reviews cover all aspects of the document - both technical and editorial. The review amounts to a thorough evaluation of the overall documentation effort, with the primary aim being the granting of final approval for production.

Section 5, *Change Control Guidelines*, should define the baseline documents that are subject to change control. The individuals and organizations responsible for making changes to baseline documents should be identified (e.g., user group, design group, programming group, quality assurance group). The functions of the change control board should also be described. The section should include procedures for changing baseline documents and explain how changes are classified (e.g., priority change, normal change, record change, etc.). Instructions for initiating a change request and change action reporting should be included.

Example:

5.1.1 Functional Baseline

The aggregate of documents produced during the analysis process establishes the functional baseline for change control. These documents include
- Functional description documents
- Data requirements documents
- Alternatives evaluation documents

Functional Description Document
A functional description document defines the functional requirements of a proposed ADS system and provides the ultimate user with a clear statement of the operational capability to be developed. If the scope of the proposed system functions is changed at any point, the document should be updated and receive user concurrence.

Data Requirements Document
The data requirements document defines the inputs required of the user, the procedures to be followed to provide this input to the system, specifications that define all standard data elements, and the data limitations of the system. Changes made to the system data requirements at any point during the development process must be reflected in the data requirements document.

Alternatives Evaluation Document
The alternatives evaluation document identifies the alternative approaches to the user problems and requirements. If a purchased package is to be considered, the evaluation and selection criteria are set forth in this document. The selection of the chosen alternative is based upon its performance against the specified criteria. Changes in these criteria or additions to the list of alternatives must, therefore, be reflected in the alternatives evaluation document.

5.1.2 Allocated Baseline

The allocated baseline for change control is established with the publication of the external design document (or preliminary design document) which provides the transition from the functional requirements to a set of user-oriented specifications.

2.4 SYSTEMS AND PROGRAMMING STANDARDS

Having defined corporate policy and established guidelines for the software development process, we can now focus on establishing *systems and programming standards*. Standards, as the term implies, are used to standardize the development of a software product. They establish the design limitations, systems and programming conventions, and the measure for quality control. Several types of standards may be applied to a software development program. They include

- Naming conventions
- Design standards
- Coding standards
- Development aids
- Data Dictionary standards

The common purpose of all standards is to promote the consistency of approach in the development of software products. To this end, the standards adopted should be organized and published in a *Systems and Programming Standards Manual*. When supported by policy, this manual becomes a vital reference work for analysts and programmers responsible for the design, programming, and maintenance of computer software systems.

At the beginning of a project, the project manager should define the specific standards to be used. The applicable standards should be referenced in the project plan and must be adhered to in the absence of any conflicting customer requirements that may arise. Any deviations from the published standards should be documented in the project plan, together with a justification. It is the project manager's responsibility to ensure that the standards are followed.

In addition to establishing the standards that will guide the system and programming functions, the manual may serve as a baseline for software quality assurance. The primary areas of QA concern that may correlate with the published standards include

- QA reviews of *program requirements* specifications prior to the onset of software design

- QA *top-level design* reviews to ensure that the requirements specifications have been properly identified

- QA *detail design* reviews to ensure that the design functions performed adhere to established standards

- QA *coding* reviews to ensure that the coding was done in compliance with coding standards and conventions

- QA *test plan and procedure* reviews to ascertain that the system/modules accomplish the requirements objectives

The suggested content arrangement of the *Systems an Programming Standards Manual* is as follows:

Cover
Foreword
Contents
Standards
- Naming Conventions
- Design Standards
- Coding Standards
- Development Aids
- Data Dictionary

The *cover* should contain the data relative to security and classification, standard classification, date of approval, title, and acquisition method.

A *foreword* should be prepared to explain the reasons for or purpose of the manual. The foreword may include a brief resume of the development history of the manual or a statement of reason for a particular format or sequence in the presentation of standards.

Example:

FOREWORD

This manual contains standards that must be used by all those who are involved in a software development process. The standards are approved by the Office of the President for use companywide. Recommended corrections, additions, or deletions shall be submitted to

Standards Committee
MIS Department
XYC Company

Section 1 presents *naming conventions* for identifying systems and subsystems, programs, data sets, procedures, jobs, data bases, and reports.

Section 2 presents *design standards* that must be applied in designing data bases, on-line systems, batch systems, reports, and programs. It also includes standards for design reviews.

Section 3 presents the *coding standards* to be followed in coding programs. It includes standards pertaining to language selection, program language applications, and common routines.

The single word CONTENTS, in capital letters, should head the contents page. Identification numbers and headings for each section and subsection should be shown. The contents may include references to appendixes and index, if needed. A separate caption or title should head each list of figures and tables.

Example:

Section 1, Naming Conventions, may include several types of naming conventions as indicated in the content example on the preceding page. The objective of these standards is to ensure a consistent approach to identifying common entities that comprise a software system.

The preparation and presentation of the standards pertaining to *naming conventions* are illustrated below and on the following pages.

System/Subsystem Names. This subsection of the *Systems and Programming Standards Manual* should present the naming conventions that must be used by the software development staff to ensure a consistent approach to identifying systems and subsystems.

Example:

1.1 SYSTEM/SUBSYSTEM NAMES

All programming personnel must adhere to the following conventions when assigning system/subsystem names:

SU
Where
    S = one-position unique number specified by the
         established convention
    U = one-position unique character or number specified by
         the established convention

Program Names. This subsection should present the naming convention standard that must be used by the software development staff to ensure a consistent approach to identifying programs.

Example:

1.2 PROGRAM NAMES

All programming personnel must adhere to the following conventions when assigning program names:

GDPTSUXX
Where:
    G = group code
    D = division code
    P = constant P
    T = program type
          1 for MP
          2 for BMP
          3 for batch programs
    S = system code
    U = subsystem code
    XX = sequential number

Data Set Names. This subsection should present the naming convention standards that must be used by the software development staff to ensure a consistent approach to identifying data sets.

Example:

1.3 DATA SET NAMES

All programming personnel must adhere to the following conventions when assigning data set names:

```
N P DIV C CA FFFFFFF(...)
VT
        1 for MP
        0 (Zero)
```

Where
First level

Position 1	N	=	non-VSAM data set
	V	=	VSAM data set
Position 2	P	=	production data set
	T	=	test data set
Positions 3 to 5	DIV	=	The center assignment three digit identifier of the owner location
Position 6	C	=	CICS data base
	I	=	IMS data base
	O	=	other
Positions 7 and 8	CA	=	The center assigned two-digit code 00 (zeros)

Procedure Names. This subsection should present the naming convention standard that must be used by the software development staff to ensure a consistent approach to identifying procedures.

Example:

1.4 PROCEDURE NAMES

All programming personnel must adhere to the following conventions when assigning procedure names:

DRSUXXXX

Where

D	=	alpha division code
R	=	a constant R to denote that it is a procedure name
S	=	system ID
U	=	subsystem ID
XXXX	=	sequential number to guarantee uniqueness

Job Names. This subsection should present the naming convention that must be used by the software development staff to ensure a consistent approach to identifying jobs.

Example:

1.5 JOB NAMES

All programming personnel must adhere to the following conventions when assigning job names:

DSUXXYYY

Where
D	=	alpha division code
S	=	system ID
U	=	subsystem ID
XX	=	sequential number to guarantee uniqueness
YYY	=	numeric division code

Data Base Names. This subsection should present the naming convention standard that must be used by the software development staff to ensure a consistent approach to identifying data bases.

Example:

1.6 DATA BASE NAMES

All programming personnel must adhere to the following conventions when assigning data base names:

GDDBBYZ

Where
GDDBBY	=	DBD Name
Z	=	"1" for ISAM; "0" for index overflow or "P" for prime data set

Report Names. This subsection should present the naming convention standard that must be used by the software development staff to ensure a consistent approach to identifying reports.

Example:

1.7 REPORT NAMES

All programming personnel must adhere to the following conventions when assigning report names:

DTSUXXN
Where
DTSUXX	=	from the program name
N	=	a unique character

Section 2, *Design Standards*, should present those standards required to standardize the technique used in performing the following design activities:

- Data base design
- On-line design
- Batch/batch mode processing (BMP) design
- Forms design
- Report design
- Program design
- Design review checkpoints

The preparation and presentation of the standards pertaining to these design activities are illustrated below and on the following pages.

Data Base Design Standards. This subsection should present the standards that establish the requirements for data base design.

Example:

2.1 DATA BASE DESIGN STANDARDS

All data base oriented systems must be designed in conformance with the following standards:

1. All on-line transactions will be governed by a class structure defined by data base services.

2. An IMS/VS program over 64K must be approved by data base services.

3. All program development will utilize COBOL/VS.

4. IMS/VS production will use PROC's supplied by OLS.

5. IMS/VS BMP programs must take SYNCH points at appropriate intervals using a standardized routine provided by OLS.

6. To achieve production status, all appropriate information must be entered in the data base dictionary.

7. IMS/VS transactions will use "MODE-SINGLE" and be designed accordingly.

8. One on-line transaction per program.

On-Line Design Standards. This subsection should present the standards that establish the design requirements for IMS message processing in an *on-line* environment.

Example:

2.2 ON-LINE DESIGN STANDARDS

All on-line systems must meet the following standard requirements:

Communications
1. The data transmission network shall consist of voice quality lines used on demand for data transmission.

2. Average holding times in the voice system should not exceed 4 to 5 minutes.

3. Connecting a terminal to the data transmission shall be done by using a common carrier modem.

System Load
1. Both the communication system and the computing system should be operating at 70 percent of saturation at peak so that terminal response is reasonable.

2. Batch jobs should be run on the third shift to reduce system load.

Batch/BMP Design Standards. This subsection should present the standards that establish the design requirements for IMS message processing in a *batch* environment.

Example:

2.3 BATCH/BMP DESIGN STANDARDS

The following standards must be applied by all analysts and programmers in designing IMS batch processing programs.

1. All batch programs, except utility programs, must be designed to execute as IMS batch message processing programs (hereinafter referred to as BMPs).

2. All BMPs will be coded utilizing COBOL/VS.

3. The overlay method of program segmentation will not be used for any BMP.

4. The use of dynamic linkage should be cleared through the project manager.

5. All BMPs will access only IMS data base files.

6. BMPs will be modular in structure.

7. All batch reporting will be accomplished by BMPs writing out report records to a report file, a GSA data base, which will subsequently be processed by an edit program.

Forms Design Standards. This subsection should present the standards that establish a consistent approach to forms design.

Example:

2.4 FORMS DESIGN STANDARDS

The following standards must be adhered to in designing forms:

Continuous Forms

1. Typical widths and lengths (depths), in inches, for continuous forms are as follows:
   WIDTH:
   4 3/4, 5 3/4, 6 1/2, 8 1/2, 9, 9 1/2, 9 7/8,
   10 5/16, 11

   LENGTH:
   2 5/6, 3, 3 1/3, 3 1/12, 3 2/3, 4, 4 1/4,
   5 5/12, 6, 7, 7 1/3

2. Continuous forms may be left unfastened or the sheets may be fastened together by any one of several methods:

   - Staple fastening

   - Glue fastening

   - Crimped fastening

   - Sewed in the margin

Report Design Standards. This subsection should present the standards that establish a consistent format for all reports that must be designed.

Example:

2.5 REPORT DESIGN STANDARDS

The following standards must be adhered to in designing reports:

Report Headings
The first three lines of all reports will be a standard heading as follows:

   Line 1:
   Positions 5-12: Report number
   Functional area (Centered)
   Positions 102-109: Run date (MM/DD/YY)
   Positions 111-115: Run time (HH:MM)

   Line 2:
   Positions 1-18: Division

Processing Options
The first page of every report should be titled *Processing Parameters* and should use specified options and selection criteria.

Design Review Standards. This subsection should present the design review standards that establish a set of checkpoints through which development projects can be systematically reviewed.

Example:

2.6 DESIGN REVIEW STANDARDS

The following standards must be applied when one is establishing checkpoints for technical reviews:

1. A software development project must undergo six technical reviews:

   - Systems requirements definition Review
   - Systems external specifications review
   - Systems internal specifications review
   - Program specifications review
   - Final system checkout review
   - Post installation review

2. During the conducting of these reviews, key members of the development team should be present in order to answer questions or expand on the material present.

3 The spacing of these reviews in the system development life cycle, the materials to be reviewed during each review, and the name of the review shall be based upon the systems development methodology.

Program Design Standards. This subsection should present the program design standards to be followed for the development of new programs and modification of old programs

Example:

2.7 PROGRAM DESIGN STANDARDS

Programming standards include

- Program organization standards
- Procedure name standards
- Program structure standards
- Program comments standards
- Program parameter standards
- Blank line and spacing standards
- Flowchart standards

Programming language use shall be as follows:

Business Applications
All business programs developed for the mainframe will be developed using ANS COBOL II.

Engineering and Scientific Applications
All engineering and scientific programs developed for workstation use will be developed using PL1, FORTRAN, and C.

Program Organization. This subsection should present the program organization standards to be followed for the development of new programs and modification of old programs.

Example:

2.7.1 Program Organization

The program organization standards to be used when one is designing programs are as follows:

1. Programs should be written in modular form. Divide programs into functional sections to achieve modularity.

2. Lengthy or complex routines should be visually separated from other routines or code.

3. Number of sections should be kept to a reasonable number to allow efficient execution of programs.

Procedure Names. This subsection should present the procedure name standards to be followed for the naming of new procedures.

Example:

2.7.2 Procedure Names

Where the prefix is a sequential set, the procedure name standards to be used when designing programs are as follows:

1. Paragraph and section name should be coded in the following format:

    XXXX-MEANINGFUL-NAME

    The combined set and name will allow identification of procedures both logically and physically.

2. Prefix XXXXX will be constructed as XKKOO where

    - X is
    I for initialization paragraph/section
    M for a mainline paragraph/section
    T for any termination paragraph/section
    S for a subroutine paragraph/standard

    - LL is
    a unique set of characters to identify a logical group of processing. This could be for one or more paragraphs or sections.

Program Structure. This subsection should present the program structure standards to be followed for development of new programs and modification of old programs.

Example:

2.7.3 Program Structure

The program structure standards to be used when one is designing new programs or modifying old programs are as follows:

1. Each source statement or clause should appear on a single line.
2. Each sentence should begin in column 14.
3. For IF statements, further indent clauses other than the IF and ELSE clauses.

Program Comments. This subsection should present the program comments standards to be followed for development of new programs and modification of old programs.

Example:

2.7.4 Program Comments

The program comments standards to be used in designing new programs or modifying old programs are as follows:

1. Any coding which cannot be easily understood by other programmers should be explained by using the asterisk (*) in column 7. Annotation should be used in all divisions as needed.
2. Use comments at the section level to describe the section's functions.

Program Parameters. This subsection should present the program parameters standards to be followed for development of new programs and modification of old programs.

Example:

2.7.5 Program Parameters

The program parameter standards to be used in designing new programs or modifying old programs are as follows:

1. Do not accept data from the console. Input parameters such as period date, type of run, etc., can be provided through the use of control cards or the PARM field of the EXEC JCL statements. For example:
   ```
   //S01 EXEC PGM-PROGA,PARm='TEST' or
   //CONTROL DD *
   TEST
   /*
   ```

Blank Lines and Spacing. This subsection should present the blank lines and spacing standards to be followed for development of new programs and modification of old programs.

Example:

2.7.6 Blank Lines and Spacing

The blank-lines and spacing standards to be used when one is designing new programs or modifying old programs are as follows:

1. To clearly indicate logical breaks, blank lines must be used preceding paragraph names, record descriptions, and 01 levels.
2. New page must be used before division names, section names, and file descriptions.
3. The EJECT facility may also be used to separate other logical sections of the program for improved readability.

Grouping Routines. This subsection should present the grouping routine standards to be followed for development of new programs and modification of old programs.

Example:

2.7.7 Grouping Routines

The grouping routines standards to be used in designing new programs or modifying old programs are as follows:
1) Significant routines which are performed may be grouped together in common area.
2) Short blocks of code which are used by more than one routine should be coded in line for each use. Use of COPY or the PANVALET + +INCLUDE functions are recommended for this purpose.

Flowcharts. This subsection should present the flowchart standards to be followed for development of new programs and modification of old programs.

Example:

2.7.8 Flowcharts

The flowchart standards to be used in designing new programs or modifying old programs are as follows:

1. Macro flowchart should be written for each program prior to coding.
2. The flowchart, together with the program special sections, should be reviewed with the system analyst prior to coding.

Section 3, *Coding Standards*, presents standards that establish control techniques for coding the software programs. They provide the programming staff with complete guidelines for code generation, compiling statements into machine-readable form, and module and integration testing. The primary areas of programming concern that should be addressed in these standards are

- Language selection
- Language standards
- Common routines

The preparation and presentation of the standards pertaining to *coding* are illustrated in this section.

Language Selection. This subsection should present the standards to be followed in selecting the program language to be used for the development of new programs. Standards should be presented for both business and scientific applications.

Example:

3.1 LANGUAGE SELECTION

The following standards should be used for program language selection:

1. For *business applications* developed on the mainframe, programs will be developed using COBOL II; assembler language may be used with prior approval by the QA organization.

   Business programs developed for the PC will be developed using either dBASE or C++.

2. For *engineering and scientific applications*, FORTRAN, PASCAL, or C programming languages may be used.

   Engineering applications developed for the workstation environment will be developed using C++.

   Modifications to existing systems will be made in the language of that system unless the function required cannot be developed within the current source language. All programs placed on a workstation will be compiled and the source code removed from the workstation and placed within the software configuration library.

Language Standards. This subsection should present the program language standards to be followed for the development of new programs and modifications of old programs. The presentation should include all programming languages applicable to the development process.

Example:

3.2.1 COBOL STANDARDS

The following standards must be adhered to when one is producing program code in COBOL.

1. For documentation purposes, programs should contain the following clauses:
   - Program ID
   - Author
   - Installation
   - Date written
   - Date compiled
   - Change history
   - Remarks
2. Use the APPLY CORE-INDEX clause when processing an indexed file randomly to allow the highest level index to be processed in core.
3. The APPLY WRITE-ONLY clause should be used for files with variable-length records opened as OUTPUT to obtain maximum use of the block.

Common Routines. This subsection should present the standards that must be adhered to in order to ensure that common routines are utilized whenever possible.

Example:

3.3 COMMON ROUTINES

The following standards must be followed to ensure that common software is utilized wherever appropriate:

To ABEND a program with a user specified completion code, and to optionally suppress the ABEND (dump) output, use ABEND99.

<u>Calling Sequence</u>
Call ABEND99, using data name.

<u>Argument</u>
"Data-Name" is any 2-byte binary data item aligned on a half-word boundary. Prior to executing the CALL statement, "data-name" should be initialized with a positive integer user ABEND code.

Section 4, *Development Aid Standards*, is needed to establish consistency in the usage of in-house utilities, system software packages, and debugging aids.

The preparation and presentation of the standards pertaining to *development aids* are illustrated in this section.

In-House Utilities. This subsection should present the guidelines that will aid staff in the use of in-house utilities. Guidelines should address all available utilities. These may include

- Data conversion utilities
- Disaster recovery utilities
- Disk/tape/file utilities
- Documentation Generators

Example:

4.1 IN-HOUSE UTILITIES

DSN404 - Scratch/Rename Data Sets
This utility is used to scratch, rename, and uncatalog cataloged data sets. The following standard must be adhered to when using this utility.

Calling Sequence

```
//SO1 EXEC DSN404
//SYSIN DD *
  Any number of input control cards go here
//*
```

Input Control Cards

Coding must start in column 1 and continue without any spaces. Data after the first space will be listed, but will be treated as comments.

Scratch

TCA.P404.ABC Data set to be scratched

The data set will be uncataloged and scratched if located on a direct access device.

Rename

TCA.P404.ABC Data set to be renamed
TCA.P404.DEF New data set name

System Software Packages. This subsection should present the guidelines that will aid the development staff in the use of system software packages such as TSO, RAMIS, PANVALET, EASYTRIEVE, etc.

Example:

4.2 SYSTEM SOFTWARE PACKAGES

TSO

The purpose of this standard is to aid MIS personnel in using TSO. The following standards must be applied:

> <u>HELP406</u>
> Provides on-line help for the current TSO release. To execute, enter
>
> > HELP406
>
> <u>PANA406</u>
> Used to add a member to TCA.P406.PANLIB.
>
> Input required is member name, member type, and user code. Allowable member types are COBOL, DATA, and CNTL.
>
> To execute enter: PANA406 member-name, member-type, user-code.

Debugging Aids. This subsection should present guidelines that will aid development staff in the use of debugging programs. Guidelines should be prepared for all available debugging aids.

Example:

4.3 DEBUGGING AIDS

ADS (ADVANCED DEBUGGING SYSTEM)

ADS is to be used in the test CICS region only. It is unavailable in production or training. Use this aid for debugging command-level CICS programs.

An interactive, language-independent test facility enables users to identify, diagnose, and resolve application problems in a CICS environment.

The program intercepts processing to prevent storage violations and detect program check errors on either a region wide or a selective basis, allowing intermittent errors to be diagnosed and corrected.

Section 5, *Data Dictionary Standards*, presents standards that define the approach to maintaining information on the data dictionary. The primary areas of concern that should be addressed involve defining programs to the data dictionary, defining modules to the data dictionary, defining files to the data dictionary, and defining jobs to the data dictionary.

The preparation and presentation of standards pertaining to maintaining data on the data dictionary are illustrated in this section.

System Information. This subsection should define the approach for maintaining information about software systems on the data dictionary.

Example:

5.1 SYSTEM INFORMATION

This standard defines a standard approach for maintaining information about MIS systems on the data dictionary.

An application system is a combination of jobs, programs, data bases, and other system resources that satisfy a complete set of data processing requirements. It is mandatory that application systems be documented on the data dictionary. A fully documented system will have a description and all its related entities as follows:

- Programs
- Modules
- Data bases
- Files
- Jobs

Program Information. This subsection should define the approach for maintaining information about programs on the data dictionary.

Example:

5.2 PROGRAM INFORMATION

This standard defines the approach for maintaining information about programs on the data dictionary.

It is essential that a set of basic information about programs be maintained on the data dictionary as follows:

- Program name
- Program description
- Type
- Language
- Size
- Files accessed and access intent
- Reports created

Data Element Definition. This subsection should define the approach for defining and maintaining *data elements* on the data dictionary.

Example:

5.2 DATA ELEMENT DEFINITION

The following standards must be adhered to in defining data elements on the data dictionary.

This standard defines the approach for maintaining information about programs on the data dictionary.

1. All elements must be defined as primary elements on Form MIS-800, Primary Element Maintenance.

2. If the element already exists, but a different picture clause is required, complete Form MIS-900, Secondary Element Maintenance.

3. An element that is also a logical group identifier must be defined on form MIS-950, Subfield Element Maintenance.

2.5 PROCEDURE MANUALS

This section provides instructions for the preparation of procedure manuals. It suggests a format arrangement and gives step-by-step guidance for writing the procedure statements.

Simply stated, procedures explain *what* work has to be done, *who* will do it, *when* it must be done, and the sequence of tasks and task steps that have to be performed. The preparation of procedure manuals requires communications skills that focus on providing readers with a medium that facilitates quick comprehension and accurate response. Incomplete procedure statements can have serious consequences on a software development project. A missing instruction or a poorly constructed procedure statement can lead to system failure and create a costly dilemma.

The techniques suggested in this section are concerned with how to organize the contents of a procedure manual and how to construct the individual procedure statements. The primary objective is to illustrate how to organize the procedural data for publication.

Procedure instructions may involve both narrative and graphic presentations. When the procedures relate to filling out forms, samples of the forms should accompany the instruction. Other visual presentations that correlate with instructions may include graphs, sketches, screen layouts, and diagrams. Many instructions, of course, cannot be accompanied with graphic aids. For those instructions that must be presented entirely in narrative form, the writer must exercise care to ensure that the instructions are presented in a manner that the reader can easily understand.

This requires the use of concise sentence construction. Long and wordy sentences tend to lose the reader and often contribute to procedure failure.

The physical characteristics of a procedure manual are also considered in this section, including the arrangement of front matter, procedure statements, and indexes (if required). As in the case of policy statements, the procedures may be arranged in sequence of publication or in groups covering related subjects. The sequencing in publication order approach may be easier for the writer, but it often poses problems to the user. From the user's standpoint, the subject arrangement is generally considered more coherent. If the statements are logically arranged, the user more readily becomes familiar with the major groupings that provide written information needed to perform specific jobs.

The day-to-day operation of a data processing organization depends, to a great extent, on written procedures that circulate within and among the user and development staff. These documents convey precise information regarding how the various entities involved in a systems development effort interact with one another.

The physical characteristics of the model for a procedure manual presented in this section include the arrangement of front matter, procedure statements, and indexes. Some of the steps involved in developing the procedure manual and constructing procedure statements parallel those suggested in constructing policy statements. In fact, many companies tend to combine the responsibility for preparing both *policy* and *procedure* statements. The policy and procedure statements are often combined and published together in a *Policy and Procedure Manual.*

The contents should be arranged in accordance with the following:

Cover
Explanation of company system of manuals
Policy statement
Table of contents
Introduction
Procedures statements
Index

The text on the cover should include information relative to security classification, procedure identification, date of approval, title, and acquisition method. For multivolume procedure manuals, the volume number should be indicated on the top right-hand corner.

The editorial preparation of the various sections of the manual is explained and illustrated on the following pages.

Explanation of Company's System of Manuals. An explanation of the company's system of manuals should appear as the first page following the cover. The statements should outline the scope and relationship of the various policy and procedure manuals used throughout the company.

Example:

THE COMPANY'S SYSTEM OF MANUALS

I. **General**
The company's system of manuals includes instructions on policies, procedures, responsibilities, and standards which are prepared and approved by persons of recognized authority. Each set of manuals is issued in a separate binder.

II. **Companywide Policies and Procedures**
The companywide manual contains policies and procedures that apply to all personnel throughout the company.

III. **Divisional/Interdepartmental Policies and Procedures**
This manual contains two types of procedural instructions: (1) operating procedure instructions to be followed in performing the work of a particular division and (2) operating procedure instructions that flow through one or more divisions of the company.

IV. **Departmental Policies and Procedures**
This manual contains only those policies and procedures that concern the supervisors of only one department. Such instructions might cover either individual jobs or subroutines affecting several sections of the department.

Review and Approval Policy Statement. The policy statement pertaining to the review and approval of departmental procedures should be included as the second page following the cover.

Example:

POLICY STATEMENT

Whenever instructions to be included in a departmental procedure manual represent that department's share of an interdivisional or companywide procedure, such instructions should not be released until they have first been cleared with the general procedures staff. This is necessary in order to coordinate the coverage and the time of issuance of all written instructions related to the same policy or procedure.

Contents. The single word CONTENTS (in capital letters) should head the contents page.

Example:

CONTENTS

Introduction. An introduction that explains the arrangement of procedures and provides the reader with information on how to use the manual should appear as the first page following the contents.

Example:

INTRODUCTION

This manual includes procedures to be followed in performing planning, design, programming, implementation, and maintenance tasks related to software development. It is divided into three levels of procedural control: (1) corporate, (2) divisional, and (3) departmental.

     Section 1 contains the procedures that must be followed at the corporate level. It includes procedures concerned with short- and long-range planning pertaining to software development projects.

     Section 2 includes procedures that must be followed in performing software development functions at the divisional level. It covers procedures pertaining to budget reviews, project initiation, and configuration management.

     Section 3 contains all the procedures that are carried out at the departmental level.

STEPS IN WRITING PROCEDURE STATEMENTS

There are six steps in writing a procedure statement:

Step 1. State, as specifically as possible, the purpose of the procedure being described.

Step 2. Identify those organizations that will be affected by the procedure.

Step 3. List all the references that apply to the procedure (e.g., company-wide manuals, vendor manuals, etc.).

Step 4. List all the attachments associated with the procedure (e.g., forms, schematics, equipment lists, etc.).

Step 5. Prepare a statement covering the general aspects of the procedure that must be known for effective performance.

Step 6. Describe, in step-by-step fashion, the procedure(s) to be performed, indicating who will be responsible for performing each step (e.g., Requestor, MIS librarian, group leader, MIS planning committee, etc.)

The narrative statement should be accompanied by graphics representations (illustrations, flowcharts, forms, etc.) wherever applicable. If the illustrations, etc., are too bulky or will interrupt the continuity if placed within the main section, they should be included in an appendix to the manual.

After the front-matter considerations are concluded, the procedure writer need only be concerned with the preparation and classification of new procedures to be added to the manual, and the updating and maintenance of the procedures already in the manual. These changes and additions to the procedure manual should, of course, be coordinated through formal review committees, responsible for defining standards within the organization.

Typically, a procedure statement is divided into six elements: purpose, organizations affected, references, attachments, general statement, and procedure statement. Each of these elements is illustrated below and on the following pages.

Purpose. This subsection should specifically state the purpose of the procedure. The purpose statement should be as concise as possible.

Example:
_____

1.0 PURPOSE
The purpose of procedure XYZ is to define the procedure for requesting MIS services for development of new systems and enhancements to existing systems.

Organizations Affected. This subsection should list all organizations affected by the procedure.

Example:

2.0 ORGANIZATIONS AFFECTED

The MIS departments of all corporate divisions are affected by procedure XYZ.

References. This subsection should provide a listing of all the references applicable to the procedures. The listing may include references to policy statements; related procedures; methods guidelines; system and programming standards; and equipment manuals.

Example:

3.0 REFERENCES

Corporate Policy and Procedure Manual
MIS Maintenance Service Report
MIS Incident Report

Attachments. This subsection should list all the attachments that relate to the procedures. The attachments may include forms, exhibits, charts, tables, and task checklists from the methods guidelines.

Example:

4.0 ATTACHMENTS

MIS Service Request
System/Program Change form
Project Certification form

General Statements. This subsection should provide information of a general nature that will help the reader better understand the procedural requirements.

Example:

5.0 GENERAL

5.1 *New systems* include all work in developing an EDP-based system for an operation that is being performed manually without any support EDP systems. New systems can also be classified as *major* or *minor*.

Major development effort is for systems that will generally take more than 6 months of effort to develop (although each installation may establish a different threshold than the one specified).

Minor development includes all new systems that fall under this threshold.

5.2   *Enhancements* pertain to all changes to the system that are made for the convenience of the user. This includes changes in the user operations or environment, new requirements, changes in the preference of report layouts, adding new data to existing reports, new reports, new features, new capabilities, etc.

Procedure Statements. This subsection should detail the procedure to be followed in step-by-step fashion. The title of the person or the organizational entity responsible for performing each task step should be noted.

Example:

Requestor	6.1 Fill out requestor information section on MIS request and include any attachments.
	6.2 Secure approval signatures of supervisor and department manager.
	6.3 Determine the appropriate project authorization number for billing purposes and enter this information on MIS Service Request.
	6.4 Forward documents to MIS librarian
Librarian	6.5 Assign sequential number from book, log in, and enter on form. Retain copy.
	6.6 Forward documents to appropriate group leader.
Group Leader	6.7 Review the request for completeness and signed approval. If not complete, return to user.

In many software development environments, analysts and programmers are quick to downgrade procedures as "red tape," but the lack of procedures may well be the primary cause of most software development failures.

Procedures are the means by which software development projects are initiated, carried forward, and terminated. It is through procedures that policies are implemented, project requests are approved, estimates are developed, methods guidelines are followed, and the system is tested, implemented, and maintained. These are just a few of the software development activities that should be considered by procedure analysts. They are sufficient, however, to point out that it is in the context of procedures that actions and control of a software development activity are achieved. Procedures govern the direction and scope of performance and guide the process by which software deliverables are produced. They enable project managers to systematically monitor the progress of a development effort.

However, procedures play a vital role in the software development process only to the extent that the project managers are willing to support their development and enforce them. The effectiveness of a software manager may be correlated with a recognition of how procedures are required to convert static plans and policies into a dynamic administrative force.

Chapter 3
Software Development Analysis Documentation

The emphasis during the analysis stage of the systems development life cycle is on both quantitative and qualitative evaluation. During the analysis stage, the systems development organization identifies the problems and sets goals and criteria by which to judge the feasibility and determine the basic requirements of the proposed project. The documentation resulting from these activities includes

- Statements of existing problems
- Preliminary estimates of costs
- Projected schedules for development of a new system
- Data that permits intelligent decision making regarding the economic justification and technical feasibility of the proposed project
- Preliminary specifications that define functional, performance, data, environmental, and organizational requirements

The analysis process begins with a request for a new system or system enhancement. The originator, usually the manager of the user department, prepares a project request document that briefly describes the problem and/or need for a new system or improvement to an existing system. The project request document is then reviewed by the system's development department to determine how the objectives stated by the request can best be met. If the request calls for a major development effort, an analyst may be assigned to conduct an *initial investigation*.

Working with the user management and key user personnel, the analyst performs a series of tasks that are aimed at evaluating the costs and benefits of the proposed project. The main objective of the initial investigation is to acquire a better understanding of the problems, opportunities, and need expressed on the project request. This involves gathering information that will enable management to make value judgments. During this phase, target schedules are developed and preliminary costs estimates are made. The initial investigation culminates with the development of a feasibility study work plan that outlines the tasks to be performed to review the present system functions (i.e., inputs, files, outputs, costs, etc.), identify and evaluate commercially available packages, and prepare an economic evaluation.

After completing the initial investigation, and authority has been granted to proceed to the next phase, the analyst conducts the *feasibility study* to determine what should be done, how it can be done, and what is the value of doing it.

The first step in conducting a feasibility study is to review the present system to learn what it does and how it does it. When this task is completed, the analyst focuses on identifying functional requirements and assessing the support necessary to satisfy these requirements. Having reviewed the present system and analyzed the requirements of the proposed system, the analyst establishes a checklist of tasks to be performed for the review of application packages that may satisfy the user requirements. The documentation resulting from the feasibility study is used by the project team to develop a project plan that describes how the project team intends to accomplish the development objectives.

The project plan reaffirms the life cycle phases of the systems development methodology and provides work-planning checklists of the tasks and task steps to be performed during each phase of development. The key personnel responsible for performing the tasks should be identified in the plan. In addition, the plan should provide a specification of the review process (i.e., who reviews the project, at what milestones, etc.), and explain how the user and development staff organizations will communicate with one another.

When the feasibility study is completed and the project plan has been published, the analyst moves on to the third phase of the development process, *requirements definition*. During this phase, the analyst expands upon the functional requirements that were identified during the feasibility phase. This involves defining the functional and performance requirements on which the proposed system must be based (e.g., accuracy requirements, timing requirements, failure contingency requirements, etc.); analyzing the input, data base, and output requirements; defining the environmental requirements (e.g., hardware, software, interface, security and privacy, control, etc.); and assessing organizational impacts of the new system.

This chapter reviews the task-documentation orientation of a systems development methodology that defines the tasks, task steps, and deliverables of the analysis process. It explains how the analysis documentation is used to define the functional baseline for configuration management and describes the evolution of analysis documentation.

Examples are shown for the various deliverables. Instructions are provided for organizing and synthesizing the deliverable items to produce initial investigation, feasibility study, and requirements definition phase end-documents. Summary guidelines for the content development of each milestone document to be produced during the analysis process are also included. Likewise, guidelines are presented for the content development of the project plan.

These content development guidelines, combined with the format and style guidelines discussed in Chapter 8, define a set of standards that will provide project managers with uniform documentation that will enable them to monitor the progress of the analysis process at significant milestones. They also provide a standardized record of the analysis data and ensure that authors of documents and managers of project development have a guide to follow in preparing and checking documentation.

3.1 THE PROJECT REQUEST: THE FIRST ANALYSIS DOCUMENT

Requests for new systems development, or for enhancements to existing systems, originate with the preparation of a formal *project request*. The project request is usually brief, generally not more than a page or two. When the request is completed, it is submitted to a steering committee or other decision-making body for review. The project request thus becomes the first document entered into the project file. The information provided by the project request usually includes the project title, a brief description of the project, and the objectives the requestor seeks to accomplish by the implementation of a new system or enhancement to an existing system. The project request data also should indicate the anticipated impact of the proposed system on the management controls, equipment requirements, and personnel. An example of a project request form is shown in Figure 3-1.

MIS DEPT.	Date Recorded by MIS Dept.	Project ID	SR No.	Project Authorization #

REQUESTOR

I. PROJECT DESCRIPTION AND AUTHORIZATION

A. Requested By: _____ Date: _____

B. Requested Due Date: _____ C. Charge to Dept.: _____ % of Cost _____

D. ☐ New Project   ☐ Project Revision

E. Project Description:

_____

_____

_____

_____

F. Requesting Department Supervisor _____ Phone Ext. _____

G. Department Manager _____ Date: _____

MIS DEPARTMENT

II. DATA PROCESSING – REVIEW AND COST ESTIMATES

A. Type of request   ☐ Development (D)   ☐ Enhancement (EN)

B. Estimate of Cost:

NON–RECURRING			RECURRING			
Expense Items	Hours	Cost	Expense Items	Freq.	Hours	Cost
1. Systems Analysis			1. Personnel			
2. Programming			2. Supplies			
3. Equipment Usage			3. Computer System			
4. Supplies			4. Other Equipment			
5. Other Expense			5. Other Expense			
6. Overhead						
TOTAL			TOTAL			

C. Data Processing Acceptance of Design & Estimate

Under 5K

1. Group Leader _____ Date: _____

2. Project Manager _____ Date: _____

3. MIS Manager _____ Date: _____

REQUESTOR

III. REQUESTOR ACCEPTANCE OF DESIGN & ESTIMATE

Under 5K	A. Requestor _____ Date: _____
	B. Supervision _____ Date: _____
5K to 15K	C. Dept. Mgr. _____ Date: _____
15K to 30K	D. Plant Mgr. _____ Date: _____
	E. OD Mgr. _____ Date: _____
Over 30K	F. General Mgr. _____ Date: _____

Figure 3-1. Project Request Document

3.2 ANALYSIS TASK-DOCUMENTATION ORIENTATION

In a structured systems environment, the software development methodology (SDM) defines the life cycle phases of the analysis process. The phases, in turn, are broken down into a series of tasks and task steps. The results of each task and task step are recorded as they are completed. When all of the tasks for a given phase have been completed and the results recorded, the document records are delivered to a project file and placed under configuration control. The items in the project file may then be recalled to produce the analysis phase end-documents. Collectively, these documents establish the functional baseline for configuration management. The process is illustrated in Figure 3-2.

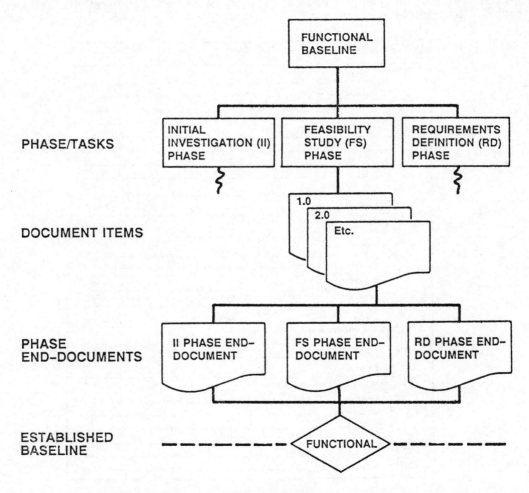

Figure 3-2. End-Document Orientation of the Analysis Process

3.3 INITIAL INVESTIGATION TASK DOCUMENT ITEMS

The initial investigation breaks down into six major tasks. Each task results in one or more document items that are deliverable to the project file. The cumulation of documentation presented in the initial investigation document provides management with the requisite information upon which to decide whether the project merits further analysis. The task document correlation of the initial investigation phase of software development is shown in Table 3-1.

Table 3-1. Initial Investigation Task-Document Item Correlation

No.	Task/Task Step	Document Item
1	Review project request.	Initial Problem and Need Statement
2	Prepare to conduct initial investigation.	Work Schedule Interview Schedule Interview Questionnaire
3	Conduct interviews.	Interview Worksheets Interview Summaries
4	Analyze information.	Project Cost Summary Target Schedule
5	Prepare feasibility study work plan.	Present System Review Proposed System Requirements Applications Package Review Economic Evaluation
6	Prepare initial investigation-report.	Initial Investigation Document

The objective of each initial investigation task and the nature of the document items resulting from these tasks are further described and illustrated on the following pages.

Task 1. Review Project Request

The analyst begins the initial investigation by assessing the project request. The objective of this task is to define the problems, needs, and requirements relative to the system requested as well as the environmental and operating constraints that must be considered. The deliverable of this task is generally a written statement that identifies all problem areas in the existing system that could be corrected by implementation of a new system.

Example:

Phase 1   *Initial Investigation*

PROBLEM AND NEED STATEMENT

The current system is not programmed for multisite operation and is not upgradable to an on-line system. These problems are compounded by the fact that documentation is virtually non-existent. The proposed system will correct these problems.

Task 2. Prepare to Conduct Initial Investigation

The next step is to prepare documents that will be used to establish schedules for conducting the initial investigation, identify those individuals and organizational units to be interviewed, formulate the questions to be asked in gathering information about the problem, and list existing documentation from which data can be gleaned. The document items resulting from this task are

- Initial investigation work schedule
- Interview schedule
- Interview questionnaire

Initial Investigation Work Schedule. This document may be prepared in the form of a Gantt chart that shows the start and completion dates of each task to be performed during the initial investigation.

Example:

Phase 1   *Initial Investigation*

INITIAL INVESTIGATION WORK SCHEDULE

1. Work Schedule	▬▬▬
2. Conduct Interview	▬▬▬▬▬
3. Analyze Info.	▬▬▬▬▬
4. Prepare FS Plan	▬▬▬▬▬
5. Prepare	▬▬▬▬▬

Interview Schedule. This document should list the individuals to be interviewed in the initial investigation. It should show the name and title of each person to be interviewed and the date and time of each scheduled interview. It should also summarize the topics of the interview in a brief form.

Example:

Phase 1   *Initial Investigation*

INTERVIEW SCHEDULE

INTERVIEWEE: F. Farnsworth TITLE: Marketing Director
DATE: 6/10-6/15 TIME: 10:30 A.M. daily
TOPICS TO BE DISCUSSED
Marketing planning functions
How is the marketing unit organized?
Market plan implementation
Establishing marketing objectives
Controlling marketing activities

Interview Questionnaire. This document should be designed to organize the list of questions to be asked during the interviews. Each question should be assigned a unique reference number. The name of the individual to whom a specific question will be asked should be identified.

Example:

Phase 1   *Initial Investigation*

INTERVIEW QUESTIONNAIRE

Interviewee: F. Farnsworth   Title: Marketing Director

Topic: Market planning

No.	Question to Be Asked
1	What is the company's overall marketing objective?
2	How are target markets selected?
3	What is the marketing mix?
4	How is the marketing unit organized?
5	How are the marketing activities coordinated?
6	How are the marketing activities controlled?

Task 3. Conduct Interviews

The purpose of this task is to gather information that will enable both data processing and user management to evaluate the costs and benefits of the proposed project. The end-items are

- Interview worksheets
- Interview summaries

These documents are further described and illustrated below.

Interview Worksheets. The function of this document is to provide a record of the interview responses. The worksheet should show the name of the organization, identify the person being interviewed, and indicate her or his position in the organization. The interview responses recorded on the worksheet should be correlated with the specific question number on the interview questionnaire. The exhibits provided by the interviewee in support of the responses should be referenced on the worksheet.

Example:

Phase 1	*Initial Investigation*

INTERVIEW WORKSHEETS

Interviewee: F. Farnsworth   Title: Marketing Director

Question 1.   What is the company's overall marketing objective?

Answer: The company's marketing objective is to increase its market share of the computer industry by 15 percent within the next 5 years. Toward this end, a new product will be introduced every 3 months.

Support Exhibits: Marketing Policy Manual (attachment A) and Five-Year Business Plan (attachment B).

Question 2. How are target markets selected?

Answer: The primary emphasis is to evaluate a target market in terms of how entry into the market will affect the firm's sales, costs, and profits Marketing management then considers whether the organization has the resources to produce a marketing mix required to meet the needs of a particular market. The size and number of competitors already selling in the target markets are also analyzed.

Support Exhibits: Marketing Policy Manual (attachment A) and Five-Year Business Plan (attachment B).

Interview Summary. This document summarizes the information gathered during the interview as it relates to the system functions and feasibility. It should reference each question asked by question number (as listed on the interview questionnaire), indicate the respondent by name or initials, summarize the respondent's answers to each referenced question, and reference specific areas that will aid in the analysis of the interviewee responses.

Example:

Phase 1   *Initial Investigation*

INTERVIEW SUMMARY

Question 1. What is the company's overall marketing objective?

Respondent's Initials: FF

Summary Statement
The objectives of the proposed system should be stated in a manner consistent with the overall objectives of the business. If the development staff fail to establish systems objectives that are consistent with the organization's 5-year marketing objectives, the system may work against the achievement of the firm's overall objective.

Task 4. Analyze Information

The purpose of this task is to analyze the collected data in order to make preliminary determinations relative to the project costs and target schedules. The analysis process should consider the extent of innovation that may be required by the proposed system and the risk inherent in the systems development process. Special emphasis is placed on the gathering of quantitative historical cost data. The document items that are deliverable at the conclusion of task 4 are

- Project costs summary
- Target schedule

These documents are further discussed and illustrated in the following paragraphs.

Project Costs Summary. This document should provide preliminary estimates for each phase of the software development process. The completed document should show the phases of development, the estimated person-weeks that will be involved for each phase, and the projected costs for each development phase.

Example:

Phase 1		*Initial Investigation*

PROJECT COSTS SUMMARY

Development Phase	Person-Weeks	Dollars
Feasibility Study	3-4	$ 7,500
Requirements Definition	3-4	7,500
External Design	4-6	10,500
Internal Design	8-16	35,000
Programming	6-8	20,000
Testing	1-2	3,500
Conversion	4-5	8,000
		$92,000

Target Schedule. This document should show the target schedules for starting and completing each of the remaining phases defined by the SDM. Each phase should be listed in the sequence in which it will take place.

Example:

Phase 1		*Initial Investigation*

TARGET SCHEDULE

Development Phase	Start Date	Complete Date
Feasibility Study	3/3	3/31
Requirements Definition	4/7	5/5
External Design	5/5	6/9
Internal Design	6/9	8/18
Programming	6/10	9/8
Testing	8/21	8/30
Conversion	9/10	10/13

Task 5. Prepare Feasibility Study Work Plan

The purpose of this task is to prepare a plan for conducting a feasibility study aimed at providing management with sufficient data to permit intelligent decision making regrading the economic and technical feasibility of the proposed project.   The documents resulting from this task are

- Present system review
- Proposed system requirements
- Applications package review
- Economic evaluation

Each of these documents is further discussed in the following paragraphs.

Present System Review.   This document should identify the tasks to be performed in reviewing the present system. It should list each task to be performed in sequential order and show the starting date and the completion date for each task.

Example:

Phase 1	Initial Investigation

PRESENT SYSTEM REVIEW

NO.	TASK TO BE PERFORMED	START DATE	COMPLETE DATE
1	Prepare present system schematic.	3/1	3/1
2	Prepare list of organization/ personnel functions required by the present system.	3/1	3/1
3	Analyze equipment requirement of the present system.	3/2	3/2
4	Prepare summary of present system requirements.	3/3	3/4
5	Prepare list of programs associated with the present system.	3/5	3/7
6	Identify the input documents and/or transactions required by the present system.	3/8	3/10
7	Identify all output of reports, displays, or transaction documents generated by the present system.	3/11	3/13
8	Summarize contents and characteristics of each data base.	3/14	3/18

Proposed System Requirements. This document should identify the tasks to be performed in conducting the proposed system requirements study. It should list each task to be performed in sequential order and show the starting date and the completion date for each task.

Example:

| Phase 1 | | | *Initial Investigation* |

PROPOSED SYSTEM REQUIREMENTS

NO.	TASK TO BE PERFORMED	START DATE	COMPLETE DATE
1	Prepare proposed system schematic.	3/30	4/1
2	Define performance require-ments.	4/1	4/2
3	Define anticipated capabili-ties of the proposed system.	4/3	4/5
4	Define the functional require-ments of the proposed system.	4/6	4/9
5	Analyze equipment impacts.	4/11	4/15
6	Analyze software impacts.	4/14	4/16
7	Analyze organizational impacts.	4/16	4/18
8	Analyze operational impacts.	4/19	4/21
9	Analyze development impacts.	4/22	4/24
10	Identify assumptions and constraints.	4/25	4/27

Applications Package Review. This document should identify the tasks to be performed in the review of commercially available application packages that may apply to the system. It should list each task to be performed in sequential order and show the starting date and the completion date for each task.

Example:

| Phase 1 | | | *Initial Investigation* |

APPLICATIONS PACKAGE REVIEW

NO.	TASK TO BE PERFORMED	START DATE	COMPLETE DATE
1	Identify available packages.	4/28	5/3
2	Identify package vendors.	4/28	5/3
3	Summarize features of each available package.	4/28	5/3

Economic Evaluation. This document should identify the tasks to be performed to evaluate the costs and benefits of developing the proposed system. It should list each task to be performed in sequential order and show the starting date and the completion date for each task.

Example:

Phase 1   *Initial Investigation*

ECONOMIC EVALUATION

NO.	TASK TO BE PERFORMED	START DATE	COMPLETE DATE
1	Identify functional improvements to be derived from the proposed system.	5/4	5/5
2	Analyze benefits to be derived from each functional improvement.	5/6	5/9
3	Determine direct and indirect savings in workforce and resources.	5/10	5/12
4	Prepare benefit statement.	5/15	5/14
5	Estimate labor costs.	5/15	5/16

Task 6. Prepare the Initial Investigation Report

All of the document items that were created during the performance of the preceding tasks (i.e., tasks 1 to 5) are stored in either an on-line or off-line repository. In task 6, select documents are retrieved from the repository for inclusion in the initial investigation phase end-document. The process is illustrated in Figure 3-3.

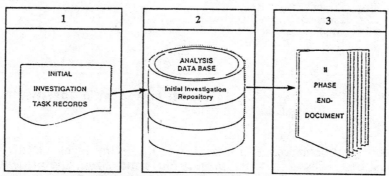

1. All initial investigation documents, including worksheets, questionnaires, and task records
2. The initial investigation documents are stored in an on-line or off-line repository.
3. Selected document items are retrieved from the repository for inclusion in the initial investigation phase end-document.

Figure 3-3. Initial Investigation Phase End-Document Evolution

The aggregate of documents items stored in the central repository at the conclusion of the initial investigation phase of development establishes the first level of analysis documents that will define the functional baseline for configuration control. In summary, they include the following documents, discussed and illustrated in this subsection:

- Problem and need statement
- Initial investigation work schedule
- Interview schedules
- Interview questionnaires
- Interview worksheets
- Interview summaries
- Project cost summaries
- Target schedules
- Feasibility study work plans

In contemplating the preparation of an initial investigation phase end-document, only those document items that serve to identify the existing problem and address the potential of the proposed system relative to costs and benefits are retrieved. The suggested content arrangement for presenting the documentation to the user and development staffs is shown in Figure 3-4.

1.0	MANAGEMENT SUMMARY
1.1	Problem and Need Statement
1.2	Projected Costs
1.3	Target Schedule
2.0	FEASIBILITY STUDY WORK PLAN
2.1	Present System Review
2.2	Proposed System Requirements Study
2.3	Applications Package Review
2.4	Economic Evaluation

Figure 3-4. Sample Table of Contents for the Initial Investigation Phase End-Document

The content outline serves as a checklist of the initial investigation document items that must be retrieved from the project file, synthesized, and presented in the initial investigation phase end-document.

The initial investigation phase end-document, and the feasibility study and requirements definition documents establish the functional baseline for configuration management and control.

3.4 FEASIBILITY STUDY TASK DOCUMENT ITEMS

The feasibility study breaks down into seven major tasks. The task document item correlation of the feasibility phase of software development is shown in Table 3-2.

Table 3-2. Feasibility Study Task Document Item Correlation

No.	Task/Task Step	Document Item
1	Review Work Outline	Updated Project Plan
2	Schedule and Conduct Interviews	Interview Schedules
		Interview Summaries
		Supporting Data and Documents
3	Review Present System	
3.1	Identify current organizational functions and relationships	Organizational Charts
		Summary of Functions Performed
		Job Descriptions
		Staffing Requirements
		Operating Budgets
3.2	Identify types and volumes of inputs and outputs	Input/Output Index
		Data Flow Diagram
		Work Volume Statements
3.3	Identify equipment	List of Equipment
3.4	Identify current system	Current System Requirement
3.5	Identify program	List of Programs
		List of Files/Data Bases
		System Flow Diagram
3.6	Identify current methods	Summary of Controls
3.7	Identify existing documentation	List of Documents
3.8	Prepare cost summary	Current Costs
3.9	Develop problem statement	Problem and Need Statement
4	Analyze Proposed System	
4.1	Identify development objectives	Statement of Objectives
4.2	Identify required outputs	List of Outputs
4.3	Analyze required inputs	Input/Output Index
4.4	Prepare initial data flow diagram	Proposed System Schematic
4.5	Analyze improvements vs. impacts	Summary of Improvements
		Summary of Impacts
5	Identify Package Alternatives	
5.1	Identify package vendors	List of Vendors
5.2	Acquire literature	Record of Requisition
5.3	Review published articles	Index of Articles
5.4	Prepare letters of inquiry	Letters of Inquiry
5.5	Review vendor literature	Literature Summaries
5.6	Perform package comparisons	Package Comparison Worksheets
		Package Evaluations
6	Analyze Costs and Benefits	
6.1	Estimate current costs;	Current Costs Worksheet
6.2	Estimate future costs	Future Costs Worksheet
6.3	Calculate ROI	ROI Worksheet
6.4	Analyze benefits	Statement of Benefits
6.5	Evaluate economic feasibility	Economic Evaluation Summary
	Package Evaluations	
7	Prepare Feasibility Study Phase End-Document	

The objective of each feasibility study task and the nature of the document items resulting from these tasks are further described and illustrated in the text that follows.

Task 1. Review Feasibility Study Work Plan

The analyst assigned to conduct the feasibility study begins by reviewing the feasibility study work plan that was prepared at the conclusion of the initial investigation. The plan defines the tasks to be performed and identifies the products of each task. (The document items that make up the work plan were explained and illustrated in Section 3.2.1.) When the review is completed, the analyst may elect to prepare a Gantt chart or PERT network to display the work plans. An example of a Gantt chart that defines the timing of the tasks to be performed is shown below.

Example:

Phase 2   *Feasibility Study*

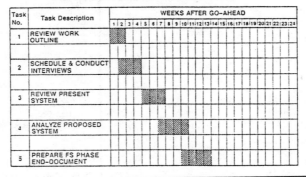

An example of a PERT network that displays the work plan is shown in below.

Example:

Phase 2   *Feasibility Study*

FEASIBILITY STUDY PERT NETWORK

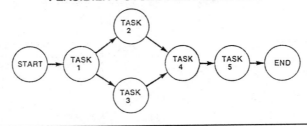

Task 2. Schedule and Conduct Interviews

As in the case of the initial Investigation, interviews are conducted to gather qualitative and quantitative information that will enable management to make sound judgments. In the feasibility study, however, the interviews are conducted to correlate the user needs that were defined in the project request and during the initial investigation with development criteria concerned with economic and technical feasibility. The document items resulting from task steps concerned with planning, scheduling, conducting, and documenting feasibility study interviews are essentially the same as those discussed and illustrated in Section 3.2.1 relative to the conduct of initial investigation interviews. Other document items that may result from the conduct of a user organization analysis are

- User organization chart
- User organization description

These documents are further discussed and illustrated in the following paragraphs.

User Organization Chart. A user organization chart may be prepared to schematically portray the user organization for which the proposed system will be developed. The chart should show the number of individuals that comprise the user organization. It should list the names of the specific individuals to be interviewed.

Example:

Phase 2   *Feasibility Study*

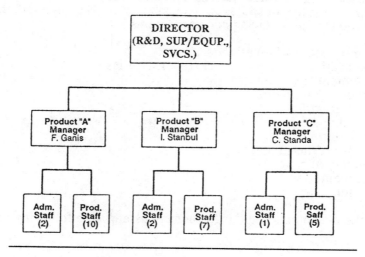

USER ORGANIZATION CHART

User Organization Description. To expand upon the information provided by the user organization chart, the analyst may also prepare a *User Organization Description* document. This document should identify the management hierarchy and explain the functions performed by the organization. It should also reference any exhibits that support the feasibility study interview process.

Example:

Phase 2	*Feasibility Study*

USER ORGANIZATION DESCRIPTION

HEADCOUNT
Management: 11
Clerical: 14
Sales: 276

MGMT HIERARCHY

Name	*Title*	*Extension*
Fred Farnsworth	Director	7755
Bill Baily	Sales Mgr	7002
Red Rivers	VP/Products	7909

PRIMARY FUNCTIONS
Product Development: Develop and market test new products
Pricing: Formulate pricing policies and determine methods used to set prices.
Promotion: Determine major types of promotions to be used.
Marketing Management: Establish marketing activities.

EXHIBITS
Marketing Plan

Task 3. Review Present System

The purpose of this task is to survey current systems and operations to achieve a general understanding of what they do and how they do it. This task is further broken down into a series of subtasks. As each subtask is completed, the results are recorded to produce the following document items:

- Present system schematic
- Organizational and personnel responsibilities
- Equipment requirements
- System requirements
- List of programs
- List of inputs
- List of outputs
- Data base/file summary
- Summary of controls
- Documentation
- Cost summary

Each of the documents listed is further discussed in the following paragraphs.

Present System Schematic. This document is used to schematically show the relationships of the functions and staffing requirements of the present system workflow. The workflow may be diagramed to show the organizational and personnel responsibilities from the top down as they relate to the functions and timing requirements of the present system.

Example:

Phase 2   *Feasibility Study*

PRESENT SYSTEM SCHEMATIC

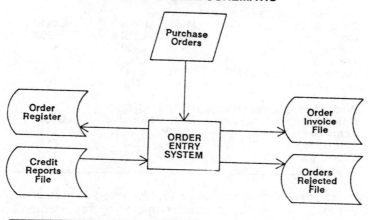

Organizational and Personnel Responsibilities. This document should list the organizational and personnel functions that are required by the present system. It should also show the *time* (i.e., hours spent per day, week, or month to perform each function), *volume* (i.e., the number of transactions, inquiries, or reports performed in the time period indicated), and the *costs* involved in performing each function.

Example:

Phase 2   *Feasibility Study*

ORGANIZATIONAL AND PERSONNEL RESPONSIBILITIES

Function	Hr/ Day	Hr/ Week	Hr/ Month	Vol/ Week	Cost/ Week
Inventory	8	40	160	1000	$400
Purchasing	4	20	80	100	$200
Packaging	4	20	80	20	$150
Data entry	80	400	1600	500	$300

Summary of Present System Equipment Requirements. This document is used to analyze the equipment requirements of the present system. It should include information relative to quantity, manufacturer, description, equipment status, model, and cost of each equipment item.

Example:

Phase 2	*Feasibility Study*

SUMMARY OF PRESENT SYSTEM EQUIPMENT REQUIREMENTS

Currently Available Equipment

Description	Qty.	Mfg.	Model	Cost
Computer	1	IBM	SYS34	$280K
Printer	3	UNIV	2400	$7K
Terminal	3	IBM	UVC1	$1.4K
Disk drive	2	IBM	D34	$18K
Tape drive	2	IBM	HT3	$13K

Additional Equipment Required by New System

Description	Qty.	Mfg.	Model	Cost
Terminal	2	UNIV	UVC1	$400
Disk pack	2	IBM	D34	$18K
Tape drive	1	IBM	HT3	$7K

Summary of Present System Computer Operating Requirements. This document summarizes the computer operating requirements of the present system. For each batch job to be performed, information should be provided that indicates the minimum, average, and maximum run time required; the minimum core requirements; the file storage requirements; equipment requirements; operating system requirements; and the name of the programming language most prevalent on the job.

Example:

Phase 2	*Feasibility Study*

SUMMARY OF PRESENT SYSTEM COMPUTER OPERATING REQUIREMENTS

Min. Run Time	Max. Core Req.	File Storage Req.	Operating System Req.	Program Language Req.
60	365	None	MAPICS	COBOL
30	556K	None	EC0010	COBOL
2	365K	None	EC140	COBOL
18	285K	3M	EC140	COBOL
25	460K	8M	EC140	COBOL

List of Present System Programs. This document should list all the programs that are included in the current system configuration. At least the following information should be provided: program name/ID, a description of the major functions of each program, and an explanation of any known deficiencies of the program as they affect the present system's operation.

Example:

Phase 2   *Feasibility Study*

LIST OF PRESENT SYSTEM PROGRAMS

Program	Function	Deficiencies
EC0010	Master list by brass tag	
EC0015	Monthly master file list	
EC0020	Equipment due for calibration	Does not provide location data
EC0030	Master file maintenance	
EC0040	Routine file update	Time-consuming process.
EC0050	On-line inquiry	Too rigid - needs user-definable selects

List of Present System Inputs. This document item should identify all of the input documents and transactions that provide the input to the system. For each input, the estimated *volume* (i.e., the number of each input type), *frequency* (i.e., how often the inputs are processed), and *media* (e.g., magnetic tape, cartridge, manual input, etc.) are indicated.

Example:

Phase 2   *Feasibility Study*

LIST OF PRESENT SYSTEM INPUTS

Input Name	Volume	Frequency	Medium
INPUT FORM	650	Weekly	KOD
ECBRASSM		On demand	Disk
ECBRASC		On demand	Disk
ECBRASB		On demand	Disk
MASTER A	400	Daily	Disk
HISTORY		Weekly	Disk

List of Present System Outputs. This document identifies all outputs of records, displays, or transactions generated by the present system. For each output, the estimated *volume* (i.e., the number of each output type), *frequency* (i.e., how often the output are processed), and *media* (e.g., magnetic tape, cartridge, paper printout, etc.) are indicated.

Example:

Phase 2			*Feasibility Study*

LIST OF PRESENT SYSTEM OUTPUTS

Input Name	Volume	Frequency	Medium
ECTRANPF FILE UPDATE	15	Daily	Report
EQUIPMENT DUE FOR CALIB.	10	Daily	Report
MASTER FILE LIST BY BRASS TAG NO.	1500	Weekly	Report
MASTER FILE MAINT. LIST	20	Daily	Report

Present System Data Base/File Summary. This document should summarize the contents and characteristics of each data base and data base file used by the present system. It should identify each data base by name, and each record by title and should indicate the medium, label, record length, and organization of the files.

Example:

Phase 2			*Feasibility Study*

PRESENT SYSTEM DATA BASE/FILE SUMMARY

File Title	Title	Medium	Label	Record Length
ECBRASSM	BRASTG	Disk	BRASRC	119
ECBRASS	BRASTG	Disk	BRASRS	81
ECTRANC	TRANC	Disk	TRANL	8
ECTRAND	BRDEPT	Disk	DEPSR	84
ECTRANE	BEMPNO	Disk	EMPNUM	86
ECTRANPF	BUORG	Disk	USRORG	121

Present System Summary of Controls. This document should be used to summarize I/O controls, user controls, data file and data base controls, access controls, file maintenance controls, and backup and recovery controls. It should describe every control function associated with the present system and should explain how the controls are being implemented.

Example:

Phase 2   *Feasibility Study*

PRESENT SYSTEM SUMMARY OF CONTROLS

Function	Performed by User	Performed by System
Input		
1. All input transactions are batched with control totals on documents, lines, and amounts.	X	
2. All employees must submit a time report each week.	X	
Processing		
1. Changes against nonexistent or closed projects are rejected.		X
2. All errors are placed on an error suspense file and will continue to print until removed.		X
Output		
1. All reports must print at least a report title		X
2. Generation data set content is required.		X
3. Control totals must balance.	X	X

List of Present System Documentation. This document should identify all of the documentation currently available for the present system. It should list each item of documentation by name and indicate the medium in which the documentation resides and its level of completeness.

Example:

Phase 2   *Feasibility Study*

LIST OF PRESENT SYSTEM DOCUMENTATION

Document Name	Statement of Completeness
User Guide	
Operations Run Book	
Program Specification	Missing Programs EC041R PCPIC43

Present System Cost Summary. This document should summarize the costs related to the functions, volumes, and staffing requirements of the present system. It should list all of the equipment or software utilized by the present system and show the cost of leasing, operating, and maintaining the equipment and software. The method of acquisition should also be indicated.

Example:

Phase 2   *Feasibility Study*

PRESENT SYSTEM COST SUMMARY

Equipment/ Software	Operating	Maintenance	Acquisition
Computer	24,000/mo	1800/mo	Lease
Operating system software		1500/mo	Lease
Communications monitor	5000/yr		
DBMS	800/mo	1200/yr	
Dictionary		1800/yr	Lease
Application		36,000/yr (labor)	Internal
NetManager		2000/mo	Lease
DASD		5000/mo	Lease

Task 4. Analyze Proposed System
The object of this task is to analyze the requirements of the proposed system and the relationship of the proposed system to the organization's short- and long-range objectives. The deliverables of this task are a series of documents that define the objectives of the proposed system and summarize the expected improvements, impacts, assumptions and constraints. They include

- Proposed system schematic
- Statement of objectives
- Summary of new capabilities
- Summary of capabilities to be upgraded
- Summary of equipment impacts
- Summary of software impacts
- Summary of organizational impacts
- Summary of operational impacts
- Summary of development impacts
- Assumptions and constraints

Proposed System Schematic. This document is used to schematically show the relationships of the functions and processing requirements to the proposed system work flow. The work flow may be diagramed, showing how each class of input will enter the system and how each class of output will flow from the system.

Example:

Phase 2	Feasibility Study

PROPOSED SYSTEM SCHEMATIC

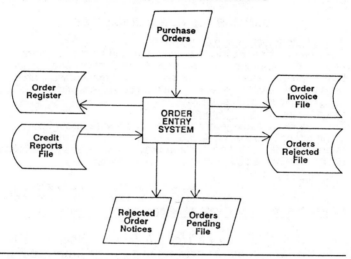

Statement of Objectives. This document should provide a concise statement of the major functional and performance requirements and objectives of the proposed system. Any anticipated operational changes that will affect the system and its use should be identified.

Example:

Phase 2	Feasibility Study

STATEMENT OF OBJECTIVES

The new system will continue to provide all of the features of the present system, but in addition the new system will provide
- Reports of work assignments versus equipment due for calibration
- A dictionary or cross-referenced list by equipment location, equipment owner department, and cumulative time for repair, calibration, etc.
- Management reports for the calibration manager and equipment control manager
- Invoices to owner departments

Summary of New Capabilities. This document should summarize the new capabilities to be obtained from the proposed system. It should list all of the functions that the new system is expected to perform which are not being performed by the present system. If the benefit from the new function is tangible, it should be so indicated. Likewise, attributes relative to cost, productivity, quality, efficiency, timeliness, reliability, and service enhancements should be indicated.

Example:

Phase 2   *Feasibility Study*

SUMMARY OF NEW CAPABILITIES

Work Assignment Report Generation
The new system will provide both on-line and hard-copy work assignment reporting. This will provide productivity and service-level improvements through the reduction of manual work order preparation. It will also reduce the time between work assignments for each employee.

Management Report Generation
The creation of management reports for average throughput, summary call reports, workload, and workforce reporting will improve management control and provide improved work leveling capability when an employee is sick or on vacation.

Invoice Generation
The ability of the sytem to produce both internal and external invoices will improve billing accuracy and reduce the number of administrative hours spent validating work performed.

Summary of Capabilities to be Upgraded. This document is used to summarize the functional improvements on existing capabilities. It should list those functions which relate to upgrading existing capabilities. It should indicate whether the benefit to be derived is tangible or intangible. It should also indicate the attributes relative to cost, productivity, quality, efficiency, timeliness, reliability, and service enhancements.

Example:

Phase 2   *Feasibility Study*

SUMMARY OF CAPABILITIES TO BE UPGRADED

Calibration Tracking
The new system will provide an automated tickler file to improve the ability to track scheduled calibration activities. This will reduce the rework required for measurements made on uncalibrated test equipment.

Equipment Location Cross-Reference Reporting
The new system will provide enhanced equipment location tracking, providing a cross-reference between equipment tag number and the equipment location. This will reduce the time spent hunting down equipment to be worked on.

Summary of Equipment Impacts. This document should discuss any required additions and modifications to the current available equipment and their impacts on the user. It should include data that explain the impact of the proposed system relative to processors, storage media, output devices, and input devices. A brief statement should be included that describes how the additions or modifications will impact the operation of the equipment items.

Example:

Phase 2   *Feasibility Study*

SUMMARY OF EQUIPMENT IMPACTS

1. Add one terminal.
   Impact: This will reduce time required for finding an available terminal in another department.
2. Add one printer.
   Impact: New report generation will require additional printer time. Current printers already overloaded.
3. Add terminal emulation boards.
   Impact: This will provide the PC base with the ability to use the new system, minimizing the number of terminals required.

Summary of Software Impacts. This document should discuss any additions and modifications that must be made to existing applications and support programs. A brief statement should be included that describes the impacts of the new system on the support software, input and equipment simulators, and test software as well as the impact of the new system on the user.

Example:

Phase 2   *Feasibility Study*

SUMMARY OF SOFTWARE IMPACTS

1. The relational requirements of the cross-referencing and scheduling features will require the existing programs to be modified to use the relational DBMS.
   Impact: The file accesses to 16 programs will require modification. Additionally, the data will have to be moved from the existing flat files to the RDBMS.
2. Files with information about owner department and calibration dates must be expanded to include equipment location.
   Impact: Will require time to track down each piece of equipment. This will have to be done by each department tracking its own equipment.
3. New modules must be added to perform all new functions such as management report generation and invoice generation.
   Impact: No effect on users during development. Will require retraining for implementation.

Summary of Organizational Impacts. This document item should identify the anticipated staffing impacts, particularly those organizational changes that will result from installation of the proposed new system. It should list by positional responsibility the addition or elimination of responsibilities that will be necessary to implement the proposed system. For each position that will require modification, a brief statement should be included that describes how the organization will be impacted.

Example:
Phase 2   *Feasibility Study*

SUMMARY OF ORGANIZATIONAL IMPACTS

1. Project Control Administrator
   Impact: The new system will give the administrator greater control of the system inputs and reports. Clerical functions associated with the system inputs and outputs will be eliminated.

2. Project Control Clerk
   Impact: The new system will create the need for a project control clerk position. The duties of the project control clerk will be to verify that timesheets are submitted on time and to assist the project control administrator in preparing analysis reports.

Summary of Operational Impacts. This document should discuss the changes in staffing and operational procedures that will be required to use the proposed system once it is installed. It should describe the impacts on the working relationship between the data center and the end-user.

Example:
Phase 2   *Feasibility Study*

SUMMARY OF OPERATIONAL IMPACTS

1. Timesheets must be kept by all technicians indicating the hours spent on each piece of equipment.
   Impact: Data entry will now be performed by the project control clerk, freeing technicians to perform their work.
2. The timesheets must be submitted daily to the project control clerk.
   Impact: Ensures that all information is monitored on a daily basis.
3. Invoice generation
   Impact: The project control clerk must trigger the printing of the system-generated invoices and mail the invoices to the appropriate on-site manager.

Summary of Development Impacts. This document should identify those functions that will be impacted during the development and installation of the proposed new system. It should describe the user effort required prior to and during installation of the new system and the requirements for modifying existing programs to be used by the new system. It should also indicate the amount of computer time that will be required for the parallel operation of the new and existing systems.

Example:

Phase 2	*Feasibility Study*

SUMMARY OF DEVELOPMENT IMPACTS

1. Equipment tracking
   Impact: Requires users to perform inventory counts of equipment currently in their possession.
2. Data base modifications
   Impact: The transfer of the system to a relational environment will require development time; however, the user community should see no impact.
3. Testing and conversion
   Impact: During the testing and conversion phases, both systems (old and new) will be up. The technicians will be required to update both systems during parallel operation. The amount of work associated with the dual entry will be minimized by the assignment of IS resources to work with the technicians.

Assumptions and Constraints. This document should identify the assumptions and constraints that will affect the development and operation of the proposed system. Any limitations affecting the desired capabilities of the proposed system should be discussed. Examples of assumptions include organizational actions, budget decisions, operational environment, and deployment requirements. Examples of constraints include operations environment, operator skill level, human factors, budget limitations, and development schedules.

Example:

Phase 2	*Feasibility Study*

ASSUMPTIONS AND CONSTRAINTS

Constraints
1. The system must be adjustable to include addition and deletion of equipment from calibration and maintenance lists.
2. Equipment inventory and location data must be updatable as equipment is moved from department to department.

Assumptions
1. The equipment identification system will remain unchanged.
2. A project control clerk will be added to perform data entry procedures.

Task 5. Identify Package Alternatives

The object of this task is to identify application packages that may satisfy the user requirements. This involves identifying package vendors, reviewing vendor literature, preparing letters of inquiry, and performing package comparisons. A variety of documents may be prepared by the analysts to facilitate performance of this task. They include

- Package evaluation matrix
- Product comparison worksheet
- Evaluation summary

These documents are discussed and illustrated in the following paragraphs.

Package Evaluation Matrix. This document is used to conduct a preliminary investigation of vendor software packages. Weights are assigned to each feature indicating the opinion of the analyst as to the degree to which the package features may be able to satisfy the objectives of the proposed system.

Example:

Phase 2   *Feasibility Study*

PACKAGE EVALUATION MATRIX

PACKAGE: ATG Shop Floor Data Collect
FEATURES: 1. Job-On/Off by employee
             2. Employee work center transfer
             3. Bar code capability
VENDOR: ATG Associates

Feature Number	Feature Weight	Product Weight
1	10	100
2	8	90
3	9	70
WEIGHT TOTALS		

Feature Weight Legend:
10   = Required
9   = Highly desirable
8   = Desirable
Product Weight Legend:
100   = Can be applied as is
90   = Applicable with minor modification
80   = Feature not available in current version but will be available in next release
70   = Feature not available in current version and probably will not be available for at least a year

---

Package Comparison Worksheet. The purpose of this document is to make a preliminary comparison of the available packages in terms of price, deliverables, installation and training, operating environment, etc.

Example:

Phase 2   *Feasibility Study*

PRODUCT COMPARISON WORKSHEET

Package Characteristics	FW/PW Totals	
	Product A	Product B
Price	110	90
Deliverables	100	90
Installation	80	70
Training	80	90
Maintenance	80	80

Evaluation Summary. This document is used to summarize the feature and product weights.

Example:

Phase 2   *Feasibility Study*

EVALUATION SUMMARY

Function	A	B	C	D	E
O/S compatible	100	100	100	100	100
Communications	75	100	50	0	100
Data base structure	60	80	100	75	60
Report generator	80	70	80	20	70
Security • Password • Encryption	100 0	90 0	90 50	100 0	50 100
Recovery • Rollback • Logging	50 100	50 100	100 100	50 100	50 50

Task 6. Analyze Costs and Benefits

The object of this task is to review the current operating costs and benefits and compare them to costs and benefits of developing or purchasing the proposed system. The documents associated with this task include

- Operating costs worksheet
- ROI worksheet
- Intangible benefits summary
- Economic evaluation summary

Operating Costs Worksheet. This document is used to make a preliminary tabulation of the anticipated costs of developing and implementing the proposed system. It projects the costs of direct labor, indirect labor, materials and supplies, data processing, and other cost factors.

Example:

Phase 2   *Feasibility Study*

OPERATING COSTS WORKSHEET

Description	Budget Allocation	Costs
Direct labor	_____	_____
Indirect labor	_____	_____
Materials and supplies	_____	
EDP	_____	_____
Grand Total	_____	_____

ROI Worksheet. This document is used to make a preliminary calculation of the rate of return, taking into consideration the cost savings anticipated from the proposed system.

Example:

Phase 2   *Feasibility Study*

RETURN ON INVESTMENT (ROI) WORKSHEET

A. Total Implementation Costs   _____
B. Direct Cost Savings ROI
   Direct cost savings

1st Year	*2d Year*	*3d Year*
(3 000)	12,000	12,000

   Discounted savings

1st Year	*2d Year*	*3d Year*
10%	20%	30%

Intangible Benefits Summary. This document lists the assumptions made in calculating the potential savings from the proposed system.

Example:

Phase 2   *Feasibility Study*

INTANGIBLE BENEFITS SUMMARY

1. Type of benefits
   The types of benefits to be derived from the proposed system are cost reduction, cost avoidance, and profit improvement.
2. Benefit description
   The system will decrease the amount of time required to prepare monthly reports and increase the quality of the reports.
3. Potential savings first year
   Current cost of preparing reports is estimated at $165,000 annually. The projected cost for preparing the same reports if the proposed system is implemented is $100,000. The potential savings therefore is $65,000.
4. Future projections
   The cost of producing reports is expected to decrease at the rate of 10 percent annually, since the application of CASE tools allows for regeneration of reports with simple modifications.

Economic Evaluation Summary. This document summarizes the principal cost data as determined in the preliminary analysis process.

Example:

Phase 2   *Feasibility Study*

ECONOMIC EVALUATION SUMMARY

	5-Year Cost Total
A. Estimated Cost	
Development	_____
Start-up	_____
Implementation	_____
B. Operating Costs	
EDP operations	_____
System maintenance	_____
System enhancements	_____
C. Cost Savings	
Total direct costs	_____
Total indirect costs	_____
Total direct and indirect costs	_____

Task 7. Prepare Feasibility Study Phase End-Document

All of the document items that were created during the performance of the preceding tasks (i.e., tasks 1 to 6) are stored in either an on-line or off-line repository. In task 6, select documents are retrieved from the repository for inclusion in the feasibility study phase end-document. The process is illustrated in Figure 3-5.

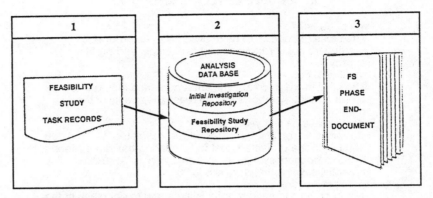

1. All feasibility study documents
2. The feasibility documents are stored in an on-line or off-line repository.
3. Selected document items are retrieved from the repository for inclusion in the feasibility study phase end-document.

Figure 3-5. Feasibility Study Phase End-Document Definition

The document items delivered to the repository during the feasibility study establish the second level of analysis documents that will define the functional baseline for configuration control, as shown in Figure 3-6.

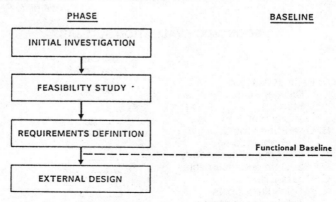

Figure 3-6. Functional Baseline Documents

In summary, the document items delivered to the repository include the following documents, discussed and illustrated in this subsection.

Feasibility Study Work Plan Documents
- Feasibility study Gantt chart
- Feasibility study PERT network

Interview Documents
- User organization chart
- User organization description

Present System Review Documents
- Present system schematic
- Organizational/personnel responsibilities
- Present system equipment requirements
- Summary of present system requirements
- Summary of present system computer operating requirements
- List of system programs
- List of present system inputs
- List of present system outputs
- Present system data base/file summary
- Present system summary of controls
- List of present system documentation
- Present system cost Summary

Proposed System Analysis Documents
- Proposed system schematic
- Statement of objectives
- Summary of new capabilities
- Summary of capabilities to be upgraded
- Summary of equipment impacts
- Summary of software impacts
- Summary of organizational impacts
- Summary of operational impacts
- Summary of development impacts
- Assumptions and constraints

Package Alternatives Evaluation Documents
- Package evaluation matrix
- Product comparison worksheet
- Evaluation summary

Cost and Benefits Analysis Documents
- Operating costs worksheet
- ROI worksheet
- Intangible benefits summary
- Economic evaluation summary

In contemplating the preparation of the feasibility study phase end-document, only those document items that serve to compare the present system to the proposed system and identify probable costs and consequences are retrieved. The suggested content arrangement for presenting the documentation is shown in Figure 3–7.

1.0 PRESENT SYSTEM REVIEW
1.1 Present System Schematic
1.2 Organizational/Personnel Responsibilities
1.3 Equipment
1.4 System Requirements
1.5 List of Programs
1.6 List of Inputs
1.7 List of Outputs
1.8 Data Base/File Summary
1.9 Cost

2.0 PROPOSED SYSTEM REQUIREMENTS
2.1 Proposed System Schematic
2.2 Statement of Objectives
2.3 Summary of Improvements
2.3.1 New Capabilities
2.3.2 Upgrading Existing Capabilities
2.4 Summary of Impacts
2.4.1 Equipment Impacts
2.4.2 Software Impacts
2.4.3 Organizational Impacts
2.4.4 Operational Impacts
2.4.5 Development Impacts
2.5 Assumptions and Constraints

3.0 APPLICATIONS PACKAGES
3.1 Available Packages

4.0 ECONOMIC EVALUATION
4.1 Benefit Statement
4.2 Cost Report

**Figure 3-7. Sample Table of Contents for the Feasibility Study
Phase End-Document**

The content outline serves as a checklist of the feasibility study document items that must be retrieved from the project file, synthesized, and presented in the feasibility study phase end-document.

When completed, the document is reviewed by the appropriate decision-making entity to determine if the development effort should continue to the next phase (i.e., the requirements definition phase), or be terminated. On approval, the feasibility study phase end-document establishes the second milestone in the configuration management functional baseline.

3.5 REQUIREMENTS DEFINITION TASK DOCUMENT ITEMS

The requirements definition breaks down into nine major tasks. The task document item correlation of the requirements definition phase of software development is shown in Table 3-3.

Table 3-3. Requirements Definition Task Document Item Correlation

No.	Task/Task Step	Document Item
1	Review Project File and Project Plan	Updated Project Plan
2	Establish User Requirements	
2.1	Conduct interviews	Interview Schedules Interview Summaries Supporting Data and Documents
2.2	Define performance requirements	Accuracy and Validity Requirements Timing Requirements
2.3	Establish failure contingency	Backup Requirements Requirements Fallback Requirements Restart Requirements
2.4	Define data collection requirements	Source Definitions Input Formats List of Interfaces
3	Determine Environmental Requirements	
3.1	Determine equipment requirements	Equipment Environment Requirements List of Interfaces
3.3	Define security requirements	Security and Privacy Requirements
3.4	Define control requirements	Control Requirements
4	Determine Organizational Requirements	Staffing Requirements Summary of Functions
5	Establish Alternatives Evaluation Criteria	Package Evaluation Criteria
6	Prepare Requirements Definition Document	Requirements Definition Document

Task 1. Analyze Feasibility Study Data

The *requirements definition* phase begins by analyzing the data that were collected during the *feasibility study*. This involves analyzing each function of the present system to establish improvement goals for the new system. The two primary documents prepared in the performance of this task are

- Present system analysis worksheet
- Proposed system objectives summary

These documents are discussed and illustrated in the following paragraphs.

Present System Analysis Worksheet. This document is used to summarize the characteristics of the present system. It identifies the system by name; shows the expenditures related to acquisition, operation, and maintenance; explains the run time and system requirements; and lists the programs and both the system and user documentation currently available.

Example:

Phase 3	Requirements Definition

PRESENT SYSTEM ANALYSIS WORKSHEET

SYSTEM NAME:

COST RUN TIME	
Acquisition: Operating Maintenance:	Minimum: Average: Maximum:
STORAGE REQUIREMENTS	
Max. Core:	File Storage:

DOCUMENTATION AVAILABLE

PROGRAM	FUNCTION

Proposed System Objectives. This document analyzes the objectives of the new system. It lists each objective and states the impact the objective will have on the user operations. It also indicates the nature of the anticipated tangible and intangible benefits.

Example:

| Phase 3 | | Requirements Definition |

PROPOSED SYSTEM OBJECTIVES

OBJECTIVE	IMPACT	BENEFIT

Legend:

CS = Cost Savings
HC = Headcount Reduction
CT = Computer Time Reduction

Task 2. Conduct Interviews

After completing the analysis of the data that were collected during the feasibility study, the analyst, once again, conducts interviews to gather information about the user problem and the requirements for the new system. The document items resulting from the performance of this task are essentially the same as those that were generated during the initial investigation and feasibility study interview processes. The deliverable documents, however, generally amplify the findings of the feasibility study and initial investigation phases by including detailed information relative to specific calculations, data formats, etc., that will be required in the design process.

Task 3. Define Performance Requirements

The object of this task is to define the specific performance requirements that must be satisfied by the new system. The documents resulting from this task define the accuracy requirements, timing requirements, failure contingency requirements, and interface requirements of the proposed system.

Accuracy and Validity Requirements. This document should provide a description of the accuracy and validity requirements that will be imposed on the system to be developed. It should specify the requirements of mathematical calculation, data validation, and data transmission.

Example:

Phase 3   *Requirements Definition*

ACCURACY AND VALIDITY

All inventory transactions must be processed as specified in the functional description document. The transactions are applied directly to the inventory transaction maintenance data base and related to the following for accuracy and validity: control, customer, work order, purchase order, inventory, parts, ID, and the products structure data bases. Reports are produced which show the transactions as they are edited, rejected transactions with error messages, and the effect of successful static inventory data transactions.

Timing Requirements. This document should provide a description of the timing requirements. It should list each program function, indicate the throughput time, specify the response time permissible for queries and updates, and provide comments that indicate priorities and changes in mode operation.

Example:

Phase 3   *Requirements Definition*

TIMING REQUIREMENTS			
Program Function	**Throughput Time**	**Response Time**	**Comments**
Inquiry	NA	2 s	User-interactive
Update	30 min	NA	5000 transactions/day
Batch	5 min	NA	150 transactions

Backup Requirements. This document should detail the backup techniques for ensuring the continuation of systems functions in the event of system failure. It should identify the specific file to be backed up, the program that accesses the file, the location of the backup site, and the name and phone number of the person to contact at the backup site. It should also explain the logistics for data transfer from the normal operating site to the backup site and should indicate the frequency and retention period of the data to be backed up. In addition, the hardware and software deficiencies and the actions to be taken at the backup site should be noted.

Example:

Phase 3	Requirements Definition

BACKUP REQUIREMENTS
FILE NAME: ECBRASS
BACKUP SITE: SANTA CLARA
PROGRAM NAME: Master List by Brass Tag (EBASS)
CONTACT: Frank T. Battle
DATA TRANSFER LOGISTICS: Data transferred to backup daily
FREQUENCY: Daily   **RETENTION PERIOD:** 14 days

Fallback Requirements. This document should describe alternate methods of performing the system functions in the event of system failure. It should explain the technique that will be used to ensure the continued satisfaction of the system requirements. It should also indicate how other systems may be used as an alternate means (e.g., manual calculation and recording) of maintaining the system functions.

Example:

Phase 3	Requirements Definition

FALLBACK REQUIREMENTS	
1	A manual time tracking system must be available in case of system failure
2	A manual system will require the retention of a service bureau for processing the manual time records.
3	An equipment maintenance agreement will have to be established for 24-hour replacement of any failing unit to bring the system back on line. Manual procedures can not be used for more than one work day.

Restart Requirements. This document should describe the restart capabilities for ensuring recovery from a temporary problem in the system hardware or software.

Example:

Phase 3   *Requirements Definition*

FALLBACK REQUIREMENTS	
1	Should the system stop during normal data collection, it may be restarted with no other action required.
2	Should the system stop during labor balancing, or shift adjustment activities, the associated files must be purged and the raw data files reloaded prior to restart.
3	Should the system halt during automatic upload, the uploaded file should be purged and the data manually transferred using standard 3270 file transfer procedures.
4	Report generation is based on system file availability. Therefore, any system stoppage will halt report processing. Adjere to the conditions outlined above for stoppage indicated by report failures.

Task 4. Correlate Functional and Performance Requirements

The documentation resulting from this task amplifies the functional requirements that were defined during the feasibility study and relates them to the performance requirements that were defined in task 3. The documents that were prepared during the feasibility study phase, which summarized the anticipated improvements and impacts, are updated based on the additional information gathered in conducting the interviews in task 2.

Task 5. Define Data Requirements

The objective of this task is to define the data requirements of the new system. The documentation resulting from this task focuses on defining each data element that is input to, output from, or stored in system data base. The document items deliverable to the project file at the conclusion of this task are

- Static system data
- Dynamic input data
- Dynamic output data
- System data constraints
- Data collection requirements
- Input formats
- Output formats
- Data base impacts

Static System Data. This document should identify each static data element (i.e., data to be used primarily as reference data). Each element should be identified by a unique name and number. The document should also provide data that indicate where the static data elements will be used.

Example:

Phase 3				*Requirements Definition*

STATIC SYSTEM DATA				
ELEMENT NAME	**NO.**	**USAGE**		
		Input	**Output**	**File**
Transaction Code	A	X	--	PART ID
Activity Code	B	X	--	PART ID
Part Number	C	X	--	PART ID
Report Distribution	D	X	--	PART ID
Engineering Data	E	X	--	PART ID
Inventory Policy	E	X	--	PART ID

Dynamic Input Data. This document should identify each dynamic input data element (i.e., an element subject to being upgraded during a normal run or during on-line operation). It should list the data elements in logical groups and identify each element by a unique number. The document should also provide information that indicates how the data will be input to the system.

Example:

Phase 3				*Requirements Definition*

DYNAMIC INPUT DATA				
ELEMENT NAME	**NO.**	**USAGE**		
		Input	**Output**	**File**
Transaction Code	A	X	--	INV. BAL
Activity Code	B	X	--	INV. BAL
Part Number	C	X	--	INV. BAL
Avg. Period Usage	D	X	--	INV. BAL
APU Trend	E	X	--	INV. BAL

Dynamic Output Data. This document should identify each dynamic output element (i.e., an element subject to being updated during a normal run or during on-line operation). It should list dynamic output data element in logical groups and identify each element by a unique number. The document should also provide information that indicates how the output will be produced.

Example:

Phase 3   *Requirements Definition*

DYNAMIC OUTPUT DATA				
ELEMENT NAME	**NO.**	**USAGE**		
		Input	Output	File
Plant	A	--	X	PART ID
Component Part No.	B	--	X	PART ID
Parent Part No.	C	--	X	PART ID
Order No.	D	--	X	PART ID
Line	E	--	X	PART ID
UM	F	--	X	PART ID
Start Date	G	--	X	PART ID
Qty. Req.	H	--	X	PART ID
Qty. Per.	I	--	X	PART ID

System Data Constraints. This document should include information that explains the limits imposed on the new system. It should include data that indicate the constraints relative to maximum file size, number of files, number of records, number of elements, and maximum record length.

Example:

Phase 3   *Requirements Definition*

SYSTEM DATA CONSTRAINTS				
MAX. FILE SIZE	**MAX. NUMBER FILES**	**MAX. NUMBER RECORDS**	**MAX. NUMBER ELEMENTS**	**MAX. RECORD LENGTH**
8 Megabytes	16,384	56,536	16,384	8192 Characters

Data Collection Requirements. This document should define the data collection requirements of the system to be designed. It should provide data that establish the values of each element (e.g., critical value, scales of measurement, coversion factor, expansion factor, and frequency of update).

Example:

Phase 3   *Requirements Definition*

DATA COLLECTION

INPUT NAME: Order demand
INPUT SOURCE: Any department from which orders are processed

INPUT TYPE: Transaction	INPUT DEVICE: Terminal

RECIPIENTS:
Sally Smith, Accounts Payable   Mel Kiyoma, Controller
Jone Nones, Purchasing Director

FREQUENCY OF UPDATE: Monthly

CRITICAL VALUE: N/A	UOM: N/A	CONVERSION FACTOR: N/A

EXPANSION FACTOR: N/A
OUTPUT: Supply and Demand Report

Input Formats. This document should describe the format of each input (i.e., card layouts, tape formats, etc.) to be used by the system.

Example:

Phase 3   *Requirements Definition*

DATA COLLECTION			
FIELD NAME	**TYPE**	**SIZE**	**COMMENTS**
Transaction Code	K	3	Example CODE=MG3
Activity Code	K	1	A=Add C=Change D=Delete
Order Number	K	12	
Order Status	M	1	(Code)
Vendor Number	M	6	
Account Code	M	12	

Output Formats. This document should describe the format of each output (e.g., reports, tape formats, etc.) to be generated by the system.

Example:

Phase 3   *Requirements Definition*

OUTPUT FORMAT				
REPORT NO: IN 0031				
REPORT NAME: INVENTORY ACTIVITY REPORT				
RUN DATE: MM/DD/YYY				
TIME: XX:XX:XX				
COMP. PART NO.	PARENT PART NO.	ORDER NO.	LINE	QTY. REQ.
XXXX	XXXXX	XXXXXX	XXXX	XXXX
XXXX	XXXXX	XXXXXX	XXXX	XXXX
XXXX	XXXXX	XXXXXX	XXXX	XXXX
XXXX	XXXXX	XXXXXX	XXXX	XXXX
XXXX	XXXXX	XXXXXX	XXXX	XXXX
XXXX	XXXXX	XXXXXX	XXXX	XXXX
XXXX	XXXXX	XXXXXX	XXXX	XXXX
XXXX	XXXXX	XXXXXX	XXXX	XXXX

Data Base Impacts. This document should describe the impacts that are associated with loading and maintaining the data base, including hardware impacts, software impacts, organizational impacts, operational impacts, and development impacts.

Example:

Phase 3   *Requirements Definition*

DATA BASE IMPACTS
DATA BASE NAME: Part Master
EQUIPMENT IMPACTS: The parts master data base will require additional DASD as all of the data are loaded.
SOFTWARE IMPACTS: None
ORGANIZATIONAL IMPACTS: The manufacturing engineering organization will be required to enter and/or validate the parts master information. With over 35,000 part to enter and validate, this could require additional temporary staffing in that organization.
DEVELOPMENT IMPACTS: None

Task 6. Define Environmental Requirements

The document items resulting from this task describe the environment needed to satisfy the performance and data requirements. They include documents that describe the equipment capabilities required for the operation of the system, the support software with which the computer programs to be developed must interact, interfaces with other systems, and documents that describe the degree of protection required. The following document items should be delivered to the project file at the conclusion of the task.

- Equipment requirements
- Support software requirements
- Interface requirements
- Security and privacy requirements
- Control requirements

Equipment Requirements. This document should list and describe the equipment presently available and any additional equipment that may be required by the proposed system. It should provide information related to the type, size, and quantity of each item of equipment (i.e., equipment items such as processors, storage media, output devices, input devices, communications hardware, etc.).

Example:

Phase 3		*Requirements Definition*

EQUIPMENT		
TYPE	**EQUIPMENT**	**NEW EQUIPMENT**
Processor	1 System 34	None
Storage	1 Disk drive	Add 1 drive
Output Device	4 Terminals 2 PCs w/emulators	Add 1 terminal Add 2 PCs Add bar code-capable printer
Input device		Add bar code reader Provide emulation capability to 2 new PCs
Communications	None	None

Support Software Requirements. This document should provide a description of the support software with which the new computer programs must interact. Specifically, it should describe the support and test software, input and equipment simulations, utility programs, and the operating and data management systems required by the proposed system. The documentation should note whether the software is presently available of would have to be purchased.

Example:

Phase 3   *Requirements Definition*

SOFTWARE		
TYPE OF SOFTWARE	**DESCRIPTION**	**REFERENCE**
Support	MAS II	1-2/1C-MM
Input	None	None
Simulation	None	None
Test	None	None
Utility	File Dump	2.1/STD/MIS
OS	Mgr	System 34
Data Mgmt.	MAS II	1-2/1C-MM

Interface Requirements. This document should provide a description of all the interfaces with other applications computer programs. It should identify each interface by name and indicate the medium and frequency of the interface. The documentation should include information pertaining to the operational implications of data transfer, the characteristics of communications media used for transfer, the current formats of interchange data, interface procedures, and the interface equipment.

Example:

Phase 3   *Requirements Definition*

INTERFACE
INTERFACE NAME: Korean Supply
BETWEEN: Inventory control and manufacturing information
MEDIUM: Electronic file interchange
FREQUENCY: On demand
NATURE OF INTERFACE: Electronic transfer across applications on same platform

Security and Privacy Requirements. This document should specify the security requirements of the new system environment. It should explain each of the functions required for security of the environment in which the system will operate.

Example:

Phase 3   *Requirements Definition*

SECURITY AND PRIVACY

SECURITY FUNCTION 1:
   Security of data during transmit and/or in the files

PURPOSE:
   To prevent embezzlement and loss of record

SECURITY FUNCTION 2:

PURPOSE:
   To prevent unauthorized terminal access, file
   modification, use of files, and use of system

Control Requirements. This document should explain the requirements for environmental control. All of the controls required (e.g., record counts, batch controls, accumulated costs, etc.) should be explained in narrative form. If no controls are to be established, this should be stated.

Example:

Phase 3   *Requirements Definition*

CONTROLS

The following controls must be considered in designing the system:

1. Controls to ensure data completeness and accuracy in updating the data base

2. Controls to ensure correct file has been mounted

3. Controls over access to the computer room must be extended

4. Controls to ensure no records have been lost during input

5. Controls to prevent unauthorized turn-on of master terminal

Task 7. Determine Organizational Requirements

The objective of this task is to define the organizational impacts of the proposed system, including the modifications of positional responsibilities and the addition or elimination of responsibilities that will be necessary to implement the new system. The documentation resulting from this task includes organizational charts that describe those parts of the organization that require significant change; estimates, by job classification, of new jobs that are to be established; estimates, by job classification, of existing jobs to be eliminated; and summary-level job descriptions for all new and revised job classifications. The document items that are used in defining organizational requirements are essentially the same as those discussed and illustrated in Section 3.2.2 (i.e., organization chart, organization description, and job descriptions).

Task 8. Establish Alternatives Evaluation Criteria

The documentation resulting from this task establishes the criteria for selecting packages to be leased of purchased from computer hardware vendors and third-party software companies. The primary document item resulting from this task is a matrix that assigns weights to each of the feature evaluation categories.

Example:

Phase 3					Requirements Definition	
PRODUCT EVALUATION MATRIX						
Feature	Weight	Prod. 1	Prod. 2	Prod. 3	Prod. 4	Prod. 5
Price Purchase Lease (5 yr) Maintenance		300K 50K 5K	410K 65K 6K	N/A 110K 10K	N/A 67K 6K	325K 49K 5K
Documentation	50	0.5	0.75	1	0.75	1
Source code	75	0	0	0	0	1
Program "hooks'	75	0.75	0.5	0.75	0	1
User group	50	0.5	0.5	1	0.75	0
Hotline support	100	0.5	1	1	0.75	0.5
Ad hoc queries	80	0	0.25	0.5	0.5	0.25
Report generator	100	0.5	0.75	0.75	0.5	0.25
Auto job off	250	1	1	1	0	0
Note: Maximum product rating = 1 Maximum feature weight = 500, implying required without exception.						

Task 9. Prepare Requirements Definition Document

The purpose of this task is to present a comprehensive written document containing a description of all user-based requirements. All of the document items that were created during the performance of the preceding tasks (i.e., tasks 1 to 8) are stored in either an on-line of off-line repository. In task 9, select documents are retrieved from the repository for inclusion in the requirements definition phase end document. The process is illustrated in Figure 3-8.

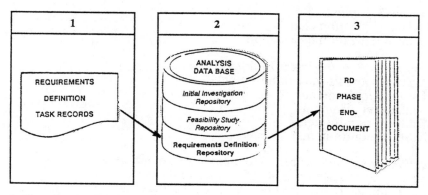

1. All requirements documents
2. The requirements documents are stored in an on-line or off-line repository
3. Selected document items are retrieved from the repository for inclusion in the requirements definition phase end-document.

Figure 3-8. Requirements Definition Document Development

When approved, this document constitutes the third milestone of analysis and, together with the initial investigation and feasibility study phase end-documents, establishes the functional baseline for configuration management as shown in Figure 3-9.

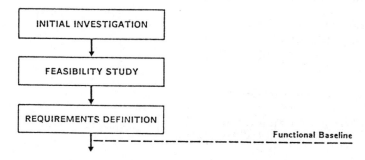

Figure 3-9. Functional Baseline Documents

In summary, these deliverables include all of the following documents that were discussed and illustrated in this subsection.

Feasibility Study Review Documents
- Proposed system analysis worksheet
- Proposed system objectives summary

Interview Documents
- User organization chart
- User organization description

Performance Requirements Documents
- Accuracy and validity requirements
- Timing requirements
- Backup requirements
- Fallback requirements
- Restart requirements

Functional and Performance Requirements Correlation Documents
- Performance requirements of new capabilities
- Performance requirements of upgraded capabilities

Data Requirements Documents
- Static system data
- Dynamic input data
- Dynamic output data
- System data constraints
- Data collection requirements
- Input formats
- Output formats
- Data base impacts

Environmental Requirements Documents
- Equipment requirements
- Support software requirements
- Interface requirements
- Security and privacy requirements
- Control requirements

Organizational Requirements Documents
- Projected organizational structure chart
- Projected personnel requirements
- Job descriptions of new job classifications

Evaluation Criteria
- Product evaluation matrix

In contemplating the preparation of the requirements definition phase end-document, only those document items that set forth requirements which must be achieved by the implementation of the proposed system are retrieved. The suggested content arrangement for presenting the documentation is shown in Figure 3–10.

1.0 GENERAL
1.1 Purpose of the Requirements Definition Document
1.2 Project References
1.3 Terms and Abbreviations
1.4 Security and Privacy

2.0 PERFORMANCE REQUIREMENTS
2.1 Accuracy and Validity
2.2 Timing
2.3 Failure Contingencies
2.3.1 Backup
2.3.2 Fallback
2.3.3 Restart

3.0 ENVIRONMENTAL REQUIREMENTS
3.1 Equipment Environment
3.2 Support Software Environment
3.3 Interfaces
3.4 Security and Privacy
3.5 Control Requirements

4.0 DATA REQUIREMENTS
4.1 Data Description
4.1.1 Static System Data
4.1.2 Dynamic Input Data
4.1.3 Dynamic Output Data
4.1.4 System Data Constraints
4.2 Data Collection Requirements
4.3 Input Formats
4.4 Output Formats
4.5 Data Base Inputs

5.0 PACKAGE EVALUATION
5.1 Evaluation Criteria

**Figure 3-10. Sample Table of Contents for the Requirements
Definition Phase End-Document**

The content outline serves as a checklist of the feasibility study document items that must be retrieved from the project file, synthesized, and presented in the requirements definition phase end-document.

When completed, the document is reviewed by the appropriate decision-making entity to determine if the development effort should continue to the design phases.

Chapter 4
Software Development Design Documentation

In Chapter 3 we saw how the vertical structure of the analysis process provided the framework for software design. As we move down the vertical structure from the analysis process through the design process, we will examine the pattern of translating needs and requirements into systems specifications and documenting the design process.

The document items produced during the software design process set forth specifications that must be followed in order to satisfy the functional requirements. They serve a variety of development functions related to the needs of programmers, operations personnel, technical writers, users, analysts, training staff, and auditors.

There are two categories of design specifications: external design specifications and internal design specifications.

External design specifications divide the system into subsystems and define the subsystem interfaces and the development and operational priorities. They also establish design criteria related to organizational constraints, the technical environment, and security and controls.

Internal design specifications spell out exactly how the system will be implemented. Documents are produced that establish specifications for designing the data bases, master files, and work files; specify how hardware/software configurations are transformed into technical requirements; explain how to modify software packages; and provide the specifications programmers need to code the programs. In addition, specification documents are written during the internal design phase that set forth plans for testing, conversion, implementation, and maintenance.

The external design specifications and internal design specifications, once approved, jointly establish the design baseline for configuration management.

This chapter establishes standards that can be used for the preparation of design specification documents. It explains the evolution of the document items that are deliverable to the project file during the design process and suggests an approach to organizing the document items for presentation in external and internal design phase end-documents.

4.1 DESIGN TASK-DOCUMENTATION ORIENTATION

As with the analysis process, design documentation evolves from a series of tasks performed. The document items resulting from each task are delivered to a project file and placed under configuration control. The phase end-documents produced at the end of the external design and internal design phases can be used to rearrange and synthesize the documentation for presentation in a manual format. The process, as it relates to design documentation, is illustrated in Figure 4-1.

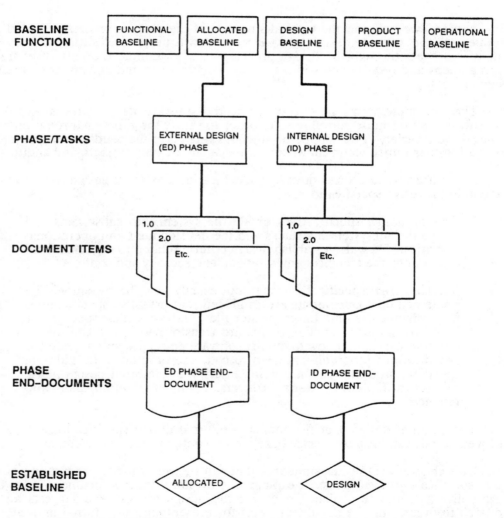

Figure 4-1. End-Document Orientation of the Design Process

4.2 EXTERNAL DESIGN TASK DOCUMENT ITEMS

The external design breaks down into seven major tasks. The task-document item correlation of the external design phase of software development is shown in Table 4-1.

Table 4-1. External Design Task Document Item Correlation

No.	Task/Task Step	Document Item
1.	Review Work Outline	Updated Project Plan
2.	Select Design Alternative	Performance Requirements Evaluation Data Requirements Evaluation Environmental Requirements Evaluation Organizational Requirements Evaluation
3.	Translate the System into Subsystems	
3.1	Identify the system functions	System Function Specifications
3.2	Define the system data	Source Document Descriptions Data Element/Source Documentation Transaction Content Definition File Content Definition Inputs from Other Systems Table Definitions Report Formats Output Screen Formats
3.3	Define processing logic	Function Algorithms Input Processing Specifications Output Processing Specifications History File Processing Specifications Data Base Logic Specifications Table Processing Specifications
4.	Define Technical Environment Specifications	
4.1	Define the hardware environment	Hardware Configuration Order Specifications
4.2	Define the software environment	Software Configuration System Schematic
4.3	Define the Operating Environment	Acceptance Response Time Criteria System Up-Time Window Down Condition Checklist
5.	Develop Security, Privacy and Control Approach	Security and Privacy Requirements I/O Controls User Controls Data File/Data Base Controls Access Controls
6.	Define Interface Requirements	Hardware Interface Requirements Software Interface Requirements
7.	Prepare External Design Document	External Design Document

The objective of each external design task and the nature of the document items resulting from these tasks are further described and illustrated in the text that follows.

Task 1. Review Analysis Documentation

The *external design* phase begins with a review of the documentation produced during the analysis process. This involves conducting a paper review of all document items in the initial investigation, feasibility study, and requirements definition project files. A checklist of analysis documentation may be used to guide the review process.

Example:

Phase 4	External Design

ANALYSIS DOCUMENTATION REVIEW CHECKLIST

Task Number	Task Description	Ck.
	REVIEW INITIAL INVESTIGATION DOCUMENTS	
1	Review Problem and Need Statement	( )
2	Review Projected Costs	( )
3	Review Target Schedule	( )
4	Review Feasibility Study Work Plan	( )
	REVIEW FEASIBILITY STUDY DOCUMENTS	
5	Review Present System Schematic	( )
6	Review Current Organization	( )
7	Review Current Equipment	( )
8	Review Current System Requirements	( )
9	Review List of Programs	( )
10	Review List of Inputs	( )
11	Review Summary of Controls	( )
12	Review List of Outputs	( )
13	Review Current Documentation List	( )
14	Review Current Cost Statement	( )
15	Review Proposed System Schematic	( )
16	Review Statement of Objectives	( )
17	Review Summary of Improvements	( )
18	Review Summary of Impacts	( )
19	Review Assumptions and Constraints	( )
20	Review Available Packages Statement	( )
21	Review Benefit Statement	( )
	REVIEW REQUIREMENTS DEFINITION DOCUMENTS	
22	Review Accuracy Requirements	( )
23	Review Timing Requirements	( )
24	Review Contingency Requirements	( )
25	Review Equipment Requirements	( )
26	Review Software Requirements	( )
27	Review Interface Requirements	( )
28	Review Security/Control Requirements	( )
29	Review Data Requirements	( )
30	Review Data Collection Requirements	( )
31	Review Input/Output Format Requirements	( )
32	Review Data Base Impacts	( )
33	Review Package Evaluation Criteria	( )

Task 2. Select Design Alternative

After reviewing the analysis documentation, the next step is to review the alternative approaches to achieving the functional requirements. The various alternatives identified in the feasibility study are measured against the criteria defined in the requirements specification to determine which are workable. The workable approaches are then compared to see which best satisfies the requirements of the proposed system. Document items resulting from this task are:

- Performance requirements alternatives evaluation
- Data requirements alternatives evaluation
- Environmental requirements alternatives evaluation
- Organizational requirements alternatives evaluation

Performance Requirements Alternatives Evaluation. This document should evaluate the features of the candidate solution relative to the accuracy and validity, timing, backup, fallback, and restart requirements defined during the requirements definition phase.

Example:

Phase 4   *External Design*

PERFORMANCE REQUIREMENTS ALTERNATIVE EVALUATION

Package:

Requirement	Weight
System Start-up	
Program Selection	
Report Generation	
Inquiry Procedures	
Output Forms	
Computer Output Microfilms	
Audit Provisions	
Response Time	
Customization	
Error Correction	
Operator/User Instructions	
Restart Procedures	
Exit Procedure	
System Documentation	

Weight Legend:
5 = Package meets 90%-100% of the requirements
4 = Package meets 80%-89% of the requirements
3 = Package meets 70%-79% of the requirements
2 = Package meetings 60 - 69% of the requirements
1 = Package meets less than 60% of the requirements

Data Requirements Alternative Evaluation. This document should evaluate the features of the candidate solution relative to the static and dynamic data requirements, system data constraints, data collection requirements, input/output formats, and data base impacts.

Example:

Phase 4   *External Design*

DATA REQUIREMENTS ALTERNATIVE EVALUATION

Package:

Requirement	Weight

Output Reports
  ■ Headings
  ■ Field selection
  ■ Line counts
  ■ Content options
  ■ Control numbers
  ■ Suppression
File Maintenance
  ■ File updating
  ■ Backup
  ■ Retention	

Environmental Requirements Alternative Evaluation. This document should evaluate the features of the candidate solution relative to the equipment, support software, interface, security and privacy, and control requirements.

Example:

Phase 4   *External Design*

ENVIRONMENTAL REQUIREMENTS ALTERNATIVE EVALUATION

Package:

Requirement	Weight

Constraints
  ■ Data entry
  ■ File maintenance
  ■ Timing
  ■ Quality Control
  ■ Edit controls
  ■ Review controls
  ■ Balancing control	

Organizational Requirements Alternative Evaluation. This document should evaluate the features of the candidate solution relative to organizational impacts.

Example:

Phase 4   *External Design*

ORGANIZATIONAL REQUIREMENTS ALTERNATIVE EVALUATION

Package:

Requirement	Weight
Functional Impacts • Reduction in manual calculations • Improved customer response • Improved data integrity • Improved audit response Economic impacts • Reduction in rework • Personnel reductions • Inventory reductions • Hardware costs • IS staffing Training Impacts • Number requiring training • Training hours required • Function-specific training	

Task 3. Translate the System into Subsystems

The next task performed by the software designer is to redefine the system into functional subsystems corresponding to the specified functional requirements. The document items resulting from this task include:

- System/subsystem schematic
- System functions description
- Source document specifications
- Record/transaction specifications
- Table content specifications
- File content specifications
- File content specifications
- Input processing logic
- Data base/file processing logic
- History file processing logic
- Table processing logic
- Output processing logic
- Output documentation formats
- Output screen formats

System/Subsystem Schematic. This document should show the relationship of the user organization to the major system components and interrelationships of the system components. This can be achieved by expanding upon or updating the proposed system schematic prepared in the feasibility study phase to show the flow from input through the system to the generation of output.

Example:

Phase 4   *External Design*

SYSTEM/SUBSYSTEM SCHEMATIC

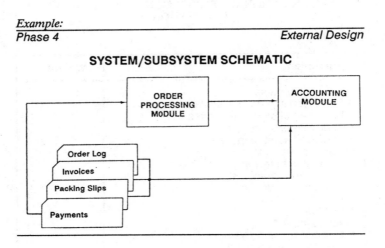

System Functions Description. This document should describe the functions to be performed by the system. This description should relate to the summary of improvements discussed in the feasibility study, but should provide descriptions of refinements and the details available as a result of the ongoing analysis and design process.

Example:

Phase 4   *External Design*

SYSTEM FUNCTIONS DESCRIPTION

The order tracking system will provide for tracking of all orders for materials purchased by the company. It will

- Track material movements, both planned and unplanned

- Track demand transactions

- Provide order detailed statistics

- Generate purchase orders

- Track purchase payments

Source Document Specifications. Specifications should be prepared for each source document that provides input to the system. The documentation should include the name of the document, the document number, a facsimile of the document, a statement of document purpose and usage, the source of data, expected volume, frequency processed, the medium of conversion, and a description of the content.

Example:

Phase 4   *External Design*

SOURCE DOCUMENT SPECIFICATIONS
Document Name: Purchase Order
Facsimile
General Purpose: To acquire stock items and notify receiving that shipment is due.
General Content:

Vendor Identification	Description
Terms of Payment	Quantity
Point of Delivery	Price
Item Number	Instructions

Record/Transaction Specifications. Specifications should be prepared for each record/transaction that provides input to the system. The documentation should include the data base/file ID, record title, length of each record, number of record characters, number of record bytes, number of records in the start-up file, a number for each element in ascending order, and a description title of each record. It should also show the start position of the data element within the record, note the label used, and indicate the length of the data element. Comments should be include when applicable.

Example:

Phase 4   *External Design*

RECORD/TRANSACTION SPECIFICATIONS

Record Name: Purchase Order

Field Name
Account Number
Start Position: 1
Label: ACCTNUM
Length: 9
Comment: Numeric

Account Name
Start Position: 10
Label: ACCTMMI
Length: 49
Comment: A/N

Street Address
Start Position: 59
Label: ACCTADD
Length: 30
Comment: A/N

City
Start Position: 89
Label: ACCTCTY
Length: 25
Comment: A/N

State
Start Position: 114
Label: ACCTSTE
Length: 2
Comment: A/N

Zip
Start Position: 116
Label: ACCTZIP

Table Content Specifications. Specifications should be prepared for each table used as input to the system. The documentation should include the name of the table, type of table classification, number of entries for variable and fixed lengths. It should indicate the dimensions of the table and specify the storage requirements. A graphic depiction of the table structure should be included in the content description.

Example:

Phase 4	External Design

TABLE CONTENT SPECIFICATIONS

Table Name:	Vendor Master
Classification:	Purchasing Vendor Master
No. Entries:	3,500
Dimensions:	3,500x850
Storage Req.:	2 Cylinders
Structure:	(See Below)

Field	Length	Type
Name	25	Alpha (Key)
Address (Order)	35	Alpha
City	25	Alpha
State	2	Alpha
Zip	9	Num (Key)
Contact	25	Alpha
Telephone	10	Num
Address (Pay)	35	Alpha
City	25	Alpha
State	2	Alpha
Zip	9	Num
Contact	25	Alpha
Telephone	10	Num
Credit Limit	8	Num
Vendor Rating	3	A/N
Product Code1	9	A/N (Key)
Product Code2	9	A/N (Key)
Product Code3	9	A/N (Key)

Content Description:

This table provides information concerning vendor order and payment locations. It also gives summary information regarding vendor's supplier rating.

The vendor rating data are supplied by purchasing.

File Content Specifications. Specifications should be prepared for files used as input to the system. The documentation should identify the file by title and type of file and should provide a brief narrative description of the file. It should include data relative to the file library, label, media, number of volumes, number of drives, organization, estimated number of records, format, record length, and key fields. It should identify each data element by number, name, length, and usage. Comments should be included when applicable.

Example:

Phase 4	*External Design*

FILE CONTENT SPECIFICATIONS	
Title of File	Inventory
Type of File	DB2 table
No. Entries	400,000
Library	TAC.PROD.LIB
Label	INV

MEDIA/STORAGE	
Media	On-line
No. Volumes	1 dedicated pack
No. Drives	
Organization	Relational
No. Records	1,800,000
Format	N/A
Record Length	130

Key Fields			
No.	**Name**	**Length**	**Usage**
7	Item Code	6 characters	Mandatory
11	Description	29 characters	Mandatory
29	Purchase Qty.	6 characters	Optional
51	Package	6 characters	Mandatory
52	UOM	3 characters	Optional

Input Processing Logic. This document should define, graphically or in narrative form, the design requirements for input processing control. It should include information pertaining to the requirement for validating inputs, maintaining data control, message processing, and algorithms to be used for input processing.

Example:

Phase 4	*External Design*

INPUT PROCESSING LOGIC

Validation
All account numbers must be checked against the Valid Number Table. Only exact matches should be accepted. Mismatches must be returned to order clerk.

Data Control Maintenance
Batching – Control totals, transaction counts, hash totals.
Verification – Key verification and visual review.

Messages
"Invalid Account Number Entered"

History File Processing Logic. This document should define, graphically or in narrative form, the design requirements for history file processing. The documentation should indicate those messages applicable to the history file process and the algorithms used for history file processing.

Example:

Phase 4	*External Design*

HISTORY FILE PROCESSING LOGIC

Logic
Filled orders -----> Diskette=Filled Purchase Order File

Canceled Orders -----> Diskette=Canceled Order File

Filled Order File + Canceled Order File=History File

Messages
"All items on Purchase Order Received"

"Partial Shipment Received"

"Purchase Order Canceled"

"Cancel Partial Issue New Purchase Order"

Table Processing Logic. This document should define, graphically or in narrative form, requirements for table processing. The documentation should indicate those messages applicable to table processing and the algorithms used for table processing.

Example:

Phase 4   *External Design*

TABLE PROCESSING LOGIC

Use
For validating account numbers versus department numbers.

Algorithm
1 Enter department number.
2 Enter account number.
3 Verify accounts number against list of allowable accounts.
4 If allowable, enter ORDER.
5 If not allowable, print applicable messages.

Messages
"Invalid Account Number"
"Valid Account Number"

Output Processing Logic. This document should define, graphically or in narrative form, the design requirements for output processing. The documentation should include data relative to design constraints for output generation and the requirements for output control. It should indicate those messages applicable to output processing and the algorithms used for output processing.

Example:

Phase 4   *External Design*

OUTPUT PROCESSING LOGIC

Output Generation Constraints
Processing date is on Friday. Orders entered after Thursday midnight will not be reflected on weekly order report.

Output Control
Password assigned and entered on validation table.

Messages
"Requestor password invalid – enter new password"
"Requestor not authorized to run report"
"Requested report sent to system printer queue."

Output Document Format. A separate document should be prepared showing the output format of each document to be created by the system. The documentation should include a facsimile of each report and a description of each line item.

Example:

Phase 4	*External Design*

OUTPUT DOCUMENT FORMAT

Output Document Name: Part Structure List

Report Facsimile

Report No: XXX   MMDDYY
Plant: XXXXX   Page: XXXX
Plan Date:

Parent Part	Component	Parent Part	Component
XXXXX	XXXXX-XXX	XXXXX	XXXXX-XXX
	XXXXX-XXX		XXXXX-XXX
	XXXXX-XXX	XXXXX	XXXXX-XXX
	XXXXX-XXX		XXXXX-XXX
	XXXXX-XXX		XXXXX-XXX
	XXXXX-XXX	XXXXX	XXXXX-XXX
XXXXX	XXXXX-XXX		XXXXX-XXX
	XXXXX-XXX		XXXXX-XXX
XXXXX	XXXXX-XXX		XXXXX-XXX
	XXXXX-XXX		XXXXX-XXX
	XXXXX-XXX	XXXXX	XXXXX-XXX
XXXXX	XXXXX-XXX		XXXXX-XXX
	XXXXX-XXX	XXXXX	XXXXX-XXX
	XXXXX-XXX	XXXXX	XXXXX-XXX
XXXXX	XXXXX-XXX		XXXXX-XXX
	XXXXX-XXX		XXXXX-XXX
	XXXXX-XXX	XXXXX	XXXXX-XXX
	XXXXX-XXX		XXXXX-XXX
	XXXXX-XXX		XXXXX-XXX
	XXXXX-XXX		XXXXX-XXX

Key Fields

No.	Line Title	Description
1	Report no.	Number of report
2	Plant	Plant ID
3	Run date	mm/dd/yy
4	Time	Time generated
5	Name	Name of report
6	Planning date	mm/dd/yy
7	Page	Page of report
8	Component no.	Numeric ID
9	Parent part	Numeric ID

Output Screen Format. A separate document should be prepared showing the output format of each screen to be created by the system. The documentation should include a facsimile of each screen and a description of each data element.

Example:

Phase 4	*External Design*

OUTPUT SCREEN FORMAT

Screen Name: Product Structure Listing

Screen Facsimile

Plant: XXXXX   MMDDYY

Product Structure Listing

Plan Date:

Parent Part	Component	Parent Part	Component
XXXXX	XXXX-XXX XXXX-XXX XXXX-XXX XXXX-XXX	XXXXX XXXXX	XXXX-XXX XXXX-XXX XXXX-XXX XXXX-XXX XXXX-XXX
XXXXX	XXXX-XXX XXXX-XXX XXXX-XXX XXXX-XXX XXXX-XXX XXXX-XXX XXXX-XXX	XXXXX XXXXX	XXXX-XXX XXXX-XXX XXXX-XXX XXXX-XXX XXXX-XXX XXXX-XXX

Scr: XXX   MMDDYY

F1 Help   F2 Save   F3 Cancel

Note: This output screen provides similar information to that available on the edit screen. However, this information is in view mode only. Users wishing to modify this information must use the edit screen.

Key Fields

No.	Field Title	Description
1	Report no.	Number of report
2	Plant	Plant ID
3	Run date	mm/dd/yy
4	Time	Time generated
5	Name	Name of report
6	Planning date	mm/dd/yy
7	Page	Page of report
8	Component no.	Numeric ID
9	Parent part	Numeric ID

Task 4. Define Technical Environment Specifications

After the subsystems have been defined, the software designers must develop specifications pertaining to the technical environment needed to satisfy the functional requirements. The documents deliverable to the project file provide specifications related to the equipment capabilities required for the operation of the system, the support software with which the computer programs to be developed must interact, the interfaces with other systems and subsystems, and the anticipated organizational, operational, and development impacts of the system. The document items resulting from this task that are deliverable to the project file are

- Hardware requirements
- Support software requirements
- Acceptance response time
- System-up time window
- Backup considerations

Hardware Requirements. This document should provide a description of the equipment capabilities required for the operation of the system. The documentation should include the number of each on- or off-line CPU and the size of internal storage and should indicate the number of diskettes, tape units, etc. required. It should also describe the communications requirements, including line speeds, and specify the number of terminals required for processing.

Example:

Phase 4	*External Design*

HARDWARE REQUIREMENTS

CPU
System IBM 3090 – 180S
8 Megabytes of core memory divided between VM and MVS using PR/SM Software (no change to CPU configuration)

Storage
2 disk packs
2 7520E disk packs must be added to the current configuration to handle the additional parts' master data

Communications
2 modems with 64-kilobaud rate. Additional equipment may be required if vendors accept EDI standards.

Terminals
6 3270 terminals

Support Software Requirements. This document should provide a description of the support software with which the computer programs to be developed must interact. The documentation would describe the storage allocation and data base organization requirements, the telecommunications requirements, and the program language requirements of the system.

Example:

Phase 4   *External Design*

SUPPORT SOFTWARE REQUIREMENTS

Data Base Support Software
Existing software base of DB2 using SPUFI with the acquisition of a compatible CASE tool.

Telecommunications Support Software
Existing telecommunication platform of CICS, VTAM, and LU 6.2 APPI to PC base will be unchanged.

Programming Support Software
APS Sage development platform interfaced to a DB2 design tool will be used. This system will be used as a test for the PC network version of the Sage software. The data base toolset will be initially tested as part of the vendor agreement.

Acceptance Response Time Requirements. This document should delineate performance criteria for acceptable response time. It should state the acceptable response time requirements in terms of best, average, and maximum. It should also relate the time criteria to the system functions and the system tests necessary for implementation.

Example:

Phase 4   *External Design*

ACCEPTANCE RESPONSE TIME REQUIREMENTS

Filled Orders
Within 2 seconds, 30 percent; within 4 seconds, 50 percent; within 8 seconds, 100 percent.

Partially Filled Orders
Within 4 seconds, 30 percent; within 8 seconds, 50 percent; within 12 seconds, 100 percent.

Unfilled Orders:
Within 2 seconds, 30 percent; within 4 seconds, 50 percent; within 8 seconds, 100% percent.

System-Up Time Window. This document should delineate performance criteria for system-up time window. The documentation should summarize the system-up time window criteria for performance of the CPU where the system resides. It should also summarize the system-up criteria for future configuration and for requested up time.

Example:

Phase 4   *External Design*

SYSTEM-UP TIME WINDOW

Current CPU
CICS − 0600 to 2200 hours − Monday through Friday.
IDMS − 0600 to 2200 hours − Monday through Friday.
CICS − 0800 to 2000 hours − Saturday and Sunday.
IDMS − 0800 to 2000 hours − Saturday and Sunday.

Future Configuration
CICS − 0200 to 2300 hours − Monday through Friday.
IDMS − 0000 to 2300 hours − Monday through Friday.
CICS − 0200 to 2000 hours − Saturday and Sunday.
IDMS − 0200 to 2000 hours − Saturday and Sunday.

Requested Up Time
0200 to 2300 − Monday through Friday.
0600 to 1800 − Saturday and Sunday.

Backup Considerations. This document should describe the backup requirements of the system. Its should list each down condition that can be anticipated and describe the backup procedure that must be established to cope with the system-down condition.

Example:

Phase 4   *External Design*

BACKUP CONSIDERATIONS

System Down Condition
1. If terminals in one building are down, reroute communications.

2. If all terminals are down, recycle CICS and VTAM. If failure persists for more than eight hours, transfer work to backup location.

3. If system CPU is down, transfer work to backup location.

4. If IDMS is down, period-end microfiche of item master catalog.

Task 5. Develop Security, Privacy, and Control Approach

The next task performed by the software designer is to define the approaches for ensuring the security of the system and data. The approach must consider the privacy and security requirements presented in the requirements definition phase of development. The document items produced during the performance of this task are:

- Security and privacy requirements
- I/O control requirements
- User control requirements
- Data file/data base control requirements
- Access control requirements

Security and Privacy Requirements. This document should describe requirements for security and privacy. It should explain the system security, environment security, and data security functions and their purposes.

Example:

Phase 4   *External Design*

SECURITY AND PRIVACY REQUIREMENTS

Access Security
1. Assign password to individual users to restrict system assess.
2. Provide work-group-level authority standards.
3. Auto log off after 20 minutes of inactivity.
4. RACF data access control.

Environmental Security
1. Limit computer room access to operations personnel to prevent unauthorized operator terminal usage.
2. Plant security to protect against unauthorized building access.
3. Backup files maintained in locked cabinet in locked storage facility.
4. Fire safety precautions observed in computer room.

Data Security
1. Maintain duplicate file of source documents to prevent loss of documents in transit.
2. Nonproduction programs prohibited from accessing production files.
3. Decision support access to files is read only.
4. Nightly incremental backups performed on data packs.
5. Weekly full-pack backups standard procedure.
6. Full disaster recovery backups are located at an off-site facility and can be retrieved in extreme emergency.

I/O Controls. This document should provide a description of the input/output controls.

Example:

Phase 4   *External Design*

I/O CONTROLS

Control Objectives
To ensure that data that provide input to the system are properly assembled and that the output requested is produced.

Control Procedure
1. Data entry is performed by the functional department responsible for the integrity of the data.
2. Full field level on-line edits are performed by the system to ensure valid data types, ranges, and no key violations.
3. Reports are routed to local printers as determined by password and terminal ID.

Corrective Action
1. Authorization for edit capability provided by cognizant user managers
2. Full audit maintained by system, monitored by accounting and external auditors

---

User Controls. This document should provide a description of the user controls.

Example:

Phase 4   *External Design*

USER CONTROLS

Control Objectives
To prescribe procedures to be followed by the user department when submitting and receiving information from data processing operations.

Control Procedures
1. Only users with IDs and passwords authorized for report generation can initiate batch reports.
2. Large jobs are held in queue for overnight processing.

Corrective Action
User department is responsible for all data validation and correction.

Data File/Data Base Controls. This document should provide a description of the data file/data base controls.

Example:

Phase 4	External Design

DATA FILE/DATA BASE CONTROLS

Control Objectives
To ensure that file integrity is maintained and that the proper files are used when programs are run.

Control Procedures
1. Data bases are bound to program during move to production.
2. Users are given only view capability of data bases from outside of production applications.
3. Daily balances are performed to ensure integrity of data bases.

Corrective Action
1. Data base errors are corrected by cognizant user departments.
2. Edit validations ensure that data type, range, and format are correct as well as ensuring against key violations.
3. All edits are recorded in the audit file, providing full recoverability in case of malicious or accidental disruption of the data base.

Access Controls. This document should provide a description of the access controls.

Example:

Phase 4	External Design

ACCESS CONTROLS

Control Objectives
To ensure that use of computer programs and access to output reports are restricted to authorized parties.

Control Procedures
1. Large batch reports are printed and maintained in the computer center until an authorized person picks them up.
2. Other reports are routed to local printers based on password and terminal ID.

Corrective Action
RACF control is maintained at the data element level. Only authorized IDs can edit specified data.

Task 6. Define Interface Requirements

The software designer then focuses on preparing specifications that establish interface controls. The documents delivered to the project file detail interface requirements pertaining to data formats, data contents, data rates, hardware interface design, applications software interface design, and data base interface design. The results of this task are summarized in two documents:

- Hardware interface requirements
- Software interface requirements

Hardware Interface Requirements. This document should describe each hardware interface required by the system and the operational implications of the hardware interface.

Example:

Phase 4	*External Design*

HARDWARE INTERFACE REQUIREMENTS

Corporate Network

The additional traffic caused by this system will require access to fractional T1 lines in addition to our current bandwidth. This access will require additional modem and multiplexor hardware.

Local Network

The addition of six new terminals in the purchasing area will require either the installation of a new communications controller to gain the additional ports, or an upgrade to the microcode to allow existing equipment to handle the multisession requirements of some of the users.

If an additional controller is attached, there will need to be some modification of current channel attachments to provide the connectivity.

Network Maintenance

The new 24-hour availability of the system will impinge on the normal network maintenance window. This will require operational changes to allow partial network outages during non-peak hours, but while the system is still up and otherwise available.

Software Interface Requirements. This document should describe each hardware interface required by the system and the operational implications of the hardware interface. The documentation should specify the type of interface, the operational implications of data transfer, and the transfer requirements to and from the system. It should describe the current formats of interchanged data, define the communications media required for data transfer, and prescribe interface telecommunications procedures.

Example:

Phase 4   *External Design*

SOFTWARE INTERFACE REQUIREMENTS

Interface Between: Receiving system and order tracking system.

Operational Implications
1. Order tracking system has built in controls to track open orders and partial shipments, thus eliminating the need for similar controls in the receiving system.
2. The two systems use separate data bases with large redundancies in the information they maintain. This interface will combine the two data bases, forcing the recompilation and rebinding of the programs in the old receiving system.
3. Users of the receiving system will have to be retrained in using the access procedures. Most changes to the system will be transparent to the user, but the access screens will change, and order tracking functions will now be handled by the new system.

Transfer Requirements
Program needed to read daily receipts from receiving system.

Current Formats
Both systems reside in the DB2 system. However, because the receiving system was in place prior to the establishment of the data dictionary, there are discrepancies in data lengths and types for several data elements. The specific changes required to implement this interface are
1. Carrier code goes from numeric only to alphanumeric. Data display length is unchanged
2. The part number field must be expanded from 8 characters to 15.

Interface Procedures
1. Receipt data matched daily against purchase order data to determine order status.
2. Only status information will be passed between the systems. Tracking data will reside in DB2 and be directly accessible from either system.

Task 7. Prepare External Design Document

The final external design task performed by the software designer is the preparation of the external design phase end-document. All of the document items that were created during the performance of the preceding tasks (i.e., tasks 1 to 6) are stored in either an on-line or off-line repository. In task 7, select documents are retrieved from the repository, reorganized, and synthesized for inclusion in the external design phase end-document. The process is illustrated in Figure 4-2.

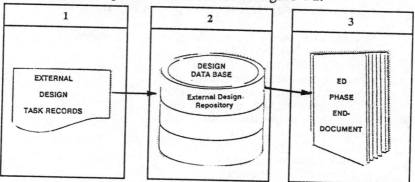

1. All external design documents, including worksheets, questionnaires, and task records
2. The external design documents are stored in an on-line or off-line repository.
3. Selected document items are retrieved from the repository for inclusion in the external design phase end-document.

Figure 4-2. External Design Phase End-Document Evolution

The document items delivered to the repository during the external design phase establish the allocated baseline for configuration management as shown in Figure 4-3.

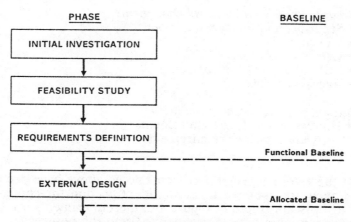

Figure 4-3. Allocated Baseline Document

In summary the deliverable items include all of the following document items that were discussed in this section.

    Package Evaluation Documents
- Performance requirements package evaluation
- Data requirements package evaluation
- Environmental requirements package evaluation
- Organizational requirements package evaluation

    System/Subsystem Documents
- System/subsystem schematic
- System function description
- Source document specifications
- Record/transaction specifications
- Table content specifications
- File content specifications
- Input processing logic
- History file processing logic
- Table processing logic
- Output processing logic
- Output document format
- Output screen format

    Technical Environment Specifications
- Hardware requirements
- Support software requirements
- Acceptance response time requirements
- System-up time window
- Backup considerations

    Security Privacy and Control Documents
- Security and privacy requirements
- I/O controls
- User controls
- Data file/data base controls
- Access controls

    Interface Requirements Documents
- Hardware interface requirements
- Software interface requirements

When all of the external design documents noted above have been delivered to the project file, they are assigned a catalog identification for configuration management purposes. As illustrated in Figure 4-3, these documents establish the allocated baseline for configuration management. From the point when the allocated baseline is established, no changes should be made to the design without formal change control processing.

The content of the external design document should be arranged in sections in accordance with the following:

Section 1.0 General
Section 2.0 System/subsystem specifications
Section 3.0 Security and Controls
Section 4.0 Technical Environment
Section 5.0 Interfacing Requirements

The breakdown of the document items contained in each subsection is shown in Figure 4-4.

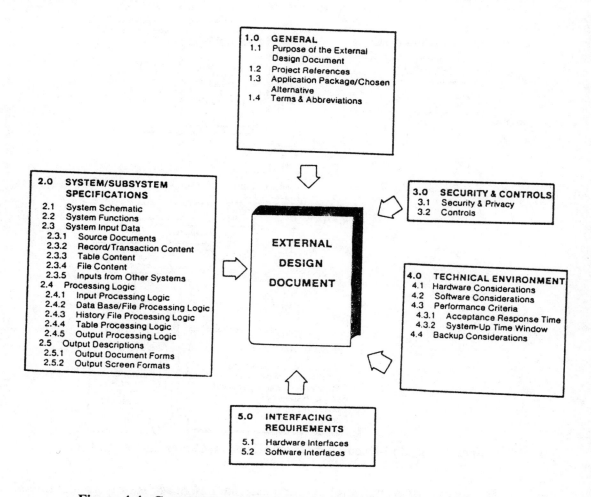

Figure 4-4. Content Arrangement of the External Design Document

4.3 INTERNAL DESIGN DOCUMENTATION

Whereas the documents delivered to the external design project file established the baseline for allocating the system functions to subsystems, the system designers can now proceed to finalize the system architecture. During this phase, documents are produced that establish specifications for designing the data bases, master files, and work files; specifications are prepared that explain how the hardware and software configurations are transformed into technical requirements; procedures are developed for modifying software packages; and instructions for transforming specifications into code are provided. In addition, documents are written that set forth plans for testing, conversion, implementation, and maintenance. The end-document orientation of the internal design process is illustrated in Figure 4-5.

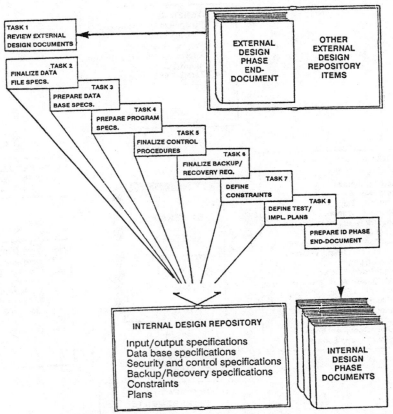

Figure 4-5. End-Document Orientation of the Internal Design Process

The specific items deliverable to the external design repository are identified in Table 4-2.

The internal design breaks down into nine major tasks. The task document item correlation of the internal design phase of development is shown in Table 4-2.

Table 4-2. Internal Design Task-Document Item Correlation

No.	Task/Task Step	Document Item
1.	Review external design documentation.	Documentation Checklist
2.	Finalize data file specifications.	Input File Specifications Output File Specifications Interface File Specifications Intermediate File Specifications
3.	Prepare data base specifications.	Data Base Applications Labeling/Tagging Conventions Data Base Organization Summary Data Base Instructions Table Layouts
4.	Prepare program specifications.	Support Software Environment Interface Specifications Storage Requirements Program Design Summary Program Design - Logic Flow -Initialization/Sign-on Procedures - Operator Messages - User Messages - Setup Instructions Table Layouts Record Layouts
5.	Finalize system control procedures.	Input Checklist Output Checklist User Control Instructions Data Base/File Control Instructions Access Control Instructions Error Control Instructions Audit Control Instructions File Maintenance Instructions
6.	Finalize backup and recovery procedures.	Backup Procedures File Retention Procedures Restart Procedures
7.	Define development constraints.	Operating Time Window Constraints Hardware Constraints Software Constraints Communications Constraints Development Staff Constraints
8.	Define test and implementation plans.	Test Plan Conversion Plan Implementation Plan Maintenance Plan Documentation Plan
9.	Prepare internal design phase end-document	Internal Design Document

Task 1. Review External Design Documentation

The *internal design* phase begins by conducting a paper review of the external design documentation in the project file that established the allocated baseline for configuration management. A checklist of external design documentation may be used to guide the review process.

Example:

Phase 5		*Internal Design*

No.	Task Description	CK.
	Review System/Subsystem Specifications	
1	Review system schematic	( )
2	Review system functions specifications	( )
3	Review input data specifications	
3A	Review source document specifications	( )
3B	Review record/transaction specifications	( )
3C	Review table content specifications	( )
3D	Review file content specifications	( )
3E	Review other systems input specifications	( )
4	Review I/O processing logic specifications	
4A	Review input processing logic specifications	( )
4B	Review DB/file processing logic specifications	( )
4C	Review history file processing specifications	( )
4D	Review table processing specifications	( )
4E	Review output processing logic specifications	( )
4F	Review output document format specifications	( )
4G	Review output screen format specifications	( )
	Review Security and Control Requirements	
5	Review security requirements	( )
6	Review privacy requirements	( )
7	Review control requirements	( )
	Review Technical Environmental Requirements	
8	Review hardware considerations	( )
9	Review software considerations	( )
10	Review performance criteria	
10A	Review acceptance response time criteria	( )
10B	Review system-up time window criteria	( )
11	Review backup considerations	( )
	Review Interfacing Requirements	
12	Review hardware interface requirements	( )
13	Review software interface requirements	( )

Task 2. Finalize Data File Specifications

After reviewing the external design documentation that defined the source documents, transactions, tables, and files that will provide input to the system and the output formats and descriptions of the reports and display to be generated by the system, the systems designers can proceed to finalize the data file specifications. The document items resulting from this task that are deliverable to the project file are

- Input file specifications
- Output file specifications
- Interface file specifications
- Intermediate work file specifications

Input File Specifications. A record layout document should be completed for each input transaction. The documentation should include descriptions of the data elements and the file characteristics. (*Note:* The data used by the system designers in preparing input transaction layouts are drawn from the file/record descriptions that were documented during the external design phase.)

Example:

Phase 5	*Internal Design*

INPUT FILE SPECIFICATIONS

Input Name: Vendor Master   ID No. PUR20
Source Library: PUR.PROD.LIB
Data Set Name: PUR.PROD.LIB.VENMSTR
File Usage: Read Only

Input to:

Subsystem	Program
Receiving	RCV-ACCPT
Receiving	RCV-RCVR
Order Tracking	ORTR-PR03

File Size:

No. Records	Record Length
3500	130

Layout:

No.	Element Name	Start Position	Length
1	Vendor	1	35
2	Terms of Payment	36	10
3	Point of Delivery	46	25
4	Item Number	61	15
5	Description	76	35
6	Quantity	111	6
7	Price	117	9

Output File Specifications. A record layout document should be completed for each file used to generate outputs. The documentation should describe all output formats.

Example:

Phase 5   *Internal Design*

OUTPUT FILE SPECIFICATIONS

Output Name: Receiver Print   ID No. RCV40
Source Library: PUR.PROD.LIB
Data Set Name: PUR.PROD.LIB.RCVR.PRN
File Usage: Read Only

Output from:
Subsystem   **Program**
Receiving   RCV-RCVR

File Size:
No. Records   **Record Length**
100-500   245

Layout: Sequenced by receiver number

No.	Element Name	Start Position	Length
1	Receiver number	1	8
2	Product code	9	12
3	P.O. number	21	18
4	Line item number1	39	3
5	Part number1	42	15
6	Qty received1	57	6
7	Qty ordered1	63	6
8	Line item number2	69	3
9	Part number2	72	15
10	Qty received2	77	6
11	Qty ordered2	83	6
12	Line item number3	89	3
13	Part number3	92	15

Interface File Specifications. A record layout document should be completed for each file required as an interface to other systems. The descriptions of the file characteristics and the layouts of data elements should be presented in the same format and style used for the presentation of input and output file specifications.

Intermediate Work File Specifications. A record layout document should be completed showing the data elements for each intermediate work file. The descriptions of the file characteristics and the layouts of data elements should be presented in the same format and style used for the presentation of input and output file specifications.

Task 3. Prepare Data Base Specifications

The objective of this task is to define the relationships between the data elements, translate the data relationships into logical data base structures, and develop the physical data base design. The documentation should include specifications that define the data base storage requirements, establish labeling and tagging conventions, describe the data base organization, and specify any special instructions for data entry and machine run. The document items resulting from this task that are deliverable to the project file are

- Data base applications
- Labeling/tagging conventions
- Data base organization summary
- Special instructions
- Table layouts

Data Base Applications. This document should identify each data base application. The documentation should include the name of the system and indicate the dates during which the data base will be used. It should also delineate the storage requirements, file media, record sequence, and the form of the file and the respective codes.

Example:

Phase 5		*Internal Design*

DATA BASE APPLICATIONS

Application	Effective Dates	
System	From	To
Technical Support	MM/DD/YY	MM/DD/YY
IHO Reporting	MM/DD/YY	MM/DD/YY
Order Status	MM/DD/YY	MM/DD/YY
Change Status	MM/DD/YY	MM/DD/YY

Storage Requirements
Data base will contain approximately 10,000 reports. Each report is not to exceed a length of 216. The data base will be stored on a dedicated disk pack.

File Characteristics

Medium	Encoding System
Disk	Binary

Record Sequence
Part No.
Inventory Source
Part Type

Labeling/Tagging Conventions. This document should specify the system labeling/tagging conventions to the extent necessary for the programmer to use the convention as a practical tool (e.g., the conventions used to identify new versions of the data base).

Example:

Phase 5   *Internal Design*

LABELING/TAGGING CONVENTIONS

Purpose and Scope
These instructions define the procedures for grouping like objects and identifying the function or language of each object or member. The purpose of this standard is to make development and maintenance easier. However, if the standard becomes unduly restrictive on production, the standard should be changed, not production.

References
MIS Policies; Naming Conventions; Index 220

Standards/Procedures
MIS Standards Manual; Index 220-25
An exception for naming will be used for the interface to the old receiving system. The interface modules will use the program number suffix of the receiving system.

Data Base Organization Summary. This document should set forth specifications concerning the organization and manipulation of the data base. The documentation should describe the general file design and format of the physical data base files and explain the design rationale for consistency.

Example:

Phase 5   *Internal Design*

DATA BASE ORGANIZATION SUMMARY

The vendor master data base is a DB2 data base indexed on vendor number, Zip code, and product code. The field definitions are provided in the input data base specifications resulting from task 2 of this development phase. Normal DB2 access rules apply to this data base. This system will have read-only authority on this data base.

Updates to the data base are made from the purchasing system which places a record level lock during the update. The receiving system will retry 5 times before notifying the user of the lock condition and instructing the user to try at a later time. The receiving system places no locks on the data base.

Data Base Instructions. This document should provide instructions for data entry and machine processing. The documentation should define the criteria and summarize procedures for data entry. It should also provide machine run instructions for generating, modifying, updating, or otherwise using the data base.

Example:

Phase 5   *Internal Design*

DATA BASE INSTRUCTIONS

Data Base Name: Problem Log

Key Definition: Log Number + Date

Duplicate Key Checking: On entry of a duplicate key, the program should notify the user to contact IS customer service and inform them that a data base error has occurred.

Update Processing: The data base will be updated (records added) from program MNT-ACT01. Edits to the existing records should be made from program MNT-ACT02. MNT-ACT01 should create the log number as a sequentially incremented number. The user should not be allowed to edit this number.

Table Layouts. This document should summarize the design specifications of tables. The documentation should include the table name and classifications and indicate the number of entries, dimensions of the core image required for storing the table, and the appropriate storage image. It should also illustrate the table structure and describe the table content.

Example:

Phase 5   *Internal Design*

TABLE LAYOUT

Field	Length	Type
Log number	9	Numeric
Receiver	25	Alpha
Contact	25	Alpha
Cont-Tel	10	Numeric
Cont-Ext	4	Numeric
Problem-Type	15	Alpha
Priority	1	Alpha
Date-Open	6	Date

Task 4. Prepare Program Specifications
The objective of this task is to prepare program design summaries that define the inputs, outputs, interfaces, and algorithms. The specifications developed in the performance of this task are used by programmers to code the programs. The document items resulting from this task that are deliverable to the project file are

- Support software environment
- Interface specifications
- Storage requirements
- Program design summary
- Program design logic flow
- Program design initialization/sign-on procedures
- Program design operator messages
- Program design user messages
- Program design setup instructions
- Table layouts
- Record layouts

Support Software Environment. This document should describe the support software with which the computer program must interact. The documentation should include the program name and indicate the function of the program. It should also include information related to run time, the frequency of runs, and hardware considerations for program operations. References to the languages and the operating system should be used when applicable.

Example:

Phase 5   *Internal Design*

SUPPORT SOFTWARE ENVIRONMENT

Program Name: CMB125

Function: Generates delinquency reports based upon aging analysis as specified by the program. This utility provides input as a flag with record number information.

Operating Considerations: Run time: 2 seconds maximum. Frequency: as requested by your program. Call this program as a standard INCLUDE function. It takes the table name and field names as parameter. It also requires specification of the delinquency criteria. The routine uses system date and time as references. Use the keyword Today, to specify the current date. For example, Today -60 yields exceptions for all records showing greater than 60-day inactivity. Now -60 would show records with more than 1 minute (Now=HH:MM:SS). Now is valid only for periods less than 24 hours.

Interface Specifications. This document should be prepared to provide a description of each interface to other applications computer programs. The documentation should include the program name and indicate the systems between which the interface takes place. Information related to the medium and frequency of the interface should also be provided.

Example:

Phase 5   *Internal Design*

INTERFACE SPECIFICATIONS

Program Name: Korean Supply System

Interface Between: Korean manufacturing and order tracking systems

Media: Tape, diskettes

Frequency of Interface: Weekly

Nature of Interface: The data are reformatted to match the file characteristics of the order tracking system and then loaded into the system though the batch procedure for order entry.

Storage Requirements. This document should provide a description of storage requirements for each program. The documentation should include information pertaining to internal storage, drum storage, disk storage, tape storage, or other storage requirements.

Example:

Phase 5   *Internal Design*

STORAGE REQUIREMENTS

Program Name: ECO70

Internal Storage
This program will load the master parts file into core in segments.

Disk Storage
The parts master file will require a total of 60 pages of data base space. It is estimated that the growth of the parts list will not require additional space for at least 3 years.

Program Design Summary. This document should summarize the program design for each program in the system. The information presented should identify the purpose of the program, the inputs to and outputs from the program, interfaces to other programs, and a description of the logic and algorithms used in the program.

Example:

Phase 5   *Internal Design*

PROGRAM DESIGN SUMMARY

Program Name: ECO70
Program Purpose:
This program is used to process the information in the BBB
Backlog Order File (MKBBP01). It then prints the HI-REL
Delinquent Backlog Report.
Inputs:
BBB Backlog Order File (MKBBP01)
Outputs:
HI-REL Delinquent Backlog Report
Interfaces:
None
Algorithms:
Delinquent Orders = Today - 30 If OrdTyp = Norm
Delinquent Orders = Today - 5 If OrdTyp = Rush

Program Design – Logic Flow. This document should provide a graphic illustration of the logic flow. It should show the decision processes, conditions tested for branching, error detection methods, and the algorithms and logical data manipulations.

Example:

Phase 5   *Internal Design*

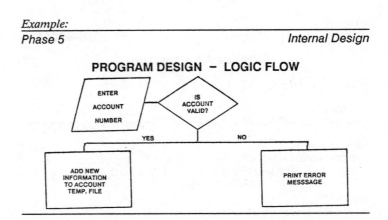

Program Design – Initialization/Sign-on Procedures. This document should define the procedures for program initialization and for system sign-on. It should show the step-by-step logic for these activities.

Example:

Phase 5	*Internal Design*

PROGRAM DESIGN - INITIALIZATION/SIGN-ON PROCEDURES

Initialization Procedures
1. Set page count and record count to zero.

2. Declare all arrays and variables and set numeric initial values to 0, alpha initial values to " ".

3. Call CMB125 setting table=ORDERS, field1 = ORD-DATE and field2 = ORDTYP. Set Delinq = 30

Sign-on Procedures
1. At the network monitor screen, type *Ship, user ID,* and *password.*

2. Enter the transaction ID SHP01.

3. Enter application password.

Program Design – Operator Messages This document should summarize all of the operator messages to be generated by the program. It should show the exact message displayed and describe the anticipated response or action to be taken by the operator.

Example:

Phase 5	*Internal Design*

PROGRAM DESIGN – OPERATOR MESSAGES

Message No. 1: "File MKBBB01 Open"
Operator Action: Wait until current job using file completes, then rerun the job.

Message No. 2: "Prepare Printer: Enter "0" to continue"
Operator Action: Check printer to ensure there is sufficient paper. Return to the console and enter a 0 and press Enter.

Message No. 3: "Job Complete"
Operator Action: Remove the reports from the printer. Burst and decollate the report and distribute copies as defined on the distribution header.

Program Design – User Messages. This document should summarize all user messages to be generated by the program. It should show the exact message to be displayed, and describe the anticipated response or action to be taken by the user when the message is displayed.

Example:

Phase 5   *Internal Design*

PROGRAM DESIGN – USER MESSAGES

Message No. 1: "XXXX password not on file"
User Action: Contact the application administrator. Request a password for the system.

Message No. 2: "XXXX Your password will expire in DD days"
User Action: At the command line, type PW to access the password update screen. Follow the instructions on the screen to change the password.

Message No. 3: "XXXX Enter the customer number, press F1 for lookup"
User Action: Enter the customer number for this report. If the customer number is unknown, the user should be able to perform a lookup function to scroll through valid customer numbers and select from the list.

Program Design – Setup Instructions. This document should provide instructions for job set-up for batch job streams. The documentation should show run frequency, time to run the job, day of the week to run the job and specific instructions for data sets, sources, and volumes to set up.

Example:

Phase 5   *Internal Design*

PROGRAM DESIGN – SETUP INSTRUCTIONS

Job Stream: N/A
Type of Run: On-line
Run Frequency: Daily
Estimated Time: 7 minutes
Job Setup:

Data File	Library	Table/Data Set Name
ORDERS	PROD.DB2	Op-Orders
CUR-INV	PROD.DB2	Act-Inv
SHIPS	PROD.DB2	Transit

Special Instructions
Prior to accepting a run instruction, the system should ensure there are no table locks active.

Task 5. Finalize System Control Procedures

The objective of this task is to define the controls for data base and file integrity and establish the procedures for error correction and system auditing. The document items resulting from this task that are deliverable to the project file are

- Input checklist
- Output checklist
- User control instructions
- Data base/file control instructions
- Access control instructions
- Error control instructions
- Audit control instructions
- File maintenance instructions

Input Checklist. This document should provide a checklist for controlling the assembly of data and requesting batch job runs for data inputs, updates, and deletions.

Example:

Phase 5   *Internal Design*

INPUT CHECKLIST

Job: Hourly labor entry

( ) Each time clerks validate the entries for employees in their sections, and clear any exceptions.
( ) Once cleared, the time clerk shall submit the entries by selecting the labor balance option from the menu.
( ) The labor data from all of the time clerks shall be cumulated in the uncosted labor file.
( ) At 2:30 each day, the operator shall submit job LAB-COST to assign cost of labor and post the cost against the general ledger.

Output Checklist. This document should provide a checklist for controlling the generation of outputs from the system.

Example:

Phase 5   *Internal Design*

OUTPUT CHECKLIST

Job: Personnel Reports
( ) Verify requestor ID is either manager or personnel.
( ) Do not allow printer destination override.
( ) Requestor must pick up report for computer center and show ID.

User Control Instructions. This document should describe the controls required by user departments in submitting data and receiving information from the system. It should include, as appropriate, procedures for batch control, correction and resubmission, special requests, and any other control procedures to be implemented.

Example:

Phase 5   *Internal Design*

USER CONTROL INSTRUCTIONS

Batch Controls. All standard batch processes are either scheduled through CA-7 or triggered on-line by user request. User-requested batch jobs are password controlled and managed by run time estimates. Long-run-time jobs are queued for overnight processing.

Special Requests. Special purpose batch runs may be requested by user managers. These requests will require scheduling with computer operations and must be validated by IS customer support representative.

Correction Control. Error correction shall be performed on-line by the cognizant user organization. Audit controls and on-line validation shall be in place to prevent unauthorized modification of data and to facilitate the entry of valid data.

Data Base/File Control Instructions. This document should describe the controls to be implemented for data base file integrity and consistency.

Example:

Phase 5   *Internal Design*

DATA BASE/FILE CONTROL INSTRUCTIONS

Integrity

1. All files are backed up daily on cartridges.
2. All programs using files work from duplicate files to ensure the integrity of the original.

Consistency

1. Initial information created by the user will be maintained in a spool file and checked by a verification program prior to inclusion in the master file.
2. The programs used to enter data into the system require verification prior to accepting the data.

Access Control Instructions. This document should summarize system access controls. It should describe all the controls to be used to restrict system and data access. Included in the description should be all controls relating to passwords, automatic log offs, physical locks, etc.

Example:

Phase 5   *Internal Design*

ACCESS CONTROL INSTRUCTIONS

1. Primary access control will be provided by the RACF system. In addition, application access will be controlled using the standard 8100 log on security and then user security codes for maintenance transactions.

2. The codes will be checked by a common security routine in the update program.

3. Attempted violations will be reported on the audit tail file.

4. Users with three unsuccessful access attempts will be logged off the system. Their terminal IDs and user IDs shall be reported to the computer security organization.

Error Control Instructions. This document should describe error correction controls. It should include error messages to be displayed when data entry edits are not passed, out-of-balance errors are detected, authorization violations are detected, and historical data are modified.

Example:

Phase 5   *Internal Design*

ERROR CONTROL INSTRUCTIONS

1. Programs must be designed to detect and report all abnormal conditions and file inconsistencies when they are encountered.

2. As with the security routine, a common error-handling routine will be called to generate a transaction to an error-handling program.

3. All data base changes which have not been saved shall be rolled back upon detection of an error.

4. The error reporting program shall determine if full transaction rollback is required based on the error code generated in the program.

Audit Control Instructions. This document should describe the audit trails to be provided by the system. It should include both manual and automated tracking and detail what is tracked at each point in the audit trail.

Example:

Phase 5	*Internal Design*

AUDIT CONTROL INSTRUCTIONS

1. An audit trail will be made of all maintenance and update transactions entered into the system.

2. When a maintenance transaction has been successfully processed, a record will be written to the audit file.

3. The record written to the audit file will contain both the "old data" and the "new data" version.

4. The audit file will be read weekly and a report listing of each transaction showing the before and after images of the updated record will be generated.

File Maintenance Instructions. This document should provide instructions for file maintenance. The documentation should address procedures and controls relative to authorization, code changes, and historical data changes.

Example:

Phase 5	*Internal Design*

FILE MAINTENANCE INSTRUCTIONS

File: Vendor Master

1. The standard access to the file shall be read only.

2. Programs which add or update records shall be bound with the application to the table with the update authorization granted to the program.

3. The application shall provide a method for determining proper authority for table updates based on password and terminal ID.

4. The program shall provide explicit record locking for the record being updated. Under no circumstance will the application prevent read against the table by other programs.

Task 6. Finalize Backup and Recovery Procedures

The objective of this task is to define the backup, file retention, and restart procedures for restoration and reapplication in a dynamic environment. The document items resulting from this task that are deliverable to the project file are

- Backup procedures
- File retention procedures
- Restart procedures

Backup Procedures. This document should identify the primary and secondary backup locations. The documentation should include the name and telephone number of the person in charge and a list that shows the hardware/software differences at the backup site that may require making modifications. The logistics of transferring data from the operating center to the backup site should also be explained.

Example:

Phase 5	*Internal Design*

BACKUP PROCEDURES

Primary Backup Location: Santa Clara

Person in Charge: John Allen
Telephone: (408) 737-2665
Hardware/Software Differences: File space is limited. Job must be run twice at backup site using different data sets.

Transfer Logistics: Data are transferred to backup location daily. No special transfer logistics needed.

Secondary Backup Location: Sunnyvale

Person in Charge: George Carlton
Telephone: (408) 737-1234

Hardware/Software Differences: System is not using COBOL II. Therefore, a special backup program must be used at this site. In addition, time availability on this system is limited. Only mission critical applications can be run at this site.

Transfer Logistics: Data are transferred to backup location daily. No further transfer logistics needed.

File Retention Procedures. This document should define the file retention periods and locations for each file used by the application. It should include the following information: file name, file type, backup medium, file retention location, and the retention period either in days or in processing generations.

Example:

Phase 5   *Internal Design*

FILE RETENTION PROCEDURES

File Name	Type	Medium	Location	Retention Period
DLINQCY	VSAM	Tape	Data Ctr	7 days
INVOICE	VSAM	Tape	Data Ctr	5 days
MTDGB	VSAM	Tape	Data Ctr	10 days
TBLB1	VSAM	Tape	Data Ctr	14 days
TBLB2	VSAM	Tape	Data Ctr	14 days
TBLB3	VSAM	Tape	Data Ctr	14 days
TBSRC	VSAM	Tape	Data Ctr	14 days

Restart Procedures. This document should define the restart specifications for the system. It should define the job name and step at which the restart occurs, the program used to run the job, the files used and the operator actions at each possible failure condition. The specific restart procedures should also be defined.

Example:

Phase 5   *Internal Design*

RESTART PROCEDURES

Job	Step	Restart Procedure
DBACK	1	Restart Job from Start.
	2	1. Delete data set DB-BAC-TMP. 2. Close all files. 3. Restart job.
	3	1. Check to ensure that file DB-BAC-TMP has been closed. 2. Delete file DB-RES. 3. Rerun DB-BACK from start point 3. 4. If job fails a second time, call the programmer specified in the on-call list. Do Not Continue With Remaining Nightly Jobs.

Task 7. Define Development Constraints

The purpose of this task is to define the constraints imposed on the system by the operating time window, hardware, software, communications environments, and staff of the development organization. The document items resulting from this task that are deliverable to the project file are

- Operating time window constraints
- Hardware constraints
- Software constraints
- Communications constraints
- Development staff constraints

Operating Time Window Constraints. This document should define the daily and week-end availability of the system. The operating window should show beginning and end times for the availability to the user.

Example:

Phase 5	*Internal Design*

OPERATING TIME WINDOW CONSTRAINTS

1. On-line system functions must be maintained as follows:
    0600 to 2300 - Monday though Friday
    0600 to 1800 - Saturday and Sunday

2. Batch processing capability must be maintained during these hours, with queued jobs running in the window from:
    1900 to 2300 - Monday through Friday
    0600 to 1800 - Saturday and Sunday

3. Holiday operations should follow the same schedule as normal weekend availability.

4. Special requests may be submitted to extend weekend operation from 0600 to 2300 hours. These requests can be negotiated based on user need and operations system maintenance requirements.

5. The allowable unscheduled down time is not to exceed 1 hour per 1000 hours of operation. Downtime is defined as the application being unavailable to the user within the normal operating time window defined above.

6. System time shall be reserved for backups, program installations, data base testing, CICS testing, etc. only during the times outside of the operating time window defined above.

Hardware Constraints. This document should describe the constraints imposed on the system by the hardware configuration.

Example:

Phase 5   *Internal Design*

HARDWARE CONSTRAINTS

1. Screen maps and transactions must be compatible to the 3270 terminals.

2. Screen and action messages must be sendable to remote 3645 printers.

3. The communications controllers in the engineering area do not permit multiple sessions. Thus, the application must handle all cross- system file transfers internally, rather than requesting users to sign on to the two systems simultaneously.

Software Constraints. This document should describe the constraints imposed on the system by the software configuration (operating system, DBMS, etc.).

Example:

Phase 5   *Internal Design*

SOFTWARE CONSTRAINTS

1. System must be maintainable with COBOL language in conjunction with 8100 software.

2. The standard DTMS data base/transaction management system will be used in the development of the system.

3. For screen/terminal interaction, the program will use DPPX/DPLS.

4. All utility programs used by the system will be copied into the production library if changes are made.

5 All utility programs must be maintained by the utility library and need not be copied if they are used intact.

6. Because of portability requirements between the primary and secondary backup locations, do not use any nonstandard COBOL functions. The program library functions can be used if explicitly INCLUDEd into the program. Document the INCLUDEs to ensure they are available at the backup locations.

Communications Constraints This document should describe the constraints imposed on the system by the communications system (dial in capabilities, network availability, etc.).

Example:

Phase 5   *Internal Design*

COMMUNICATIONS CONSTRAINTS

1. Line rate is 9600 bits per second (BPS).

2. Line control will be the synchronous data link control as established by IBM.

3. Message prioritizing shall be controlled though the operating system based on usage/response time.

4. Channels will be available only during the prime shift (0800 - 0400).

Development Staff Constraints. This document should describe the constraints imposed on the development effort by the availability of development staff resources.

Example:

Phase 5   *Internal Design*

DEVELOPMENT STAFF CONSTRAINTS

1. The data communications organization is understaffed and will not be available except on a scheduled basis of 5 hours per week.

2. The experience of the development staff with the application generator is very limited. This will be the first project using the generator for three of the programmers. This will require the two programmers who are experienced with the tool to devote as much as 50 percent of their time in assisting the remaining team members.

3. With the loss of M. Watkins, we are without a DBA for this project. While the data structures and logical models have been developed, the need to create the physical data bases is still present. This can be done by some of the more experienced programmers, but it will impact scheduling.

4. Two of the key programmers on this project are contract personnel. The permanent staff must be brought up to speed as soon as possible to reduce the risk of losing the expertise on the system.

Task 8. Define Test and Implementation Plans

The documents produced as a result of this task outline the steps necessary for program testing, file conversion, and implementation of the system. The document items resulting from this task that are deliverable to the project file are

- Test plans
- Conversion plans
- Implementation plans
- Maintenance plans
- Documentation plans

Test Plans. These documents outline the plans for the various levels of testing to be performed to ensure system functionality. The plans should indicate the task to be performed and the individual or group responsible for the performance of the task.

Example:

Phase 5	*Internal Design*

TEST PLANS

Task No.	Task Description/Responsibility
1	Finalize order tracking simulation input. *Responsibility*: TBD
2	Finalize ADCM simulation input. *Responsibility*: TBD
3	Finalize order component status simulation input. *Responsibility*: TBD
4	Finalize IHO status report simulation input. *Responsibility*: TBD
5	Finalize error message test input. *Responsibility*: TBD
6	Finalize action message test input. *Responsibility*: TBD
7	Finalize order deletion text input. *Responsibility*: TBD
8	Log-on test. *Responsibility*: TBD

Conversion Plans. These documents outline the plans for the file conversions, organizational changes, training, etc., required before the system can be implemented. The plans should indicate the task to be performed and the individual or group responsible for the performance of the task.

Example:

Phase 5	*Internal Design*

CONVERSION PLANS

Task No.	Task Description/Responsibility/Start-End Dates
1	Operations Training *Responsibility*: TBD *Start Date*: 9/09 *End Date*: 9/09
2	User Training *Responsibility*: TBD *Start Date*: 9/09 *End Date*: 9/09

Implementation Plans. This document should define the tasks for implementation. It should describe what must be done in moving files from the development environment to production and in conducting any phased-implementation activities. The plans should indicate the task to be performed and the individual or group responsible for the performance of the task.

Example:

Phase 5	*Internal Design*

IMPLEMENTATION PLANS

Task No.	Task Description/Responsibility
1	Operations Training *Responsibility*: TBD
2	User Training *Responsibility*: TBD
3	Management Review *Responsibility*: TBD

Maintenance Plans. This document should describe the plans for maintaining the system after it is placed into production. It should indicate who will be responsible for its maintenance, whether there is a warranty period from the developers, etc.

Example:

Phase 5 *Internal Design*

MAINTENANCE PLANS

Maintenance activities are divided into three categories: *emergency takeover, permanent modification,* and *temporary patches.*

Emergency takeover relates to those situations in which programmers unfamiliar with a system are required to implement changes to a program.

Permanent modifications are needed to fix a bug in the system or to meet new requirements for the system.

Temporary patches will be performed in emergency situations or when short-term requirements must be met.

Documentation Plans. This document should define the documentation plans for the remainder of the development effort. It should identify the documents to be developed, the schedule for their development, and the people responsible for their generation.

Example:

Phase 5 *Internal Design*

DOCUMENTATION PLANS

Documentation shall, at a minimum, consist of the following:

Initial Investigation Phase Document – Completed
Feasibility Study Phase Document – Completed
Requirements Definition Phase Document – Completed
External Design Phase Document – Completed
Internal Design Phase Document
Test Plans
Test Reports
Program Package Documentation
Conversion Specifications
User Guides
Operations Guides

Task 9. Prepare Internal Design Phase End-Document.

The final internal design task performed by the software designer is the preparation of the internal design phase end-document. All of the document items that were created during the performance of the preceding tasks (i.e., tasks 1 to 8) are stored in either an on-line or off-line repository. In task 9, select documents are retrieved from the repository, reorganized, and synthesized for inclusion in the internal design phase end-document. The process is illustrated in Figure 4-6.

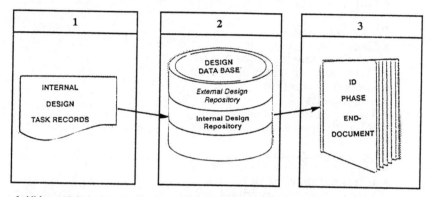

1. All internal design documents, including worksheets, questionnaires, and task records
2. The internal design documents are stored in an on-line or off-line repository.
3. Selected document items are retrieved from the repository for inclusion in the internal design phase end-document.

Figure 4-6. Internal Design Phase End-Document Evolution

The document items delivered to the repository during the internal design phase establish the design baseline for configuration management as shown in Figure 4-7.

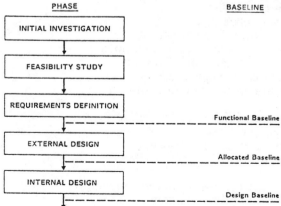

Figure 4-7. Design Baseline Document

In summary these deliverables include all of the following document items that were discussed in this subsection.

I/O Specifications
- Input document formats
- Input screen formats
- Output document formats
- Output screen formats

Data Base Specifications
- Data base applications
- Labeling/tagging conventions
- Data base organization summary
- Special instructions
- File layouts
- Table layouts
- Record layouts

Program Specifications
- Support software requirements
- Interface specifications
- Program design summary
- Program design logic flow
- Program design initialization/sign-on procedures
- Program design operator messages
- Program design user messages
- Program design setup instructions
- Table layouts
- Record layouts

Control Procedures
- Input checklist
- Output checklist
- User control specifications
- Data base control specifications
- Access control specifications
- Error control specifications
- Audit control specifications

Backup and Recovery Procedures
- Backup procedures
- File retention procedures
- Restart procedures

Development Constraint Documentation
- Operating time window constraints
- Hardware constraints
- Software constraints

- Communications constraints
- Development staff constraints

Testing and Implementation Documentation
- Test plans
- Conversion plans
- Implementation plans
- Maintenance plans
- Documentation plans

When all of the internal design documents noted above have been delivered to the project file, they are assigned a catalog identification for configuration management purposes. As illustrated in Figure 4-7, these documents establish the design baseline for configuration management. From the point when the design baseline is established, no changes should be made to the system design without formal change control processing. The content arrangement of the internal design document is shown in Figure 4-8.

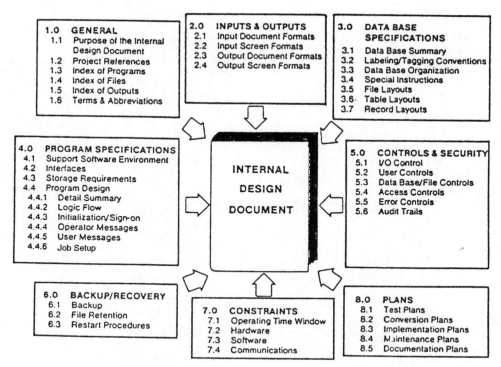

Figure 4-8. Content Arrangement of the Internal Design Document

Chapter 5

Software Programming and Test Documentation

Whereas the analysis and design phases were peculiarly the province of the analysts and design personnel, the responsibility for developing the programs and their associated documentation is shared with the programmers. A new battery of skills, those of coding, testing, and debugging, come into play. The analysis and design development groups, however, may continue their leadership roles.

The extent of the documentation to be produced is determined by the scope of the system, the language in which it is to be written, whether the developers will also provide maintenance, whether the software is for internal use or for market, and similar issues. Program documentation consists of both external and internal documentation. That is, it consists of manuals (either hard copy or on-line) and comments embedded in the code. The decision as to the scope of documentation to be produced must be made by that level of management with which the success of the project rests.

The program and test documentation provides the information necessary for program design, coding, debugging, delivery, and maintenance. The documentation resulting from these activities may include

- Program description documents
- Program package documents
- Test plans
- Test specifications
- Test procedures
- Test reports

The programming and testing phases of systems development are cyclic rather than strictly sequential. The linear task to task flow is replaced by a process of interpreting a specification for a particular module, translating the specification into computer-readable code, testing the code, debugging, and retesting. When a related module has been through this process, the two modules are tested together, debugged, and retested.

Because of the linear nature of a published work, the document guidelines presented in this chapter are presented as distinct sections. Keep in mind, however, that the program and test documentation is produced as part of the cycle just described.

5.1 PROGRAM DEVELOPMENT

Program development breaks down into eight major tasks, starting with the physical creation of the data bases and files designed in the previous phase. The task-documentation orientation of the programming phase of systems development is shown in Table 5-1.

Table 5-1. Programming Task Document Item Correlation

No.	Task/Task Step	Document Item
1.	Create data base files.	Record Layouts Data Dictionary Indexes
2	Prepare contol program.	Program Logic Diagrams Array Definitions Variable Definitions Constants Flags Data Base References Library Programs Function Calls
3.	Code on-line modules.	Program Logic Diagra,s Transaction Definitions Arrays Variables Constants Flags Data Base References Library Programs Function Calls Interfaces
4.	Code batch procedures.	Program Logic Diagrams Arrays Variables Constants Flags Data Base References Library Programs Function Calls Interfaces
5.	Code reports.	Program Logic Diagrams Output Formats
6.	Code screens.	Program Logic Diagrams Screen Formats Transaction Definitions
7.	Code interfaces.	Program Logic Diagrams Arrays Variables Constants Flags
8.	Prepare and publish program development documentation.	Program Performance Specifications Program Design Specifications Program Description Program Package

The objective of each programming task and the nature of the document items resulting from these tasks are further described and illustrated below and on the following pages.

Task 1. Create Data Base/Files

The first task in the programming process is to create the physical data bases. Special programming emphasis is often required to create the physical structure of the data base. The performance of this task requires that the programmer, in consultation with the data base analyst, implement the physical design of the database that was specified during the internal design phase. The deliverables of this task are

- Physical data base
- Record layouts
- Updated data dictionary
- Data base indexes

The physical data base resides in computer storage/memory, the remaining deliverables of this task are further described and illustrated in the following paragraphs.

Record Layouts. A record layout should be prepared for each record to be handled by the DBMS. The documentation should include the record name, length, data source, record purpose, and comments. The record should also define the position for each field in the order it appears and denote the data type codes and applicable key identifiers.

Example:

Phase 6   *Program Development*

RECORD LAYOUT

Data Base/File Name: Personnel
Segment Name: Accounts Payable
Parent Name: Accounting
Source Library: PROD.HR.LIB
Length: 230
Key Size: 48
Occurrences: 200

D.E. No.	D.E. Name	Positions From	To
23	Title	12	37
27	Location	38	45
28	Mail Stop	54	59

Data Dictionary. The data dictionary document should provide a detailed description of each data element in the data base. It should include the data element name, data element length, the number used to identify the data element, and the full name of the element. It should denote the input and output data types, indicate the number of words the field occupies in the record, and provide all other pertinent information about the data element.

Example:

Phase 6				*Program Development*

DATA DICTIONARY

System Name: Maintenance Management
System Prefix: MNT

D.E. No.	Element Name	Source	Length	Type
41	mntname	pwd file	25	Alpha
49	cstfacil	cust list	30	Alpha
63	cstcont	cust list	25	Alpha
64	cstphon	cust list	10	Num.
66	mntlgnmr	sys gen	05	Num.
67	mnttype	entry	15	Alpha
68	mntprior	entry	3	Alpha
69	mntstatus	entry	4	Alpha

Data Base Indexes. This document should identify each index included in the subprogram data base. The documentation should indicate the title of the index with the mnemonic label in parentheses and briefly state the use of each index.

Example:

Phase 6	*Program Development*

DATA BASE INDEXES

Data Base: Customer

Primary Index: Customer Number

Secondary Indexes:

Zip Code	Used in purchasing module sales volume by location.
Product Code + Zip Code	Used in sales projection for products by location. Also in credit projections to search customer accounts and product preferences.

Task 2. Prepare Control Program

The objective of this task is to write the main program which controls the flow of the system. This program generally calls other programs that perform the various system functions. The documentation generated during this task includes source listing comments as well as the following deliverable items

- Control program source code
- Program logic diagram
- Array definitions
- Variable definitions
- Constants used
- Flags used
- Data bases referenced
- Library programs used
- Special function calls used

The program code resides in the computer program library. Other documentation that serves maintenance and operations purposes is deliverable to the project file. These documents are further described and illustrated in the following paragraphs.

Program Logic Diagram. This document should provide a graphic representation of the program process flow. It should show procedural relationships, control transfers, loops, decision points, and the program structure.

Example:

Phase 6   *Program Development*

PROGRAM LOGIC DIAGRAM

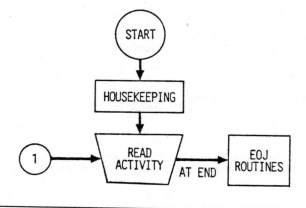

Array Definitions. This document should identify the arrays used by each subprogram. The documentation for each array should include the array name and a statement of the use and attributes of the array. It should indicate the number of words for each array. The meaning and purpose of each subfield should also be described.

Example:

Phase 6	Program Development

ARRAY DEFINITIONS

Array Name: NAME
Purpose and Attributes: This array provides the names of the individuals being tested.
Size: 5500
Indexes: First name and last name
Scaling Factors:

Bits 1 - 20	Fist Name
Bits 21-40	Last Name
Bits 41-49	Social Security
Bits 60-100	Address

Variable Definitions. This document should describe each variable used in the subprogram. The documentation for each variable should include the variable name and a statement of the use and attributes of the variable. It should indicate the number of bits and sign (if numeric) or number of characters (if alphanumeric) and should also define scaling factors for each variable.

Example:

Phase 6	Program Development

VARIABLE DEFINITIONS

Variable Name: FNAME
Purpose and Attributes: To identify first name
Size: 20 characters
Type: Alpha

Variable Name: LNAME
Purpose and Attributes: To identify last name.
Size: 25 bits
Type: Alpha

Variable Name: SSN
Purpose and Attributes: To identify social security number of testee
Size: 9
Type: Numeric string

Constants. This document should describe each constant used in the subprogram. The documentation for each variable should include the title of the constant with the mnemonic label in parentheses. It should briefly state the use and attributes of the constant.

Example:

Phase 6   *Program Development*

CONSTANTS

Constant Name: MinScore
Purpose and Attributes: 2-digit percentage value indicating the minimum passing score of the test
Size: 2 digits
Scaling Factors: X100 for raw score
Bit Layout: NM, where N and M = 0 -9

Constant Name: PerScore
Purpose and Attributes: Equals maximum number of points on test.
Size: 3 digits
Scaling Factors: Not applicable
Bit Layout: LMN, where L = 1 or 2, M and N = 0 -9

Flags. This document should define each flag included in the subprogram data base. The documentation should indicate the title of the flag (with the mnemonic label in parentheses) and briefly state the use and status of each flag. It should also specify the initial condition of the flag.

Example:

Phase 6   *Program Development*

FLAGS

Flag Name: FlPerScr
Purpose and Attributes: To indicate perfect test score
Initial Condition: False
Bit Layout: L = Logical

Flag Name: FlFail
Purpose and Attributes: To indicate failing test score
Initial Condition: False
Bit Layout: L = Logical

Flag Name: FlReTst
Purpose and Attributes: To indicate second attempt at test
Initial Condition: False
Bit Layout: L = Logical

Data Base References. This document should provide a complete list of all references to local and common data base items. The listing should be cross-referenced to the data base specifications that were delivered to the internal design project file and included in the internal design phase document.

Example:

Phase 6			Program Development

DATA BASE REFERENCES

Data Base Items	Program Ref.	Functional Ref.	Design Ref.
Name	CB-10	ETS ED	ETS ID
Address	CB-10	ETS-ED	ETS ID
Telephone	CB-10	ETS-ED	ETS ID
Age	CB-10	ETS-ED	ETS ID
Sex	CB-10	ETS-ED	ETS ID
Score	DB-10	ETS-ED	ETS ID
Test ID	CB-10	ETS-ED	ETS ID

Library Programs. This document should list, in alphabetical order, the library routines used by each subprogram. The documentation should indicate the name of the routine (with the mnemonic label in parentheses) and describe where the routine is used. It should also provide a list of all the documents which define the subroutine (e.g., program performance specification, etc.).

Example:

Phase 6			Program Development

LIBRARY PROGRAMS

Subroutine Name	Where Used	Where Located	Doc. Ref.
Calndr	EICB-02	UTIL. LIB.	Stds Ut-02
	EICB-05	UTIL. LIB.	Stds Ut-02
	EITST-02	UTIL. LIB.	Stds Ut-02
	EITST-06	UTIL. LIB.	Stds Ut-02
RSort	EICB-02	UTIL. LIB	Stds Ut-05
	EICB-03	UTIL. LIB	Stds Ut-05
	IETSR-02	UTIL. LIB	Stds Ut-05
	IETSR-04	UTIL. LIB	Stds Ut-05
Stats	EICB-04	UTIL. LIB	Stds Ut-23
	EITST-01	UTIL. LIB	Stds Ut-23
	EITSR-01	UTIL. LIB	Stds Ut-23

Task 3. Code On-Line Modules

Once the central calling program is completed, the functional program modules that were specified during the internal design phase can be written. Each module should be written and documented according to prescribed standards. The documentation generated during this task includes

- On-line program code
- Program logic iagram
- Transaction definitions
- Array definitions
- Variable definitions
- Constants used
- Flags used
- Data bases referenced
- Library programs used
- Special function calls used

    The source listing includes comments which may be useful in debugging operations. The other document items generated during this task are of the same format as those of the preceding task. There will, of course, be a set of these document items for each on-line program written.

Task 4. Code Batch Procedures

The objective of this task is to write the batch program modules that were specified during the internal design phase. Each module should be written and documented according to prescribed standards. The documentation generated during this task includes

- Batch program code
- Program logic diagram
- Array definitions
- Variable definitions
- Constants used
- Flags used
- Data bases referenced
- Library programs used
- Special function calls used

    The source listing includes comments which may be useful in debugging operations. The other document items generated during this task are of the same format as those documents produced in task 2. There will, of course, be a set of these document items for each batch program written.

Task 5. Code Reports

The objective of this task is to code the report programs that were specified during the internal design phase. Each report should be written and documented according to prescribed standards. The documentation generated during this task includes

- Report program code
- Program logic diagram
- Output format
- Array definitions
- Variable definitions
- Constants used
- Flags used
- Data bases referenced
- Library programs used
- Special function calls used

The source listing includes comments which may be useful in debugging operations. The output format document item is described and illustrated in the following paragraph. The other document items generated during this task are of the same format as those documents produced in task 2. There will, of course, be a set of these document items for each report program written.

Output Format. This document should graphically illustrate and describe each output message, card format, tape format, etc. to be processed by the subprogram. The documentation should provide a facsimile of each input format and define the data elements of the format. If the description concerns a common system subroutine, the documentation should explain the input registers and provide any pertinent scaling and bit-position information.

Example:

Phase 6	Program Development

OUTPUT FORMAT

OUTPUT NAME Employee Test Results	OUTPUT TYPE Report

Employee Test Result **Test Date 11/21/91**		
Employee Name	ID No.	Score
Adams, Jonh	21.221	84
Ashton, Doug	21-910	89
Ager, Stan	84-165	92
Bush, Harry	32-009	73

Task 6. Code Screens

The objective of this task is to code the screen programs that were specified during the internal design phase. Each screen should be written and documented according to prescribed standards. The documentation generated during this task includes

- Screen program code
- Program logic diagram
- Screen format
- Array definitions
- Variable definitions
- Constants used
- Flags used
- Data bases referenced
- Library programs used
- Special function calls used

The source listing includes comments which may be useful in debugging operations. The screen format document item is described and illustrated in the following paragraph. The other document items generated during this task are of the same format as the documents produced in task 2. There will, of course, be a set of these document items for each report program written.

Screen Format. This document should describe each output screen format created by the system. It should include a facsimile of a screen produced by the system and explain all the data items referenced.

Example:

Phase 6   *Program Development*

SCREEN FORMAT

MASTER FILE STATISTICS

	Date of Last Calib.	Calibration Due Date	Purchase Date
Last 3 Months	XXXXXX	XXXXXX	XXXXXX
Last Month	XXXXXX	XXXXXX	XXXXXX
This Month	XXXXXX	XXXXXX	XXXXXX
Next 3 Months	XXXXXX	XXXXXX	XXXXXX

(1)

Task 7. Code Interfaces

The objective of this task is to code the interfaces to other modules and other systems as specified during the internal design phase. Each interface should be written and documented according to prescribed standards. The documentation generated during this task includes

- Interface program code
- Program logic diagram
- Array definitions
- Variable definitions
- Constants used
- Flags used

The source listing includes comments which may be useful in debugging operations. The other document items generated during this task are of the same format as those documents produced in task 2. There will, of course, be a set of these document items for each report program written.

Task 8. Prepare and Publish Program Development Documentation

The function of this task is to reorganize and synthesize the documents produced during the programming activity and present them in a coherent form useful for anyone responsible for the maintenance of the system. Program development documentation may be organized to prepare the following manuals:

Program Performance Specifications. This manual should describe the operational and functional requirements necessary to design, test, and maintain the required programs. It includes all the documentation needed to control the program development and testing processes. The documentation enables management to assess the satisfactory completion of the computer programs.

Program Design Specifications. This manual should be comprised of document items that specify the programming approach for coding the computer programs. These items identify the allocation of functions and the tasks to be performed by the individual computer subprograms or modules. They also specify the guidelines to be observed by the system programmer when producing the computer program.

Program Description. This manual should provide technical descriptions of all computer subprogram functions, structures, operation environments, and operating constraints. It should include source and object code listings and diagrammatic and narrative flow descriptions. The documentation is used by operational and maintenance personnel in diagnosing troubles, designing and implementing modifications to the system, and introducing or adding new subprogram functions to the completed program.

Program Package. This manual should include a source form listing, an error-free source/object listing, a complete cross-reference listing, and any data which are necessary for programs to run properly.

Figure 5-1 depicts the evolution of program development document in the software development process.

SOURCE	DOCUMENTATION
Requirements Definition Phase	**PROGRAM PERFORMANCE SPECIFICATION** ▪ General Information ▪ System Description Documentation ▪ Program Function Documentation ▪ Test Requirements Documentation ▪ Test Verification Documentation
Internal Design Phase	**PROGRAM DESIGN SPECIFICATION** ▪ General Information ▪ System Requirements Documentation ▪ Quality Assurance Documentation
Programming Phase	**PROGRAM DESCRIPTION DOCUMENT** ▪ General Information ▪ Program Description Documentation **PROGRAM PACKAGE DOCUMENT** ▪ General Information ▪ Programs ▪ Program Listings ▪ Data Base Design ▪ Subprogram Flowcharts

Figure 5-1. Evolution of Program Development Documentation

5.2 TEST DOCUMENTATION

The testing phase of the systems development process involves defining the criteria by which the system will be tested and measuring the criteria against the acceptable failure rate. During this phase, documents are produced that outline a general plan of action for each level of testing, define test requirements and overall objectives to be met, provide specifications for the required test cases, and report the results of the tests performed. The testing phase breaks down into seven major steps. The task-document item correlation of the testing phase is shown in Table 5-2.

Table 5-2. Testing Phase Task-Document Item Correlation

No.	Task/Task Step	Document Item
1	**Prepare Test Plan**	
1.1	Define tasks and responsibilities	Task Responsibility Checklist
1.2	Define Test Monitoring Methods	Monitoring Methods
1.3	Determine Test Software Requirements	Test Software Requirements
1.4	Define Test Schedules	Test Schedules
1.5	Define Test Environment Requirements	Test Environment Requirements
2	**Prepare Test Case Specifications**	
2.1	Prepare Unit Test Specifications	Unit Test Specifications
2.2	Prepare Module Integration Test Specification	Module Integration Test Specification
2.3	Prepare Verification Test Specifications	Verification Test Specifications
2.4	Prepare Acceptance Test Specification	Acceptance Test Specification
3	**Define Acceptance Criteria**	
3.1	Define Unit Test Acceptance Criteria	Unit Test Acceptance Criteria
3.2	Define Module Integration Test Criteria	Module Integration Test Acceptance Criteria
3.3	Define Acceptance Test Criteria	Acceptance Test Criteria
4	**Define Test Procedures**	
4.1	Define Unit Test Procedures	Unit Test Procedures
4.2	Define Module Integration Test Procedure	Module Integration Test Procedures
4.3	Define Verification Test Procedures	Verification Test Procedures
4.4	Define Acceptance Test Procedures	Acceptance Test Procedures
5	**Conduct the Tests**	Test Results
		Discrepancy Reports
		Recommendations
6	**Conduct Acceptance Review**	Functional Audit Report
		Physical Audit Report
7	**Prepare Phase End-Document**	Test Document

The objective of each level of testing and the nature of the document items resulting from the tasks performed are further described and illustrated in this section.

Task 1. Prepare Test Plan

The objective of this task is to define what testing will be performed. The test plan should define the tasks to be performed for each level of testing and indicate the individuals and organizations responsible for performing the tests. The document items resulting from this task are

- Task responsibility checklist
- Monitoring methods
- Test software requirements
- Test schedules
- Test environment requirements

Task Responsibility Checklist. This document should define the tasks to be performed for each level of testing. The documentation should identify the organization or individual responsible for performing each test step.

Example:

Phase 7		Testing

TASK RESPONSIBILITY CHECKLIST

Task No.	Task Description	Responsibility
10	Prepare test case specifications	C. Lamar
20	Define acceptance criteria	J. Petticord
30	Define test procedures	R. Dean
40	Conduct the tests	
41	Conduct unit tests	R. Dean
42	Conduct module integration tests	R. Dean
43	Conduct verification tests	C. Lamar
44	Conduct acceptance tests	

Monitoring Methods. This document should explain the methods to be used in monitoring each level of testing. The documentation should define the method to be employed in monitoring and controlling the execution of tests and in correcting unit test discrepancies. It should also define the methods to be used in validating the test completion.

Example:

Phase 7   *Testing*

MONITORING METHODS FOR UNIT TESTS

Execution Monitoring
Individual modules shall be tested by the programmer who developed the module. The programmer is responsible for ensuring that all planned tests are properly executed. The project leader shall verify compliance.

Correction
Errors detected during unit testing shall be corrected by the programmer and the module shall be completely retested. The project leader shall verify compliance.

Reporting
Test results shall be recorded and reported using the standard test report format.

Validation
Programs passing unit test shall be reviewed by QA along with the test documentation.

Test Software Requirements. This document should define the software test requirements for each level of testing. The documentation should identify the data generators required to conduct the tests, the test drivers/environmental simulators to be used, and the analysis programs required for analyzing test results.

Example:

Phase 7   *Testing*

TEST SOFTWARE REQUIREMENTS

Data Generator
All test data shall be generated using the ADF rules generation with literals added by the programmer.

Test Drivers/Environmental Simulators
Many ADF transactions can be run by the same ADF transaction driver/IMS transaction. The IMS transaction defines the PSB so only those transactions with the same PSB can use the same IMS transaction. Therefore, ADF transactions must be clustered.

Analysis Programs
Analysis programs shall be developed for all special algorithms generating internally used data. Outputs from the system shall be manually checked.

Test Schedules. This document should provide a description of the sequence of the test activities at each level of testing. The documentation should provide a brief description of each test step, identify the location where the tests will take place, and indicate the scheduled start and complete dates of each test step.

Example:

Phase 7   *Testing*

TEST SCHEDULE

Test Step	Description	Test Location	Start	Complete
1	Verify program unit logic	Desk	12/1	12/5
2	Verify computational adequacy	Desk	12/1	12/5
3	Verify data-handling capability	Desk	12/4	12/8
4	Verify interfaces	Desk	12/8	12/12
5	Test every path of each logical branch	Desk	12/8	12/14

Test Environment Requirements. This document should define the test environment requirements for conducting each level of testing. The documentation should identify both hardware and software requirements for conducting the tests.

Example:

Phase 7   *Testing*

TEST ENVIRONMENT REQUIREMENTS

Hardware Requirements

No special hardware is required for unit testing. Testing will be conducted using standard 3270 type IBM terminals.

Software Requirements

The data generator and test drivers previously specified must be available in the test environment. Additionally, the stub programs required for each of the menu tests must be available prior to approval of these modules

Task 2. Prepare Test Case Specifications

The objective of this task is to prepare specifications for the test cases required at each level of testing. The document items resulting from this task are

- Unit test case specifications
- Module test case specifications
- Verification test case specifications

Unit Test Case Specifications. A specification document should be prepared for each unit test case specified in the test plan. The documentation should identify the test case by name, indicate the test case number, and describe the purpose of the test. It should indicate the number of iterations and the data combinations for each iteration.

Example:

Phase 7	Testing

UNIT TEST CASE SPECIFICATIONS
Case 1: DMPB10

Requirement to Be Verified	Functional Baseline Ref.	Allocated Baseline Ref.
Input Validation Logic ■ Invalid Data ■ Valid Data ■ Invalid range (high and low)	RD-03	ED-18
Selection Logic ■ AND logic ■ NOT logic ■ OR logic	RD-04	ED-19
Computational Accuracy ■ Logic result ■ Input/output validation	RD-7,9	ED-12,14
Data Load Handling ■ All valid data stream ■ Mixed valid and invalid data	RD-16	ED-12,13,18
Branches ■ Valid data type test ■ Logic branches	RD-16	ED-12

Test Configuration
All integration tests shall be conducted from the development library with all data files moved from the PANTSTLIB and generated as defined in the test data requirements specification.

Test Software Required
The data generator and test driver software specified previously will be required in the test environment.

Module Integration Test Case Specifications. A specification document should be prepared for each module integration test case specified in the test plan. The documentation should identify the test case by name, indicate the test case number, and describe the purpose of the test. It should indicate the number of iterations and the data combinations for each iteration and identify the test components, data types, operating considerations, and any prerequisite test cases.

Note

The format and style of all written test specifications are essentially the same as illustrated for the unit test specifications.

Verification Test Case Specifications. A specification document should be prepared for each verification test case specified in the test plan. The documentation should identify the test case by name, indicate the test case number, and describe the purpose of the test. It should indicate the number of iterations and the data combinations for each iteration and identify the test components, file volumes, data types, operating considerations, and any prerequisite test cases.

Acceptance Test Case Specifications. A specification document should be prepared for each acceptance test case specified in the test plan. The documentation should identify the test case by name, indicate the test case number, and describe the purpose of the test. It should indicate the number of iterations and the data combinations for each iteration and identify the test components, file volumes, data types, operating considerations, and any prerequisite test cases.

Task 3. Define Acceptance Criteria

The objective of this task is to define the criteria by which the test results will be measured to determine acceptability. Criteria should be defined for each level of testing: *unit testing* to verify each unit performs according to design, *module integration testing* to verify that the modules properly interface with one another, *verification testing* to verify that the system correlates with the documentation, and *acceptance testing* to verify that the system performs in the operating environment. The document items resulting from this task are

- Unit test acceptance criteria
- Module integration test criteria
- Verification test criteria
- Acceptance test criteria

Unit Test Acceptance Criteria. This document should define the criteria by which the results of unit tests will be measured. The documentation should include criteria for verifying program unit logic, computational adequacy, data-handling capability, interfaces, and acceptance of branch executions.

Example:

Phase 7	Testing

UNIT TEST ACCEPTANCE CRITERIA

Each input, process, and output unit of the computer program must be tested to verify that it performs as specified in the internal design. Each unit test must be performed separately from the tests of other units and should be performed in two stages:

Stage 1. The unit must be compiled and errors corrected as indicated by the compiler.

Stage 2. Each program branch must be tested to verify that it can be properly executed. The tests must be repeated until all known errors are eliminated and the program matches the design.

Module Integration Test Acceptance Criteria. This document should define the criteria by which the results of module integration test will be measured. The documentation should establish criteria for the acceptable integration of program units into modules and into the software system.

Example:

Phase 7	Testing

MODULE INTEGRATION TEST ACCEPTANCE CRITERIA

Module integration tests are conducted to ensure compatibility between computer programs and to establish compatibility with the program interfaces. The module integration tests must adhere to the following criteria:

1. Testing must be performed to ensure that the program units properly interface with each other to form the module.

2. Tests should be conducted using dynamic and static input data.

3. Mathematics and utility routines, including testing and debugging aids, must be available.

4. The QA group must review the module integration testing procedures prior to their use by the development organization.

5. The tests must be conducted by an independent test group.

Verification Test Criteria. This document should define the criteria by which the results of verification tests should be measured to verify software performance and interface requirements.

Example:

Phase 7   *Testing*

VERIFICATION TEST ACCEPTANCE CRITERIA

To verify that the software meets the functional requirements, a thorough examination of the software hierarchy and functional flow diagrams must be conducted. To accomplish this objective, a combination of verification methods should be used:

- The comparison method should be used to compare the performance of the new system against the requirements specified for the system.

- An analysis should be conducted to validate the program's equations and logic of the program outputs.

- Demonstration methods should be used to verify that the system on-line functionality meets specifications.

Acceptance Test Criteria. This document should define the criteria by which the results of acceptance tests can be measured to determine if the software performs in the operational environment as it did in the test environment.

Example:

Phase 7   *Testing*

ACCEPTANCE TEST CRITERIA

The same tests as used in the verification testing are used in acceptance testing. These tests shall be conducted jointly by the quality assurance and user organizations. The following criteria shall be adhered to in acceptance testing:

- All items on the test plan shall be successfully completed, including file conversion and data loading tasks.

- Test inputs shall demonstrate the system performance to the limit of its design capability.

- Performance shall be measured against a standard program to eliminate test biases caused by machine load.

- The test hardware configuration must be sufficiently installed to adequately evaluate performance in the operating environment.

Task 4. Define Test Procedures

The objective of this task is to provide detailed instructions for test execution and evaluation of test results at each level of testing. The documentation should specify test materials, input data, test routines, and the required hardware configuration; describe the step-by-step sequence to be followed in performing tests; explain when and how test data should be input; and provide for the quantitative evaluation of test results. The document items resulting from this task are

- Unit test procedures
- Module integration test procedures
- Verification test procedures
- Acceptance test procedures

Unit Test Procedures. This document should set forth the procedures for verifying that the software unit meets the defined requirements. The documentation should briefly describe the procedures for test initialization, list the steps to be followed, and explain the procedures for terminating a test.

Example:

Phase 7	*Testing*

UNIT TEST PROCEDURES

Test: UT0100   *Program:* DPMB030

Test Setup
1. Move test file DMTST from PANLIB to the development library
2. Clear output file DPMF-105.

Test Initialization
1. Load the test driver program ATD-100.
2. Select Sequential Numeric from the Test Data Type menu.
3. Type 00000 as the initial value.
4. Specify DMBTF as the output file.

Test Steps
1. Execute the test with the parameters noted above.
2. Upon completion of the number sequence, print out the contents of the output file.

Test Termination
Visually inspect the file dump to ensure that all data types were properly read by the program. Identify data types that should have resulted in errors and ensure that the errors were trapped.

Note

The format and style of all written test procedures are essentially the same as illustrated for the preparation of unit test procedures.

Module Integration Test Procedures. This document should set forth the procedures for verifying that the units properly interface with the system modules. The documentation describes the procedures for test initialization, lists the steps to be followed, and explains the procedures for terminating a test.

Verification Test Procedures. This document should set forth the procedures for verifying that the units and modules function properly in the total software and hardware environment to provide the functionality specified in the requirements definition phase. It should describe the procedures for test initialization, list the steps to be followed, and explain the procedures for terminating a test.

Acceptance Test Procedure. The acceptance test procedure should be identical to the verification test procedure. The difference between the two tests is that verification testing is performed by the IS organization, whereas the acceptance testing is performed by the user organization.

The test procedures should be analyzed by the QA organization to determine if they are sufficient to adequately verify the acceptability of the program units, modules, etc. The QA analysis should answer the following questions:

- Are the procedures adequate to recover from abnormal terminations?

- Do the procedures identify the correct testing organization for each level of testing to be performed?

- Do the procedures enable the testers to verify compliance with the requirements set forth in the *functional* baseline documentation?

- Do the procedures enable the testers to verify compliance with the requirements set forth in the *design* baseline documentation?

- Do the procedures enable the testers to verify compliance with the requirements set forth in the *product* baseline documentation?

- Should test be run through all possible paths through the system or only on representative paths?

- Do the procedures correlate with the test acceptance criteria defined for each level of testing and are they consistent with the test objectives?

Task 5. Conduct the Tests

The objective of this task is to conduct various tests to ensure that the requirements specifications are met. This includes testing the modules and programs to ensure their correct integration into subsystem, testing for file recovery and reconstruction, verifying user procedures required to effectively implement the system, and performing acceptance tests to ensure that all criteria are met. The document items resulting from this task are

- Test results
- Discrepancy reports
- Recommendations

Test Results. A test report should be prepared for each test specified in the test plan. The documentation should identify the test case by name and number, analyze the test performance, and summarize suggested refinements to improve the performance of the system.

Example:

Phase 7	*Testing*

System Title:
LAPS
Test Series No: AT
Test Case Name: Customer Inquiry Function Verification
Unit ID: LACU
Description of Problem: Switching to table view did not retain customer number.
Corrective Action Taken: Changed code to retain index

Type of Test:
Demonstration
*Test Case No.:*120

Program ID: LACU-010,020, 030

Discrepancy Reports. A discrepancy report should be prepared whenever a discrepancy occurs between the design documents and a program. The report should contain information on the criticality and recommended priority for change, as well as any solution or corrective actions that may have been taken.

Example:

Phase 7	*Testing*

Report No: DR-37	*Criticality:* Moderate
Discrepancy: Checks written against accounts payable do not post against the general ledger until after all checks have been printed.	
Programs Affected: DMPB 22	*Files Affected:* General Ledger File

Recommendations. This document should provide recommendations as to the improvements that can be realized in design and operation, based on the test results. It should summarize the recommendations incorporated in the summaries of each test level, indicating those recommendations already implemented.

Example:

Phase 7	*Testing*

Upon review of the results of all test sequences, it is recommended that the system be moved to the production library and control passed to the applications support organization. The suggestions pertaining to the addition of the multiple record entry capability, made during the early test phases, has not been supported by the actual use of the system. It is therefore recommended that the change be reserved until other modifications are required on the system.

Task 6. Conduct Acceptance Review

The objective of this task is to conduct a formal audit of the test results to determine if the software is ready to be released to production. Two types of audit should be conducted: functional audit and physical audit. The documents resulting from this tasks are

- Functional audit report
- Physical audit report

Functional Audit Report. A functional audit report should be prepared that verifies compliance with the software requirements and notes discrepancies in the test results. The documentation should verify conformity with test plans and the validity of interface simulations, analysis methods, and configuration documentation.

Example:

Phase 7	*Testing*

Validation of Test Plan Compliance
The test data and test results have been reviewed by the audit team and have been found to comply with the test plan.

Validation of Interfaces
The hardware and software simulation used to conduct the tests were 90 percent effective, but the simulation did not allow for high volumes of invalid data types, thus the stress testing was inconclusive.

Validation of Analysis
Since analysis was used as a substitute for testing, a more detailed explanation of the methods used is required before a determination of their validity is made.

Physical Audit Report. This document should report on the accuracy and completeness of the function design and product baseline documentation. Any discrepancies between the documentation and the system should be reported.

Example:
Phase 7	*Testing*

Functional Baseline Documentation
The reporting function added during the external design is not reflected in the requirements specification.

Design Baseline Documentation
Changes in data base characteristics and storage allocation requirements are not adequately reflected.

Product Baseline Documentation
Source code listing included with the program package is 1 revision behind the code.

Version Description Document
The version description does not reflect the changes made in DMPS06 and DMPB07. The correct release level is 2.3, but the document shows 2.1.

Corrective Active Requirements. This document should itemize the corrective actions that must be taken before the system can be validated for production use.

Example:
Phase 7	*Testing*

Requirements Definition
1. Update document to include the biweekly reporting function specified in the internal design.
2. Incorporate the requirements change specification dated 4/24 to increase the acceptable response time from milliseconds to 1 second.

External Design
1. Update document to include the biweekly reporting function specified in the internal design.
2. Change allocation of data base inquiry function from separate module to subfunction within each module.

Internal Design

1. Incorporate change specification for overhead rate calculation.
2. Update report specifications to show changes incorporated as a result of user acceptance testing.
3. Data base specification is missing.

Task 7. Prepare Test Phase End-Document

The objective of this task is to provide a published repository for the presentation of the accumulated test documentation, including test plans, test specifications, test procedures, and test reports for all levels of testing. Summary guidelines for developing the content for various types of test documents are provided in Chapter 7.

The program and test document items, combined with the media containing the source and object code, establish the product baseline for configuration management as shown in Figure 5-2.

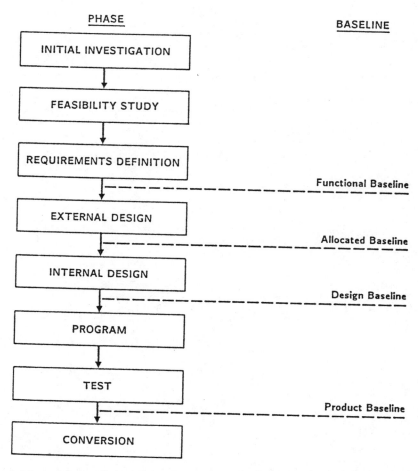

PHASE   BASELINE

- INITIAL INVESTIGATION
- FEASIBILITY STUDY
- REQUIREMENTS DEFINITION — Functional Baseline
- EXTERNAL DESIGN — Allocated Baseline
- INTERNAL DESIGN — Design Baseline
- PROGRAM
- TEST — Product Baseline
- CONVERSION

Figure 5-2. Product Baseline for Configuration Management

Chapter 6
Implementation Documentation

The preparation of implementation documentation is often viewed as the total sum of the software documentation process. In a well-defined software development environment, however, the preparation of implementation documents is essentially an iterative process that synthesizes and reorganizes document items that were produced during the analysis and design phases for presentation to a user audience. In this chapter, we will examine three types of implementation documents: conversion documents, user guides, and operations guides.

Conversion documents define those tasks that are required to place the system into an operable mode. They amplify the conversion plan that was defined during the internal design phase and define file conversion, file creation, and data entry requirements.

User guides summarize the system application and operation functions, describe the overall performance capabilities of the system, and define procedures the user must follow to operate the system.

Operations guides provide instructions for setting up and running the system and define the procedures for system backup and file retention.

Figure 6-1 shows the documentation sources that provide input to implementation documents.

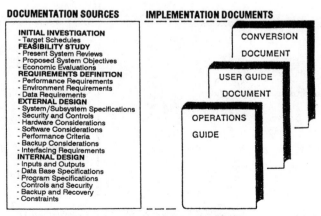

Figure 6-1. Documentation Sources

6.1 CONVERSION DOCUMENTATION

The conversion phase of the implementation process encompasses those tasks that are required to place the system into an operable mode. The conversion phase breaks down into seven major tasks. The task-documentation orientation of the conversion phase is shown in Table 6-1.

Table 6-1. Conversion Task Document Item Correlation

No.	Task/Task Step	Document Item
1	Review conversion plan.	Conversion Task Plan Conversion Support Requirements
2	Identify data sources.	File Conversion Data Source Summary New Table Data Source Summary
3	Define purging/error correction procedures.	Data Purging Procedures History File Procedures Error Correction Procedures
4	Obtain user commitments.	Resource Commitment Summary Organizational Commitment Summary Hardware Commitment Summary
5	Define training requirements.	EDP Personnel Training Requirements User Personnel Training Requirements
6	Develop conversion programs.	Conversion Program Schematic Conversion Program Logic Definitions Program Test Cases Program Code Program Operation Instructions
7	Prepare conversion document.	Conversion Document

Task 1. Review Conversion Plan

The conversion process begins by reviewing the conversion plan that was prepared during the internal design phase. Following the review, documents are prepared that summarize the requirements and identify the conversion activities to be performed. Such documents may include

- Conversion task plan
- Conversion support requirements

Conversion Task Plan. This document should list all the tasks and subtasks to be performed during the conversion process. The name of the person who will be responsible for the performance of each task and the start and end dates during which the task will take place should be noted.

Example:

Phase 8	Conversion
CONVERSION TASK PLAN	

Task No. 1. Convert files Start Date: July 1	Responsibility: Project team End Date: July 23
Task No. 2. Confirm integrity Start Date: July 24	Responsibility: QA End Date: July 28

Conversion Support Requirements. This document should describe the support requirements for conversion. It should identify the organizations that will participate in the conversion process and identify the hardware configuration that must be installed and the support aids that will be used during the conversion effort. It should also indicate any special considerations that may be required in the execution of the conversion plan.

Example:

Phase 8	Conversion
CONVERSION SUPPORT REQUIREMENTS	

Participants: Project Team	Quality Assurance Accounts Receivables

Hardware Configuration:
IBM 3090-180S Processor
Xerox 5200 Printer
Dual Disk Drives
  (10 Gigabytes)
Magnetic Tape Drive
  (800 Bits/Inch)
Five Keystations
	Software Support Requirements:
	Data Entry Package
	System Utilities
	Report Generator Package
	File Maintenance Package

Task 2. Identify Data Sources

The objective of this task is to identify the sources for collecting data for the start-up master files and system tables. The documents resulting from this task are

- File conversion data source summary
- New table data source summary

File Conversion Data Source Summary. This document should identify the sources from which data are to be extracted to create the start-up master files. The documentation should provide data that compare the old file with the new file. It should also list the data elements of the new file, showing the starting and ending positions of each data element.

Example:

| Phase 8 | | Conversion |

FILE CONVERSION DATA SOURCE SUMMARY

Item	Existing File	New File
Name ID No. Type Sequence	Sales Order SO-321 Single Record Customer Quantity Price	Order Entry OE-543 Multirecord Customer No. Items Ordered Quantity Price
Data Element		

No.	Name	From	To	Source
101	Account ID	01	10	File
120	Customer	11	30	Customer data base
130	Order No.	31	41	Receivables Ledger
150	Amount	71	80	Cost File

New Table Data Source Summary. This document should identify the sources from which data are extracted to set up the initial system tables.

Example:

| Phase 8 | | Conversion |

NEW TABLE DATA SOURCE SUMMARY

Table	Source	Access Method
Invoice Number Current Pricing Valid Accounts	A/R Ledger Costing System Acct. Validation File	Sequential Key-Sequenced Indexed Relational

Task 3. Define Purging/Error Correction Procedures

The objective of this task is to define the procedures for purging old file records, storing them in a history file, or making corrections to the records in the old file so that they can be used in creating new files. The documents resulting from this task are

- Data purging procedures
- History file procedures
- Error correction procedures

Data Purging Procedures. This document should define the procedures for purging old file records.

Example:

Phase 8	*Conversion*

DATA PURGING PROCEDURES

File Name	Procedure
ACT-RCV	1. Ensure that all tables using the valid data records have been created and populated. 2. Remove all access authority to the file and let it stay in place for 3 weeks. 3. If no problems have been encountered with the new file data, purge the old file.

History File Procedures. This document should define the criteria for moving old file records to a history file.

Example:

Phase 8	*Conversion*

HISTORY FILE PROCEDURES

File Name	Procedure
PAID-INV	1. Run the extract program for all paid invoice records with the aging parameter set at 180 days. 2. Ensure that the load program properly updates the invoice and checks written data bases. 3. Specify the file name in the weekly archive. Label the archive tape as "FINAL PAID-INV."

Error Correction Procedures. This document should define the criteria for correcting old file records so that they can be used in generating new files.

Example:

	Conversion
Phase 8	

ERROR CORRECTION PROCEDURES

File Name	Procedure

ACT-RCV	1. Process the file through the extract program. The extract will perform the following validity checks:
	  ▪ Customer number
	  ▪ Pick number
	  ▪ Product codes
	2. Review the error file records and determine the source of the errors.
	3. Do <u>not</u> purge error records! Contact the accounting manager for assistance in correcting records.

Task 4. Obtain User Commitments

The objective of this task is to confirm the user commitments relative to resources, organizational revisions, and hardware requirements. The document items resulting from this tasks are

- Resource commitment summary
- Organizational commitment summary
- Hardware commitment summary

Resource Commitment Summary. This document should affirm the user commitment to conversion efforts that may exceed normal workloads. The documentation should address user commitments to the costs and time involved in carrying out conversion activities related to data purification, input preparation, and file balancing.

Example:

	Conversion
Phase 8	

RESOURCE COMMITMENT SUMMARY

Organization	Activity/Commitment	Estimate
Accounting	File purification/validation	3 person-weeks
Accounting	Input of initial vendor qualification data	6 person-weeks
Purchasing	Input of product codes	4 person-weeks

Organizational Commitment Summary. This document should affirm the user commitment to organizational requirements. The documentation should address user commitments to staff reductions and interorganizational adjustments. It should also address organizational contingency plans in the event of implementation problems.

Example:

Phase 8   *Conversion*

ORGANIZATIONAL COMMITMENT SUMMARY

Organization	Commitment
Accounting	Temporary transfer of three persons to purchasing
Accounting	Permanent transfer of one person to new position of system administrator
Purchasing	Temporary addition of three persons to staff
Purchasing	Reduction of permanent staff by two persons following initial data entry functions.

Hardware Commitment Summary. This document should affirm the user commitment to the hardware requirements. The documentation should address user commitments to hardware installation and site preparation.

Example:

Phase 8   *Conversion*

HARDWARE COMMITMENT SUMMARY

Hardware	Site Preparation	Schedule
MICR printer	▪ Add new 220-V power outlet ▪ Replace lock on printer room door	4/1 4/15
Data terminals	Purchasing ▪ Add 1 controller ▪ Clear desk area for 5 terminals Accounting ▪ Clear desk area for 3 terminals	4/7 4/15 4/15
Remote printer	▪ Add local printer connection in purchasing ▪ Provide cover for printer	4/7

Task 5. Define Training Requirements

The objective of this task is to define the strategies for training both user and EDP personnel. The document items resulting from this task are

- EDP personnel training requirements
- User personnel training requirements

EDP Personnel Training Requirements. This document should outline the training strategies for training EDP personnel. It should list the manuals required for training, include schedules for classroom instruction, and summarize any plans that have been developed for on-the-job training.

Example:

Phase 8	Conversion

EDP PERSONNEL TRAINING REQUIREMENTS

Manuals Required
Project Control Manual – PC/1 Console Schedule File Guide
Project Control Manual – PC/2 I/O Operator Guide

Classroom Materials	**On-the-Job Training**
Session outlines	Operators will have 3
Flip charts and/or transparencies	weeks of supervised training
Sample problems	after classroom training is
Handouts	completed.

User Personnel Training Requirements. This document should summarize the user training requirements. It should describe the requirements for training materials, identify the personnel to be trained, define the techniques to be used for user training (e.g., overhead transparencies, practice time, etc.), show the schedules that have been determined for user training, and note the staffing assignments for conducting training sessions.

Example:

Phase 8	Conversion

USER PERSONNEL TRAINING REQUIREMENTS

Training Materials:	User Manual, Terminal Guide
Personnel:	Accounting manager, accounting supervisor, accounting staff, purchasing staff
Technique:	Hands-on classroom training
Schedule:	Group 1: 3 days, Mon-Wed, July 16-18 Group 2: 2 days, Thurs-Fri, July 19, 20
Staffing:	J. Miller – HR, R. Swanson – IS, training both classes

Task 6. Develop Conversion Programs

The objective of this task is to develop programs required for conversion. The documentation should define the processing logic for coding, establish test cases for coding and debugging the programs, and provide instructions for running the required conversion programs. The document items resulting from this task are

- Conversion program schematic
- Conversion program logic definitions
- Program test cases
- Program test specification

Conversion Program Schematic. This document should depict the sequence and processes required for the conversion of old files to new ones. The documentation should indicate when manual procedures are to be used and when conversion aids for control purposes should be applied.

Example:

Phase 8   *Conversion*

CONVERSION PROGRAM SCHEMATIC

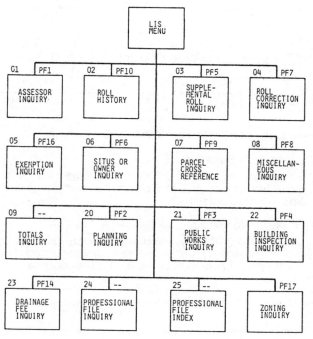

Conversion Program Logic Definitions. This document should define the program logic for each program required for conversion.

Example:

Phase 8	Conversion

CONVERSION PROGRAM LOGIC DEFINITION

Program Initialization Logic

Step 1. Verify error file ACT-RCV-ERR is empty.

Step 2. Verify source file OPN-ACT-RCV exists and contains records.

Step 3. If either step 1 or step 2 returns a nonzero return code, exit the program with an error message indicating the problem.

Edit Validation Check

Step 1. Sequentially read the records of the OPN-ACT-RCV file.

Step 2. Validate field 1 – Cust-ID against the customer data base.

Step 3. If the ID does not exist, prefix the ID with error flag 9E.

Step 4. Validate field 2 – Prod-Code against the PROD data base.

Step 5. If the product code does not exist, flag the product code with the 9E error prefix.

Program Test Cases. A program test case definition document should be prepared for each test case to be used in the conversion process.

Example:

Phase 8	Conversion

PROGRAM TEST CASE

Conversion Program Name: OPN-RCV-CHK

Test Case 1. Records in error file.

Enter three records in the error file prior to program initialization. Verify that the program returns the proper error message, and does not continue processing.

Test Case 2. No Records in OPN-ACT-RCV file.

Copy the OPN-ACT-RCV file and delete all records from the copy. Initiate the conversion program and verify that the program returns the proper error message and does not continue processing.

Test Case 3. Records in error file and no records in OPN-ACT-RCV.

Using the files from the two previous test cases, initiate the program and verify that both error messages are generated.

Program Operations Instructions. This document should provide job instructions for running the one-time conversion programs.

Example:

Phase 8	*Conversion*

PROGRAM OPERATIONS INSTRUCTIONS

Program Name
OPN-RCV-CHK
Files Used
OPN-ACT-RCV, OPN-RCV-ERR, PROD.PROD-CODE, PROD.PICK-LST, PROD.CUST-MSTR
Job Setup
1. If a copy of OPN-RCV-ERR exists, rename the file and copy an empty copy of the file into OPN-RCV-ERR. 2. Ensure no locks exist on the production files that would prevent the program from reading the files. 3. Move a copy of the OPN-ACT-RCV file into the test region.
Job Initiation
Submit the job OPN-RCV-CHK from TSO
Job Termination
A message will be displayed on the operator's console indicating that the job has been completed and specifying the number of records written to the error file. If the number of records does not equal zero, notify the accounting department and have them contact the analyst to coordinate cleanup. Carbon-copy the IS manager on the communication to the accounting manager.

Task 7. Prepare Conversion Document

The final task in the conversion process is to gather and organize all pertinent documentation for presentation in a *system turn-over document*. All documents relevant to the user interaction with the system are retrieved from the various repositories and synthesized to specifically address system turnover needs.

Summary guidelines for developing the content of a conversion document are provided in Chapter 7.

6.2 USER GUIDES

In the realm of information systems, the content of a user guide must be developed to coincide with criteria that define the characteristics of one of the following methods of data processing:

- Off-line (batch) processing
- Direct access processing
- Real-time on-line processing
- Timesharing network processing
- Distributed network processing

In a general context, *all* user documentation, regardless of the processing method, should include document items that may be categorized as follows.

General Information Documentation. The document items that comprise this category describe how the user can make use of the documentation delivered to the project file and/or presented in a user guide manual. They include document items that explain any terminology with which the user may be unfamiliar.

System Summary Documentation. The document items that comprise this category summarize the system application and operation functions and describe the overall performance capabilities of the system. They include document items that describe the system configuration and present a general overview of the organization of the system.

I/O Requirements Documents. The document items in this group detail the I/O process. They describe each input, the flow of data through the processing cycle, and the resultant outputs.

While all user guides generally contain document items from the documentation categories described above, user guides prepared for a real-time, timesharing, or distributed network system will also require the inclusion of document items that include

File Query Procedures. The document items in this category provide the instructions necessary for preparing and processing of a query applicable to the data base.

Network Access Procedures. The document items in this category provide instructions for network access.

Thus, in planning the content of a user guide, the preparer must be aware of the functional differences between the various methods of information processing.

6.2.1 Off-Line (Batch) System User Guide

An *Off-Line (Batch) System User Guide* should describe all of the batch functions in a system. The primary purpose of a batch system user guide is to instruct the user in how to

- Prepare source documents, input transactions, and other hard-copy media that may require user interaction
- Interact with the display screens
- Make use of output reports
- Perform post-processing activities related to balancing and reconciling the system control totals
- Perform error control functions.

Figure 6-2 shows the documentation categories and the document items that should be considered in planning the sectional breakdown of an off-line (batch) system user guide.

GENERAL	SYSTEM SUMMARY	I/O REQUIREMENTS	FILE QUERY	NETWORK ACCESS
PURPOSE OF THE USER GUIDE	SYSTEM APPLICATION	SYSTEM INPUTS	Not Applicable	Not Applicable
PROJECT REFERENCES	SYSTEM FUNCTIONS	DATA ENTRY PROCEDURES		
TERMS AND ABBREVIATIONS	SECURITY PROCEDURES	INTERFACING WITH OPERATION		
		SYSTEM SCHEDULES		
		OUTPUT DISTRIBUTION		
		ERROR CORRECTION AND RESUBMISSION.		

Figure 6-2. Sectional Breakdown Considerations for an Off-Line (Batch) System User Guide

In a batch processing environment, source documents are organized into batches and processed at given time intervals (daily, weekly, quarterly, annually, on request, etc.). If the source documents are to be processed against a master file, they are usually sorted into the same sequence as the master file before they are processed. The jobs are planned and organized into a job stream well in advance of actual processing. Transactions are collected, grouped by application, and processed at a scheduled time and in a scheduled sequence. The batch process has certain inherent disadvantages. These include the time required to prepare the batched input and the delays that can be created by periodic scheduling. These same characteristics, however, can prove advantageous. For instance, when certain transactions occur infrequently during the day, they can be batched together and processed overnight. The process is illustrated in Figure 6-3.

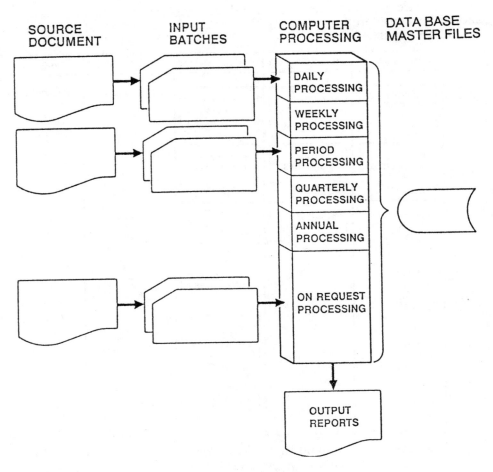

Figure 6-3. Batch Processing Environment

Batch system user guides may be further categorized as follows:

- Functionally oriented batch system user guide
- Single-function batch system user guide
- Batch system user guide with error procedures
- Batch system user guide with audit and change request procedures
- Batch system user guide with fallback procedures

Functionally oriented batch system user guides provide a detailed overview of the system for orientation purposes, followed by a series of step-by-step data preparation and batch processing procedures. The documents are functionally oriented, providing quick access to data pertaining to each of the system's processing procedures. The arrangement may be sequentially organized in the order in which the business transactions occur.

Single-function batch user guides are organized for a system which performs a single function or one function with optional processing activities. Numerous single function user guides may be prepared where different organizational entities will each be working with only one or two functions of a large system. A system summary explains the application of the system within the user organization. A summary description permits someone not involved with the day-to-day functioning of the system to gain an understanding of its use and operational characteristics. This summary is followed by detailed instructions for preparing data for input and for using system outputs.

Batch user guides with error procedures describe procedures for preparing the inputs, utilizing the outputs, and detecting and correcting errors within the output reports. They describe the procedures for job submission, whether submitted on-line or through the computer center. These user guides are suitable for either single- or multi-function batch systems.

Batch user guides with audit and change request procedures modify the organization of the previous document with the addition of two sections: one describing the audit trails provided by the system to enable error detection and correction or define improper accesses; the other defining the procedures for requesting changes to the system.

Batch user guides with fallback procedures describe the system inputs, operation, and procedures for user-operations interfacing. In addition, they describe the fallback procedures to be used in the event that the computer system fails or for some other reason becomes unavailable. This information is needed in user guides for systems performing critical functions within the organization. It may alternatively be included in a separate disaster recovery document.

Summary guidelines for preparing each of these types of batch system user guides are provided in Chapter 7.

6.2.2 On-Line System User Guides

The documentation contained in an on-line user guide must relate to user functions that are directly tied to and controlled by a central processing unit (CPU) and involves devices that are capable of direct two-way communications with the CPU. On-line systems may be classified as follows: inquiry systems, update systems, real-time systems, timesharing systems, integrated systems, distributed network systems, and multiprogramming/multiprocessing systems. Regardless of the on-line environment, the document items contained in the user guide must explain how to sign on and sign off the system, what security measures must be taken, and how to use the terminal. Document items should also be included that explain how the user interacts with the various menus and how to update and query the system data base. On-line system may be categorized as shown in Figure 6-4. The user instructions for each type of system must reflect the special processing considerations of that system classification.

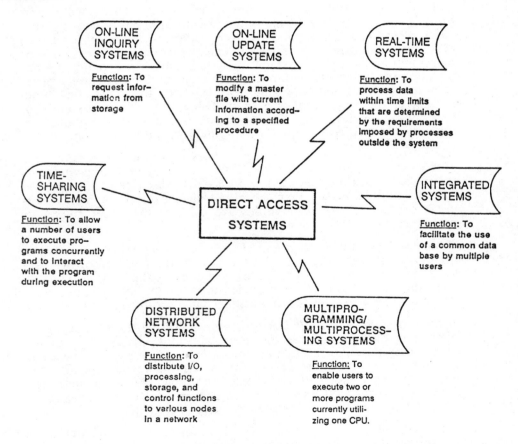

Figure 6-4. On-Line Systems Classifications

On-Line Update System User Guides. The documentation contained in a user guide for an on-line update system should provide instructions that facilitate two-way communications between the user responsible for updating the data base and the central processing unit. In addition, the documentation included in an on-line update system user guide should provide general information related to the use of the user guide and a summary related to the application, operation, and configuration of the system. Document items should be included that define user functions pertaining to data entry and on-line batch processing. In addition, document items should include summary instructions for general system usage, including sign-on/sign-off, use of terminal, and security procedures. An on-line update user guide may be published as a separate manual or as a subset of a manual that details user procedures in a more comprehensive direct access system. In either case, the user instructions should explain the frequency, restrictions, and sources of input data and provide procedures for data base access, updating, and error correction. Figure 6-5 shows the sectional breakdown of a typical on-line update system user guide.

GENERAL	SYSTEM SUMMARY	I/O REQUIREMENTS	FILE QUERY	NETWORK ACCESS
PURPOSE OF THE USER GUIDE	SYSTEM APPLICATION	DATA SOURCES	Not Applicable	Not Applicable
PROJECT REFERENCES	SYSTEM OPERATION	ACCESS PROCEDURES		
TERMS AND ABBREVIATIONS	SYSTEM CONFIGURATION	UPDATE PROCEDURES		
	SECURITY PROCEDURES	RECOVERY AND ERROR CORRECTION		
		TERMINATION PROCEDURES		

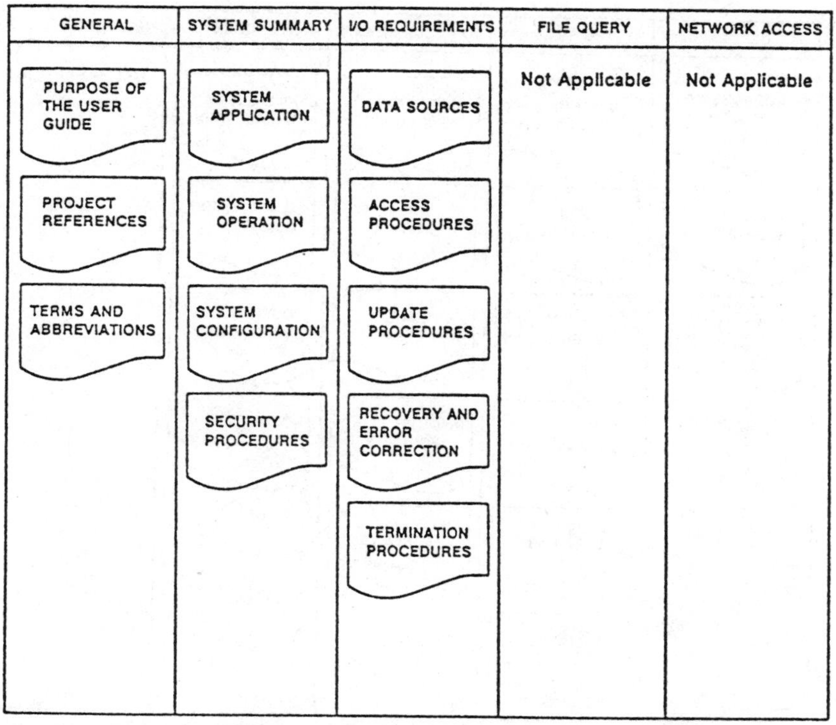

Figure 6-5. Sectional Breakdown Considerations for an On-Line Update System User Guide

On-Line Inquiry Systems User Guide. The function of an on-line inquiry system is to request information from storage. For example, the user may execute a machine statement to initiate a search of library documents stored in a bibliographic data base. Thus, if the user guide is prepared for an on-line inquiry system, the documentation should include instructions for the preparation and processing of system queries. The document items contained in the user guide should detail the system query capabilities, explain the data base format, and provide guidance for the preparation of query titles, requests, and parameter inputs. Since the system components in an on-line inquiry system are a terminal, data communication lines, an inquiry program contained in memory, an I/O message control unit, and one or more data files that the central processor can access, the user instructions contained in the user guide must enable inquiry operations to take place within the total configuration. Figure 6-6 shows the document items in each documentation category that should be considered when the content arrangement of an on-line inquiry system user guide is being planned.

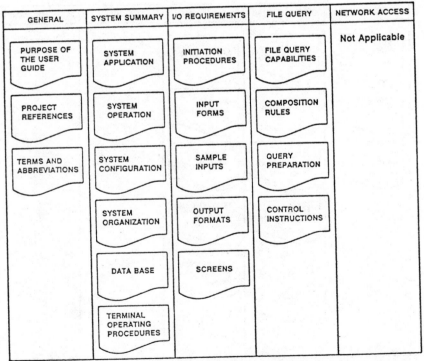

GENERAL	SYSTEM SUMMARY	I/O REQUIREMENTS	FILE QUERY	NETWORK ACCESS
PURPOSE OF THE USER GUIDE	SYSTEM APPLICATION	INITIATION PROCEDURES	FILE QUERY CAPABILITIES	Not Applicable
PROJECT REFERENCES	SYSTEM OPERATION	INPUT FORMS	COMPOSITION RULES	
TERMS AND ABBREVIATIONS	SYSTEM CONFIGURATION	SAMPLE INPUTS	QUERY PREPARATION	
	SYSTEM ORGANIZATION	OUTPUT FORMATS	CONTROL INSTRUCTIONS	
	DATA BASE	SCREENS		
	TERMINAL OPERATING PROCEDURES			

Figure 6-6. Sectional Breakdown of Considerations for an On-Line Inquiry System User Guide

On-Line Real-Time System User Guide. Although an on-line system is not always a real-time system, a real-time system always consists of equipment with an on-line capability. Therefore, the documentation in this category may be more appropriately referred to as *on-line real-time system documentation.* In this environment, the documentation considerations must relate to the system query capabilities and the user functions that impact the time delays between the creation of data to be processed and the actual processing of these data. User instructions are needed that explain how to initiate and interact with the system through the user terminal. The documentation should include descriptions of any menus, input screens, output screens, and all physical reports as well as procedures for querying the system. It should also include information that describes the purpose of the user guide and explains the system application, operation, configuration, and organization. The documentation categories to be considered in the organizing the content of an on-line real-time system user guide are shown in Figure 6-7.

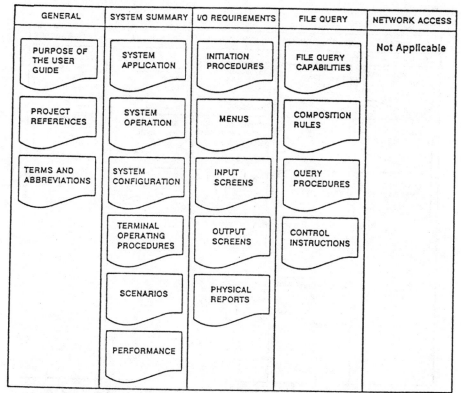

Figure 6-7. Sectional Breakdown of Considerations for an On-Line Real-Time System User Guide

Timesharing System User Guide. User documentation in a timesharing environment focuses on two basic modes of processing: *conversational mode* and *remote batch-processing mode.* In conversational mode, documentation is required that explains how each statement or request input by the user through a terminal is processed and an appropriate reply sent back to the terminal. In a remote batch-processing mode, the terminals used in the system may be quite different from those used in conversational mode. They can consist of an I/O device such as a card reader and printer, which are connected to a local computer. Although timesharing systems may differ, they all share the common features of concurrent access, rapid response time, independent capabilities, flexibility of handling multiple operations, and security controls. A timesharing user guide will most likely incorporate the documentation considerations of a multiprogramming on-line interaction and real-time response system. Figure 6-8 shows the documentation categories and document items that should be considered when the sectional breakdown of a timesharing user guide is planned.

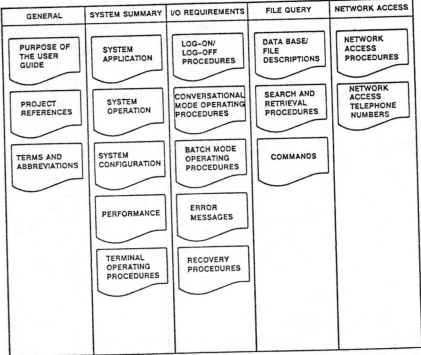

Figure 6-8. Sectional Breakdown of Considerations for a Time-sharing User Guide

Network Data Processing User Documentation. A distributed network system combines the advantages of both centralized and decentralized systems. While tasks such as design and program development are, by necessity, centralized, the functions related to I/O processing, storage, and control are distributed to the various network nodes. The documentation contained in a distributed network user guide, therefore, should provide instructions for performing functions that utilize a host computer to which several remote terminals may be attached or for performing satellite operations in a network that consists of several computers interconnected by a single communication line with no single computer acting as a host. The user documentation associated with a distributed network processing system permits the distributed sites to use existing applications software in a network environment. The documentation categories that should be considered in planning the sectional breakdown of a distributed network user guide are shown in Figure 6-9.

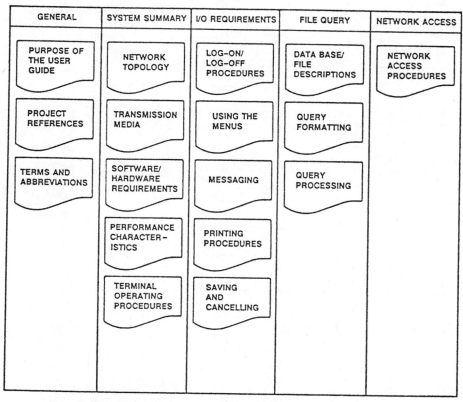

Figure 6-9. Sectional Breakdown of Considerations for a
Distributed Network User Guide

6.3 OPERATIONS DOCUMENTATION

The function of an operations guide is to define the control requirements of a system and provide instructions for initiating, running, and terminating the computer system. The document items contained in an operations guide may be grouped as follows:

- General information documents
- System overview documents
- Run description documents

The document items that comprise each category of documentation applicable to an operations guide are shown in Figure 6-10.

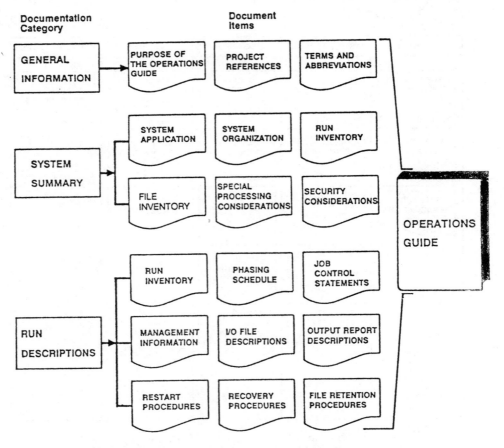

Figure 6-10. Operations Guide Document Items

Chapter 7
Management Options
for Document Preparation

As we discussed in the preceding chapters, the document items that record the results of tasks performed during the development cycle of a computer system are generally intended as deliverables to a project file. The decision of whether to accumulate these documents and publish them as a compilation of phase documentation must be made by the appropriate managers. Since the requirements for documentation vary widely depending on the management techniques employed by both the development and user groups for whom the documentation is intended, decisions regarding the preparation of phase documents and decisions regarding the methods of preparation will vary. For example, when the user group is also the development group, the approach to serving audience communications needs will be entirely different than when these two groups function as separate entities.

7.1 DOCUMENT TYPES

Not all the document types discussed in the previous chapters may be needed on a particular project. The determination of which document types should be produced is usually the responsibility of the project manager. The level of complexity of the system to be documented is generally the essential determinant.

Responsibility for the preparation of each document type to be produced must also be identified early in the systems development process. Some document types are logically the responsibility of the development group; others, the responsibility of the user group; and still others, the joint responsibility of both groups.

The documents to be prepared may range from a few pages to several hundred pages. The size of a document will depend on the magnitude and complexity of the project. The sectional arrangement for a given document type, however, should be consistent regardless of the size of the document. A primary factor to be considered in determining the scope and size of a document is the environment in which the system will operate.

7.1.1 Combining Document Types

It may be necessary in some operational environments to combine two or more document types into a single volume as illustrated in Figure 7-1.

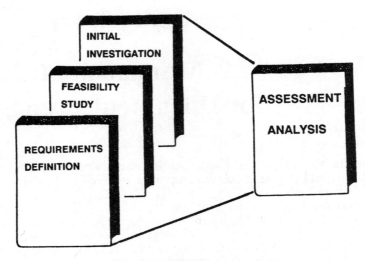

Figure 7-1. Combining Document Types

7.1.2 Splitting Document Types

Conversely to combining document types, it is sometimes appropriate to split the contents of a specific document type to produce several different manuals. See Figure 7-2.

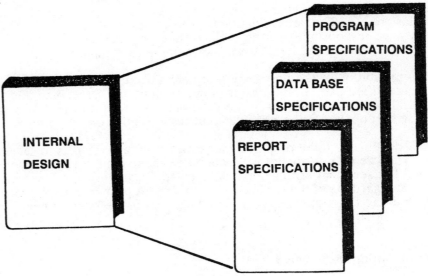

Figure 7-2. Splitting Document Types

7.2 MANAGEMENT OPTIONS FOR PRESENTATION

Decisions regarding the method of presentation should be made before the documentation process gets underway. Three options for presentation are discussed and illustrated in this section:

- Narrative method
- Forms method
- On-line method

The content structure is essentially the same regardless of the method of presentation. Each method, however, has distinct advantages and disadvantages that must weighed when the method of presentation is chosen. In the subsections that follow, we illustrate each method of presentation and point out certain advantages and disadvantages of each.

7.2.1 Narrative Method

The narrative method is the most commonly used method of presenting phase documents. Despite the popularity, however, the writer of a narrative manual does not have the luxury of prestructured forms or screen structures (see Sections 7.2.2 and 7.2.3) to guide the content development process. The challenge of the narrative approach is further increased if the materials prepared by the development group (from which data will be gleaned) are haphazardly organized.

Generally speaking, this approach to manual preparation uses a free-form text narrative based on a standard outline. To assist the reader, the writer may also use drawings and illustrations to reinforce the narrative descriptions and directions. To demonstrate the narrative approach, we have developed a model for an on-line inquiry user manual that is structurally organized as follows:

1.0 System Overview
2.0 General System Usage
3.0 Detailed Description

This, of course, is not a comprehensive outline of sections and subsections that typically comprise an on-line inquiry user manual. The authors have simply chosen these sections to illustrate the technique of presenting documentation in a narrative form. Along with these sections, the complete content arrangement may include an introduction section that states the manual's purpose and scope, an operations section that defines procedures the computer operator must follow to perform certain operations, and a section that provides information about service and maintenance.

The examples that follow coincide with the model for sectional arrangement we developed to illustrate the narrative approach to preparing phase documents that evolve during the development life cycle.

Example:

1.0 SYSTEM OVERVIEW

The land information system (LIS) was developed to provide an automated system for obtaining information on specific parcels of land. The following departments were involved in planning and implementing LIS:

Assessor
Public Works
Planning
Building Inspection

The purpose of LIS is to make land information readily available to the various county departments as well as to the public. A primary objective of LIS is to reduce the necessity of maintaining duplicate manual files of land information in the separate county departments.

2.0 GENERAL SYSTEM USAGE

Subsection 2.1, *Sign-on/Sign-off Procedures,* provides step-by-step instructions for signing on and signing off the system.

Subsection 2.2, *Security Procedures,* describes all security functions and procedures for physical access to the system, password controls, procedural differences for inquiry versus update of data base, abnormal termination and system failure, accounting controls, and audit trails.

Subsection 2.3, *Use of Terminal,* provides a clear, complete description of how the system works and how to use it. It also explains the functions of the controls and indicators on the display station, describes the keyboard and what each key does, interprets the messages that appear on the status line of the display, and prescribes procedures for analyzing and solving most problems that may occur while using the terminal.

3.0 DETAILED DESCRIPTION

This section provides instructions for accessing the information contained in the land information system (LIS) data base.

Subsection 3.1, *LIS Menu,* explains and illustrates the use of the LIS Main Menu.

Subsection 3.2, *General Inquiry Functions,* describe the functions that relate to LIS in general. It describes the purpose of these functions, explains how to get to each screen, provides step-by-step procedures for updating LIS files, and references the PF key functions.

Subsection 3.3, *General Update Functions,* provides step-by-step input procedures and references PF key functions.

7.2.2 Forms Method

The forms approach to documentation has many advantages. These include the following:

- The forms provide for uniformity of format and consistency of content throughout the system development cycle.

- The predetermined tables of content can serve as automatic *checklists* of the documentation to be included in a particular document type.

- The forms provide a measure of control for ensuring the completeness of required documentation.

- Clerical and support staff can be used to prepare phase-end documents.

- Documentation can be prepared concurrently with the systems development effort, not retrospectively.

The forms approach revolves around the use of prestructured forms for all components and items of documentation. Each form is intended for use in a specific section or subsection of a particular phase document. The forms cover a wide range of systems development functions and can be formatted to present all types of documentation (e.g., descriptive narratives, flowcharts, table content descriptions, logic and algorithms, layouts and facsimiles, screen displays, etc.).

In preparing the forms, the functions of the audience to which communications are directed should be considered. As previously noted, the two audiences generally involved in the systems development process are the development group and the user group. The forms intended to communicate to the development group should emphasize the design and programming functions of the system. The forms directed to the user group should focus on provisions for inputs to the system and outputs generated by the system.

Titles of sections should be preprinted and carried on every form relating to that section. Titles at the first subsection level (e.g., 1.1) should also be preprinted on the forms, but the title of the second-level subsection (e.g., 1.1.1) and fourth-level subsection (e.g., 1.1.1.1) will have to be added during the documentation process to reflect terms and titles that are unique to the system being documented (e.g., program names, file names, etc.)

Each form should be accompanied by instructions for filling out the form. Programmers and systems analysts can use the forms as a checklist of the task to be performed. Management can use them to monitor the work performed. Both groups will find the forms useful in easing the burden of preparing systems documentation.

Forms Design. The first step in designing forms that can be used to document the development of a computer system is to design a basic form with a standard heading. The form should provide blocks for the company name, the name of the system, and the page number, release date, and revision date.

Example:

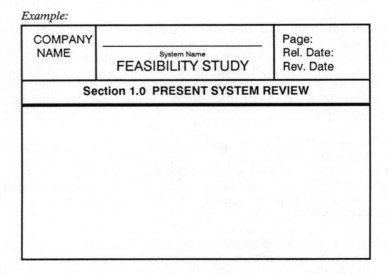

The second step is to expand upon the form design to allow for inclusion of the main section heading.

Example:

The third step is to incorporate primary subsection headings into the forms design, allowing space for addition sub-subsection identifications that are autonomous to the system to be documented.

Example:

COMPANY NAME	System Name FEASIBILITY STUDY	Page: Rel. Date: Rev. Date
Section 1.0 PRESENT SYSTEM REVIEW		
1.8 DATA BASE/FILE SUMMARY 1.8.1 Marketing Data Base 1.8.1.1 North American Sales		

The fourth and final step is to prestructure the forms to facilitate recording of all component items of system and program documentation pertinent to a particular task. Considerable judgment has to be exercised to determine the data elements to be incorporated in the forms' design.

Example:

COMPANY NAME	System Name FEASIBILITY STUDY	Page: Rel. Date: Rev. Date

Section 1.0. PRESENT SYSTEM REVIEW

1.8 DATA BASE/FILE SUMMARY
1.8.1 Marketing Data Base
1.8.1.1 North American Sales

FILE TITLE	RECORD TITLE	MEDIUM	LABEL	RECORD LENGTH

Instructions for completing each form may be printed on the reverse side of each form or in a separate document.

Example:

FEASIBILITY STUDY

Form Number: TCA-FS-140

PURPOSE OF FORM

The purpose of this form is to summarize the contents and characteristics of each data base/file used by the present system.

INSTRUCTIONS FOR FILLING OUT FORM

1. *Data Base Title*: Enter the appropriate heading number and the data base name. For example

 1.8.1 Marketing Data Base

2. *File Title*: List the files contained within the data base in either file name or number sequence.

3. *Record Title*: List the records within each file.

4. *Medium*: Indicate the storage medium (e.g., disk, tape, etc.).

5. *Label*: Note the file label used by programs for referencing the file.

6. *Record Length*: Indicate whether the record length is fixed or variable and the maximum and minimum length of a physical or logical record.

7. *Organization:* Show the type of file organization (sequential, random, indexed, etc.).

NOTE

Forms packets that correlate with the deliverables of each phase of the system's life cycle discussed in Chapters 2 to 6 are available from UMMA, 1250 Oakmead Parkway, Suite 210, Sunnyvale, CA 94088.

To demonstrate the forms method for presenting documentation, we will expand the model used in Section 7.2.1 to illustrate the narrative approach to preparing an on-line inquiry user manual. The expanded model defines the subsections of the of the manual as follows:

1.0 System Overview
  1.1 Information Flow Diagram

2.0 General System Usage
  2.1 Sign-on/Sign-off Procedures

3.0 Detailed Description
  3.1 Display Content Description

Example:

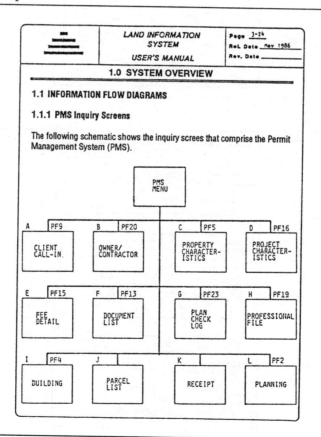

Example:

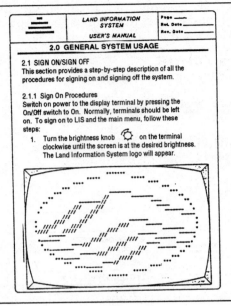

Example:

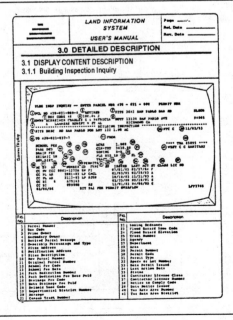

7.2.3 On-Line Approach

Both the narrative method and the forms method discussed in the preceding subsections may be adapted to an on-line approach to documentation.

Numerous word and text processing systems are available to facilitate adapting the *narrative method* to documentation to an on-line system. Packages such as Page Maker, Interleaf, DCF, and Ventura Publisher have broad capabilities for document formatting, text editing, page composition, and graphics design. In combination with laser printer technologies, these and other software tools can produce near-typeset-quality output and page mechanicals that can be used for conventional printing of phase documents.

In adapting the *forms method*, specific considerations may include the development of a menu-driven documentation system that enables the documentalist to call up screen structures that can be used for document preparation. For example, a main menu may be designed that shows all of the document types that correlate with the systems development cycle. The documentalist could select from the main menu the specific document to be prepared. On command, a primary task menu could be displayed. This menu, in turn, could identify the content structure for the selected document type. On selection of the applicable menu item, a subtask menu could be called up which lists the sections and subsections of the document and enables the writer to call up a screen format that can be used for on-line document preparation. As a final step, a print option can allow the recorded data to be output in a hard-copy form. The process is described below and on the following pages.

Menus and Screens. The specifications for developing screen formats and defining user interactions should focus on providing options that can be selected by the documentalist at any point in the systems development life cycle. Instructions for performing the tasks and subtasks that comprise the systems development methodology (SDM) should be organized to facilitate *branching*.

The methodological approach discussed in this section may be viewed as the branching of a tree. The tree has a *trunk* (the Phase Selection Menu), *large branches* (the Primary Task Menus), *smaller branches* (the Subtask Menus), perhaps *smaller branches still* (Information/Instruction Screens), and *leaves* (screens to record the task results). The end-item deliverables prescribed by the methodology may be correlated with the *fruit* of the tree. Most of the tasks and subtasks prescribed can be accomplished in four "jumps" or less – from the *Phase Selection Menu* to the *Primary Task Menu* to the *Subtask Menu* to the *Task-Record Screen*.

The main menu lists the available options at any stage of the development process. From the main menu, the documentalist can get to all the other screens that can be used to record task results and prepare phase end-documents. The illustrations on the following pages will guide you through the process.

Phase Selection Menu. The system begins with the Phase Selection Menu. The menu shows the SDM life cycle phases and provides for selecting the desired phase.

Example:

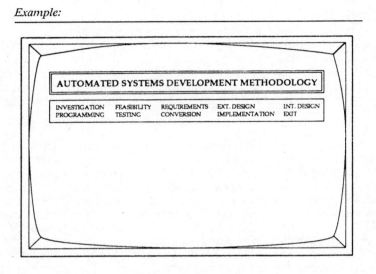

Primary Task Menu. After the appropriate life cycle phase has been selected, the display switches to the Primary Task Menu which shows all the tasks that comprise the selected phase.

Example:

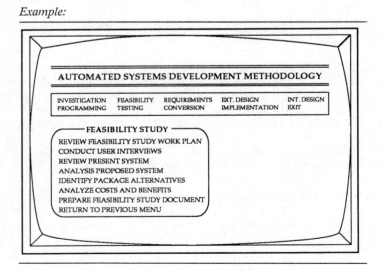

The Subtask Menu. The menu path from the Primary Task Menu then takes the user to a Subtask Menu which lists the task steps and provides options for selection.

Example:

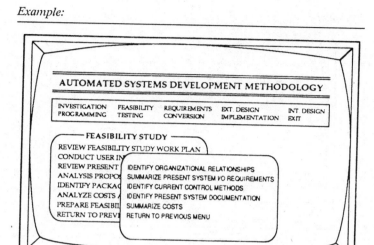

In some instances, the options on the Subtask Menu will lead to a Sub-Subtask Menu which further breaks down the task steps to be performed.

Example:

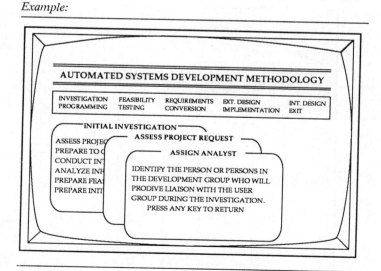

The Task-Record Screen. After completing the work to be performed for a given task or subtask, the user calls up the prescribed Task-Record Screen to record the task results.

Example:

Printing the Task Record. A print option is provided to print the task records using prestructured forms that correlate with the data on the task record screens.

Example:

Company Name/Logo	SYSTEM NAME FEASIBILITY STUDY		PAGE: REL. DATE: REV. DATE:

Section 1.0 – PRESENT SYSTEM REVIEW							

1.11 COST							
EQUIPMENT/SOFTWARE	OPERATING		MAINTENANCE PER. MO.		METHOD OF ACQUISITION		
	PER RUN	PER MONTH	ROUTINE	ENHANCEMENT	LEASED	PURCHASE	DEV'PT
EQUIPMENT System 34 Disk Drive	$ 50	$ 500	$ 1000 100				
SOFTWARE DB Security MUSM 1			500 500				
STORAGE DISK–DYSAM MAG. TAPES			150 150				

Instruction/Information Screens. The automated documentation system includes a variety of screens that provide special instructions or information that relate to a specific task or task step. Examples of these screens are shown below.

Administrative Task Instructions. This category of screens provides instructions for performing *administrative* tasks that are essential to carrying out the tasks and task steps prescribed by the SDM.

Example:

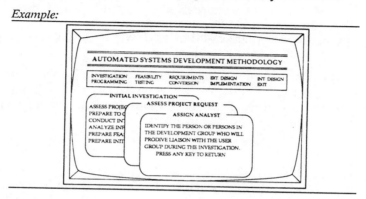

Project Control Instructions. This category of screens provides instructions for performing project control functions prescribed by the SDM that do not require a document deliverable.

Example:

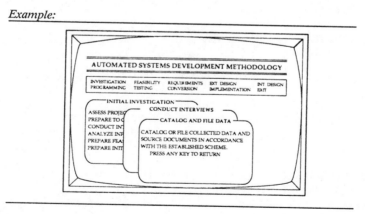

NOTE

A software package that correlates with the deliverables of each phase of the systems life cycle discussed in Chapters 2 to 6 is available from Neurosystems, Inc., 230 E. 48th St., Suite 1D, New York, NY 10017.

7.3 FORMAT AND STYLE CONSIDERATIONS

Regardless of the presentation method, format and style guidelines should be established for

- Dividing a manual into parts, chapters, sections, and subsections
- Numbering of these divisions
- Organizing user procedures and supporting information
- Illustration and table development
- The placement, capitalization, and style requirements for various subdivisions of the manual

Several alternatives may exist for presentation of systems manuals. In these cases, selection criteria should be included in a format and style handbook to guide the selection of the best alternative. These criteria are generally environment oriented, based on the size and complexity of the project.

7.3.1 Divisions

Systems manuals are generally organized in divisions and subdivisions to make the information easy to understand, find, and correlate with the system objectives. The usual divisions and subdivisions are

- Front matter
- Parts (chapters, sections, subsections
- Paragraphs
- Subparagraphs
- Illustrations/table/graphs)
- Appendixes
- Glossary
- Index

The front matter of a systems manual generally consists of the following:

- Cover
- Sign-off sheet
- Change control grid
- Foreword/Preface
- Table of Contents
- List of Illustrations
- List of Tables

Samples of each of the front matter components are provided on the following pages.

Cover. The cover of systems manual should indicate the name of the system, the catalog number, and the company name and logo.

Example:

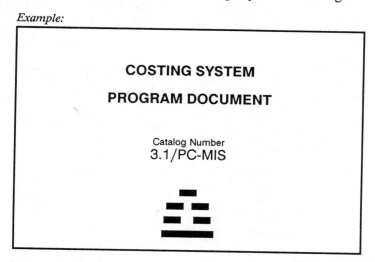

Sign-off Sheet. Once the document is officially approved, a sign-off sheet may be prepared bearing the signatures of any or all of the following: the MIS manager, project team leader, QA manager, user manager, analyst, and the programmer(s). The sign-off sheet should be reproduced and included as the first page following the cover of the manual.

Example:

	DOCUMENT SIGN-OFF

CATALOG NUMBER: _____ RELEASE DATE: _____

COSTING SYSTEM

PROGRAM DOCUMENT

Approved By: _____ Date: _____
Approved By: _____ Date: _____
Approved By: _____ Date: _____
Approved By: _____ Date: _____

Change Control Grid. A *change control grid* may be used to ensure that all corrections and additions that are made at various intervals are included in the published document. As each change is released, the document holder crosses off the proper revision number on the grid.

Example:

FEASIBILITY STUDY							
INSTRUCTIONS: 1. Place this revision control grid in front of your document. 2. Cross off each revision number as revisions are received and filed in your document.							
1	11	21	31	41	51	61	71
2	12	22	32	42	52	62	72
3	13	23	33	43	53	63	73
4	14	24	34	44	54	64	74
5	15	25	35	45	55	65	75
6	16	26	36	46	56	66	76
7	17	27	37	47	57	67	77
8	18	28	38	48	58	68	78
9	19	29	39	49	59	69	79
10	20	30	40	50	60	70	80

Foreword/Preface. A Foreword or a Preface, when included in a systems manual, should contain the purpose and scope of the manual, plus any other information that may be required. The Foreword/Preface should define abbreviations and symbols and should contain general information regarding the project being documented.

Example:

PREFACE

The objectives of this feasibility study for the On-line maintenance tracking system is to provide management with the information necessary to determine the costs and benefits of implementing an on-line system for tracking the status and history of maintenance activities at each property.

The concept for an on-line tracking system originated when the general manager found that there was no ready source of information regarding the history or the cost of maintenance of any of the remote properties.

The information contained in this document is supplemented by both the initial investigation documents, and the documentation contained in the project file. Both are available for review.

Table of Contents. Each document must, of course, have a table of contents. Each numbered section, subsection, and sub-subsection (or paragraph) in the completed document should be referenced by page number on the contents page.

Example:

COMPANY NAME	Equipment Calibration System System Name **Program Document**	Page: Rel. Date: Rev. Date
	CONTENTS	

List of Illustrations. A systems manual containing five or more flow charts, logic diagrams, or other illustrations should have a list of illustrations showing the figure number, title, and page number of each figure.

Example:

COMPANY NAME	Equipment Calibration System System Name **Program Document**	Page: Rel. Date: Rev. Date
	LIST OF ILLUSTRATIONS	

List of Tables. A systems manuals containing five or more tables should have a list of tables showing the table number, title, and page number of each table.

Example:

COMPANY NAME	Equipment Calibration System System Name Program Document	Page: Rel. Date: Rev. Date
	LIST OF TABLES	
2-1 Program/File Cross-Reference ....2-2 2-2 File/Program Cross-Reference ....2-4 3-1 Program/Screen Cross-Reference 3-8		

7.3.2 Parts, Chapters, Sections, and Subsections

The division of a systems manual into parts, chapters, sections, and subsections will depend on the scope of the project and the coverage requirements in the published document.

The following paragraphs describe the structure and numbering scheme for dividing a manual into parts, chapters, and sections.

Parts. A systems manual should be divided into parts only when it is desired to separate the coverage for the various design, programming, or implementation activities being documented. For example, the content of an internal design document may be divided into parts as follows:

Part I	System Design Overview
Part II	System Design Specifications
Part III	Data Base Schema
Part IV	Output Design
Part V	Program or Module Design

A document intended for user or operations audiences may be divided into parts as follows:

Part I	Systems Information
Part II	Operating Schedules
Part III	Job-Related Information
Part IV	Security
Part V	File Backup and Recovery

A part should always be a division of a volume and never a separate volume in itself. Roman numerals should be used to number parts as shown in the examples above.

Chapters. Depending on manual size and project complexity, a system manual may be divided as follows:

- Chapters and sections
- Sections only

When a manual exceeds 3 inches in thickness, it may be desirable to divide it by *chapters and sections.* In this event:

- Arabic numerals should be used to number chapters consecutively throughout all volumes of the publication
- Roman numerals should be used to number sections consecutively within each chapter.

Example:

Chapter 3	Job-Related Information
Section I	Batch Processing
Section II	On-Line Processing
Section III	Job Control Listings

The more common practice in preparing a systems manual is to divide it into *sections* only. In this event, sections are numbered using Arabic numerals with decimal separators for indicating the sectional level of presentation.

Example:

Part III	Job-Related Information
Section 1.0	Batch Processing
Section 2.0	On-Line Processing
Section 3.0	Job Control Listings

In either case there should be at least two of each subdivision used. That is, if there is a Chapter 1, there should be a Chapter 2; if there is a Section 1, there should be a Section 2; etc.

Subsections. In a manual that is divided into chapters *and* sections, the subsections (i.e., paragraphs) are numbered with Arabic numerals. The numbering sequence begins with the chapter number (e.g., 3), followed by a dash and the paragraph or subparagraph number. Decimal separators are used to indicate the divisional level.

Example:

Chapter 3 Job-Related Information
Section I Batch Processing
3-1 Job Stream Descriptions
3-1.1 System Backup Job Stream
3-1.2 DSS Load Job Stream
3-2 Job Step Instructions

While this approach is not commonly used in the preparation of commercially produced manuals, it does meet the requirements set forth in various industrial and government specifications that define standards and establish the general style and format for preparing systems development documents.

In a manual that is divided by sections *only*, the subsections are numbered with Arabic numerals with decimal separators to indicate the divisional level.

Example:

Section 3 Job-Related Information
3.1 Job Stream Descriptions
3.1.1 System Backup Job Stream
3.1.2 DSS Load Job Stream
3.2 Job Step Instructions

7.3.3 Illustrations, Tables, Charts, and Graphs

Alternatives to text presented in the various sections of a manual may include the following:

- Illustrations
- Tables
- Charts
- Graphs

Each alternative is further described and illustrated in the following paragraphs.

Illustrations. Illustrative material should be used to describe a system function when this can be done more efficiently and effectively by graphic methods, or to clarify text and supplement information which is difficult to describe by text alone.

The following should be considered when one is using illustrations in a systems manual:

- All illustrations should be assigned figure titles.
- The title should follow the figure number and should be centered below the illustration.
- Figure titles should be short and describe the content or purpose of the illustration.
- Figures should be numbered sequentially within each section with the section number preceding the sequence number.
- Use a dash to separate the section number from the sequence number. (e.g., Figure 3-1, Figure 4-1, Figure 5-1, etc.).

Tables, Charts, and Graphs. Reference data, other than illustrations, should be presented in tabular, chart, or graph form. Tables, charts, and graphs should be handled in the same manner as illustrations except that the title should appear on top of the presentation rather than below it.

7.3.4 Appendixes

If appendixes are needed to complement the documentation presented in a systems manual, they should immediately follow the last chapter or section of the manual. Appendix headings should be identified by capital letters with the title of the appendix in upper- and lowercase.

Example:

```
APPENDIX A   Screen Formats
APPENDIX B   Report Samples
APPENDIX C   Command Structure
```

The pages of the appendixes should be consecutively numbered in Arabic numerals preceded by the capital letter of the appendix (e.g., A-1, A-2, etc.).

7.3.5 Glossary

In some documentation environments, it is customary to include a listing of terms, definitions, or acronyms unique to the system documented as part of the sectional content. In others, a glossary may be appended at the end of the document to define or explain terms unique to the document or subject to interpretation. The former approach is incorporated in some of the content alternatives presented later in this chapter. If a glossary is used as an independent unit, the pages should be consecutively numbered with Arabic numerals with the word GLOSSARY or the letters GL preceding the sequential numbers (e.g., GL-1, GL-2, etc.).

7.3.6 Index

Indexing an ADS manual may involve the preparation of any or all of the following index types:

- Alphabetic index
- Table of contents
- Chapter indexes
- Special indexes

Alphabetic Index. An alphabetic index should be provided when the manual size exceeds 35 pages. For a multivolume manual, each volume should contain its own alphabetic index. The alphabetic index should enable the user to find important items under those names most likely to be used.

Example:

```
                        ALPHABETIC INDEX

        A                           F
        Arrays, 5,11,17,34          File layouts, 99-118
                                    Function keys, 7,11-13
        B
        Bit layout, 142             H
                                    Help screens, 168-173
        C
        Change procedures, 121-136  I
        Command syntax, 4           Input processing, 52-69
        Constants, App A            Interfaces, 58,74-86

        D                           K
        Data dictionary - App B     Key indexes, 122-124
                                    Keys, 7, 11-21
        E
        Edit functions, 5,23        L
        Error messages, 63          Log-on procedure, 4-5
```

Table of Contents. A table of contents is located in the front and should identify by title and page number, the chapter and section headings plus any major subheadings.

Chapter and Section Indexes. When chapter and/or section indexes are deemed applicable, they should be located at the front of each chapter or section of the manual.

Example:

```
                      SECTION 4 INDEX
4.1 Support Software Environment ........................................ 46

4.2 Interfaces ............................................................. 49

4.3 Storage Requirements ................................................ 53

4.4 Program Design ...................................................... 55
4.4.1 Detail Summary ................................................... 55
4.4.2 Logic Flow ........................................................ 57
4.4.3 Initialization/Sign-on ............................................ 68
```

Special Indexes. Special indexes may be used to facilitate troubleshooting or in referencing procedural steps. Such indexes may be by symptom, job function, or any other key locator.

Example:

```
                      Symptom Index
Screen
   Screen dim or dark ................................................. 197
   Improper colors ................................................... 198

Program Functions
   Function not available ............................................. 203
   Function expecting an argument .................................... 203
```

7.3.7 Style of Writing

Since the paramount consideration in preparing a systems manual is its technical content, the presentation should be in a language free of vague and ambiguous terms, using the simplest words and phrases which will convey the intended meaning. To facilitate such communications, a style guide is needed that establishes rules for using

- Abbreviations and symbols
- Mathematical equations
- Numerals
- Cross-references

These topics are amply dealt with in numerous books concerned with the element of style and are therefore not elaborated upon in this book. *The Harbrace College Handbook*, for example, provides guidelines for grammar, mechanics, punctuation, spelling and diction, and writing effective sentences. Another comprehensive guide to technical writing style is HDBK-63038-2 which is available from the U.S. Government Printing Office.

7.4 DOCUMENTATION REVIEWS

The logical step to ensure accuracy and completeness of a phase end-document is to conduct formal management review of the document prior to publication. The reviewers must answer the following questions:

> Did the writer interpret the information correctly?
> Is the presentation complete and accurate?
> Does the document convey the information intended?
> Does the document conform to presentation standards?

7.4.1 Review Types

Document reviews may be classified as *technical reviews* or *editorial reviews*. A technical review measures the technical accuracy of the document. An editorial review focuses on ensuring that the format and style of presentation comply with established standards. Reviews can also be classified by when they are held. Three types of reviews fall in this classification: checkpoint reviews, draft reviews, and approval-for-production reviews.

> *Checkpoint reviews* are used to assess the status of the documentation effort after the completion of a particular chapter, section, or subsection. Not all projects may require checkpoint reviews. For large projects, however, checkpoint reviews can be critical in ensuring that manuals are being prepared in compliance with the requirements set forth in the documentation plan.

> *Draft reviews* are conducted to ensure the technical integrity of the documentation and the consistency of the editorial format and style. In some instances both technical reviews and editorial reviews are conducted by the same review team. In larger projects, however, draft documents are reviewed by two separate review teams: a technical review team, and an editorial review team. Since most computer systems manuals are published as accumulations of phase documentation, these reviews generally coincide with overall project phase reviews that are conducted to evaluate the phase outputs and assess the project status. Once approved, the phase end-document establishes a baseline for configuration management and control.

> *Approval-for-production reviews* are comprehensive reviews generally conducted by the project manager, selected team members, and cognizant users. These reviews cover all aspects of the document - both technical and editorial. The review amounts to a thorough evaluation of the overall documentation effort, with the primary aim being the granting of final approval for production.

Since each document type is intended for a different audience, a responsibility grid should be constructed that makes explicit the involvement of various groups in the review process. Such a grid can be a useful tool for communicating between the development and user organizations on matters relative to the review process. The following matrix summarizes the review and approval points and the expected participation of project team members in the review process.

PHASE	REVIEWERS						
	MIS Manager	Project Leader	QA Manager	User Manager	Analyst	Programmer	Operations Manager
Initial Investigation	X	X	X	X	X		
Feasibility Study	X	X	X	X	X		
Requirements Definition	X	X	X	X	X		
External Design	X	X	X	X	X		
Internal Design	X	X	X		X	X	X
Program Document		X	X		X	X	X
Test Document	X	X	X		X	X	
Conversion Document	X	X	X	X	X	X	X
User Guide	X	X	X	X	X	X	X
Operations Guide	X	X	X	X		X	X

7.4.2 Review Process

The review process starts with providing review copies to the responsible reviewers. The following should be considered when a document review is planned.

Status Notation. The status of a document (i.e. first draft, second draft, etc.), should be indicated on the cover of all review copies submitted to reviewers in anticipation of a formal review session.

Example:

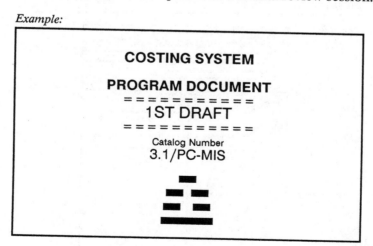

Document Review Control Form. A document review control form should accompany each copy review process.

Example:

DOCUMENT REVIEW CONTROL

Document Title: _____   Catalog Number: _____

_____
_____

☐ Initial Documentation   ☐ Change Documentation   ☐ Additions

TRANSMITTAL COMMUNICATIONS

Sent To: _____   Date: _____

Date Requested For Response: _____

Action Required: ☐ Acknowledgement Of Receipt
                   ☐ Review & Response
                   ☐ Fill In The Gaps On Papers ___ ___ ___ ___ ___ ___
                   ☐ Formal Concurrence & Sign-off

ACKNOWLEDGEMENT OF RECEIPT

Received By: _____   Date: _____

Tentative Date For Completion Of Review _____

Comments: _____

ROUTING LIST

Name	Action	By Date
_____	_____	_____
_____	_____	_____
_____	_____	_____

Marking Review Copies. Corrections and changes should be neatly made between lines and margins. Professional editing symbols are not generally necessary, but all corrections and changes should be indicated in an orderly manner.

Example:

PICS-LOOK-ALIKE USERS GUIDE	Page : 3-4 Rel. Date : Oct. 1982 Rev. Date:

Section 3.0 – I/O REQUIREMENTS

3.3 PRODUCTION CONTROL REPORTS (Continued)
  3.3.1 PRODUCT/LOCATION SUMMARY REPORT (Continued)

OUTPUT CONTENT

REF. NO.	COLUMN OR LINE TITLE	DESCRIPTION & INTERPRETATION
14	YLD%	Monthly OUT divided by monthly IN
15	YLD$	Monthly OUT times standard cost
16	LAB	Standard labor cost
17	Item Number	The identifier of an item. The key to the item master file.
18	Item Description	A description of the item in the general form package, PBS, chip, product, modification code.

Conducting the Review Meeting. The writer is the logical person to preside over the formal review. The meeting itself should be somewhat informal, with the only rules being those of simple courtesy. Those reviewing the document should focus on its accuracy. The reviewers should keep in mind that the writer is a human being and is prone to mistakes. They should always use tact when pointing out an error. The writer, most likely, will appreciate corrections of facts and sloppy grammar. If a different style of writing is suggested than that prescribed in established standards, the reviewer must direct her or his suggestions to the policymakers rather than the writer.

During the meeting, the document is reviewed page by page, while questionable points are discussed and changes and corrections noted. After the formal review, the writer should collect all review copies. Parts of the review copies will appear pretty garbled after changes (and changes to changes) have been made, so the writer should transfer the corrections and changes to a previously unmarked copy. As each change or correction is transferred, the writer should read back the sentence or phrase, as modified, to confirm it has been transferred correctly.

Concurrence and Sign-off. Once a document is officially concurred, the reviewers should formalize the concurrence by signing a sign-off sheet. The sign-off sheet should then be made part of the published work, appearing as the first page of the document.

Example:

◆	DOCUMENT SIGNOFF

CATALOG NUMBER:_____ RELEASE DATE:_____

CUSTOMER SERVICE
USER GUIDE

Approved By _____ Date _____

Approved By _____ Date _____

Approved By _____ Date _____

Approved By _____ Date _____

7.5 ANALYSIS DOCUMENTS CONTENT ALTERNATIVES

In Chapter 3, we proposed that the documentation resulting from analysis activities be organized for presentation in three phase end-documents: initial investigation, feasibility study, and requirements definition. In this chapter, we will consider three alternate document types that may be produced to present analysis documentation: functional description document, data requirements document, and alternatives evaluation document.

7.5.1 Functional Description

The primary objective of a functional description document is to establish a communications vehicle between development personnel and the ultimate users of the proposed system. The document describes the proposed system in terms of the functions and outputs the system is expected to provide. The contents should be organized to reflect the requirements of the proposed system and provide the user group with information on performance, preliminary design, and user impacts, including fixed and continuing costs.

Figure 7-3 presents a table of contents for a functional description document.

```
FUNCTIONAL DESCRIPTION DOCUMENT
         TABLE OF CONTENTS


SECTION 1.0 GENERAL
1.1  Purpose of the Functional
     Description Document
1.2  Project References
1.3  Terms and Abbreviations

SECTION 2.0 SYSTEM SUMMARY
2.1  Background
2.2  Objectives
2.3  Existing Methods and Procedures
2.4  Proposed Methods and Procedures

SECTION 3.0 DETAILED CHARACTERISTICS
3.1  Specific Performance Requirements
3.1.1  Accuracy and Validity
3.1.2  Timing
3.2  Functional Area System Functions
3.3  Inputs and Outputs
3.4  Data Base Characteristics
3.5  Failure Contingencies
3.6  Security
```

Figure 7-3. Content Arrangement of a Functional Description Document

```
┌─────────────────────────────────────────────────────┐
│              FUNCTIONAL DESCRIPTION DOCUMENT          │
│                   TABLE OF CONTENTS                   │
│                      (continued)                      │
│                                                       │
│   SECTION 4.0 DESIGN DETAILS                          │
│   4.1  System Description                             │
│   4.2  System Functions                               │
│   4.2.1  Accuracy and Validity                        │
│   4.2.2  Timing                                       │
│   4.3  Flexibility                                    │
│   4.4  System Data                                    │
│   4.4.1  Inputs                                       │
│   4.4.2  Outputs                                      │
│   4.4.3  Data Base                                    │
│                                                       │
│   SECTION 5.0 ENVIRONMENT                             │
│   5.1  Equipment Environment                          │
│   5.2  Software Environment                           │
│   5.3  Interfaces                                     │
│   5.4  Summary of Impacts                             │
│   5.4.1  Organizational Impacts                       │
│   5.4.2  Operational Impacts                          │
│   5.4.3  Development Impacts                          │
│   5.5  Failure Contingencies                          │
│   5.5.1  Restart                                      │
│   5.5.2  Fallback                                     │
│   5.6  Security                                       │
│   5.7  Assumptions and Constraints                    │
│                                                       │
│   SECTION 6.0  COST FACTORS                           │
│                                                       │
│   SECTION 7.0  SYSTEM DEVELOPMENT PLAN                │
└─────────────────────────────────────────────────────┘
```

**Figure 7-3.   Content Arrangement of a Functional
Description Document (continued)**

A narrative description of each section and subsection of the functional description document follows.

1.0 GENERAL. *This section should provide a summary description of purpose of the functional description document; a listing of publications, instructions, specifications, and standards applicable to the preparation of the document; and an explanation of the terms and abbreviations unique to the document.*

1.1 Purpose of the Functional Description Document. This subsection should describe the purpose, background, and intent of the document.

1.2 Project References. This subsection should provide a brief summary of the references applicable to the development of the project.

1.3 Terms and Abbreviations. This subsection should provide a listing of any terms, definitions, or acronyms unique to the document.

2.0 SYSTEM SUMMARY. *This section should provide a general description of the existing system and the requirements for the proposed system.*

2.1 Background. This subsection should provide information concerning the background, uses, and purposes of the system.

2.2 Objectives. This subsection should summarize the major performance requirements and goals of the proposed system.

2.3 Existing Methods and Procedures. This subsection should provide a description of the methods and procedures currently used to satisfy the existing information requirements. It should include a chart showing the existing data flow through the functional system from data acquisition through processing and eventual output. A brief narrative describing the sequence in which the operational functions are performed may be included. At a minimum, the description should include information regarding organizational/personnel responsibilities, equipment being utilized, inputs and outputs, and brief description of limitations or deficiencies associated with the current procedures.

2.4 Proposed Methods and Procedures. This subsection should explain how the proposed system will interact with the functional processes which the system will support. It should include a chart showing how the proposed data flow should be provided to present an overall view of the planned capabilities. A brief narrative describing the alternative methods and procedures that have been considered should also be included. A chart showing the interacting organizations may be included to complement the narrative.

3.0 DETAILED CHARACTERISTICS. *This section should provide a detailed description of the performance requirements of the proposed system.*

3.1 Specific Performance Requirements. This subsection should describe the specific performance requirements to be satisfied by the proposed system and the system tests necessary to demonstrate those requirements. A quantitative presentation of requirements should be included (e.g., number of records, maximum allowed time from query to response, etc.).

3.1.1 Accuracy and Validity. This subsection should provide a description of the accuracy requirements, including accuracy requirements of mathematical calculations, accuracy requirements of data, and accuracy of transmitted data.

3.1.2 Timing. This subsection should provide a description of the timing requirements to be placed on the system, including the requirements related to the following: response time from receipt of input data to availability of the system products, response time to queries and to updates of data files, sequential relationship of functions, priorities imposed by types of inputs and changes in modes of operation, and any deviations from specified response times for peak load periods.

3.2 Functional Area System Functions. This subsection should amplify and describe the individual function of the major processing steps outlined in Subsection 2.4.

3.3 Inputs and Outputs. This subsection should describe each data element in the inputs to and outputs from the ADS. Information such as the following should be included: data element name, synonymous name, definition, format, range of values, unit of measurement, data item names, and abbreviations and codes. If the information is published in a data dictionary, reference should be made to the entry in the dictionary. When practical, the various input data formats and output data formats should be shown in the appropriate medium (e.g., disk, cards, tape, etc.).

3.4 Data Base Characteristics. This subsection should provide a discussion concerning the data elements to be used in the data base. It should include information such as data element name, synonymous name, definition, format, range of values, unit of measurement, and abbreviations and codes. If the information is published in a data dictionary, reference should be made to the entry in the dictionary. A description of the expected growth of the data should be included.

3.5 Failure Contingencies. This subsection should provide a discussion of the alternative courses of action that may be taken to satisfy the information requirements if the proposed ADS fails. It should include information related to backup requirements and/or fallback requirements for ensuring the continued achievement of the system functions.

3.6 Security. This subsection should describe the degree of sensitivity of the data, data files, and the inputs and outputs of the system.

4.0 DESIGN DETAILS. *This section should provide a description of how the proposed system will satisfy the functional requirements identified in Section 2.0 and Section 3.0.*

4.1 System Description. This subsection should provide a general description of the proposed system. It should reference any interfacing systems and related documentation. A chart showing the relationship of the user organizations to the major components of the proposed system should be included.

4.2 System Functions. This subsection should describe the functions of the proposed system. It should include both quantitative and qualitative descriptions of how the functions will satisfy the requirements identified Section 3.1.

4.2.1 Accuracy and Validity. This subsection should provide a description of the accuracy that will be achieved by the system. Accuracy requirements related to mathematical calculations, data, and data transmission should be considered.

4.2.2 Timing. This subsection should provide a description of the timing considerations. The descriptions should consider requirements related to throughput time, response time to queries and to updates of data files, sequential relationship of system functions, priorities imposed by types of inputs and changes in modes of operation, and timing requirements for the range of traffic load under varying operating conditions.

4.3 Flexibility. This subsection should provide a description of the capability to be incorporated for adapting the system to changing requirements (e.g., requirements for interacting with anticipated operational changes, new or improved systems, and planned periodic changes). It should identify the components and procedures subject to change.

4.4 System Data. This subsection should provide a description of the inputs, outputs, and data used.

4.4.1 Inputs. This subsection should include the following information pertaining to inputs: title and tag, format, and acceptable range of values; number of items; means of entry and input; initiation procedures (e.g., card, tape, sensor, internal, etc.); expected volume and frequency, including special handling for peak-load periods; priority (e.g., routine, emergency, etc.); sources, form of source, and disposition of source document; security considerations of input and individual items; and requirements for timeliness.

4.4.2 Outputs. This subsection should include the following information pertaining to outputs: title and tag; format (including headings, line spacing, arrangement, totals, etc.); number of items; preprinted form requirements; means of display (e.g., CRT, printer, etc.); expected volume and frequency, including special handling; priority (e.g., routine, emergency, etc.); timing requirements (e.g., response time); requirements for accuracy; and user recipients and use of displays.

4.4.3 Data Base. This subsection should include the following information pertaining to the data base: title and tag, description and content, number of records or entries, storage media and size, security considerations, and data retention.

5.0 ENVIRONMENT. *This section should describe the current system environment and the environment needed to satisfy the requirements delineated for the proposed system.*

5.1 Equipment Environment. This subsection should provide a description of the equipment capabilities required for the operation of the proposed system. It should include broad descriptions of the equipment presently available and the characteristics of any new equipment that may be acquired to meet the requirements of the proposed system. The following equipment types should be discussed: processor(s), including the number of each on-line/off-line processor and the size of internal storage; storage media, including number of disk units, tape units, etc.; input/output devices, including the number of each on-line and off-line device; and communications net, including line speeds.

5.2 Software Environment. This subsection should provide a description of the software with which the computer programs to be developed must interact. The description should cover both support software and test software. The documentation should include references to the language, operating system, and data management system to be used.

5.3 Interfaces. This subsection should provide a description of the interfaces with other systems and subsystems. The following should be specified for each interface: a description of operational considerations of data transfer (e.g., security considerations; a general description of data transfer requirements to and from the subject system and characteristics of communications media/systems used for transfer; format, unit of measurement, range of values, and data codes; type of anticipated interface (e.g., manual or automatic); and anticipated interface procedures, including telecommunications considerations.

5.4 Summary of Impacts. This subsection should describe the anticipated organizational, operational and development impacts of the proposed system on the user and development organizations.

5.4.1 Organizational Impacts. This subsection should describe the organizational impacts, including the modifications of positional responsibilities and the addition or elimination of responsibilities that will be required by the proposed system. The documentation should identify the number and skills of additional personnel required and the changes in authorized strength, location, and position.

5.4.2 Operational Impacts. This subsection should describe the impacts on the operational procedures of the data processing center. The documentation should include impacts caused by a change in equipment configuration.

5.4.3 Development Impacts. This subsection should assess the personnel and data processing commitment necessary in the development and testing of the system. The documentation should include a discussion of the requirements for program and data conversion and development impacts that may result from these requirements.

5.5 Failure Contingencies. This subsection should provide a discussion of possible failures of the hardware or software system, the consequences of such failures, and the alternative courses of action that may be taken to satisfy the information requirements.

5.5.1 Restart. This subsection should include a discussion of the restart capabilities for ensuring effective and efficient recovery from a temporary problem with the hardware or software systems.

5.5.2 Fallback. This subsection should expand upon the fallback and backup contingencies described in Subsection 3.5.

5.6 Security. This subsection should expand upon the security requirements identified in Subsection 3.6. The documentation should describe the degree of protection for the levels of availability, integrity, and confidentiality that must be provided by the overall system and its components.

5.7 Assumptions and Constraints. This subsection should address any data automation assumptions and constraints that relate to the development and operation of the proposed system.

6.0 COST FACTORS. *This section should provide a summary of cost factors for the proposed system. The documentation should include a discussion of cost factors relative to security considerations, telecommunications considerations, and the need to interface with other automated systems. Consideration may also be given to equipment, software, supporting telecommunications requirements, organization, and operation.*

7.0 SYSTEM DEVELOPMENT PLAN. *This section should discuss the overall management approach to the development and implementation of the proposed system. The documentation should in-*

clude a discussion of the time frames for development, interorganizational liaison requirements, and any other factors that must be known prior to initiating development.

7.5.2 Data Requirements Document

The data requirements document is a technical document. Its objectives are to define the data elements which the system must handle and to communicate the data collection requirements to the user. The contents of a data requirements document should define the inputs required by the user, explain the procedures the user must follow to provide this input to the system, describe the expected output data, provide specifications of all uses of the data elements, and explain the data limitations of the system. A suggested arrangement follows.

Figure 7-4 presents a table of contents for a data requirements document.

```
               DATA REQUIREMENTS DOCUMENT
                   TABLE OF CONTENTS

      SECTION 1.0 GENERAL
      1.1  Purpose of the Data Requirements
           Document
      1.2  Project References
      1.3  Terms and Abbreviations
      1.4  Change Management
      1.5  Data Security

      SECTION 2.0 DATA DESCRIPTION
      2.1  Static System Data
      2.2  Dynamic Input Data
      2.3  Dynamic Output Data
      2.4  Data Constraints

      SECTION 3.0 DATA COLLECTION
      3.1  Requirements and Scope
      3.1.1  Input Sources
      3.1.2  Input Device
      3.1.3  Recipients
      3.1.4  Range of Values
      3.1.5  Scales of Measurement
      3.1.6  Conversion Factors
      3.1.7  Output Form/Device
      3.1.8  Expansion Factors
      3.1.9  Frequency of Update
      3.2  Source of Input Data
      3.3  Data Collection Procedures
      3.3.1  Input Formats
      3.3.2  Output Formats
      3.4  Data Base Impacts
```

Figure 7-4.   Content Arrangement of a Data Requirements Document

A narrative description of each section and subsection of the data requirements document follows.

1.0 GENERAL. *This section should explain the purpose, provide a brief summary of references, explain unique terms and abbreviations, describe procedures for making modifications, and describe the security considerations.*

1.1 Purpose of the Data Requirements Document. This subsection should describe the purpose and intent of the document.

1.2 Project References. This subsection should provide a brief summary of the references applicable to the history and development of the project. It should reference the project request and related functional description document by title, date, and security classification. It should also indicate the project sponsor, user, and operating center that will run the system and explain the relationship of this project to other projects.

1.3 Terms and Abbreviations. This subsection should provide a listing of any terms, definitions, or acronyms unique to the document or subject to interpretation. It should not include item names or data codes.

1.4 Change Management. This subsection should describe the procedures for managing changes to the system data requirements.

1.5 Data Security. This subsection should describe the degree of sensitivity of the data, data files, inputs, and outputs of the system. It should also identify the authority sources for levels of availability, integrity, and confidentiality.

2.0 DATA DESCRIPTION. *This section should define the static data and dynamic data requirements of the system. It should provide descriptions of each data element that include synonymous name, definition, format, range of values, units of measurement, and data item names, abbreviations, and codes.*

2.1 Static System Data. This subsection should list the titles of static data elements used by the system for either parametric control or reference purposes. The data elements should be presented in logical groups (e.g., functions, subjects, etc.).

2.2 Dynamic Input Data. This subsection should list the titles of dynamic input data elements which are intended to be updated by a system run or during on-line operation. The data elements should be presented in logical groups (e.g., functions, subjects, etc.).

2.3 Dynamic Output Data. This subsection should list the titles of dynamic output data elements which are intended to be updated by a system run or during on-line operation. The data elements should be presented in logical groups (e.g., functions, subjects, etc.).

2.4 Data Constraints. This subsection should describe any data constraints which were not previously defined in the document. The information should provide an indication of the limits of the system with regard to expansion or utilization, with emphasis on limits which could prove critical to future system development.

3.0 DATA COLLECTION. *This section should describe the data collection support the user needs to gather the data values for use by the particular system.*

3.1 Requirements and Scope. This subsection should describe the information required by the system developer in order to establish the data values of each data element. It should include information needed for the data element dictionary (e.g., data element name, synonymous name, definition, format, range of values, unit of measurement, data item names, abbreviations, and codes).

3.1.1 Input Sources. This subsection should list the sources from which the data element will be fed into the system (e.g., an operator, station, organizational unit, etc.).

3.1.2 Input Device. This subsection should identify the hardware devices to be used for entering the data into the system.

3.1.3 Recipients. This subsection should identify those users who should be cognizant of the data elements input to the system, generated by a program and output, and that are inputted to the system but are not outputted by it.

3.1.4 Range of Values. This subsection should describe the range of values associated with each data element.

3.1.5 Scales of Measurement. This subsection should specify the numeric and nonnumeric scales for measuring a data element.

3.1.6 Conversion Factors. This subsection should specify the measured quantities that must go through analog and digital conversion processes.

3.1.7 Output Form/Device. This subsection should identify the form of output and the device on which output is to be generated (e.g., graphics output from a plotter, warning signal from a buzzer, or screen data on a CRT).

3.1.8 Expansion Factors. This subsection should specify the expansion factor for systems that are expected to undergo future expansion (e.g., if the maximum number of input devices is now 6, but is expected to be 12 within a year, the expansion factor should be noted).

3.1.9 Frequency of Update. This subsection should specify the frequency that data elements input to the system are expected to be modified.

3.2 Source of Input Data. This subsection should delineate the source(s) of input data.

3.3 Data Collection Procedures. This subsection should identify the procedures and formats for data collection for entry to and output from the system.

3.3.1 Input Formats. This subsection should describe all input formats, including master file formats used by the system.

3.3.2 Output Formats. This subsection should describe all output formats created by the system.

3.4 Data Base Impacts. This subsection should describe the impacts associated with collection and maintenance of the data base on equipment, software, organizational, operational, and development environments.

7.5.3 Alternatives Evaluation Document

The primary objective of an alternatives evaluation document is to identify and evaluate the alternatives to solving the user needs and requirements. The contents should be organized to summarize the proposed system conceptual design, define the assumptions and constraints that will govern the selection of alternatives, identify the viable alternatives, present the standard criteria for package evaluation, and provide comparative analyses of the benefits and objectives of each presented alternative.

Figure 7-5 presents a table of contents for an alternatives evaluation document.

```
ALTERNATIVES EVALUATION DOCUMENT
TABLE OF CONTENTS

SECTION 1.0 GENERAL
1.1 Purpose of the Alternatives
    Evaluation Document
1.2 Terms and Abbreviations

SECTION 2.0 SYSTEM DESCRIPTION
2.1 Data Flow Schematic
2.2 System Functions
2.3 Constraints
2.4 System Design
2.4.1  Inputs
2.4.2  Files
2.4.3  Outputs
2.5 System Controls

SECTION 3.0 VIABLE ALTERNATIVES
3.1 Potential Packages
3.2 Evaluation Criteria
3.2.1   User Requirements
3.2.2   Availability
3.2.3   Equipment Configuration
3.2.4   Software Environment
3.2.5   Design Features
3.2.6   Flexibility
3.2.7   Expansibility
3.2.8   Documentation
3.2.9   Vendor Support
3.2.10  Vendor Reputation

SECTION 4.0 COMPARATIVE ANALYSIS
4.1 Current Operating Costs
4.2 Future Operating Costs
4.3 Benefits
4.4 Payback Period and ROI

SECTION 5.0 RECOMMENDATIONS
```

Figure 7-5. Content Arrangement of an Alternatives Evaluation Document

Summary guidelines for developing the content of an alternatives evaluation document are provided below and on the following pages.

1.0 GENERAL. *This section should provide a summary description of purpose of the alternatives evaluation document and an explanation of the terms and abbreviations unique to the document.*

1.1 Purpose of the Alternatives Evaluation Document. This subsection should describe the purpose, background, and intent of the document.

1.2 Terms and Abbreviations. This subsection should provide a listing of any terms, definitions, or acronyms unique to the document.

2.0 SYSTEM DESCRIPTION. *This section should include a graphical explanation of the system components and an explanation of the functions to be performed by the proposed system. It should also define the constraints and assumptions that will govern the selection of the viable alternatives and describe the principal inputs, files, and outputs to be considered in the system design.*

2.1 Data Flow Schematic. This subsection should present a graphical representation that shows the flow of data and the points of interaction between the user and the system.

2.2 System Functions. This subsection should explain the functions to be performed by the proposed system.

2.3 Constraints. This subsection should identify the constraints that will impact the selection of the viable alternative to solve the user needs and requirements. It should also include any assumptions that may govern the design considerations.

2.4 System Design. This subsection should describe the inputs, files, and outputs.

2.4.1 Inputs. This sub-subsection should describe the inputs to the system.

2.4.2 Files. This sub-subsection should explain the content and purpose of all key files.

2.4.3 Outputs. This sub-subsection should include content descriptions and facsimiles of all reports and displays.

2.5 System Controls. This subsection should describe the controls for maintaining data integrity, security, and for auditability.

3.0 VIABLE ALTERNATIVES. *This section should identify the possible alternatives that will satisfy the user needs and present the criteria for evaluating each alternative.*

3.1 Potential Packages. This subsection should identify all the packages to be evaluated.

3.2 Evaluation Criteria. This subsection should present the criteria against which each package will be evaluated.

3.2.1 User Requirements. This sub-subsection should describe the required features of the new system and present criteria for comparison against package features.

3.2.2 Availability. This sub-subsection should present criteria for evaluating the availability of the package and the operational status at other locations.

3.2.3 Equipment Configuration. This sub-subsection should list the equipment constraints and present criteria for comparison to package requirements.

3.2.4 Software Environment. This sub-subsection should list the software constraints of the proposed system and present criteria for evaluating programming language, operating system, data base, and data communications requirements.

3.2.5 Design Features. This sub-subsection should describe the design features of the proposed system and present criteria for evaluating design features provided by each alternative relative to control and audit trails, input and output options, provisions for file maintenance, exit routines, and ease and flexibility of operation.

3.2.6 Flexibility. This sub-subsection should present criteria to be used to review a package's ability to accommodate changing user requirements.

3.2.7 Expansibility. This sub-subsection should present criteria for reviewing the sensitivity of the application packages to increases in production volumes and frequency of operation.

3.2.8 Documentation. This sub-subsection should present criteria for evaluation ability of the package documentation for satisfying the user and information systems organization requirements.

3.2.9 Vendor Support. This sub-subsection should present criteria for evaluating vendor provisions for support relative installation, maintenance, and enhancements.

3.2.10 Vendor Reputation. This sub-subsection should present criteria for evaluating items related to assessing the risk of vendor business failure and the quality of vendor personnel.

4.0 COMPARATIVE ANALYSIS. *This section should present analysis summaries relative to current and future operating costs and intangible benefits.*

4.1 Current Operating Costs. This subsection should present documentation that shows the current operating costs for user operation over a minimum of three past periods.

4.2 Future Operating Costs. This subsection should present documentation used to determine future operating costs for each of the alternatives being considered.

4.3 Benefits. This subsection should include documentation used to project the tangible and intangible savings contribution that can be achieved from each proposed alternative.

4.4 Payback Period and ROI. This subsection should include documentation used to determine the payback period and return on investment for each of the alternatives.

5.0 RECOMMENDATIONS. *This section should present staff recommendations for each alternative selected and explain reasons behind the selection.*

7.6 DESIGN DOCUMENT CONTENT ALTERNATIVES

In Chapter 4, we proposed that the documentation resulting from the design activities be organized for presentation in two phase end-documents: external design and internal design. In this chapter, we will consider two other document types that may be produced to present design documentation: system/subsystem specification and data base specifications.

7.6.1 System/Subsystem Specification

The primary objective of a system/subsystem specification document is detail the interfaces with other systems and subsystems and the facilities to be utilized for accomplishing the interfaces. The contents this document should be organized to provide a definition of the system/subsystem functions and to communicate details of the ongoing analysis between the user's operational personnel and the appropriate development personnel.

Figure 7-6 presents a system/subsystem specification table of contents.

```
SYSTEM/SUBSYSTEM SPECIFICATIONS DOCUMENT
             TABLE OF CONTENTS

SECTION 1.0  GENERAL
1.1    Purpose of the System/
       Subsystem Specification
1.2    Project References
1.3    Terms and Abbreviations
SECTION 2.0  SUMMARY OF REQUIREMENTS
2.1  System/Subsystem Description
2.2  System/Subsystem Functions
2.2.1   Accuracy and Validity
2.2.2   Timing
2.3  Flexibility
SECTION 3.0  ENVIRONMENT
3.1  Equipment Environment
3.2  Support Software Environment
3.3  Interfaces
3.4  Security
3.5  Controls
SECTION 4.0  DESIGN DETAILS
4.1  General Operating Procedures
4.2  System Logic Flow
4.3  System Data
4.3.1   Inputs
4.3.2   Outputs
4.3.3   Data Base
4.4  Program Descriptions
```

**Figure 7-6   Content Arrangement of a Systems/
Subsystem Specifications Document**

A narrative description of each section and subsection of the systems/subsystems specifications follows:

1.0 GENERAL. *This section should provide a summary description of purpose of the system/subsystem specification; a listing of publications, instructions, specifications, and standards applicable to the preparation of the document; and an explanation of the terms and abbreviations unique to the system/subsystem specification.*

1.1 Purpose of the System/Subsystem Specification. This subsection should describe the purpose, background, and intent of the system/subsystem specification.

1.2 Project References. This subsection should provide a brief summary of the references applicable to the development of the project.

1.3 Terms and Abbreviations. This subsection should provide a listing of any terms, definitions, or acronyms unique to the system/subsystem specification.

2.0 SUMMARY OF REQUIREMENTS. *This section should provide a specification for each program in the system (or subsystem).*

2.1 System/Subsystem Description. This subsection should provide a general description of the system or subsystem. The description should be written to provide a frame of reference for the remainder of the document. It should include a chart depicting the relationship between the user organization and the system functions.

2.2 System/Subsystem Functions. This subsection should describe the functions as to the system or subsystem, providing details of how the functions will satisfy requirements documented in earlier phases.

2.2.1 Accuracy and Validity. This subsection should provide a description of the accuracy requirements imposed on the system/subsystem. The description should include accuracy requirements of mathematical calculations, accuracy requirements of data, and accuracy of transmitted data.

2.2.2 Timing. This subsection should provide a description of the timing requirements placed on the system/subsystem. The description should include requirements related to

- Throughput time
- Response time to queries and to updates of data files
- Sequential relationship of program functions
- Priorities imposed by types of inputs and changes in modes of operation
- Timing requirements for the range of traffic load under varying operating conditions
- Sequencing and interleaving programs and systems
- I/O transfer time required
- Internal processing time requirements

2.3 Flexibility. This subsection should provide a description of the capability for adapting the program to changing requirements.

3.0 ENVIRONMENT. *This section should provide an expansion of the environment given in the functional description document. Changes should be discussed in terms of the impacts on the currently available environmental components (e.g., equipment, software, etc.).*

3.1 Equipment Environment. This subsection should provide a description of the equipment environment required for the operation of the systems/subsystem. A guideline for equipment to be described follows:

- Processor(s), including number of each on-line/off-line and size of internal storage
- Storage media, including number of disk units, tape units, etc.
- Input/output devices, including number on- and off-line
- Communications net, including line speeds

3.2 Support Software Environment. This subsection should provide a description of the support software with which the computer programs to be developed must interact.

3.3 Interfaces. This subsection should provide a description of the interfaces with other application computer programs, including those of other operational capabilities and from other organizations. The following should be specified for each interface:

- Type of interface (e.g., operator control of a terminal, or program interfaces with other programs)
- Descriptions of operational implications of data transfer, including security considerations
- Data transfer requirements to and from the subject program and characteristics of communications media used for transfer
- Formats of data for both the sending and receiving systems, including the data item names, codes, or abbreviations that are to be interchanged
- Interface procedures, including telecommunications
- Interface equipment
- Data conversion requirements

3.4 Security. This subsection should be related to the functional description document and should reflect the levels of availability, integrity, and confidentiality of the system and its components.

3.5 Controls. This subsection should provide a discussion of the program controls. Control data such as record counts, accumulated counts, batch controls, etc., should be included.

4.0 DESIGN DETAILS. *This section should provide a general description of the operating procedures, system logic flow, system data, and programs.*

4.1 General Operating Procedures. This subsection should provide a general description of the operating procedures (e.g., load, start, stop, recovery, and restart).

4.2 System Logic Flow. This subsection should describe the logic flow of the system/subsystem, primarily in the form of higher-level charts.

4.3 System Data. This subsection should describe the inputs, outputs, and data base.

4.3.1 Inputs. For each input record, the following should be included:

- Title and tag
- Source, medium, and disposition of source medium
- Expected volume and frequency
- Priority (e.g., routine, emergency, etc.)
- Degree of sensitivity
- Requirements for timeliness

For each input data element, the following should be included:

- Name and tag
- Position in the input data record type
- Synonymous name
- Definition
- Unit of measurement
- Format and acceptable range of values
- Degree of sensitivity
- Data item names, abbreviations, and codes

4.3.2 Outputs. For each output type, the following should be included:

- Title and tag
- Format, including headings, line spacing, arrangement, totals, etc.
- Means of display (e.g., CRT, printer, etc.)
- Expected volume and frequency, including special handling
- Priority (e.g., routine, emergency, etc.)
- Timing requirements (e.g., response time)
- User recipients and use of displays
- Preprinted form requirements
- Degree of sensitivity

For each output data element, the following should be included:

- Name and tag
- Definition
- Unit of measurement
- Format and acceptable range of values
- Data item names, abbreviations, and codes

4.3.3 Data Base. For each data base, the following should be included:

- Title and tag
- Narrative summary of content
- Number of records or entries
- Storage media and size
- Degree of sensitivity
- Retention schedule (including provisions for backup)

For each data base element, the following should be included:

- Name and tag
- Position in data base
- Definition
- Unit of measurement
- Format and acceptable range of values
- Data item names, abbreviations, and codes

4.4 Program Descriptions. This section should describe the functions of the computer programs in the system/subsystem. A chart showing the interrelationships of the different functions may be included.

7.6.2 Data Base Specification

A *data base specification* may be prepared when there are many analysts and programmers are involved writing programs that utilize the same data. The document should be sufficiently detailed to permit program coding and data base generation. The contents should be organized to thoroughly describe the data base identification and provide complete data definitions. If the system will use an integrated data base, it should also be identified. Graphical representations should be used when deemed necessary to support the text. Each graphic representation should be consistent with standardized data element names as shown in data element libraries.

Figure 7-7 presents a table of contents for a data base specification.

```
                DATA BASE SPECIFICATION
                   TABLE OF CONTENTS

SECTION 1.0  GENERAL
  1.1  Purpose of the Data Base Specification Document
  1.2  Project References
  1.3  Terms and Abbreviations
SECTION 2.0  DATA BASE DESCRIPTION
  2.1  Data Base Identification
  2.1.1    System Identification
  2.1.2    Effective Dates
  2.1.3    Storage Requirements
  2.1.4    Physical Description
  2.2  Labeling/Tagging Conventions
  2.3  Data Base Organization
  2.4  Special Instructions
  2.5  Support Programs
  2.6  Security
SECTION 3.0  DATA DEFINITIONS
  3.1  Data Files
  3.1.1    General Description
  3.1.2    Physical Characteristics
  3.1.3    Logical Characteristics
  3.2  Tables
  3.3  Items
  3.4  Records and Entries
SECTION 4.0  INTEGRATED DATA BASE
```

**Figure 7-7   Content Arrangement of a Data Base
Specifications Document**

A narrative description of each section and subsection of the data base specification document follows:

1.0 GENERAL. *This section should provide a summary description of the purpose of the data base specification document, a listing of publications, and an explanation of terms and abbreviations unique to the ID document.*

1.1 Purpose of the Data Base Specification Document. This subsection should describe the purpose, background, and intent of the document.

1.2 Project References. This subsection should provide a brief summary of the references applicable to the development of the project, including

- The reference or catalog number for the item referenced
- The title of the item referenced
- The source or author of the item referenced
- The classification status of the item referenced

1.3 Terms and Abbreviations. This subsection should provide a listing of any terms, definitions, or acronyms unique to the internal design document or subject to interpretation by the user.

2.0 DATA BASE DESCRIPTION. *This section should provide all the information necessary to identify and describe the data base being documented. It should include various kinds of background information essential for proper utilization of the data base.*

2.1 Data Base Identification. This subsection should give the code name, tag, or label by which each data base may be uniquely identified. It should also provide descriptive information, whether or not it is implied in the identification code.

2.1.1 System Identification. This subsection should accurately and thoroughly identify the system of which the data base being documented is a part. The identification should include the full system name, system code name, tag or label, system model, modification, or version number. If more than one system uses this data base, each should be identified.

2.1.2 Effective Dates. This subsection should give the first and last dates of the period during which this data base may be used. It should also indicate whether the data base is complete or incomplete, pre- or post-system delivery to the customer, experimental or permanent, and whether it supersedes or will be superseded by another data base.

2.1.3 Storage Requirements. This subsection should contain the estimated internal and peripheral storage assignments for all of the programs and data of a system. In addition, it should contain information relevant to certain constraints and conditions under which the programs must operate.

2.1.4 Physical Description. This subsection should identify the physical characteristics of the master data base file(s) and any duplicate working copies. The identification should include the file media (i.e., disk, tape, etc.), form of the file (e.g., symbolic or binary), and the respective codes used.

2.2 Labeling/Tagging Conventions. This subsection should discuss the system labeling/tagging conventions to the extent necessary for the programmer to use the conventions as a practical working tool. For example, the conventions used to identify new versions of the data base should be specified.

2.3 Data Base Organization. This subsection should provide system implementers with a single, central source of major design considerations for the handling of the data base. The general file design and format and the rationale of the design should be given for each kind of file medium (i.e., tape, disk, etc.).

2.4 Special Instructions. This subsection should contain the instructions to be followed by all personnel who will contribute to the generation of the new data base and who will use it for both testing and operational purposes. The instructions should include

- Criteria for entering data into the data base
- Rules and procedures to be followed when submitting data for entry into the data base
- Identification of a data control unit, if applicable
- Formats for data description sheets and cards
- Machine run instructions for generating, modifying, updating, or otherwise using the data base files

2.5 Support Programs. This subsection should reference or, if required, discuss briefly the support programs directly related to the data base. Descriptions should include program name, functions, and major program operating considerations (e.g., operating time, hardware setup required, etc.).

2.6 Security. This subsection should contain an overview and discussion of the security considerations associated with the data of the overall system.

3.0 DATA DEFINITIONS. *This section should include thorough, detailed definitions and descriptions of all the data utilized by the system. The specific details of information required for each form of data may vary from system to system and will depend on the design characteristics of the operating system.*

3.1 Data Files. This subsection should describe the general, physical, and logical characteristics of each data file.

3.1.1 General Description. This sub-subsection should provide general information pertinent to each data file. The documentation should include

- Name and tag or label
- A brief statement of the purpose of the file and logical criteria used for its compilation
- The degree of sensitivity
- Conditions under which the file is modified or updated
- Restrictions and limitations on usage

3.1.2 Physical Characteristics. This sub-subsection should describe the physical characteristics of each data file. The documentation should include

- File content and format
- Forms of the contents (e.g., symbolic, binary, mixed, etc.)
- File control information used by programs (e.g., storage control items, directories, pointers, skip continue features, and end-of-file markers)
- A representative of the file structure including tables, records, entries, items, or other subelements of the file

3.1.3 Logical Characteristics. This sub-subsection should describe the logical characteristics of each data file. The documentation should include:

- Data element name
- Synonymous name
- Definition
- Format
- Range of values
- Unit of measurement
- Data item names, abbreviations, and codes

Any variations in either the inputs or outputs from the format or data items that will be used on the data base must be specifically identified.

3.2 Tables. This sub-subsection should provide an adequate table definition as applicable to the data base. The documentation should include

- Table tag or label
- Full name or purpose of the table
- Data file containing the table
- Program subsystem that uses this table
- Logical divisions within table (i.e., internal table blocks or parts − not entries)
- Basic table structure (fixed or variable length, fixed or variable entry structure)

3.3 Items. The word *item* refers to a specific category of detailed information that has a defined position within a table. This sub-subsection should define these items. The definitions should include

- Table tag or label
- Purpose of the item
- The degree of sensitivity of the item and whether it maintains a specific degree of sensitivity or changes under certain conditions (e.g., removal or introduction of data files or specific data)
- Table type in which it is found
- Position in table (i.e., word number and bit positions, level numbers, etc.)

- Item use (e.g., table control item, entry structure key item, string control item, data item, etc.)
- Item type (e.g., symbolic character, integer, fraction, mixed number, string, bead, status, etc.)
- Item coding (e.g., character code, binary or binary-coded decimal, scaling factor, etc.)
- Accessibility factor (e.g., coded to indicate machine instruction modifiers that can expedite retrieving and storing of the item)

3.4 Records and Entries. If the basic unit of the data file is a record or an entry, it should be defined to the same degree as tables. In addition, the documentation should include

- Full name and purpose
- An explanation of each item
- Maximum size
- Graphics representation

4.0 INTEGRATED DATA BASE. If the system will use an integrated data base, that integrated data base should be identified in this section. The discussion should include any impacts on the integrated data base of the data that are to be used in this system as described in Section 2.0. Such impacts may include recommended changes in the organization of the data in the integrated data base that would enhance system efficiency, the addition to the integrated data base of the new data elements needed for this system, etc. Recommendations concerning changes in existing support software may be included.

7.7 PROGRAM DOCUMENT CONTENT ALTERNATIVES

Various types of documents may be produced to present program development data. This chapter presents guidelines for the content development of the following document types that may result from programming functions:

- Program performance specification
- Program design specification
- Program description document
- Program package document

A suggested content arrangement and summary guidelines for developing the content of each of the above program documents are provided in this section.

7.7.1 Program Performance Specification

This document elaborates on the requirements specified during the requirements definition phase and the program specifications outlined during the internal design phase. The primary intent of the document is to guide the design of the computer programs and to provide management with a vehicle for monitoring program development and assessing if the computer programs have been satisfactorily completed.

The suggested content arrangement of the program performance specification document is shown in Figure 7-8.

```
┌─────────────────────────────────────────────────────────┐
│          PROGRAM PERFORMANCE SPECIFICATION              │
│                  TABLE OF CONTENTS                      │
│                                                         │
│  SECTION 1.0 GENERAL                                    │
│   1.1   Purpose                                         │
│   1.2   Scope                                           │
│   1.3   References                                      │
│  SECTION 2.0 SYSTEM DESCRIPTION                         │
│   2.1   Program Descriptions                            │
│   2.2   Equipment Descriptions                          │
│   2.3   Input/Output Utilization Table                 │
│   2.4   Interface Block Diagram                         │
│   2.5   Inter-system Program Interfaces                 │
│  SECTION 3.0 PROGRAM FUNCTIONS                          │
│   3.N    (Function N)                                   │
│   3.N.1     Inputs                                      │
│   3.N.2     Processing                                  │
│   3.N.3     Outputs                                     │
│   3.N.4     Special Requirements                        │
│  SECTION 4.0 TEST/VERIFICATION REQUIREMENTS            │
│   4.1   Test Requirements                               │
│   4.2   Acceptance Test Requirements                    │
└─────────────────────────────────────────────────────────┘
```

**Figure 7-8   Content Arrangement of a Program
Performance Specification**

Summary guidelines for developing the content of a program performance specification document are provided below and on the following pages.

1.0 GENERAL. *This section of the program performance specification contains document items that describe the purpose and scope of the program performance specification, and list the references applicable to the history and development of the project.*

1.1 Purpose. Describe the purpose, background, and intent of the program performance specification.

1.2 Scope Describe the scope and objectives of the program performance specification. Identify each program by the appropriate naming convention and briefly describe the major function(s) of each program.

1.3 References. List all documents which impact the performance requirements. This subsection should include, but not be limited to, the following:

- *Planning and Management Documents.* Identify all policies, standards, and guidelines that define the performance requirements.
- *Functional, Allocated, and Design Baseline Documents.* Identify the baseline documents that define the performance requirements.

2.0 SYSTEM DESCRIPTION. *This section of the program performance specification contains document items that describe the system and operating environment in which the programs will function, as well as design constraints and standards that must be adhered to in order to ensure proper program development and maintenance.*

2.1 Program Descriptions. Describe the system within which each program will operate. The role assigned to each program shall be defined in relation to the defined functions the system must perform.

2.2 Equipment Descriptions. Provide a detailed description of the relationships of the program with interfacing equipment. The documentation should include

- *Equipment Requirements.* Describe the requirements imposed on the program by each piece of interfacing equipment (e.g., displays, plotters, storage devices, etc.).
- *Equipment Options and Controls.* Briefly describe the equipment options and controls and how they relate to the specified program.

If no peripheral equipment is required other than the equipment that comprises the operating system configuration, this subsection is not applicable.

2.3 Input/Output Utilization Table. Summarize the I/O requirements placed on the computer programs by the system equipment. The requirements may be presented in tabular form. If no peripheral equipment is handled by the program, this subsection is not applicable.

2.4 Interface Block Diagram. Prepare a block diagram of the equipment-computer relationships to facilitate presentation of the material. If all peripheral equipment is handled by standard interface with the operating system, this subsection is not applicable.

2.5 Intersystem Program Interfaces. Describe the interfaces between each computer program and other programs of this or other systems. Include

- A statement of purpose for each interface
- Description of the data to be exchanged between the programs
- An estimate of the quantity of data to be transferred between the programs
- An estimate of the transfer rates per second

3.0 PROGRAM FUNCTIONS. *This section of the program performance specification contains document items that provide detailed textual, logical, and mathematical descriptions for each function performed by a computer program.*

3.N   Function N. Each subsection of Section 3.0 should provide details specific to a particular system function. Each function should be separately presented.

3.N.1 Inputs. This subsection shall contain detailed descriptions of the input data. The documentation should include

- An identification of the source of the data
- Estimates of the quantity of the data
- Timing requirements imposed on the data
- Data security requirements

3.N.2 Processing. Provide a textual and mathematical description of the processing requirements of the function. The documentation should include

- Requirements definitions relative to the operation(s) of the function
- Specifications that show the derived equations and explanations of the derivations
- A diagram showing the sequencing of processing events, timing requirements, and restrictions or limitations

3.N.3 Outputs. Provide a detailed description of all output data. The documentation should include

- The name of the output
- A description of the contents of each output
- A facsimile of each output

3.N.4 Special Requirements. Provide a detailed description of special data processing requirements. The documentation should include

- Instructions for preparing special formats to accommodate testing and simulation
- An identification of requirements for future expansion
- Special recovery requirements in case of program failure

4.0 TEST/VERIFICATION REQUIREMENTS. *This section of the program performance specification contains document items that specify the requirements for the levels of testing that must be performed (e.g., subprogram testing, program testing, acceptance testing, etc.).*

4.1 Test Requirements. Specify the requirements for performing each level of testing, except acceptance testing. The documentation should specify

- The tools and facilities required for each test level
- The required formulas and algorithms to be used for testing
- The tolerances allowable at each level of testing

4.2 Acceptance Test Requirements. Explicitly define those performance requirements which become a part of acceptance testing. The documentation should define

- The required capacities to be demonstrated
- The required accuracies to be demonstrated
- The limitations of the test environment

7.7.2 Program Design Specification

This document is based on the performance requirements defined in the program performance specification. The purpose of the program design specification is to document the program design structure and input/output processing functions to be performed.

The suggested content arrangement of a program design specification document is shown in Figure 7-9.

```
PROGRAM DESIGN SPECIFICATION
        TABLE OF CONTENTS
SECTION 1.0  GENERAL
1.1  Purpose
1.2  Scope
1.3  References
SECTION 2.0  SYSTEM REQUIREMENTS
2.1  Function Allocation
2.1.1  Input Functions
2.1.2  Output Functions
2.2  Storage Allocation
2.3  Processing Allocation
2.4  Functional Flow Diagram
2.5  Programming Guidelines
SECTION 3.0  QUALITY ASSURANCE
3.1  Peer Review Procedures
3.2  Periodic Review Procedures
3.3  Technical Review Procedures
3.4  Configuration Audit Procedures
```

Figure 7-9   Content Arrangement of a Program Design Specification

Summary guidelines for developing the content of a program design specification document are provided below and on the following pages.

1.0 GENERAL. *This section of the program design specification contains a summary description of the computer program design structure and input/output processing functions.*

1.1 Purpose. Describe the purpose and intent of the program design specification.

1.2 Scope. Describe the scope and objectives that are intended by the program design specification. Identify each program by the appropriate naming convention and briefly describe the major functions of each program.

1.3 References. List all documents which define or constrain the design requirements. This subsection should include, but not be limited to, the following:

- *Planning and Management Documents.* Identify all policies, standards, and guidelines affecting the development effort.

- *Functional Baseline Documents.* Identify the functional baseline documents that define the performance requirements.

2.0 SYSTEM REQUIREMENTS. *This section of the program design specification contains document items that describe the computer program design structure and processing functions.*

2.1 Function Allocation. This subsection should identify and describe the allocation of functions and tasks to be performed by the individual computer program modules.

2.1.1 Input Functions. Provide a general summary of the input functions to be performed for each subprogram, module, and subroutine. The documentation should

- List the subprogram designator
- Provide a list of input functions performed by the subprogram
- Identify the specific data required as input
- Define the interface source of each input to the subprogram

2.1.2 Output Functions. Provide a general summary of the output functions to be performed for each subprogram, module, and subroutine. The documentation should

- List the subprogram designator
- Provide a list of output functions performed by the subprogram
- Identify the specific data required as output
- Indicate why this output is required by the user

2.2 Storage Allocation. Describe the allocation of memory storage space. The documentation should describe

- The allocation of memory storage to subprograms or modules
- The allocation of memory storage to executive and interrupt routines
- The allocation of memory storage to common subroutines
- The allocation of memory storage to the common data base

2.3 Processing Allocation. Describe the allocation of processing time. The documentation should describe

- The processing allocations related to the timing
- The processing allocations related to sequencing
- Any equipment constraints that impact the peripheral processing allocations

2.4 Functional Flow Diagram. Show the general flow of program data and execution control. Provide a narrative description. If the program is designed to operate in more than one mode, each mode should be clearly distinguished in both the text and flow diagram(s).

2.5 Programming Guidelines. Specify the programming guidelines to be observed by the programmer(s) when producing the computer program. The documentation should

- Name the programming language and its supporting system (e.g., monitor, loader, debug, utilities, etc.)
- Reference the appropriate user's manuals and specifications for the language and system should be referenced

- State in concise terms the mnemonic labeling conventions to be observed

3.0 QUALITY ASSURANCE. *This section shall define the review procedures for verification of the computer program design.*

3.1 Peer Review Procedures. Define the procedures for conducting peer reviews to detect errors in the program design. The documentation should

- Describe the purpose and objective of program design peer reviews
- List the step-by-step procedure for conducting peer reviews
- Establish when program design peer reviews will be held
- Determine the duration of each program design review
- Identify the individuals responsible for conducting program design peer reviews

3.2 Periodic Review Procedures. Define the procedures for conducting periodic reviews to determine project status, discover problems, and inform the project team of the current project status. The documentation should

- Describe the purpose and objective of periodic reviews
- Define the scope of periodic reviews
- Establish when periodic reviews will be held
- Determine the duration of each periodic review
- Identify the individuals responsible for periodic reviews

3.3 Technical Review Procedures. Define the procedures for conducting technical reviews to ensure the technical quality and architectural consistency of the program design. The documentation should

- Describe the purpose and objective of technical reviews
- Define the scope of technical reviews
- Establish when technical reviews will be held
- Determine the duration of each technical review
- Identify the individuals responsible for conducting technical reviews

3.4 Configuration Audit Procedures. Define the configuration audit procedures for validating the program design. If configuration management (CM) guidelines have been established, the following documentation should be included:

- Procedures for verifying accuracy and validity
- Procedures for verifying data integrity
- Procedures for performance verification

7.7.3 Program Description Document

This document describes and completely defines the basic subprogram logic and program procedures for each application subprogram and for each system control subroutine. It is used by operational and maintenance personnel to diagnose troubles, design and implement system modifications, and introduce or add subprogram functions to the completed program.

The suggested content arrangement of a program description document is shown in Figure 7-10.

PROGRAM DESCRIPTION DOCUMENT
TABLE OF CONTENTS

SECTION 1.0 GENERAL
1.1 Purpose
1.2 Scope
1.3 References

SECTION 2.0 PROGRAM DESCRIPTION
2.1 Subprogram Detailed Description
2.2 Subprogram Data Design
2.2.1 Arrays
2.2.2 Variables
2.2.3 Constants
2.2.4 Flags
2.2.5 Indexes
2.2.6 Common Data Base References
2.3 Input Formats
2.4 Output Formats
2.5 Library Subroutines
2.6 Conditions for Initiation
2.7 Subprogram Limitations
2.8 Interfacing Description

Figure 7-10.   Content Arrangement of a Program
Description Document

Summary guidelines for developing the content of a program description document are provided below and on the following pages.

1.0   GENERAL. *This section of the program description document contains a summary description of the structure and functions of the subprograms.*

1.1   Purpose. Describe the purpose and intent of the program description document.

1.2   Scope. Describe the scope and objectives that are intended by the *Program Description Document*. Identify each subprogram by the appropriate naming convention and list the functions to be performed by each subprogram.

1.3   References. List all documents which define the performance and design requirements. This subsection should include, but not be limited to, the following:

- *Planning and Management Documents.* Identify all policies, standards, and guidelines that pertain to the development effort.
- *Baseline Documents.* Identify the functional baseline documents that define the performance and design requirements and the allocated baseline documents that establish the allocation of functions.

2.0   PROGRAM DESCRIPTION. *This section of the program description document contains document items that explain the structure and function of each subprogram.*

2.1 Subprogram Detailed Description. Describe the detailed design of each subprogram. The description should indicate the mnemonic tag that identifies the code segment in the subprogram listing. Each section of code in the subprogram listing should be described.

2.2   Subprogram Data Design. This subsection should contain a summary description of the subprogram data base.

2.2.1 Arrays. Describe the arrays used by each subprogram. The documentation should

- Indicate the title of the array and its mnemonic label
- State the use and attributes of each array
- Indicate the number of words for each array and describe the purpose of each index
- Define applicable scaling factors for each array (e.g., inches, feet, etc.
- Describe the range of values for each array
- Describe the meaning and purpose of each subfield

2.2.2 Variables. Describe each variable included in the subprogram data base. The documentation should

- Indicate the title of the variable with the mnemonic label in parentheses;
- State the use and attributes of each variable
- Define the applicable scaling factors for each variable (e.g., inches, feet, etc.)
- Indicate the number of bits and sign (if numeric) or number of characters (if alpha-numeric)
- Define the range of values for each variable
- Describe the meaning, purpose, and range of each subfield

2.2.3 Constants. Describe each constant included in the subprogram data base. The documentation should

- Indicate the title of the constant and its mnemonic label
- Briefly state the use and attributes of each constant
- Define the applicable scaling factors for each constant (e.g., inches, feet, etc.)
- Indicate the number of bits and sign (if numeric) or number of characters (if alpha-numeric)
- Describe the meaning, purpose, and range of each subfield

2.2.4 Flags. Describe each flag included in the subprogram data base. The documentation should

- Indicate the title of the flag and its mnemonic label
- Briefly state the use and status of each flag
- Specify the initial condition of the flag
- Describe the meaning, purpose, and range of each subfield within the computer word

2.2.5 Indexes. Describe each index included in the subprogram data base. The documentation should

- Indicate the title of the index and its mnemonic label
- Briefly state the use of each index

2.2.6 Common Data Base References. Provide a complete list of all references to local and common data base items. The listing should be cross-referenced to the data base specifications in the internal design document.

2.3 Input Formats. Graphically illustrate and describe each input message, card format, tape format, etc., processed by the subprogram. The documentation should

- Provide a facsimile of each input format
- Define the data elements of each input format

If the description concerns a common system subroutine, explain the input registers and provide any pertinent scaling and bit-position information.

2.4 Output Formats. Graphically illustrate and describe each output message, card format, tape format, etc., processed by the subprogram. The documentation should

- Provide a facsimile of each output format
- Define the data elements of each output format

If the description concerns a common system subroutine, explain the output registers and provide any pertinent scaling and bit-position information.

2.5 Library Subroutines. List, in alphabetical order, the library subroutines used by each subprogram. The documentation should

- Indicate the name of the subroutine and its mnemonic label
- Describe where use is made of each library subroutine
- Identify the location of the subroutine in the program
- Reference all the documents which define the subroutines (e.g., program performance and design specifications, etc.)

2.6 Conditions for Initiation. Identify system conditions that must be met for each subprogram to be initiated for processing. The documentation should

- Define the static conditions for initiating subprograms
- Explain the variable conditions for initiating subprograms
- If the conditions are based on certain value settings, define the required values

2.7 Subprogram Limitations. Summarize any known or anticipated limitations of each subprogram. The documentation should

- List all requirements that impact timing
- Explain the limitations of any algorithms and formulas
- Specify the design limits of the input and output data
- State the provisions for error checking

2.8 Interfacing Description. Graphically show the sequential and functional relationships of each subprogram with other subprograms and system subroutines with which it interfaces. The documentation should show

- The entry point of each subprogram interface
- Each interface input variable
- Each interface output variable

7.7.4 Program Package Document

This document consists of a processor program source listing; a source/object listing produced by an assembly or compilation of source code, a cross-reference listing produced by a compilation of the source; and any data which are necessary to cause programs to run properly (e.g., adaptation data, data file contents, setup data, program parameter values, etc.).

The suggested content arrangement of the program package document is shown in Figure 7-11.

```
PROGRAM PACKAGE DOCUMENT
TABLE OF CONTENTS

SECTION 1.0  GENERAL
1.1 Purpose
1.2 Scope
1.3 References

SECTION 2.0  PROGRAMS
2.1 Source Program
2.2 Object Program

SECTION 3.0  LISTINGS
3.1 Source Listing
3.2 Source/Object Listing
3.3 Cross-Reference Listing

SECTION 4.0  DATA BASE DESIGN SUMMARY
4.1 Record Layouts
4.2 Data Dictionary
4.3 Subprogram References

SECTION 5.0  SUBPROGRAM FLOWCHARTS
```

Figure 7-11 Content Arrangement of a Program Package Document

Summary guidelines for developing the content of a program package document are provided below and on the next page.

1.0 GENERAL. *This section of the program package document (PPD) briefly defines each of the required items in the processor program package.*

1.1 Purpose. Describe the purpose, background, and intent of the program package document.

1.2 Scope. Describe the scope and objective intended by the program package document.

1.3 References. List all those instructions, specifications, standards, and other documents applicable to the preparation of the PPD.

2.0 PROGRAMS. *This section of the program package document contains the complete source and object forms of the processor program suitable for assembly or compilation. The physical form may be card decks, disks, or magnetic tape.*

2.1 Source Program. Include the source form of the program with the package. The program should be in the standard machine readable format in which it will be maintained (i.e., disk, tape, punched card, etc.). In either case, the source program form must be compatible with production facility to which the program is delivered. For example card readers may differ in their interpretation of the physical punches on a card may differ in their interpretation of the physical punches on a card for certain alphanumeric symbols.

2.2 Object Program. This section of the program package document should include the complete object form of the processor program suitable for loading and execution in the operational digital processor. The object program shall be obtained from an assembly or compilation of the source processor program. The physical form of the object program should be cards, disks, or magnetic tape. In either instance, the object program tapes must be compatible to the production facility to which the program is delivered.

3.0 LISTINGS. *This section of the program package document should include a listing of the source and object programs as well as all cross-reference listings.*

3.1 Source Listing. Each compiler source statement should be annotated with comments. If the source contains any assembly-level code, then a comment should be listed for each assembly-level line or group of lines with not less than an average of one comment per five statements.

3.2 Source/Object Listing. This section of the program package document should contain a listing of the combined source statement and resulting objects machine instructions generated during an assembly or compilation of the delivered source programs. The source/object listing should be free from compiler-generated errors or warnings and should be an exact presentation of the delivered source and object program. If the supporting compiler or assembler system does not provide source/object listings, then the minimum requirement is the object listing.

3.3 Cross-Reference Listing. This section of the program package document should include a cross-reference table of each mnemonically labeled statement in the digital processor program and each statement in the processor program that references the labeled item. The table should be ordered alphabetically according to the mnemonic labels and generated as the result of an assembly or compile of the delivered source digital processor program.

4.0 DATA BASE DESIGN SUMMARY. *This section of the program package document should summarize the design specifications of the data base. It should provide a complete detailed description of all common data items necessary to carry out the functions of the computer program. The terminology employed in the data base design summary must conform to the programming guidelines.*

4.1 Record Layouts. Provide a detailed description of each category of data handled by the data base management system (DBMS). The documentation should

- Indicate the category name
- Indicate the minimum and maximum Record length in words
- Identify the source of the data
- Briefly state the purpose of the record
- Include any additional pertinent information about the record (e.g., relationship to other records)
- Define the word position for each field in the order it appears in the input record and label with mnemonic name
- Denote the data type codes and key field identifier if applicable

4.2 Data Dictionary. This section of the program package document should contain a detailed description of each data element in the data base. The documentation should

- Indicate the record name
- Indicate the minimum and maximum record length
- Indicate the number used to identify the record
- Note the full name of the element
- Note the input and output data type
- Indicate the number of words the field occupies in the record
- Provide all other pertinent information about the data element

4.3 Subprogram References. This section of the *Program Package Document* should include a complete list of all common data base items with a cross-reference which includes all referencing subprograms. The list may be presented in the form of a matrix.

5.0 SUBPROGRAM FLOWCHARTS. *This section of the program package document should include graphic representations of the subprogram process flows. The documentation should show procedural relationships, transfer of control, loops, decision points, and block structure.*

7.8 TEST DOCUMENT CONTENT ALTERNATIVES

This section presents guidelines for the content development of the following document types that may be produced during the testing phase of an automated data system:

- Test plan
- Test specification
- Test procedures
- Test report

7.8.1 Test Plan

This document defines the scope of the testing to be performed. The purpose of the test plan is to ensure that the technical requirements have been effectively met and that system integration is ensured.

The suggested content arrangement of a test plan is shown in Figure 7-12.

```
                    TEST PLAN
                TABLE OF CONTENTS


    SECTION 1.0 INTRODUCTION
    1.1    Purpose
    1.2    Scope
    1.3    References

    SECTION 2.0 UNIT TEST PLAN
    2.1    Task Responsibility Checklist
    2.2    Monitoring Methods
    2.3    Test Software Requirements
    2.4    Schedule
    2.5    Test Environment Requirements
    2.6    Test Cases
    2.6.N  Test N

    SECTION 3.0 MODULE INTEGRATION TEST PLAN
    3.1    Task Responsibility Checklist
    3.2    Monitoring Methods
    3.3    Test Software Requirements
    3.4    Schedule
    3.5    Test Environment Requirements
    3.6    Test Cases
    3.6.N  Test N

    SECTION 4.0 VERIFICATION TEST PLAN
    4.1    Task Responsibility Checklist
    4.2    Monitoring Methods
    4.3    Test Software Requirements
```

Figure 7-12. Content Arrangement of a Test Plan

```
┌─────────────────────────────────────────────────┐
│                   TEST PLAN                      │
│               TABLE OF CONTENTS                  │
│                                                  │
│  SECTION 4.0 VERIFICATION TEST PLAN (Continued)  │
│  4.4   Schedule                                  │
│  4.5   Test Environment Requirements             │
│  4.6   Test Cases                                │
│  4.6.N  Test N                                   │
│                                                  │
│  SECTION 5.0 ACCEPTANCE TEST PLAN                │
│  5.1   Task Responsibility Checklist             │
│  5.2   Monitoring Methods                        │
│  5.3   Test Software Requirements                │
│  5.4   Schedule                                  │
│  5.5   Test Environment Requirements             │
│  5.6   Test Cases                                │
│  5.6.N  Test N                                   │
│                                                  │
└─────────────────────────────────────────────────┘
```

Figure 7-12. Content Arrangement of a Test Plan (continued)

Summary guidelines for developing the content of a test plan document are provided below and on the following pages.

1.0 INTRODUCTION. *The Introduction of the test plan should state the purpose and scope of the document. It should identify all levels of testing required and reference all applicable standards and specifications for each level of testing.*

1.1 Purpose. Describe the purpose and intent of the test plan.

1.2 Scope. Describe the scope and objectives that are intended by the test plan. The documentation should

- Identify the levels of testing to be performed
- Define the methods of testing to be used at each test level
- Describe the system environments for each test level

1.3 References. List those specifications, standards, and all other documents related to the development of the test plan. The documentation should list each document title and the document control number assigned to each document and should identify the date of issue for each document.

2.0 UNIT TEST PLAN. *This section of the test plan provides the documentation required to perform tests aimed at compiling the unit and correcting errors indicated by the compiler. It also includes documentation needed to verify that each program branch, equation, and logic flow are properly executed.*

2.1 Task Responsibility Checklist. Define the tasks to be performed for unit testing, indicating the organizational/individual responsibilities for executing each task. The documentation should

- List the tasks to be executed to verify unit performance

- Identify the organization or individual responsible for performing each test step

2.2 Monitoring Methods. Define the methods to be used in monitoring the unit testing process. The documentation should

- Define the method to be employed in monitoring and controlling the execution of the unit tests
- Explain the method to be employed in monitoring and correcting unit test discrepancies
- Explain the methods to be used to validate test completion

2.3 Test Software Requirements. Define the software requirements for unit testing. The documentation should identify

- The data generators to be employed to conduct the unit testing
- The test drivers/environmental simulators to be used in conducting unit tests
- The analysis programs required for analyzing unit test results

2.4 Schedule. Provide a description of the sequence of the unit test activities, noting the test locations and start and complete dates. The documentation should

- Indicate the sequence number of each unit test step
- Provide a brief description of each test step
- Identify the location where unit testing will take place
- Indicate the scheduled start and complete dates of each test step

2.5 Test Environment Requirements. Define the test environment requirements for conducting unit tests. The documentation should identify:

- The hardware requirements for conducting unit tests
- The software requirements for conducting unit tests

2.6 Test Cases. This subsection should identify and separately describe each test case to be conducted during unit testing.

2.6.N Test N. Provide a description of the requirements to be verified by the unit test. The documentation should

- List the requirements to be verified by the unit test and reference the functional and allocated baseline documents that relate to the specified requirement
- Define the configuration required to perform the unit test
- Identify the software requirements for conducting the unit test

3.0 MODULE INTEGRATION TEST PLAN. *This section of the test plan provides the documentation for module integration testing. It includes documentation that establishes the procedures for verifying that program units properly interface with one another, that the modules have been properly coded, and that all logic paths operate as designed.*

3.1 Task Responsibility Checklist. Define the tasks to be performed for module integration testing, indicating the organizational/individual responsibilities for executing each task. The documentation should identify the following:

- The tasks to be executed to verify unit performance
- The organization or individual responsible for performing each test step

3.2 Monitoring Methods. Define the methods to be used in monitoring the module integration testing process. The documentation should define the following:

- The method to be employed in monitoring and controlling the execution of the module integration tests
- The method to be employed in monitoring and correcting module integration test discrepancies
- The methods to be employed in validating module integration test completion

3.3 Test Software Requirements. Define the software requirements for module integration testing. The documentation should identify the following:

- The data generators to be employed to conduct the module integration testing
- The test drivers/environmental simulators to be used in conducting module integration tests
- The analysis programs required for analyzing module integration test results

3.4 Schedule. Provide a description of the sequence of the module integration test activities, noting the test locations and start and complete dates. The documentation should include

- Sequence number of each module integration test step
- A brief description of each test step
- The location where module integration testing will take place
- The scheduled start and complete dates of each module integration test step

3.5 Test Environment Requirements. Define the test environment requirements for conducting module integration tests. The documentation should identify the following:

- The hardware requirements for conducting module integration tests
- The software requirements for conducting module integration tests

3.6 Test Cases. This subsection should identify and separately describe each test case or the module integration testing.

3.6.N Test N. Provide a description of the requirements to be verified by the module integration test. The documentation should include

- A list of the requirements to be verified by the module integration test;
- References to the functional and allocated baseline documents that relate to the specified requirement
- A description of the configuration required to perform the module integration test

- The software requirements for conducting the module integration test

4.0 VERIFICATION TEST PLAN. *This section of the test plan consists of document items that prescribe tests to be performed to demonstrate that the integrated software system satisfies the requirements specified in the functional and allocated baselines. The documentation includes correlations between specified requirements and the test plan activities.*

4.1 Task Responsibility Checklist. Define the tasks to be performed for verification testing, indicating the organizational/individual responsibilities for executing each task. The documentation should identify the following:

- The tasks to be executed to verify unit performance
- The organization or individual responsible for performing each test step

4.2 Monitoring Methods. Define the methods to be used in monitoring the verification testing process. The documentation should define the following:

- The method to be employed in monitoring and controlling the execution of the verification tests
- The method to be employed in monitoring and correcting verification test discrepancies
- The methods to be employed in validating verification test completion

4.3 Test Software Requirements. Define the software requirements for verification testing. The documentation should identify the following:

- The data generators to be employed to conduct the verification testing
- The test drivers and environmental simulators to be used in conducting verification tests
- The analysis programs required for analyzing verification test results

4.4 Schedule. Provide a description of the sequence of the verification test activities, noting the test locations and start and complete dates. The documentation should include

- The sequence number of each verification test step
- A brief description of each test step
- The location where verification testing will take place
- The scheduled start and complete dates of each verification test step

4.5 Test Environment Requirements. Define the test environment requirements for conducting verification tests. The documentation should identify the following:

- The hardware requirements for conducting verification tests
- The software requirements for conducting verification tests

4.6 Test Cases. This subsection should identify and separately describe each test case to be conducted during module integration testing.

4.6.N Test N. Provide a description of the requirements to be verified by the verification tests. The documentation should include

- A list of the requirements to be verified by the verification test
- References to the functional and allocated baseline documents that relate to the specified requirement
- A description of the configuration required to perform the verification test
- The software requirements for conducting the verification test

5.0 ACCEPTANCE TEST PLAN. *This section of the test plan contains document items that establish the approach for acceptance testing. The documentation reflects the user orientation of the same test cases used to conduct verification testing.*

5.1 Task Responsibility Checklist. Define the tasks to be performed for acceptance testing, indicating the organizational/individual responsibilities for executing each task. The documentation should identify the following:

- The tasks to be executed to verify unit performance
- The organization or individual responsible for performing each test step

5.2 Monitoring Methods. Define the methods to be used in monitoring the acceptance testing process. The documentation should define the following:

- The method to be employed in monitoring and controlling the execution of the acceptance tests
- The method to be employed in monitoring and correcting acceptance test discrepancies
- The methods to be employed in validating acceptance test completion

5.3 Test Software Requirements. Define the software requirements for acceptance testing. The documentation should identify the following:

- The data generators to be employed to conduct the testing
- The test drivers and environmental simulators to be used in conducting acceptance tests
- The programs required for analyzing acceptance test results

5.4 Schedule. Provide a description of the sequence of the acceptance test activities, noting the test locations and start and complete dates. The documentation should include

- The sequence number of each acceptance test step
- A brief description of each test step
- The location where acceptance testing will take place
- The scheduled start and complete dates of each acceptance test step

5.5 Test Environment Requirements. Define the test environment requirements for conducting acceptance tests. The documentation should identify the following:

- The hardware requirements for conducting the tests
- The software requirements for conducting acceptance tests

5.6 Test Cases. This section should identify and separately describe each test case to be conducted during acceptance testing.

5.6.N Test N. Provide a description of the requirements to be verified by the acceptance test. The documentation should include:

- a list of the requirements to be verified by the acceptance test;
- references to the functional and allocated baseline documents that relate to the specified requirement;
- a description of the configuration required to perform the acceptance test;
- the software requirements for conducting the acceptance test.

7.8.2 Test Specification

This document is derived from the corresponding system or program specifications. It establishes the test criteria and explains the test methods. A test specification should be included for each test identified in the test plan. The test specification is generally prepared before test procedures are developed.

The suggested content arrangement of a test specification is shown in Figure 7–13.

```
                    TEST SPECIFICATION
                    TABLE OF CONTENTS

SECTION 1.0  GENERAL
1.1 Purpose
1.2 Scope
1.3 References

SECTION 2.0  UNIT TEST SPECIFICATIONS
2.N  Unit Test Case N

SECTION 3.0  MODULE INTEGRATION TEST SPECIFICATIONS
3.N  Module Integration Test Case N

SECTION 4.0  VERIFICATION TEST SPECIFICATIONS
4.N  Verification Test Case N

SECTION 5.0  ACCEPTANCE TEST SPECIFICATIONS
5.N  Acceptance Test Case N
```

Figure 7-13. Content Arrangement of a Test Specification

Summary guidelines for developing the content of a test specification are provided below and on the following pages.

1.0 GENERAL. *This section of the test specification should state the purpose, scope, objective, and support requirements. It should provide sufficient information to clearly establish the basis for developing the test and evaluating its results.*

1.1 Purpose. Describe the purpose and intent of the test specification.

1.2 Scope. Describe the scope and objectives that are intended by the test specification. The documentation should identify the following:

- The levels of testing to be performed
- The methods of testing to be used at each test level

1.3 References. List those specifications, standards, and all other documents related to the development of the test specifications. The documentation should

- List each document title and the control number assigned to each document
- Indicate the date of issue for each document

2.0 UNIT TEST SPECIFICATIONS

This section of the test specification contains document items that identify the basis methods for conducting unit tests and establish criteria for evaluating the results of these tests.

2.N Unit Test Case N. Prepare a specification sheet for each test case specified in the test plan. The documentation should include

- The unit test case by name
- The test case number
- A description of the purpose of the test
- The number of iterations and the data combinations of each iteration
- The test components, file volumes, data types, operating considerations, and prerequisite test cases
- A brief description of the results of the test case
- A definition of the criteria for successful completion
- A description of any special methods used to validate unit test results

3.0 MODULE INTEGRATION TEST SPECIFICATIONS. *This section of the test specification contains document items that identify the basis methods for conducting module integration tests and establish criteria for evaluating the results of these tests.*

3.N Module Integration Test Case N. Prepare a specification sheet for each test case specified in the test plan. The documentation should include the following data:

- The test case name

- The test case number
- An explanation of the purpose of the test
- The number of iterations and the data combinations of each iteration
- An identification of the test components, file volumes, data types, operating considerations, and prerequisite integration test cases
- A brief description of the results of each test case
- A definition of the criteria for successful completion of each test
- A description of any special methods used to validate test results

4.0 VERIFICATION TEST SPECIFICATIONS. *This section of the test specification contains document items that identify the basis methods for conducting verification tests and establish criteria for evaluating the results of these tests.*

4.N Verification Test Case N. Prepare a specification sheet for each test case specified in the test plan. The documentation should

- Identify the unit test case by name
- Indicate the test case number
- Describe the purpose of the test
- Indicate the number of iterations and the data combinations of each iteration
- Identify the test components, file volumes, data types, operating considerations, and prerequisite verification test cases
- Briefly describe the results of the test case
- Define the criteria for successful completion
- Describe any special methods used to validate test results

5.0 ACCEPTANCE TEST SPECIFICATIONS. *This section of the test specification contains document items that identify the basis methods for conducting acceptance tests and establish criteria for evaluating the results of these tests.*

5.N Acceptance Test Case N. Prepare a specification sheet for each test case specified in the test plan. The documentation should

- Identify the unit test case by name
- Indicate the test case number
- Describe the purpose of the test
- Indicate the number of iterations and the data combinations of each iteration
- Identify the test components, file volumes, data types, operating considerations, and prerequisite acceptance test cases
- Briefly describe the results of the test case
- Define the criteria for successful completion
- Describe any special methods used to validate test results

7.8.3 Test Procedures

This document provides detailed instructions for test execution and evaluation of test results at each level of testing. The procedures are developed from the specifications contained in the test specifications document. The document should include test procedures for

- Unit testing
- Module integration testing
- Verification testing
- Acceptance testing

Procedures may be combined into one document or produced as separate documents for each level of testing. The test procedures procedures document, in any case, should also specify the specific test materials, input data, test routines, control and reporting, and hardware configuration requirements for each level of testing. The individuals and organizations responsible for applying the procedures should be identified.

The suggested content arrangement of a test procedures document is shown in Figure 7-14.

```
┌─────────────────────────────────────────────────┐
│              TEST PROCEDURES                     │
│              TABLE OF CONTENTS                   │
│                                                  │
│                                                  │
│   SECTION 1.0  GENERAL                           │
│   1.1 Purpose                                    │
│   1.2 Scope                                      │
│   1.3 References                                 │
│                                                  │
│   SECTION 2.0  UNIT TEST PROCEDURES              │
│   2.N Unit Test Case N                           │
│                                                  │
│   SECTION 3.0  MODULE INTEGRATION TEST PROCEDURES│
│   3.N Module Integration Test Case N             │
│                                                  │
│   SECTION 4.0  VERIFICATION TEST PROCEDURES      │
│   4.N Verification Test Case N                   │
│                                                  │
│   SECTION 5.0  ACCEPTANCE TEST PROCEDURES        │
│   5.N Acceptance Test Case N                     │
│                                                  │
└─────────────────────────────────────────────────┘
```

Figure 7-14. Contents of a Test Procedures Document

The summary guidelines for developing the content of a test procedures document are provided on the following pages.

1.0 GENERAL. *This section of the test procedures document should contain items that describe the purpose and use of the test procedures. It should explain the organization and structure of the procedures and any assumptions or constraints imposed on their usage.*

1.1 Purpose. Describe the purpose and intent of the test procedures.

1.2 Scope. Describe the scope and objectives that are intended by the test procedures document. The documentation should identify

- The levels of testing to be performed
- The methods of testing to be used at each test level
- The system environments for each test level

1.3 References. List those specifications, standards, and all other documents related to the development of the test procedures. The documentation should

- List each document title and the control number assigned to each document
- Identify the date of issue for each document

2.0 UNIT TEST PROCEDURES. *This section of the Test Procedures contains document items that define the procedures for conducting unit tests.*

2.N Unit Test Case N. Prepare a procedures analysis sheet for each test case specified in the test plan to verify the software unit meets the defined requirements. The documentation should

- Identify each test case by number
- Identify the program being tested by name
- Identify the test sequence or grouping series
- Briefly describe the procedures for unit test initialization
- List the test steps to be followed
- Briefly explain the procedures for terminating the test

3.0 MODULE INTEGRATION TEST PROCEDURES. *This section of the test procedures contains items that prescribe procedures for conducting module integration tests.*

3.N Module Integration Test Case N. Prepare a procedures analysis sheet for each test case specified in the test plan to verify that the units properly interface with the system modules. The documentation should

- Identify each test case by number
- Identify the program being tested by name
- Identify the test sequence or grouping series
- Briefly describe the procedures for test initialization
- List the test steps to be followed
- Briefly explain the procedures for terminating the test

4.0 VERIFICATION TEST PROCEDURES. *This section of the test procedures contains document items that prescribe procedures for conducting verification tests.*

4.N Verification Test Case N. Prepare a procedures analysis sheet for each test case specified in the test plan to verify that the units/modules function properly in the total software/hardware environment. The documentation should

- Identify each test case by number
- Identify the program or module being tested
- Identify the test sequence or grouping series
- Briefly describe the procedures for test initialization
- List the test steps to be followed
- Briefly explain the procedures for terminating the test

5.0 ACCEPTANCE TEST PROCEDURES. *This section of the test procedures document contains items that prescribe procedures for conducting acceptance tests.*

5.N Acceptance Test Case N. Prepare a procedures analysis sheet for each test case specified in the test plan to verify that the software performs properly in the operational environment. The documentation should

- Identify each test case by number
- Identify the program or module being tested
- Identify test sequence or grouping series
- Briefly describe the procedures for test initialization
- List the test steps to be followed
- Briefly explain the procedures for terminating the test

7.8.4 Test Report

This document defines and evaluates discrepancies between the intended system or program design and the program capability as produced in code. The documentation contained in the test describes the purpose and nature of the test, details deviations from the test specification or test procedures, and recommends changes to previous documentation. A test report should be prepared for each of the following stages of testing.

- Unit testing
- Module integration testing
- Verification testing
- Acceptance testing

The suggested content arrangement of a test report is shown in Figure 7-15.

```
┌─────────────────────────────────────────────────────┐
│                    TEST REPORT                        │
│                 TABLE OF CONTENTS                      │
│                                                       │
│  SECTION 1.0  INTRODUCTION                            │
│  1.1  Purpose                                         │
│  1.2  Scope                                           │
│  1.3  References                                      │
│                                                       │
│  SECTION 2.0  UNIT TEST REPORT                        │
│  2.1  Test Analysis                                   │
│  2.2  Test Summary                                    │
│                                                       │
│  SECTION 3.0  MODULE INTEGRATION TEST REPORT          │
│  3.1  Test Analysis                                   │
│  3.2  Test Summary                                    │
│                                                       │
│  SECTION 4.0  VERIFICATION TEST REPORT                │
│  4.1  Test Analysis                                   │
│  4.2  Test Summary                                    │
│                                                       │
│  SECTION 5.0  ACCEPTANCE TEST REPORT                  │
│  5.1  Test Analysis                                   │
│  5.2  Test Summary                                    │
│                                                       │
│  SECTION 6.0  RECOMMENDATIONS                         │
│                                                       │
└─────────────────────────────────────────────────────┘
```

Figure 7-15. Content of a Test Report

The summary guidelines for developing the content of a test report are provided below and on the following pages.

1.0 INTRODUCTION. *This section of the test report should contain document items that describe the purpose and nature of the testing. It should explain any deviations from test specifications or test procedures required in the complete performance of the test and their impact on the validity of the test results.*

1.1 Purpose. Describe the purpose and intent of the test report.

1.2 Scope. Describe the scope and objectives that are intended by the test report. The documentation should identify

- The levels of testing reported
- The methods of testing used at each test level
- The system environments for each test level

1.3 References. List those specifications, standards, and all other documents that relate to the testing process. The documentation should

- List each document title and identify the control number assigned to the document
- Identify the date of issue for each document

2.0 UNIT TEST REPORT. *This section of the test report should present the results of the unit test activities. The documentation should include test analyses of each test performed and a summary of the overall test process.*

2.1 Test Analysis. Present a brief analysis of each test performed during the unit test activity. The documentation should

- Identify the test case by name and number
- Analyze the performance of the program module as tested compared to the criteria for successful completion as defined in the test plan

2.2 Test Summary. Summarize the results of the complete unit test process. The documentation should

- Summarize the capabilities demonstrated by the program module
- Identify any deficiencies uncovered during the unit test
- Summarize suggested refinements to improve the performance of the system/program module and reference the impact such refinements would have on the design specifications

3.0 MODULE INTEGRATION TEST REPORT. *This section of the test report should present the results of the module integration test activities. The documentation should include test analyses of each test performed and a summary of the overall test process.*

3.1 Test Analysis. Present a brief analysis of each test performed during the module integration test activity. The documentation should

- Identify the test case by name and number
- Analyze the performance of the system as tested compared to the criteria for successful completion as defined in the test plan

3.2 Test Summary. Summarize the results of the complete module integration test process. The documentation should

- Summarize the capabilities demonstrated by the integrated system modules
- Identify any deficiencies uncovered during the integration test
- Summarize suggested refinements to improve the performance of the program modules and reference the impact such refinements would have on the design specifications

4.0 VERIFICATION TEST REPORT. *This section of the test report should present the results of the verification test activities. The documentation should include test analyses of each test performed and a summary of the overall test process.*

4.1 Test Analysis. Present a brief analysis of each test performed during the verification test activity. The documentation should

- Identify the test case by name and number
- Analyze the performance of the system as tested compared to the criteria for successful completion as defined in the test plan

4.2 Test Summary. Summarize the results of the complete verification test process. The documentation should

- Summarize the capabilities demonstrated by the system
- Identify any deficiencies uncovered during the verification test
- Summarize suggested refinements to improve the performance of the system and reference the impact such refinements would have on the design specifications

5.0 ACCEPTANCE TEST REPORT. *This section of the test report should present the results of the acceptance test activities. The documentation should include test analyses of each test performed and a summary of the overall test process.*

5.1 Test Analysis. Present a brief analysis of each test performed during the acceptance test activity. The documentation should

- Identify the test case by name and number
- Analyze the performance of the system as tested compared to the criteria for successful completion as defined in the test plan

5.2 Test Summary. Summarize the results of the complete acceptance test process. The documentation should

- Summarize the capabilities demonstrated by the system
- Identify any deficiencies uncovered during the acceptance test
- Summarize suggested refinements to improve the performance of the system and reference the impact such refinements would have on the design specifications

6.0 RECOMMENDATIONS. *This section should itemize recommendations as to the improvements that can be realized in design and operation, based on the test results. It should summarize the recommendations incorporated in the summaries of each test level, indicating those recommendations already implemented.*

7.9 IMPLEMENTATION DOCUMENT CONTENT ALTERNATIVES

This section presents guidelines for the content development of the following implementation document types that may be produced to facilitate the implementation of a computer system:

- Conversion document
- Implementation procedures
- Users manual
- Operations manual

A suggested content arrangement for each document type and summary guidelines for the development of their content follow.

7.9.1 Conversion Document

This document defines those tasks that are required to place the system into an operable mode. The suggested content arrangement of a conversion document (CD) is shown in Figure 7-16.

```
┌─────────────────────────────────────────────────┐
│              CONVERSION DOCUMENT                 │
│              TABLE OF CONTENTS                   │
│                                                  │
│                                                  │
│   SECTION 1.0  CONVERSION PLAN                   │
│   1.1 Conversion Plan Update                     │
│   1.2 Conversion Plan Checklist                  │
│                                                  │
│   SECTION 2.0  CONVERSION REQUIREMENTS           │
│   2.1 Resources                                  │
│   2.2 Organization                               │
│   2.3 Hardware                                    │
│                                                  │
│   SECTION 3.0  FILE CONVERSION and DATA ENTRY    │
│   3.1 File Conversion                            │
│   3.1.1  Creating New Files                      │
│   3.1.2  Updating Existing Files                 │
│                                                  │
│   SECTION 4.0  TRAINING REQUIREMENTS             │
│   4.1 EDP Personnel                              │
│   4.2 User Personnel                             │
│                                                  │
│   SECTION 5.0  SYSTEM TURNOVER                   │
│   5.1 Task/Schedule Summary                      │
│                                                  │
└─────────────────────────────────────────────────┘
```

Figure 7-16. Content Arrangement of a Conversion Document

Summary guidelines for developing the content of a conversion document are provided below and on the following pages:

1.0 CONVERSION PLAN. *This section of the CD contains document items that update the conversion plans that were defined during the internal design phase. It also includes a checklist of all activities that must be considered in system conversion.*

1.1 Conversion Plan Update. Update the conversion plan presented in the internal design (ID) phase end-document.

1.2 Conversion Plan Checklist. Prepare a checklist of all activities that must be considered in system conversion. The documentation should include the following:

1. *Activity.* List in sequential order each activity to be performed in the conversion process. The checklist should include program requirements, computer processing resource require-

ments, workload estimates and processing schedules, forms and procedures, manual support requirements, balancing and control functions, special testing requirements, and maintenance requirements.

2. *Date Started.* Indicate the projected start date for each activity.

3. *Date Complete.* Indicate the expected completion date for each activity.

2.0 CONVERSION REQUIREMENTS. *This section of the CD defines the user commitments relative to resources and describes the organizational revisions associated with the new system. It also confirms and/or updates the hardware requirements for conversion that were previously defined in the internal design document.*

2.1 Resources. The budgetary and personnel schedule data are combined to reflect the resource requirements. These data are then presented in this subsection. The various tasks are identified, and estimates of time and costs are projected. The documentation should include data pertaining to the following:

1. *Data Purification.* Summarize the data purification requirements for conversion.

2. *Input Preparation.* Summarize the input preparation requirements for conversion.

3. *File Balancing.* Summarize the file-balancing requirements for conversion.

4. *Other.* Summarize any other requirements for conversion.

2.2 Organization. The revisions required in the organizational structure prior to implementation are documented and presented in this subsection. The areas of documentation concern are

1. *Staff Reductions.* Discuss any reductions in the present staff that can take place after conversion.

2. *Staff Additions.* List additional staff that may be required for conversion and initial implementation (e.g., data entry personnel).

3. *Adjustments.* Explain any adjustments that must be made to the mix of capabilities within user areas.

4. *Contingencies.* Summarize any contingency plans prepared so that the organization can cope with unexpected problems that arise during implementation.

2.3 Hardware. This subsection should provide instructions for modifying the current equipment configuration. The presentation should include instructions for site preparation and schedules for installation. Include

1. *Changes/Updates.* Indicate any changes or reconfirm the hardware requirements specified in the requirements definition and design documents.

2. *Site Preparation.* Indicate changes and adjustments relative to site preparation that impact computer run-time requirements or the need for mass storage (e.g., physical space, security controls, air-conditioning, and furniture).

3. *Schedule*. Show the schedule for acquisition of equipment that has not yet been installed (e.g., the acquisition of new disk drives, disk packs, or tapes).

3.0 FILE CONVERSION AND DATA ENTRY

This section of the CD contains document items that review the approach to converting and controlling new and existing files.

3.1 File Conversion. This subsection should identify all file conversion requirements.

3.1.1 Creating New Files. This subsection should contain data that provides guidance for the generation of new files. It should detail the size, position, and source of each data element to be entered in the file. The data may be presented in either a narrative or a checklist form. Include procedures for ensuring file integrity and identify any data discrepancies.

3.1.2 Updating Existing Files. Explain, in narrative or checklist form, the procedures that must be followed for updating and controlling the conversion of existing files. Include procedures for ensuring file integrity and identifying data discrepancies.

4.0 TRAINING REQUIREMENTS. *This section of the CD contains document items that outline the training strategies for training both user and EDP personnel.*

4.1 EDP Personnel. The training strategies for training EDP personnel should be outlined in this section. The following training requirements should be addressed:

1. *Manuals*. List the manuals required for training EDP personnel.

2. *Classroom*. Provide a schedule for classroom instructions, if applicable, and orientation sessions to be considered.

3. *On-the-Job Training*. Summarize any plans that have been developed for on-the-job training.

4.2 User Personnel. This subsection should summarize the user training requirements. The following should be addressed:

1. *Training Materials*. Describe the requirements for training materials. Specify the materials required for each user area (e.g., data preparation, data entry, report usage, etc.).

2. *Personnel*. Identify the personnel to be trained. Describe any orientation programs developed for new personnel.

3. *Techniques*. Define the techniques to be used for user training (e.g., overhead transparencies, practice time, etc.).

4. *Schedules*. Show the schedules that have been determined for user training.

5. *Staffing*. Note the staffing assignments for conducting training sessions.

5.0 SYSTEM TURNOVER. *This section of the CD contains document items that summarize the tasks and schedules for system turnover.*

5.1 Task/Schedule Summary. This subsection should present the planned tasks and schedules for transferring the system from the development team to operations. Include all tasks associated with system verification testing and plans for resolving system problems as they are detected.

7.9.2 Batch System User Guide

In a batch processing environment, jobs are planned and organized into a job stream well in advance of actual processing. Transactions are collected, grouped by application, and processed at a scheduled time and in a scheduled sequence. A batch processing user guide should describe all the batch functions of the system.

The suggested content arrangement of a batch system user guide is shown in Figure 7-17.

```
          BATCH SYSTEM USER GUIDE
             TABLE OF CONTENTS


SECTION 1.0  GENERAL
1.1 Purpose of the User Guide
1.2 Terms and Abbreviations

SECTION 2.0  SYSTEM SUMMARY
2.1 System Application
2.2 General Description of Inputs, Processing, and Outputs

SECTION 3.0  I/O REQUIREMENTS
3.1 Screens
3.2 Input Documents
3.3 Reports
```

Figure 7-17. Content of a Batch System User Guide

Summary guidelines for developing the content of a batch system user guide are provided below and on the following pages.

1.0 GENERAL. *This section of the batch system user guide contains document items that explain the purpose of the user guide and the terms and abbreviations that are subject to interpretation by the user of the document.*

1.1 Purpose of the User Guide. This subsection should describe the purpose of the users guide in the following words, modified when appropriate:

"The objective of the user guide for (project name) (project number) is to provide the user personnel with the information necessary to effectively use the system."

1.2 Terms and Abbreviations. This subsection should provide a list of terms, definitions, or acronyms unique to this document or subject to interpretation by the user of the document. This list should not include item names or data codes.

2.0 SYSTEM SUMMARY. *This section of the batch system user guide contains document items that summarize the system application and provides a general description of the system's inputs, outputs, and processing functions.*

2.1 System Application. The uses of the software system in supporting the activities of the user's staff should be stated and explained in this subsection. The description should include

- The purpose, reason, or rationale of the system
- Capabilities and operating improvements provided by the system
- Additional features, characteristics, and advantages considered appropriate in furnishing a clear, general description of the system and the benefits derived from it
- Functions performed by the system, such as preprocessing or postprocessing data files

2.2 General Description of Inputs, Processing, and Outputs. This subsection should present a general narrative description of the inputs, the flow of data through the processing cycle, and the resultant outputs. The descriptions should include the following data:

1. *Input.* Use standard flowchart symbols to represent documents, files, etc., used as inputs to the system. Label the items to facilitate readability.
2. *Process.* Describe the relationship of the input to the output, with a general description of the flow of data through the processing cycle.
3. *Output.* Use standard flowchart symbols to represent reports, files, etc., which are generated as outputs from the system. Label the items to facilitate readability.

3.0 I/O REQUIREMENTS. *This section of the batch system user guide contains document items that define the user interaction with the system screens, input documents, and reports.*

3.1 Screens. A display screen that serves a specific input/output function should be shown in this subsection, along with instructions for user interaction with the display. The documentation should include

1. *Display Content.* Mount a facsimile or a reduced photocopy of the display in this space.
2. *User Interaction with Display.* Give step-by-step instructions for the user interaction with the display.

3.2 Input Documents. This subsection should show each input document. It should include

2. *Input Content.* Explain each item referenced.

3.3 Reports. This subsection should show each report to be generated by the system and explain its contents. The documentation should include

1. *Output Sample.* Mount a sample of the report in this space. Use a reduction of the report if necessary. Reference specific items with a bubbled number.

2. *Output Content.* Explain each item referenced.

7.9.3 On-Line System User Guide

Data processed in an on-line data base/direct access environment must satisfy processing requirements greater than those of specific applications. Therefore, unlike in batch systems, job planning and scheduling are not the primary concerns of the user because job requests arrive randomly and are processed according to the priority accompanying the request. The user involvement in an on-line processing system depends, to a large extent, on the type of system implemented.

The suggested content arrangement of an on-line system user guide is shown in Figure 7-18.

```
┌─────────────────────────────────────────────────────┐
│            ON-LINE SYSTEM USER GUIDE                 │
│               TABLE OF CONTENTS                      │
│                                                      │
│   SECTION 1.0  GENERAL                               │
│   1.1 Purpose of the User Guide                      │
│   1.2 Project References                             │
│   1.3 Terms and Abbreviations                        │
│   SECTION 2.0  SYSTEM SUMMARY                        │
│   2.1 System Application                             │
│   2.2 System Operation                               │
│   2.3 System Configuration                           │
│   2.4 System Performance                             │
│   SECTION 3.0  I/O REQUIREMENTS                      │
│   3.1 Terminal Operation                             │
│   3.2 Sign-On/Sign-Off Procedures                    │
│   3.3 Security Procedures                            │
│   3.4 Menus                                          │
│   SECTION 4.0  QUERY/UPDATE PROCEDURES               │
│   4.1 Query Procedures                               │
│   4.1.1   Scenarios                                  │
│   4.1.2   Inquiry Function                           │
│   4.1.3   Inquiry Screen                             │
│   4.1.4   Codes                                      │
│   4.2 Update Procedures                              │
│   4.2.1   Update Menu                                │
│   4.2.2   Update Function                            │
└─────────────────────────────────────────────────────┘
```

Figure 7-18. Content Arrangement of an On-Line System User Guide

Summary guidelines for developing the content of an on-line system user guide are provided below and on the following pages.

1.0 GENERAL. *This section of the on-line system user guide contains document items that explain the purpose of the user guide and the terms and references that are subject to interpretation by the user of the document.*

1.1 Purpose of the User Guide. This subsection describes the purpose of the user guide.

1.2 Project References. This section provides references applicable to the history and development of the project.

1.3 Terms and Abbreviations. This subsection provides a list of terms, definitions, or acronyms unique to this document and subject to interpretation by the user of the document. The list does not include item names or data codes.

2.0 SYSTEM SUMMARY. *This section of the on-line system user guide describes the system application, operation, configuration, and performance characteristics.*

2.1 System Application. This subsection describes the uses of the system in supporting user activities. The documentation describes the

- Purpose of the system
- Operating improvements provided by the system
- System benefits
- Functions performed by the system

2.2 System Operation. This subsection explains the relationships of the system functions with the organizations that are sources of input to the system and those that are recipients from it. The documentation includes

- A graphic representation showing the who, what, and where of the I/O functions
- A brief narrative description of the purpose and characteristics of each I/O function
- The personnel responsible for performing the I/O functions

2.3 System Configuration. This subsection provides a narrative description of the system configuration. The documentation includes descriptions of

- The system computer used to accept, process, and output data in the required format
- The software or composite of all routines and programs necessary to operate the system
- The terminals which will accept user input or inquires and produce or display system output
- The communication network which links the terminals to the computer
- The database files

2.4 System Performance. This subsection describes the performance capabilities of the system and explains how these capabilities serve user needs. The documentation includes descriptions of

- The type, volumes, and rates of inputs and outputs
- The response time
- The input limitations
- The system capabilities for detecting errors
- The processing times
- The flexibility and reliability of the system

3.0 I/O REQUIREMENTS. *This section of the on-line system user guide describes the terminal operation, provides instructions for sign-on and sign-off, outlines security procedures, and identifies each menu of the system.*

3.1 Terminal Operation. This subsection provides a clear, complete description of how the system terminal works and how to use it. The documentation includes explanations of

- The controls and indicators on the display station
- The keyboard functions
- Error messages and status line displays
- Problem analysis and correction procedures

3.2 Sign-on/Sign-off Procedures. This subsection provides step-by-step instructions for signing on and signing off the system. The documentation includes a list of user responses for each system message that appears on the terminal screen.

3.3 Security Procedures. This subsection describes the security functions and procedures for access to the system. The documentation includes

- Password controls
- Procedural differences for inquiry versus updates
- Abnormal termination and system failure procedures
- Accounting controls
- Audit trails

3.4 Menus. This subsection describes each menu of the system. It details the procedures for accessing the menu and the user interactions with the menu. Each option is explained as are the PF key functions available from the menu. All error messages likely to occur when the menu is displayed are described and the appropriate user action is detailed.

4.0 QUERY/UPDATE PROCEDURES. *This section provides procedures querying and updating the data base.*

4.1 Query Procedures. This subsection should detail the procedures for creating and executing queries against the system data.

4.1.1 Scenarios. This subsection presents case studies that illustrate common activities performed within the system. Each scenario provides step-by-step procedures for accomplishing the various activities.

4.1.2 Inquiry Function. This subsection provides the step-by-step procedures for querying the system data files. The documentation for each inquiry function explains

- The purpose of the inquiry function
- The procedures for reaching the inquiry screen
- The procedures for querying the system for the particular data being sought

4.1.3 Inquiry Screen. This subsection presents a facsimile of the screen associated with the inquiry function of the previous subsection. The screen facsimile includes descriptions of each field within the display.

4.1.4 Codes. This subsection explains all codes used within the query procedures. Codes are grouped according to the associated inquiry functions and are presented in tabular form with the code explanations adjacent to the codes.

4.2 Update Procedures. This subsection should detail the procedures for updating the data base records.

4.2.1 Update Menu. This subsection describes each menu used within the update procedures. It details the procedures for accessing the menu and the user interactions with the menu. Each menu option is explained as is each PF key function available from the menu. All error messages likely to occur when the menu is displayed are described and the appropriate user action is detailed.

4.2.2 Update Function. This subsection details the update procedures for each function that can be updated by the system. It presents the procedures in a step-by-step fashion illustrating the steps with the update screens associated with each step. Each field the user may update is described and the valid data types are detailed.

7.9.4 Operations Guide

This document should contain precise and detailed information on the control requirements and operating procedures necessary to successfully initiate, run, and terminate the system. The document items contained in an operations guide, therefore, should be designed to explain the functions of the system and the relationsips among the system elements to facilitate error correction and recovery in the computer operations area. If the system operates with on-line elements, the files required and the communications monitor requirements. The operations guide is, in essence, a user guide for the computer operations organization. It is formatted as a functionally oriented user guide.

The suggested content arrangement of an operations guide is shown in Figure 7-19.

```
┌─────────────────────────────────────────────────────┐
│                    OPERATIONS GUIDE                   │
│                    TABLE OF CONTENTS                  │
│                                                       │
│  SECTION 1.0  GENERAL                                 │
│  1.1 Purpose of the Operations Guide                  │
│  1.2 Project References                               │
│  1.3 Terms and Abbreviations                          │
│                                                       │
│  SECTION 2.0  SYSTEM OVERVIEW                          │
│  2.1 System Application                               │
│  2.2 System Schematic                                 │
│  2.3 Program Index                                    │
│  2.4 File Index                                       │
│  2.5 Security and Privacy                             │
│                                                       │
│  SECTION 3.0  RUN DESCRIPTIONS                         │
│  3.1 Job Setup                                        │
│  3.2 Job Step Instructions                            │
│  3.3 Job Outputs                                      │
│  3.3.1   Output Descriptions                          │
│  3.3.2   Output Distribution                          │
│  3.4 Job Halts and Messages                           │
│  3.5 Aborts and Restart Procedures                    │
│                                                       │
│  SECTION 4.0  BACKUP/RECOVERY                          │
│  4.1 System Backup                                    │
│  4.2 File Retention                                   │
│                                                       │
└─────────────────────────────────────────────────────┘
```

Figure 7-19. Content Arrangement of an Operations Guide

Summary guidelines for developing the content of an operations guide are provided below and on the following pages.

1.0 GENERAL

This section of the operations guide contains document items that explain the purpose of the operations guide and the terms and abbreviations that are subject to interpretation by the users of the document.

1.1 Purpose of the operations guide. This subsection should describe the purpose of the Operations Guide in the following words, modified when appropriate:

"The objective of the operations guide for (project name) (project number) is to provide computer control and computer operator personnel with a detailed operational description of the system and associated environment with which they will be concerned during the performance of their duties."

1.2 Project References. This subsection should provide a list of documents applicable to the system. The following data should be included:

1. *Reference Number.* Enter the number of the item referenced.

2. *Title.* Enter the title of the item referenced.

3. *Source/Author.* Note the source or author of the item referenced.

4. *Security Classification.* Indicate the classification status of the items referenced (i.e., confidential, proprietary, etc.).

1.3 Terms and Abbreviations. This section should include a listing of terms, definitions, or acronyms unique to the operations guide and subject to interpretation by the user of this document. The presentation should include

1. *Terminology.* List the terms requiring interpretation in alphabetical order.

2. *Explanation.* Define or explain the items listed in the "Terminology."

2.0 SYSTEM OVERVIEW

This section of the operations guide explains the system applications and presents a system schematic. It also includes indexes of programs and files and outlines the security and privacy considerations.

2.1 System Application. This subsection should explain the uses of the system in supporting the activities of the user's staff. It should include descriptions of

- The purpose of the system
- The functions performed by the system, such as maintenance of data files

2.2 System Schematic. A system schematic should be presented in this subsection. The schematic should show how the different operations are interrelated. If sets of runs are grouped by periods of time cycles, then each set of integrated operations required on a daily, weekly, etc., basis should be presented. If runs may be grouped logically by organizational level, the groups of runs that can be performed by each organizational level (e.g., headquarters processing, field activity processing, etc.) should be presented.

2.3 Program Index. An inventory of the various programs used in the operation of the system should be prepared and presented in this subsection. The data should include the program name and number; the language in which it is written; the name of the procedure, if applicable, used to run the program; and all files used by the program.

2.4 File Index. A list of all permanent files that are referenced, created, or updated by the system should be included in this section. The documentation should include the file label name, the name of the file as used in programs, the file organization, record length, and the programs that use the file.

2.5 Security and Privacy. This subsection should describe the operations requirements for security and privacy. Include information related to

1. *System Security.* Explain the system security functions and the purpose of the security.

2. *Environmental Requirements.* Identify the environmental requirements for the system operation.

3. *Data Requirements.* Identify the data requirements for the system operations (e.g., data files required, tapes to be mounted etc.).

3.0 RUN DESCRIPTIONS. *This section of the operations guide provides step-by-step instructions for running each job within the system. Specific documentation items include job setup and job step instructions, output descriptions and distribution requirements, descriptions of job halts and messages, and abort and restart procedures.*

3.1 Job Setup. This subsection should provide information necessary to set-up and run the job. It should include information pertaining to

1. *Run Frequency.* Show the frequency with which the job is run.

2. *Estimated Time.* Note the time estimated to run the job.

3. *Job Is Run on.* Enter the day of the week the job is normally run.

4. *Batch/On-line.* Indicate how the job is intiated.

5 *Job Setup.* Provide the data set/file name, label, ID no., I/O, media, source, and location for each data set/file required to run the job.

6. *Special Instructions.* Define any special instructions that may apply to the jobstream.

7. *Run Diagram.* Describe the job-stream in flowchart form, showing the job steps.

3.2 Job Step Instructions. This subsection should provide step-by-step instructions for running the job. The documentation should include

1. *Display.* Mount a facsimile of the display screen with which the operator must interact.

2. *Job Steps.* For each job step, indicate the job step number, show the console message associated with that step, and explain the operator action required.

3.3 Job Outputs. This section should describe each output of the system and provide distribution requirements for those outputs.

3.3.1 Output Descriptions. This subsection should provide the operator with a description of each output generated by the system. The documentation should include

1. *Output Name.* Enter the name of the output.

2. *Output Number.* If the output is a report, enter the report number.

3. *Forms.* Indicate the preprinted-form requirements.

4. *Output Queue.* Note any special output queue requirements.

5. *Number of Copies.* Show the number of copies required.

6. *Special Instructions.* Provide any special instructions that pertain to job outputs (e.g., timing requirements, accuracy requirements, etc.).

3.3.2 Output Distribution. This subsection should show the distribution of all outputs. The following should be included:

1. *Output Number.* Enter the output number.
2. *Output Name.* Enter the name of the output.
3. *Copy Number.* Indicate the copy number.
4. *Department Name/Recipient Name.* Enter the name of the department or recipient, for example, purchasing department, accounts receivable, and/or receiving.
5. *Mail Stop.* Show the mail stop of the department and/or recipient.

3.4 Job Halts and Messages. This section should summarize the messages that may occur during the running of the job. Data should include

1. *Message Number and Type.* Enter the number that identifies the message and the message type (e.g., fatal, warning, etc.).
2. *Message Text.* Enter the exact text of the message.
3. *Required Action.* State the action that must be taken by the operator when the message appears.

3.5 Aborts and Restart Procedures. This subsection should provide information concerning aborts and restart procedures that the personnel may follow in the event of a system failure. The documentation should include data pertaining to

1. *User Aborts.* Show the user code, cause, and response requirements for each user abort.
2. *Restart Procedures.* Provide step-by-step procedures for system restart.

4.0 BACKUP/RECOVERY. *This section of the operations guide details system backup and recovery procedures and defines the file retention requirements for backup data.*

4.1 System Backup. This subsection should define the backup procedures in the event of system failure. It should include the following data:

1. *Primary Backup.* Identify the location of primary backup sites, name of person in charge, and telephone number; list the hardware and software differences at the backup site that may require making modifications; and describe the logistics of transferring data from the operating center to the backup site.
2. *Secondary Backup.* (Provide same information as given for primary backup.)

4.2 File Retention. This subsection should provide instructions for the retention of all system files. Include the following data:

1. *File Name.* List by name each file used by the system.
2. *Type.* Indicate whether the file is an input or output file.
3. *Media.* Indicate the storage medium (e.g., disk, tape, card, etc.).
4. *Location.* Enter the retention location.
5. *Retention Period.* Show the period of retention in days or in number of processing generations.

Chapter 8

Integrating CASE Tools with a Systems Development Methodology

This chapter addresses itself to the integration of *computer-aided software engineering (CASE)* tools with a systems analysis and design methodology. Systems managers contemplating the application of CASE tools to accomplish the analysis objectives must first define a methodology that breaks the analysis process into a series of manageable tasks and defines the end-item deliverables of each task. The alternatives available to the MIS organization are to purchase an analysis methodology from an outside vendor or to develop a methodology in-house. In either case, the analysis methodology with which CASE tools may be integrated must be task-oriented and tailored specifically to meet particular analysis requirements. It must clearly define the analysis phases, prescribe tasks and task steps for each phase, and identify the end-item deliverable of each task step. The task document item correlation of each phase of the analysis process establishes the foundation for planning and implementing a CASE-oriented analysis methodology.

The CASE tools that support the technical functions of the analysis and design methodology discussed in this and preceding chapters are categorized as follows:

- Diagraming CASE tools
- Syntax verifier CASE tools
- Repository CASE tools
- Prototyping CASE tools
- Reengineering CASE tools

The CASE tools that support the managerial functions of the methodology are categorized as follows:

- SDM CASE tools
- Project management CASE tools

Diagraming CASE tools can be used to identify organizational relationships, describe the flow of data between the user organizations and the development group, and graphically show the function and performance of inputs, outputs, interfaces, and methods.

Syntax verifier CASE tools can be used for checking and analyzing structures that show the functional decomposition of the present system, define the requirements of the proposed system, and cross-reference the design logic against design rules and functional requirements.

Repository CASE tools can be used to facilitate storage of structure diagrams, screen and menu definitions, report layouts, record descriptions, process logic, data models, organizational models, process models, source code, business rules, data elements, and system information components.

Prototyping CASE tools can be used to construct models that define system requirements, answer questions about the emerging system, and build prototype simulations to discover system requirements and test behavior.

Reengineering CASE tools can be used to structure existing code or for reverse engineering (i.e., to create structure charts, data dictionaries, etc.).

Systems development methodology (SDM) CASE tools can be used to guide the user in the correct use of a structured analysis and design methodology.

Project management CASE tools can be used to track progress, control schedules, and manage resources.

8.1 INTEGRATING CASE WITH THE ANALYSIS METHODOLOGY

As discussed in Chapter 3, analysis involves a methodical investigation of a problem and the separation of the problem into smaller related units for further detailed study. It includes assessing the activities of the current system, comparing the scope of the proposed system to the existing system, and determining the functional requirements of the proposed system. Achieving the benefits of CASE in the accomplishment of analysis objectives requires, of course, an understanding of the scope of CASE tools that can be integrated with the task activities that comprise the analysis process. Diagraming CASE tools, for example, may be integrated to generate data flow, decomposition, and control flow diagrams. Repository CASE tools can be integrated to provide the mechanism needed to store and retrieve data to and from a central repository. If the systems development methodology used by the MIS organization to guide the analysis process provides structures for recording data, these structures can be linked to CASE tools to accomplish the task result. For example, questionnaires, interview summary sheets, etc., provided by the SDM (either in hard-copy form or as screen formats) may be interfaced with diagraming CASE tools to record the tasks results. Likewise, project management CASE tools can be integrated with the analysis methodology to accomplish tasks related to cost analysis (e.g., current operating costs, ROI calculations, etc.). Configuration management CASE tools may also be applied to the analysis process to support documentation control and baseline management functions.

The documentation considerations of a CASE-oriented analysis methodology are detailed on the following pages.

8.1.1 Model for a CASE-Oriented Analysis Methodology

A model for a CASE-oriented analysis methodology that coincides with the three-phase analysis methodology defined in Chapter 3 is shown in Figure 8-1. The initial investigation phase addresses the potential of the proposed system relative to costs and benefits. The feasibility study phase focuses on comparing the present system to the proposed system and identifying probable costs and consequences. The requirements definition phase establishes the functional requirements for the proposed system. Each phase is broken down into tasks and task steps with which certain types of CASE tools can be integrated to accomplish the task objectives. Figure 8-1 shows the end-item/CASE tool correlation of the analysis process.

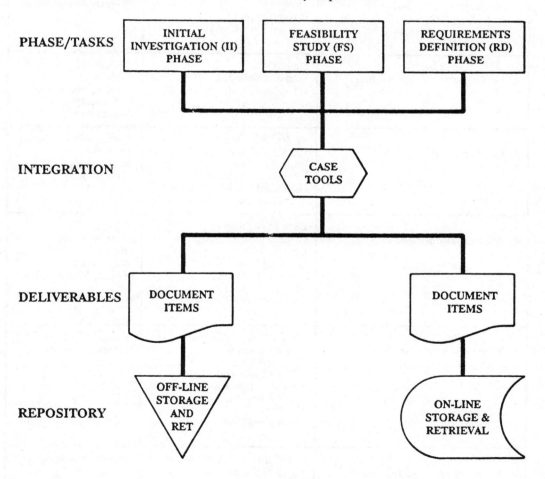

Figure 8-1. End-Item/CASE Tool Correlation of the Analysis Process

8.1.2 Initial Investigation CASE Integration

The initial investigation phase breaks down into six major tasks. Each task produces one or more end-items that can be prepared by using specified case tools. Table 8-1 shows the end-item/CASE tool correlation for each initial investigation task.

Table 8-1. Initial Investigation End-Item/CASE Tool Correlation

Task/Task Step	End-Item	Applicable Tool(s)
1. Assess project request.	Activated Project Request Project Team Organizational Chart	Diagraming Project Management
2. Prepare investigation outline.	Gantt Chart Interview Schedule Interview Questionnaire	Project Management SDM Configuration Management Diagraming
3. Conduct interviews.	Project File Structure Indexing Scheme Interview Notes Interview Summary Cataloged Data and Source Documents	Configuration Management Repository Diagramming
4. Analyze information.	Data Flow Diagrams Organizational Charts Current I/O Descriptions Updated Problem and Need Statement Budget Constraints Cost and Time Estimates	Diagraming Reengineering SDM Repository Project Management
5. Prepare feasibility study work plan.	Present System Review Task Checklist Proposed System Requirements Task Checklist Systems Alternatives Study Task Checklist Economic Evaluation Task Checklist	Project Management SDM
6. Prepare initial investigation report.	Initial Investigation Report Sign-Off Sheet Initial Project Plan	Project Management SDM

The starting point of the initial investigation process is the issuance of a *project request*. When a request is approved, the data processing organization will embark on the development effort. If the request is for a major enhancement to an existing system, an analyst or a team of analysts may be assigned to conduct an *initial investigation* for the purpose of further defining the problems and needs identified by the project request. The initial investigation phase breaks down into six major tasks.

1. *Assess Project Request.* The analyst begins the analysis process by assessing the project request. The objective of this task is to define the problems, needs, and requirements relative to the system requested and the various environmental and operating constraints that must be considered.

2. *Prepare Investigation Outline.* The next step is to prepare a work plan that defines the approach to conducting the initial investigation. This involves the preparation of documents that establish schedules for conducting interviews and provide information the analyst can use in making quantifiable judgments relevant to the problems and needs defined in the previous step.

3. *Conduct Interviews.* When the investigation outline is completed, the analyst then conducts user interviews to acquire a more detailed understanding of existing problems and needs and to define the objectives and goals of the proposed system. The interview notes and other data collected during the interviews should be cataloged and maintained in a reference file.

4. *Analyze Information.* After conducting the interviews, the analyst proceeds to analyze the collected data to clarify the information pertaining to the current organizational structure and the functions performed in the current system, and the problems or business opportunity identified in the project request.

5. *Prepare Feasibility Study Work Plan.* In anticipation of a follow-up study to determine the technical and economic feasibility of the proposed project, the analyst prepares a plan for conducting the feasibility study. The plan is then reviewed by both the user and systems management and approved for resource allocation and scheduling.

6. *Prepare Initial Investigation Report.* The initial investigation concludes with the preparation of a phase end-document that presents the findings of the study to both the user and data processing management. The task is accomplished by synthesizing and reorganizing the items that document the results of the feasibility study.

Each task is further broken down into a series of task steps, and a definable end-item is identified for each task step. The integration of CASE tools to serve the end-item orientation of the initial investigation process is explained and illustrated below and on the following pages.

Task 1. ASSESS PROJECT REQUEST

Analyze Content. The objectives of this task step are (1) to determine if the objectives and purposes are clearly defined and if the expected economic and operational benefits have been accurately stated and (2) to prioritize the project request. The end-item deliverable is an activated project request. A project management CASE tool may be integrated with this task step to initialize the project request and track status.

Assign Analyst. The objective of this task step is to identify the person or persons in the development group who will provide liaison with the user group during the initial investigation phase of the development life cycle. The end-item deliverable is a project team organizational chart. A project management CASE tool may be integrated with this task step that provides support for directing the systems development effort, particularly as regards delegation and assignment of responsibility and authority for the performance of specific tasks. A diagraming CASE tool may be integrated that provides automated support for drawing an organizational chart.

Task 2. PREPARE INVESTIGATION OUTLINE

Prepare Work Schedules. The objectives of this task step are to define the tasks appropriate to conducting the initial investigation and to determine the start and completion dates for each task to be performed. The end-item deliverable is a Gantt chart or other schedule diagram that shows the start and completion dates of each task to be performed. A project management CASE tool may be integrated with this task step that provides support for preparing milestone schedules and tracking progress. A diagraming CASE tool may also be used to prepare schedule diagrams.

Prepare for Interviews. The objectives of this task step are to identify organizational units to be included in the initial investigation study, prepare questionnaires, and schedule interviews. The end-item deliverables are an interview questionnaire and an interview schedule. A project management CASE tool may be integrated with this task step that provides support for preparing interview schedules. An SDM CASE tool may be used that provides structures for the preparation of interview questionnaires.

Identify Available Documentation. The objective of this task step is to identify existing internally or externally produced documentation that can provide input to the data collection effort. The end-item deliverables are (1) a list of internally produced documents and (2) a list of externally produced documents. A configuration management CASE tool may be integrated with this task step to track document items pertinent to the analysis process.

Task 3. CONDUCT INTERVIEWS

Establish Data Collection Control and Indexing Scheme. The objective of this task step is to establish a scheme for maintaining and identifying the collected data. The end-item deliverable is a project file structure and an indexing scheme. A configuration management CASE tool may be integrated with this task step that can be used to create an indexing scheme. A repository CASE tool may be integrated that can be used to store graphics and other information in a central repository.

Conduct the Interviews. The objectives of this task are to conduct the interviews and record responses, review the interview notes and prepare summary statements, and review summary statements with the individuals who were interviewed to ascertain accuracy. The end-item deliverables are (1) interview notes and (2) interview summary statements. A repository CASE tool may be integrated with this task step to track and store the data collected during the interviews in a central repository. A diagraming CASE tool may be used during the interviews to create flow diagrams based on interview responses.

Catalog and File Collected Data and Source Documents. The objective of this task is to catalog and file collected data and source documents. The end-item deliverables are the cataloged data and source documents. A configuration management CASE tool may be integrated with this task step that can be used to create a cataloging scheme. A repository CASE tool may be integrated that can be used to store collected data and source documents in a central repository.

Task 4. ANALYZE INFORMATION

Analyze Organizational Structure. The objectives of this task are to analyze the existing flow of data between user groups and to identify the organizational interfaces. The end-item deliverables are (1) data flow diagrams and (2) organizational charts. A diagramming CASE tool may be integrated with this task step to generate diagrams that show the flow of data between user groups and identify the organizational interfaces.

Analyze the Inputs and Outputs of the Current System. The objective of this task is to analyze document inputs and outputs and data base/file inputs and outputs. The end-item deliverables are I/O descriptions. A diagramming CASE tool may be integrated with this task step to create models that show the path of input and output data through the system. A reengineering CASE tool may be used to create structural charts of the existing system.

Prepare Updated Problem and Need Statement. The objective of this task is to prepare an updated problem and need statement. The end-item deliverable is an updated problem and need statement. An SDM CASE tool that provides a structure for the preparation of a problem and need statement may be integrated with this task step. A repository CASE tool may be used to store documents that defines the problem and need.

Identify Budget Constraints. The objective of this task is to identify budget constraints. The end-item deliverable is a budget constraint statement. A project management CASE tool may be integrated to analyze budget constraints relative to the functions, transaction volumes, and staffing requirements of the proposed system.

Prepare Preliminary Cost and Time Estimates. The objective of this task is to prepare preliminary cost and time estimates. The end-item deliverable is a cost and time estimates statement. A project management CASE tool may be integrated with this task step that can be used to generate preliminary estimates of costs and time requirements. An SDM CASE tool that provides the structure for presenting a cost and time estimate may be integrated with this task step.

Task 5. PREPARE FEASIBILITY STUDY WORK PLAN

Prepare Plan for Present System Review. The objective of this task is to prepare a plan for reviewing existing documentation, defining present system functions: identifying present system inputs, files, and outputs; defining current operating costs; and identifying problems and needs. The end-item deliverable is a present system review task checklist. A project management CASE tool may be integrated with this task step to prepare the task checklist. An SDM CASE tool that provides a structure for the task checklist may also be used.

Prepare Plan for Analyzing Proposed System Requirements. The objective of this task step is to prepare a plan for analyzing proposed system requirements. The end-item deliverable is a proposed system requirements task checklist. A project management CASE tool may be integrated with this task step to prepare the task checklist. An SDM CASE tool that provides a structure for the task checklist may also be used.

Prepare Plan for Conducting a Systems Alternative Study. The objective of this task step is to prepare a plan for identifying alternative approaches and evaluating development alternatives. The end-item deliverable is a system alternatives study task checklist. A project management CASE tool may be integrated with this task step to prepare the task checklist. An SDM CASE tool that provides a structure for the task checklist may also be used.

Prepare Plan for Evaluating Costs and Benefits. The objective of this task step is to prepare a plan for evaluating tangible costs and benefits and for evaluating intangible costs and benefits. The end-item deliverable is an economic evaluation task checklist. A project management CASE tool may be integrated with this task step to prepare the task checklist. An SDM CASE tool that provides a structure for the task checklist may also be used.

Task 6. PREPARE INITIAL INVESTIGATION REPORT

Prepare Initial Investigation Report. The objectives of this task step are to prepare a draft of the initial investigation phase end-document, review the initial investigation Document draft with both user and data processing management, make corrections and changes pursuant to the management review process, and obtain signatures for sign-off and approval. The end-item deliverables are (1) an initial investigation report, and (2) a concurrence and sign-off sheet. An SDM CASE tool that provides a structure for preparing an initial investigation report and/or a concurrence and sign-off sheet may be integrated with this task step.

Initiate Project Plan. The objectives of this task step are to establish a table of contents and work planning checklist for the preparation of a project plan and to prepare the initial project plan. The end-item deliverable is an *initial project plan*. A *project management CASE tool* may be integrated with this task step to prepare the project plan. When the plan is ready for delivery, it can be included in the initial investigation phase end-document. The presentation does not ask for final commitment to the project. It seeks only limited authority to continue through the next step − the feasibility study.

8.1.3 Feasibility Study CASE Integration

The feasibility study phase breaks down into seven major tasks. Each task produces one or more end-items that can be prepared using specified CASE tools. Table 8-2 shows the feasibility study task document correlation and identifies the type of CASE tool that may be integrated to accomplish a particular feasibility study task result.

Table 8-2. Feasibility Study Task/CASE Tool Correlation

Task/Task Step	End-Item	Applicable Tool(s)
1. Review feasibility study work plan.	Gantt or PERT Chart	SDM Project Management Diagraming Repository
2. Conduct user interviews.	User Organization Chart Job Description Forms Interview Questionnaires Interview Worksheets Interview Notes Interview Summaries Cataloged Data and Source Documents	Diagraming SDM Configuration Management Repository Project Management

3. Review present system.	Present System Schematic
	Existing System Analysis
	Data Base/File Contents
	  Summary
	Record/Document Contents
	  Summary
	Report/Output Contents
	  Summary
	Summary of Controls
		SDM
		Diagraming
		Configuration Management
		Reengineering
		Repository

4. Analyze proposed system.	Proposed System Schematic
	Summary of Functions
	Organization Charts
	Statement of Objectives
	Summary of New Capabilities
	Summary of Upgrades
	Summary of Equipment Impacts
	Summary of Software Impacts
	Summary of Organizational
	  Impacts
	Summary of Operational
	  Impacts
	Summary of Development
	  Impacts
	List of Assumptions and
	  Constraints
		Diagraming
		Repository
		SDM
		Project Management

Table 8-2. Feasibility Study Task/CASE Tool Correlation *(continued)*

Task/Task Step	End-Item	Applicable Tool(s)
5. Identify package alternatives.	List of Vendors Vendor Literature Literature Review Summary Letters of Inquiry Package Evaluation Summary	

6. Analyze costs and benefits.	Future Operating Cost
	  Worksheet
	Current Operating Cost
	  Worksheet
	ROI Worksheet
	Intangible Benefits Worksheet
	Economic Evaluation Summary
		Project Management
		SDM
		Repository

7. Prepare feasibility study document	Table of Contents and Work Planning Checklist Feasibility Study Document	SDM Repository

During the initial investigation phase, the analyst focused primarily on identifying the problem and need. In the feasibility study phase, the analyst concentrated on gathering information that might lead to a solution of the problem. This was accomplished through interviews and reviewing historical records. As the analyst focused on seeking solutions, he or she may have pursued the following line of questioning. *What are the functions of the present system? What new capabilities are being sought by the proposed system? What are the viable alternatives? What are the costs and benefits of the present system versus the proposed system?*

The data collected by the analyst can be used at the conclusion of the feasibility study to develop a *physical model* comprised of four elements: objectives, inputs, processes, and outputs. The *objectives* element of the model represents the desired results expressed in the project request and amplified during the initial investigation and feasibility study phases. The objectives are supported by more narrowly circumscribed subobjectives (e.g., upgrading the capabilities of the existing system). The *inputs* from the present system are correlated with the objectives of the proposed system and represented in the model as subsystems that provide the flow of data into the computer. The *processes* represent the transformation of information into courses of action that are consistent with the kinds of outputs required. *Outputs* in the system model are represented as the results sought by the proposed system.

The model may be presented as a diagrammatic model using CASE tools. A model of the proposed system at this stage in the development process, of course, can only depict the *physical system* of data processing. Conceptual elements that are needed to manage the physical system will be added as the life cycle of the development effort progresses.

The objective of the feasibility study is to provide management with predictable results of implementing the proposed project. The tasks to be performed to determine the feasibility of the proposed project are geared to answering three questions: *What needs to be done? How can it be done? What is the value of doing it?* To answer these questions, the study team must review the present system and analyze the proposed system requirements. This activity involves performing the following tasks.

1. *Review Feasibility Study Work Plan.* The analyst assigned to conduct the feasibility study begins by reviewing the feasibility study work plan that was prepared during the initial investigation phase. The plan defines the tasks to be performed and identifies the product(s) of each task.

2. *Conduct User Interviews.* The fact-finding objectives of this task are more probing than those related to the initial investigation. During the initial investigation study, the interviews were directed primarily to top-level managers. In the feasibility study, interviewees include operating-level managers and first-line supervisory personnel.

3. *Review Present System.* In addition to interviews, the analysts collect and review data that will provide a cumulative understanding of the present system, its costs, functions, inputs, outputs, problems, and opportunities for improvement.

4. *Analyze Proposed System.* The next task is to analyze the requirements of the proposed system. Toward this end, the analyst identifies the system objectives and, based on the objectives, lists the output and input requirements. The task also involves developing conceptual models for meeting the objectives of the requested system.

5. *Identify Package Alternatives.* Having developed a conceptual model, the analyst proceeds to identify application packages that may satisfy the user requirements. Using a variety of sources, the analyst reviews package features and makes a preliminary evaluation of available options.

6. *Analyze Costs and Benefits.* The object of this task is to review the current operating costs and benefits and compare them to anticipated costs and benefits of developing or purchasing the proposed system.

7. *Prepare Feasibility Study Document.* The feasibility study concludes with the preparation of a phase end-document that presents the findings of the study to both the user and data processing management for review and subsequent determination of whether to proceed to the requirements definition phase of development. The task is accomplished by synthesizing and reorganizing the items that document the results of the feasibility study.

Each task is further broken down into a series of task steps, and a definable end-item is identified for each task step.

The integration of CASE tools to serve the end-item orientation of the feasibility study process is explained and illustrated below and on the following pages.

Task 1. REVIEW FEASIBILITY STUDY WORK PLAN

Define the Tasks to be Performed. The objective of this task step is to break down the work to be performed in conducting a feasibility study into a series of tasks and task steps and to identify the product(s) of each activity. The end-item deliverable is a Gantt chart or PERT network that shows the work breakdown structure. An SDM CASE tool that defines the tasks to be performed may be integrated with this task step. A project management CASE tool may be used to create Gantt charts and PERT networks that list the activities of the project and show the order in which they are to be performed. A diagramming CASE tool may be used to generate the network diagrams. A repository CASE tool may be used to store the Gantt charts or PERT networks in a central repository.

Task 2. CONDUCT USER INTERVIEWS

Conduct User Organization Analysis. The objective of this task step is to conduct a user organization analysis to identify each individual to be interviewed, explain the position of the individual in the management hierarchy, and summarize the primary functions performed by the individual to be interviewed. The end-item deliverables are a user organization chart that schematically portrays the user organization and job description forms that describe the duties and interfaces of the individuals to be interviewed. An SDM CASE tool that provides structures for preparing organization charts and job descriptions may be integrated with this task step. A diagraming CASE tool may be used to create the organizational charts. A repository CASE tool may be used to store the user questionnaire and job description forms in a central repository.

Plan Interviews. The objectives of this task step are to prepare questionnaires that list the questions to be asked during the interviews and worksheets that are used to document the responses. The end-item deliverables are interview questionnaires and interview worksheets. An SDM CASE tool that provides structures for the preparation of interview questionnaires and interview worksheets may be integrated with this task step. A repository CASE tool may be used to store the user interview questionnaires and interview worksheets in a central repository.

Schedule and Conduct Interviews. The objectives of this task step are is to schedule and conduct the interviews and record interview responses. The end-item deliverables are (1) interview notes, and (2) interview summary statements. An SDM CASE tool that provides structures for recording interview notes may be integrated with this task step. A project management CASE tool may be used to update the project plan with the interview schedule information. A diagraming CASE tool may be used during the interviews to create flow diagrams based on interview responses. A repository CASE tool may be used to store interview notes and interview summary statements in a central repository.

Document Interview Responses. The objectives of this task are to review the interview notes and prepare summary statements to be reviewed with the individuals who were interviewed to ensure accuracy, prepare formal interview summary statements that summarize the gist of all the information gathered during the interview, and catalog the summary statements and support source documents. The end-item deliverables are (1) interview notes, (2) interview summary statements, and (3) cataloged data and source documents. An SDM CASE tool that provides structures for preparing interview summary statements may be integrated with this task step. A diagraming CASE tool may be used during the interviews to create flow diagrams based on interview responses. A configuration management CASE tool may be integrated with this task step that can be used to create a cataloging scheme. A repository CASE tool may be integrated that can be used to store collected data and source documents in a central repository.

Task 3. REVIEW PRESENT SYSTEM

Summarize Key Characteristics of Present System. The objective of this task step is to summarize the key characteristics of the present system relative to costs, run time, system requirements, documentation, and programs. The end-item deliverables are (1) a present system schematic and (2) an existing system analysis form. An SDM CASE tool that provides structures for preparing schematics may be integrated with this task step. A decomposition diagraming CASE tool may be integrated to identify organizational structures and their basic business functions. A repository CASE tool may be used to store the present system schematics and analysis forms in a central repository. A configuration management CASE tool may be integrated to identify the equipment configuration.

Summarize Present System I/O Requirements. The objectives of this task are to summarize the input/output requirements of the present system relative to the content and characteristics of each data base or file, record, or input document and report or other output mediated generated by the system. The end-item deliverables include (1) data base/file contents analysis summary, (2) record/document contents analysis summary, and (3) output/report contents analysis summary. An SDM CASE tool that provides structures for analyzing I/O requirements may be integrated with this task step. A reengineering CASE tool may be integrated to reverse engineer code, generate structure charts, and define existing input, output, and file structures. A diagraming CASE tool may be used to create system flow diagrams. A repository CASE tool may be used to store the I/O requirements data in a central repository.

Identify Current Control Methods. The objective of this task is to identify the present system's control methods, including methods for I/O control, user control, data file/data base control, access control, file maintenance, and recovery control. The end-item deliverable is a summary of controls. An SDM CASE tool that provides structures for summarizing controls may be integrated with this task step. A decomposition diagraming CASE tool may be integrated to identify the procedural controls. A reengineering CASE tool may be used to create structural charts that identify the present system's control methods. A repository CASE tool may be integrated that can be used to store collected data and source documents in a central repository.

Identify Present System Documentation. The objective of this task is to identify present system documentation by document name, noting the completeness and quality of each document. The end-item deliverable is a documentation list that identifies the document items associated with the present system and shows the completeness of content and its quality. An SDM CASE tool that provides structures for developing documentation lists may be integrated with this task step. A configuration management CASE tool may be integrated to identify the present system documentation.

Task 4. ANALYZE PROPOSED SYSTEM

Define the Relationships of Functions to the Proposed System Flow. The objective of this task is to define the relationships of currently performed functions to the proposed system flow. The end-item deliverables are (1) proposed system schematics, (2) summaries of functions, and (3) organization charts. An SDM CASE tool that provides structures for defining the relationships of functions may be integrated with this task step. A diagraming CASE tool may be integrated to generate diagrams that define the relationship of the functions performed by the present system to those to be performed by the proposed system. A repository CASE tool may be integrated that can be used to store collected data and source documents in a central repository.

Define the Objectives of the Proposed System. The objective of this task is to identify what the proposed system will accomplish. The end-item deliverable is a statement of objectives. An SDM CASE tool that provides structures for defining the system objectives may be integrated with this task step. A repository CASE tool may be used to store documents that define the objectives in a central repository.

Summarize the Expected Improvements. The objective of this task is to summarize the new capabilities and upgrades to existing capabilities of the proposed system. The end-item deliverables are (1) a summary of new capabilities and (2) a summary of upgrades. An SDM CASE tool that provides a structure for the preparation of a summary of capabilities and upgrades may be integrated with this task step. A repository CASE tool may be used to store documents that define the capabilities and upgrades of the proposed system.

Summarize the Expected Impacts. The objective of this task is to identify the expected impacts of the proposed system. The end-item deliverables are (1) summary of equipment impacts, (2) summary of software impacts, (3) summary of organizational impacts, (4) summary of operational impacts, and (5) summary of development impacts. An SDM CASE tool that provides structures for summarizing the expected impacts may be integrated with this task step. A decomposition diagraming CASE tool may be integrated with this task step to identify the expected impacts of the proposed system. A repository CASE tool may be used to store the impact statements in a central repository.

Identify Assumptions and Constraints. The objective of this task is to identify the assumptions and constraints used in developing the feasibility analysis. The end-item deliverable is a list of assumptions and constraints. An SDM CASE tool that provides a structure for analyzing the assumptions and constraints of the proposed system may be integrated with this task step. A repository CASE tool may be used to store the statements of assumptions and constraints in a central repository.

Task 5. IDENTIFY PACKAGE ALTERNATIVES

Identify Package Vendors. The objective of this task is to identify vendors of possible alternatives that will satisfy the user needs, objectives, and requirements of the proposed system. The end-item deliverable is a list of vendors that may provide alternative solutions. (No specific CASE tools are identified that can be integrated with this task, but a variety of on-line literature search services may be utilized to accomplish the task objectives.)

Acquire Literature. The objective of this task step is to acquire literature that may provide information regarding the features and characteristics of software packages that are commercially available. The end-item deliverable is a catalog of applicable literature. (No specific CASE tools are identified that can be integrated with this task, but a variety of on-line literature search services may be utilized to accomplish the task objectives.)

Review Published Articles. The objective of this task step is to review the published articles that provide information regarding the features and characteristics of available packages. The end-item deliverable is a literature review summary. (No specific CASE tools are identified that can be integrated with this task, but a variety of on-line literature search services may be utilized to accomplish the task objectives.)

Prepare Letters of Inquiry. The objective of this task step is to prepare letters of inquiry asking the vendors to provide additional literature that describes the cost, timing, and features of the packages offered. The end-item deliverables are letters of inquiry. (No specific CASE tools are identified that can be integrated with this task, but a variety of word processing technologies are available to generate the letters of inquiry.)

Review Vendor Literature. The objective of this task step is to review the literature provided by the prospective vendors. The end-item deliverables are package review summary statements. (No specific CASE tools are identified that can be integrated with this task.)

Perform Package Comparisons. The objective of this task step is to compare the alternative packages relative to application structure, environment, programming interfaces, and common communications support. The end-item deliverables are package evaluation summary statements. (No specific CASE tools are identified that can be integrated with this task.)

Task 6. ANALYZE COSTS AND BENEFITS

Estimate Future Operating Costs. The objective of this task step is to tabulate the future user operating costs that would be associated with the new system, including costs of direct labor, indirect labor, materials and supplies, electronic data processing, and miscellaneous costs. The end-item deliverable is a future operating costs worksheet. An SDM and/or project management CASE tool that provides a structure for cost estimating may be integrated with this task step. A repository CASE tool may be used to store the operating costs worksheets in a central repository.

Analyze Current Operating Costs. The objective of this task step is to tabulate the current user operating costs that would be associated with the areas of the proposed system under investigation, including costs of direct labor, indirect labor, materials and supplies, electronic data processing, and miscellaneous costs. The end-item deliverable is a current operating costs worksheet. An SDM and/or project management CASE tool that provides a structure for cost accounting may be integrated with this task step. A repository CASE tool may be used to store the operating costs worksheets in a central repository.

Calculate Return on Investment. The objectives of this task step are to calculate the rate of return on investment (ROI) anticipated from implementation of the proposed system, taking into consideration direct cost savings, discounted savings, and rate of return on investments. The end-item deliverable is a return-on-investment worksheet. An SDM and/or project management CASE tool that provides a structure for calculating the rate of return earned by the investment may be integrated with this task step. A repository CASE tool may be used to store the ROI worksheets in a central repository.

Analyze Intangible Benefits. The objective of this task step is to identify improvements in service, control, management performance, and operation, taking into consideration the type of benefits, first-year assumptions and calculations, and future years' projects. The end-item deliverable is an intangible benefits worksheet. A project management CASE tool that provides a structure for analyzing intangible benefits may be integrated with this task step. A repository CASE tool may be used to store the benefit statements in a central repository.

Summarize Economic Feasibility of Development. The objectives of this task step are to summarize the principal cost data, taking into consideration estimated costs, operating and maintenance costs, cost savings, worker-time requirements, system availability, payback period, and return on investment. The end-item deliverable is an economic evaluation summary. An SDM and/or project management CASE tool that provides a structure for cost control may be integrated with this task step. A repository CASE tool may be used to store the economic evaluation summaries in a central repository.

Task 7. PREPARE FEASIBILITY STUDY DOCUMENT

Prepare Feasibility Study Document Content Outline. The objective of this task step is to prepare a table of contents and work planning checklist for the preparation of a feasibility study phase end-document. The end-item deliverable is a table of contents and work planning checklist. An SDM CASE tool that provides a structure for preparing a table of contents and work planning checklist may be integrated with this task step.

Synthesize Task Documentation. The objective of this task step is to synthesize and reorganize the document items delivered to the project file during the feasibility study for inclusion in a feasibility study phase end-document. The end-item deliverables are document items to be included in the feasibility study phase end-document. A repository CASE tool may be integrated with this task step that enables the compilation of task results stored throughout the feasibility study process.

Finalize Feasibility Study Document. The objectives of this task step are to prepare the feasibility study phase end-document that communicates the results of the tasks performed during this development phase, to review the document with management, and to print and publish the document. The end-item deliverable is a published feasibility study phase end-document that provides management with a decision-making tool that will help determine whether to terminate the system project or to approve its next phase.

8.1.4 Requirements Definition CASE Integration

The requirements definition phase breaks down into 10 major tasks. Each task produces one or more end items that can be prepared using specified CASE tools. Table 8-3 shows the requirements definition task document correlation and identifies the type of CASE tool that may be integrated to accomplish a particular requirements definition task result.

Table 8-3. Requirements Definition Task/CASE Tool Correlation

Task/Task Step	End-Item	Applicable Tool(s)
1. Review project file and phase end-documents.	Updated Project Plan	Project Management Configuration Management Repository
2. Conduct requirements definition interviews.	List of Interviewees Interview Worksheet Interview Records Interview Schedule I/O Requirements File Access Requirements Contol Update Requirements Policies and Procedures	Project Management SDM Repository Diagraming
3. Determine functional requirements.	Function Description Statement Detailed Functional Requirements Statement Functional Flow Schematic	SDM Diagraming Repository
4. Define performance requirements.	Mathematical Calculation Requirements Data Accuracy Requirements Response Time Requirements Backup Requirements Fallback Requirements Restart Requirements Interface Requirements	SDM Diagraming Repository
5. Amplify statements of improvement	Updated Summary of Improvements Updated Summary of Organizational Impacts Updated Summary of Operational Impacts Updated Summary of Developmental Impacts	SDM Repository

Table 8-3. Requirements Definition Task/CASE Tool Correlation *(continued)*

Task/Task Step	End-Item	Applicable Tool(s)
6. Define data requirements.	Data Attributes Input Description Document File Record Document Output Description Document Output Content Record Output Distribution List Data Base Organization and Structure Logical Structure Worksheet	SDM Repository

7. Define environmental requirements.	Equipment Requirements
	Support Software
	  Requirements
	Interface Requirements
	Security and Privacy
	  Requirements
	Control Requirements
		SDM
		Repository

8. Determine organizational requirements.	Organization Chart Job Descriptions Personnel Detail	SDM Diagraming Repository
9. Establish alternatives evaluation criteria.	List of Alternatives Evaluation Criteria Evaluation Matrix Summary of Recommendations	SDM Repository
10. Prepare Requirements definition document.	Requirements Definition Document	

Prior to conducting the requirements definition study, the needs of the proposed system were defined only in general terms. As a result of the tasks performed during the requirements definition phase, the analyst can now develop a *conceptual model* that shows how the physical system (inputs, process, and outputs) will be controlled. The conceptual model expands upon the physical model developed at the conclusion of the feasibility study to show the control elements required to monitor system output and make necessary changes to system input. The control element depicted in the model represents the measurement, evaluation, or regulation of the input-process-output flow to determine if the system meets the defined requirements.

The control element of the model may be further broken down into sub-elements that categorize the previously defined requirements as follows: functional requirements, performance requirements, data requirements, environmental requirements, and organizational requirements. The functional requirements sub-element identifies all the functions the new system must perform and correlates them with the *performance requirements.* The *data requirements* subelement identifies the information required to support each function. The *environmental requirements* subelement considers all the significant constraints imposed on the proposed system. The *organizational requirements* subelement quantifies the organizational impacts associated with the proposed system.

The conceptual model, as in the case of the physical model developed at the conclusion of the feasibility study, may be presented in diagrammatic form utilizing CASE tools to prepare the structures.

Once a decision has been made to continue with a new software development project, a more detailed review of both the present system and the proposed system is required. The objective of the requirements definition phase is to define functional requirements, performance requirements, data requirements, environmental requirements, and organizational requirements of the proposed system. This activity involves performing the following tasks.

1. *Review Project File and Phase End-Documents.* The requirements definition phase begins by reviewing the document items stored in the project file and the document items contained in the initial investigation and feasibility study phase end-documents.

2. *Conduct Requirements Definition Interviews.* After reviewing the document items in the project file and the documentation contained in the initial investigation and feasibility study phase end-documents, the analyst then proceeds to prepare a checklist of systems requirements that must be satisfied by the new system. Interviews are then scheduled and conducted to gather additional data needed to complete the requirements definition study.

3. *Determine Functional Requirements.* The definition of functions to be performed expands upon the system objectives defined during the feasibility study. In the feasibility study phase, the functional objectives were presented in outline form. In the requirements definition phase, the functional requirements are detailed, and function flow schematics are prepared to illustrate the interrelationship of the various functions to be performed.

4. *Define Performance Requirements.* The specific performance requirements to be satisfied by the proposed system are stated in such a manner that the system designers are provided with definitive guidelines to follow in preparing design specifications relative to accuracy, timing, failure contingency, and interface requirements.

5. *Amplify Statements of Improvement and Impact.* The objective of this task is to amplify the statements that were prepared during the feasibility study phase to identify the anticipated improvements and impacts. The organizational, operational, and development

impacts of the proposed system are assessed and updated during the requirements definition phase.

6. *Define Data Requirements.* The objectives of this task are to define the data requirements of the new system and to standardize the names and codes of the data elements to facilitate data exchange and commonality of data structures.

7. *Define Environmental Requirements.* The document items resulting from this task describe the environment needed to satisfy the performance and data requirements. The end products of this task include document items that define operating constraints, policy issues, and control requirements.

8. *Define Organizational Requirements.* The objective of this task is to determine the organizational requirements based on functions to be performed and staffing needs.

9. *Establish Alternatives Evaluation Criteria.* The documentation resulting from this task establishes the criteria for selecting packages to be leased or purchased from computer hardware and software vendors.

10. *Prepare Requirements Definition Document.* The feasibility study concludes with the preparation of a comprehensive written document containing a description of all user- and MIS-based requirements.

Each task is further broken down into a series of task steps, and a definable end-item is identified for each task step.

The integration of CASE tools to serve the end-item orientation of the requirements definition process is explained and illustrated below.

Task 1. REVIEW PROJECT FILE AND PHASE END-DOCUMENTS

Review Project File. The objective of this task step is to review the documentation stored in the project file that was generated during the initial investigation and feasibility study phases. A configuration management CASE tool may be integrated with this task step to identify and track the documentation. A repository CASE tool may be used to access documentation that is available on-line.

Assess Project Plan. The objective of this task step is to assess the structure and timetable for development of the proposed project as defined in the project plan. The end-item deliverable is an updated project plan. A project management CASE tool may be integrated with this task step to make any adjustments to the project plan that are deemed necessary.

Task 2. CONDUCT REQUIREMENTS DEFINITION INTERVIEWS

Identify Individuals to be Interviewed. The objective of this task step is to identify individuals to be interviewed, specifically top-level managers, operating-level managers, and supervisory personnel. The end-item deliverable is a list of interviewees that shows the names, titles, job functions, and telephone extensions of the personnel to be interviewed. An SDM CASE tool that provides structure for the preparation of a list of interviewees may be integrated with this task step.

Design Structures to Record Interview Responses. The objective of this task step is to develop structures that the interviewer can use to record interview responses. The structural design should provide for the name of the analyst conducting the interview, the name of the person to be interviewed, the assigned question number as indicated on the questionnaire form that was developed during feasibility study, and the response to the question. The end-item deliverables may include (1) an interview worksheet, (2) an interview tape record, or (3) an interview on-line record. An SDM and/or project management CASE tool that provides structures for recording interview responses be integrated with this task step.

Schedule Interviews. The objective of this task step is to schedule interviews with all of the individuals to be interviewed. The end-item deliverable is an interview schedule that lists the name and title of each person to be interviewed and indicates the date, time, and location of the interview. An SDM CASE tool that provides structures for the preparation of interview schedules may be integrated with this task step. A project management CASE tool may be used to update the project plan with interview schedule information.

Conduct Interviews. The objectives of this task step are to collect data required to define the outputs and inputs associated with the proposed system, define the file requirements of the proposed system, document the proposed system's work flows and controls, and document relevant policies, practices, and constraints that will impact the design of the proposed system. The end-item deliverables are structures that delineate (1) input/output requirements, (2) file access requirements, (3) control and update requirements, and (4) policies and procedures. An SDM CASE tool that provides structures for the preparation of requirements documents may be integrated with this task step. A diagraming CASE tool may be used during the interviews to create diagrams based on interview responses. A repository CASE tool may be used to store collected data and source documents in a central repository.

Task 3. DETERMINE FUNCTIONAL REQUIREMENTS

Identify the Functions to be Performed. The objective of this task is to prepare statements that identify and describe the purpose of each function to be supported by the computer program. Each function description statement should include a simplified functional diagram that illustrates the function. The end-item deliverable is a function description statement for each function to be performed by the proposed system. An SDM CASE tool that provides structures for preparing function descriptions may be integrated with this task step. A diagraming CASE tool may be used to create the functional diagrams. A repository CASE tool may be used to store the function description statements in a central repository.

Detail the Functional Requirements. The objective of this task is to detail the requirements of each function to be performed by the computer program. Each detailed statement should include a description of all inputs, including data from other functions and from sources external to the computer, a textual and mathematical description of the processing requirements of each function, a description of all output data, and descriptions of special data processing requirements (e.g., growth requirements, recovery requirements, etc.). The end-item deliverable is a detailed functional requirements statement for each function to be performed by the proposed system. An SDM CASE tool that provides structures for preparing detailed functional requirements statements may be integrated with this task step. A diagraming CASE tool may be used to create functional diagrams. A repository CASE tool may be used to store the detailed functional requirement statements in a central repository.

Prepare Functional Flow Schematic. The objective of this task is to prepare a functional flow schematic that illustrates the interrelationship of the various functions to be performed and shows at what point of time, relative to each other, the functions must be performed. The end-item deliverable is a functional flow schematic. A diagraming CASE tool may be integrated with this task step to create a functional flow schematic. A repository CASE tool may be used to store the functional flow schematics in a central repository.

Task 4. DEFINE PERFORMANCE REQUIREMENTS

Define Accuracy Requirements. The objective of this task is to define the accuracy requirements placed upon the proposed system, specifically the accuracy requirements of mathematical calculations and data. The end-item deliverables are documented statements of (1) mathematical calculation requirements, and (2) data accuracy requirements. An SDM CASE tool that provides structures for preparing accuracy requirements statements may be integrated with this task step. A repository CASE tool may be integrated to store the accuracy requirements statements in a central repository.

Define Timing Requirements. The objective of this task is to define the timing requirements to be placed on the system, specifically response time requirements from receipt of input data to availability of system products and response time requirements to queries and to updates of data files. The end-item deliverables are documented statements of (1) input response time requirements, and (2) query/update response time requirements. An SDM CASE tool that provides structures for preparing response time requirements statements may be integrated with this task step. A repository CASE tool may be integrated to store the timing requirements statements in a central repository.

Define Failure Contingency Requirements. The objective of this task is to define the requirements for failure contingencies, specifically backup requirements, fallback requirements, and restart requirements. The end-item deliverables are documented statements of (1) backup requirements, (2) fallback requirements, and (3) restart requirements. An SDM CASE tool that provides a structure for document contingency requirements may be integrated with this task step. A repository CASE tool may be used to store documents that define the contingency requirements statements in a central repository.

Define Interface Requirements. The objective of this task is to provide a description of the interfaces with other systems and subsystems, specifically requirements related to the operational considerations of data transfer (e.g., security considerations), data transfer to and from the subject system, and format, range of values, and data codes.

The end-item deliverables are documented statements of (1) interface data requirements and (2) interface design requirements. An SDM CASE tool that provides a structure for documenting interface requirements may be integrated with this task step. A repository CASE tool may be used to store the documents that define the interface requirements in a central repository.

Task 5. AMPLIFY STATEMENTS OF IMPROVEMENT AND IMPACT

Amplify Requirements for Improvements. The objective of this task is to amplify the functional requirements for improvements defined during the feasibility study by relating them to the performance requirements defined in task 4. The end-item deliverable is an updated summary of improvements statement. An SDM CASE tool that provides a structure for preparing qualitative and quantitative summaries of the benefits to be obtained from the proposed system may be integrated with this task step. A repository CASE tool may be used to store the documents that summarize the anticipated improvements in a central repository.

Amplify Organizational Impacts. The objective of this task step is to amplify the organizational impacts defined during the feasibility study by relating them to the functional and performance requirements. The end-item deliverable is an updated summary of organizational impacts statement. An SDM CASE tool that provides structures for documenting the anticipated impacts of the proposed system on the user organization may be integrated with this task step.

Amplify Operational Impacts. The objective of this task step is to amplify the operational impacts defined during the feasibility study by relating them to the functional and performance requirements. The end-item deliverable is an updated summary of operational impacts statement. An SDM CASE tool that provides structures for documenting the anticipated impacts of the proposed system on the operational environment may be integrated with this task step.

Amplify Development Impacts. The objective of this task step is to amplify the development impacts defined during the feasibility study by relating them to the functional and performance requirements. The end-item deliverable is an updated summary of development impacts statement. An SDM CASE tool that provides structures for documenting the anticipated impacts of the proposed system on the development organization may be integrated with this task step.

Task 6. DEFINE DATA REQUIREMENTS

Describe Data Attributes. The objective of this task step is to describe the attributes of the data required by the proposed system, specifically in terms of timeliness, reliability, usefulness and completeness, efficiency of usage, necessity, and security. The end-item deliverable is a data attributes statement for each function/operation to which the data apply. An SDM CASE tool that provides a structure for documenting data attributes may be integrated with this task step. A repository CASE tool may be used to store the documents that define the data attributes in a central repository.

Define Input Requirements. The objective of this task step is to identify the input requirements, specifically the sources from which data will be fed into the system, the input devices used for entering the data into the system, and the input formats, including master file formats to be used by the system. The end-item deliverable is (1) an input description document that describes the system inputs and the devices to use in entering the data and (2) a file record document that lists the content of files and records within files. An SDM CASE tool that provides structures for documenting input requirements may be integrated with this task step. A repository CASE tool may be used to store the documents that define the input requirements in a central repository.

Define Output Requirements. The objective of this task step is to define the output requirements, specifically requirements related to the characteristics of the outputs to be generated by the system (e.g., size, use, access security, etc.), formats and content descriptions of all outputs to be generated by the system, and recipients of the system outputs. The end-item deliverable is (1) an output description document that describes the system inputs and the devices to use in entering the data, (2) an output content record that accompanies facsimiles of reports, and (3) an output distribution list. An SDM CASE tool that provides structures for documenting output requirements may be integrated with this task step. A repository CASE tool may be used to store the documents that define the output requirements in a central repository.

Define Data Base Characteristics. The objective of this task step is to identify data base requirements, specifically requirements related to the logical organization of static systems data and dynamic input data. The end-item deliverables are (1) a data base organization and structure document that summarizes the principal considerations that are relevant to file structures, organizations, and storage space management and (2) a logical structure worksheet that can be used for mapping logical structures to meet the input and output requirements. An SDM CASE tool that provides a structure for documenting data base characteristics may be integrated with this task step. A repository CASE tool may be used to store the documents that describe the data base characteristics in a central repository.

Task 7. DEFINE ENVIRONMENTAL REQUIREMENTS

Define Equipment Requirements. The objective of this task step is to define the equipment requirements of the proposed system, specifically requirements pertaining to the type, size, and quantity of each item of equipment required. The end-item deliverable is an equipment environment document that lists the equipment presently available and additional equipment required by the proposed system. An SDM CASE tool that provides structures for documenting equipment requirements may be integrated with this task step. A repository CASE tool may be used to store the documents that identify the equipment requirements in a central repository.

Define Support Software Requirements. The objective of this task step is to define support software requirements, specifically requirements pertaining to input and equipment simulations, test software, utilities, operating system, and data management. The end-item deliverable is a support software environment document. An SDM CASE tool that provides structures for documenting support software requirements may be integrated with this task step. A repository CASE tool may be used to store the documents that define the support software requirements in a central repository.

Amplify Interface Requirements. The objective of this task step is to amplify previously defined interface requirements, specifically requirements pertaining to operational implications of data transfer, data transfer requirements to and from subject system, characteristics of communications media used for transfer, current formats of interchange data, interface procedures, and interface equipment. The end-item deliverable is an interface requirements document that identifies each interface by name and indicates the medium and frequency of the interface. An SDM CASE tool that provides structures for documenting interface requirements may be integrated with this task step. A repository CASE tool may be used to store the documents that define the interface requirements in a central repository.

Define Security and Privacy Requirements. The objective of this task is to define security and privacy requirements. The end-item deliverable is a security and privacy document that details the requirements of the new system. An SDM CASE tool that provides a structure for documenting security and control requirements may be integrated with this task step. A repository CASE tool may be used to store the documents that define the security and control requirements in a central repository.

Define Control Requirements. The objective of this task step is to define control requirements, specifically requirements pertaining to validation controls, completeness controls, accuracy controls, and access controls. The end-item deliverable is a control requirements document that describes all the controls required. An SDM CASE tool that provides a structure for documenting control requirements may be integrated with this task step. A repository CASE tool may be used to store the documents that define the control requirements in a central repository.

Task 8. DETERMINE ORGANIZATIONAL REQUIREMENTS

Assess Organizational Impacts of New System. The objective of this task step is to assess the organizational impacts by schematically showing those parts of the organization that will be impacted by the proposed system and providing detail related to the management hierarchy and functions that will be impacted by the new system. The end-item deliverable is an organization chart that shows those parts of the organization that will be impacted by the proposed system. An SDM CASE tool that provides structures for documenting the impacts of a proposed system may be integrated with this task step. A diagraming CASE tool may be used to create organization charts. A repository CASE tool may be used to store the organization chart(s) in a central repository.

Identify Personnel Impacts of New System. The objective of this task step is to identify personnel impacts of the proposed system, including estimates of new jobs that are to be established, estimates of existing jobs to be eliminated, and summary job-level descriptions for all new and revised job classifications. The end-item deliverable is a personnel detail document that identifies, by job classification, personnel impacts of the proposed system. An SDM CASE tool that provides structures for documenting personnel impacts may be integrated with this task step. A repository CASE tool may be used to store the documents that describe the personnel impacts in a central repository.

Task 9. ESTABLISH ALTERNATIVES EVALUATION CRITERIA

Identify Alternatives. The objective of this task step is to identify the alternatives that can satisfy the user requirements. The end-item deliverable is a considered alternatives document that lists viable alternatives. An SDM CASE tool that provides structures for documenting viable alternatives may be integrated with this task step.

A repository CASE tool may be used to store the evaluation documents in a central repository.

Summarize and Recommend Alternative. The objectives of this task step is to summarize and recommend viable alternatives. The end-item deliverable is a summary of recommendations document that provides an analysis of trade-offs and advantages. An SDM CASE tool that provides structures for making package recommendations may be integrated with this task step. A repository CASE tool may be used to store the recommendation statements in a central repository.

Task 10. PREPARE REQUIREMENTS DEFINITION DOCUMENT

Review Requirements Definition Content Outline. The objective of this task step is to prepare a table of contents and work planning checklist for the preparation of a requirements definition phase end-document. The end-item deliverable is a table of contents and work planning checklist. An SDM CASE tool that provides a structure for preparing a table of contents and work planning checklist may be integrated with this task step.

Synthesize Task Documentation. The objective of this task step is to synthesize and reorganize the document items delivered to the project file during the requirements definition phase in a feasibility study phase end-document. The end-item deliverables are document items be included in the requirements definition phase end-document. An repository CASE tool may be integrated with this task step that enables the compilation of task results stored throughout the requirements definition phase.

Finalize Requirements Definition Phase End-Document. The objective of this task step is to synthesize and reorganize the document items delivered to the project file during the feasibility study for inclusion in a feasibility study phase end-document. The end-item deliverables are document items to be included in the requirements definition phase end-document.

8.2 INTEGRATING CASE WITH THE DESIGN METHODOLOGY

The goal of the design phases of systems development is to specify the functional structure of the system and prepare precise descriptions of each system component. The process involves making design decisions regarding physical facilities and operational requirements based on the functional objectives defined during the analysis phases. In Chapter 4, we explained how the design functions were accomplished in two phases: external design and internal design. In this chapter we will examine how CASE tools can be applied to support the documentation objectives of the tasks performed. During the design phases, the inputs, outputs, and internal logic of each system component are defined. The internal logic may be described with equations, flow diagrams, or decision tables using CASE tools to prepare the appropriate structures. Likewise, the overall system may be described using CASE-generated flow diagrams or hierarchical input-process-output (HIPO) diagrams. Clearly, there are numerous design functions to which CASE technologies may be applied.

As in the analysis process, systems managers contemplating the application of CASE tools to accomplish the design objectives must first define a methodology that breaks the design process into a series of manageable tasks and defines the end-item deliverables of each task. The design methodology with which CASE tools may be integrated must be task-oriented and tailored specifically to meet particular design requirements. It must clearly define the design phases, prescribe tasks and task steps for each phase, and identify the end-item deliverables of each task step. The task end-item correlation of each phase of the design process establishes the foundation for planning and implementing a CASE-oriented systems design methodology.

Achieving the benefits of CASE requires, of course, an understanding of the importance of documentation. The objectives of documentation at the design level are to provide programmers with the specifications necessary to code the programs and to establish the design baseline for configuration management. The set of documents resulting from the design process may include flow diagrams, logic diagrams, and schematics to which *diagraming* and *syntax verifier CASE tools* may be applied and output reports and screen formats that can be generated using *prototyping CASE tools*. *Repository CASE tools* can be integrated to provide the mechanism needed to store and retrieve data to and from a central repository. If the systems development methodology used by the MIS organization to guide the design process provides structures for presenting systems design specifications, security and control specifications, procedural requirements, and conversion and implementation data, these structures can be linked to CASE tools to accomplish the task result.

As the data processing community moves ahead in its rapid development of CASE tools and workbenches, it is inevitable that such tools will increasingly be used to enhance the systems design process. It is the hope of the authors that this book will stimulate systems designers to define policies that must be in place to ensure that the CASE tools used coincide with an established methodology and to develop training programs to train staff on the application of CASE tools.

8.2.1 Model for a CASE-Oriented Design Methodology

This section presents a model for a design methodology that has two phases: external design and internal design. The external design phase addresses those tasks that must be performed to translate the system into subsystems and to define the interface requirements. The internal design phase focuses on those tasks involved in generating detailed descriptions of all inputs and outputs, defining the data base structure, and developing program specifications. It defines the system and process necessary to implement and operate the system. The result of the design phases is a complete system specification from which the programmers can code the system modules and the data administration staff can create the required data base structures. The information developed also provides the user community with a basis for developing user procedures.

Each phase is broken down into tasks and task steps with which certain types of CASE tools can be integrated to accomplish the task objectives. Figure 8-2 shows the end-item/CASE tool correlation of the design process.

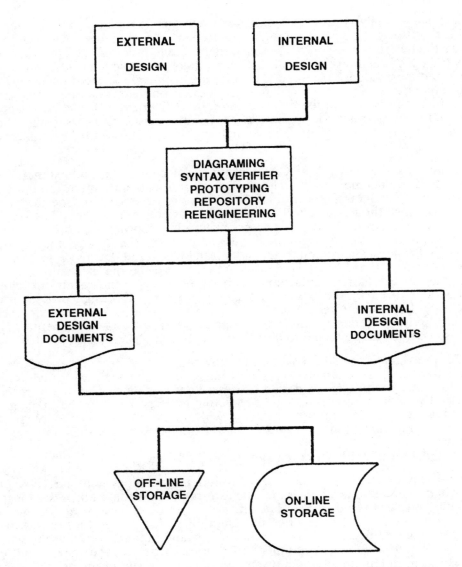

Figure 8-2. End-Item/CASE Tool Correlation of the Design Process

8.2.2 External Design CASE Integration

The external design phase breaks down into seven major tasks. Each task produces one or more end-items that can be prepared using specified CASE tools. Table 8-4 shows the end-item/CASE tool correlation for each external design task.

Table 8-4. External Design End-Item/CASE Tool Correlation

Task/Task Step	End-Item	Applicable Tool(s)
1. Review functional baseline documentation.		Repository Configuration management

2. Select design alternative.	Data Flow Diagrams
	Control Flow Diagrams
	Data Structure Outlines
	Request for Proposals
	Software Package Evaluation
	   Matrix
	Cost Analysis Statement
	Package Implementation Plan
	Letter of Commitment
	Functional Evaluation
	   Comparative Summaries
	Economic Evaluation
	   Comparative Summaries
	Vendor Evaluation
	   Comparative Summaries
	Resource Allocation
	   Authorization
		Diagraming
		Repository
		SDM
		Project management

3. Translate system into subsystems.	Structure Chart for Subsystem
	   Design
	System Components Schematic
	Subsystem Relationship Diagram
	Document Content Description
	Record/Transaction Description
	Table Content Description
	Interface Flow Diagram
	Calculation Logic Algorithms
	Data Base/File Processing Logic
	   Diagrams
	History File Processing Logic
	   Diagrams
	Table Processing Logic
	   Diagrams
	Output Processing Logic
	   Diagrams
	Report Content Descriptions
	Screen Content Descriptions
		Diagraming
		Repository
		SDM
		Prototyping
		Configuration Management

4. Amplify hardware/software requirements.	Equipment Requirements Hardware Architecture Requirements Support Software Requirements	Repository SDM Reengineering

Table 8-4. External Design End-Item/CASE Tool Correlation *(continued)*

Task/Task Step	End-Item	Applicable Tool(s)
5. Amplify system impacts.	User Organization Impact Document Organization Chart Operational Impact Statement	Diagraming Repository SDM
6. Develop security, privacy, and control approach.	Data Security Requirements Data Control Requirements	Diagraming Repository SDM
7. Prepare external design phase end-document.	External Design Phase Document Sign-off Sheet Internal Design Task Planning Checklist Committed Cost Estimate Target Schedule Milestone Charts	SDM Diagraming Project Management Repository

The external design phase of the system life cycle provides the transition from the functional requirements to a set of user-oriented design specifications. The tasks performed are aimed at enabling the user organization to monitor the internal design and subsequent implementation of the system to ensure that the requirements have been met. The external design phase is divided into seven major tasks.

1. *Review Functional Baseline Documentation.* The analyst begins by reviewing the documentation that established the functional baseline. This includes all of the questionnaire forms, interview summaries, and other document items delivered to the project file during the initial investigation, feasibility study, and requirements definition phases that were not included in the published phase end-document.

2. *Select Design Alternative.* After reviewing the functional requirements set forth in the functional baseline documents, the system designer identifies the alternative approaches to achieving the specified requirements. The various alternatives are then measured against the criteria specified in the requirements specification to determine which are workable.

3. *Translate System into Subsystems.* This task focuses on redefining the system into functional subsystems that correspond to the specified functional requirements.

4. *Amplify Hardware/Software Requirements.* After the subsystems have been defined, the system designers must develop specifications that pertain to the hardware and software environment that are needed to satisfy the functional requirements.

5. *Amplify System Impacts.* The objective of this task is to fully document the organizational and operational impacts of implementing the new system.

6. *Develop Security, Privacy, and Control Approach.* The objective of this task is to define the approaches for ensuring the security of the system and data. The approach should consider the privacy and security requirements presented in the requirements definition document.

7. *Prepare External Design Phase End-Document.* The purpose of this task is to present a comprehensive written document that establishes the design framework.

Each task is further broken down into a series of task steps, and a definable end-item is identified for each task step. The integration of CASE tools to serve the end-item orientation of the external design process is explained and illustrated on the following pages.

Task 1. REVIEW FUNCTIONAL BASELINE DOCUMENTATION

Review Initial Investigation Documentation. The objective of this task step is to conduct a paper review of all the document items contained in the initial investigation project file and/or included in the initial investigation phase end-document, especially the problem and need statement, projected cost statements, and target schedules. In an on-line environment, a repository CASE tool may be integrated with this task step to retrieve data stored in the initial investigation project file. In an on-line or off-line environment, a configuration management CASE tool may be used to identify and retrieve initial investigation documentation contained in the project file or in the initial investigation document.

Review Feasibility Study Documentation. The objective of this task step is to conduct a paper review of all the document items contained in the feasibility study project file and/or included in the feasibility study phase end-document, especially the documentation related to the current system, the documentation pertaining to the proposed system requirements, and the documentation that identifies package alternatives. In an on-line environment, a repository CASE tool may be integrated with this task step to retrieve data stored in the feasibility study project file. In an on-line or off-line environment, a configuration management CASE tool may be used to identify and retrieve feasibility study documentation contained in the project file and/or in the feasibility study document.

Review Requirements Definition Documentation. The objective of this task step is to conduct a paper review of all the document items contained in the requirements definition project file and/or included in the requirements definition phase end-document, especially the documentation related to the functional, performance, environment, and organizational requirements; and the documentation that established the criteria for selecting packages to be leased or purchased from vendors. In an on-line environment, a repository CASE tool may be integrated with this task step to retrieve data stored in the requirements definition project file. In an on-line or off-line environment, a configuration management CASE tool may be used to identify and retrieve requirements definition documentation contained in the project file and/or in the requirements definition document.

Task 2. SELECT DESIGN ALTERNATIVE

Diagram Design Alternatives. The objective of this task step is to prepare high-level flow diagrams for each alternative recommended at the conclusion of the requirements definition phase. The diagrams and associated documentation should identify the inputs required for capturing data, depict the data groupings that will form the basis for file structures, identify the outputs to be produced, and indicate the control mechanisms to be considered. The end-item deliverables are (1) data flow diagrams, (2) control flow diagrams, and (3) data structure outlines. A diagraming CASE tool may be integrated with this task step to create the data flow and control flow diagrams. A repository CASE tool may be used to capture the data grouping information. An SDM CASE tool that provides structures for identifying design alternatives may also be integrated with this task step.

Request Vendor Proposals. The objective of this task step is to prepare formal requests for proposals from vendors to request information regarding special features and technical constraints of the package offerings; detailed costs, including purchase and lease prices, maintenance, and any other costs that may be associated with the package; customer reference information; and contract requirements. The end-item deliverable is a request for proposals. An SDM CASE tool that provides structures for preparing requests for proposals may be integrated with this task step.

Evaluate Vendor Proposals. The objective of this task step is to evaluate each vendor response in terms of compatibility to user requirements, technical support capability, technical design approach, adaptability, expandibility, installation/implementation schedules, training requirements/support, documentation, vendor support, and vendor qualification. The end-item deliverables are (1) a software package evaluation matrix, (2) a cost analysis statement, and (3) a package implementation plan. An SDM CASE tool that provides structures for evaluating available packages may be integrated with this task step. A project management CASE tool may be used to prepare the package implementation plans.

Obtain Vendor Commitments. The objective of this task step is to obtain vendor commitments relating to delivery schedules, cost commitments, vendor support, and performance. The end-item deliverable is a letter of commitment. A repository CASE tool may be integrated with this task step to collect pertinent vendor commitments. An SDM CASE tool that provides structures for creating requests for commitment may be used to create the request for vendor commitment.

Finalize Make-or-Buy Decision. The objective of this task step is to determine whether to acquire a vendor package or to develop the system internally. Key comparative data are summarized and presented to management for the make-or-buy decision and final alternative selection. The end-item deliverables are (1) functional evaluation comparative summaries, (2) economic evaluation comparative summaries, and (3) vendor evaluation comparative summaries. An SDM CASE tool that provides structures for creating the comparative summaries may be integrated into this task step.

Authorize Resource Allocation. The objective of this task step is to obtain authorization for allocating the required resources to purchase a selected package or to develop the selected alternative. Resource authorizations may include financial resources, human resources, and equipment resources. The end-item deliverable is a resource allocation authorization. An SDM CASE tool that provides structures for creating the resource allocation authorization may be integrated into this task step.

Task 3. TRANSLATE SYSTEM INTO SUBSYSTEMS

Prepare System Schematic. The objective of this task step is to prepare schematics that redefine the system into functional subsystems. The end-item deliverables are (1) a structure chart for subsystem design and (2) a system components schematic. A diagraming CASE tool may be integrated with this task to generate structural charts for the subsystem design and system component schematics. A repository CASE tool may be used to store graphics and other information in a central repository.

Allocate System Functions. The objective of this task is to redefine how the system functions are allocated to the various programs and modules. The end-item deliverable is a subsystem relationship diagram that describes the data structures of each subsystem and shows the relationships between the subsystems. A diagraming CASE tool may be integrated with this task to generate entity relation charts for the subsystem design. A repository CASE tool may be used to store graphics and other information in a central repository.

Prepare Input Data Descriptions. The objective of this task step is to prepare data descriptions of the content of source documents, record/transactions, tables, files, and inputs from other systems. The end-item deliverables are (1) document content descriptions, (2) record/transaction contents descriptions, (3) table content descriptions, and (4) an interface flow diagram that shows the flow of inputs from other systems. An SDM CASE tool that provides structures for preparing input data descriptions may be integrated with this task. A repository CASE tool may be integrated that can be used to store the content description forms/screens in a central repository.

Define Processing Logic. The objective of this task step is to define processing logic relative to required calculations, data base/file processing, history file processing, table processing, and output processing. The end-item deliverables include: (1) calculation logic algorithms, (2) data base/file processing logic diagrams, (3) history file processing logic diagrams, (4) table processing logic diagrams, and (5) output processing logic diagrams. A diagraming CASE tool may be integrated with this task to generate logic diagrams. A repository CASE tool may be integrated that can be used to store graphics and other information in a central repository.

Prepare Output Descriptions. The objective of this task is to prepare output descriptions of all output document forms and output screen formats. The end-item deliverables include (1) report content descriptions and (2) screen content descriptions. A prototyping CASE tool may be integrated with this task to define the screen formats. A configuration management CASE tool may be used to track screen and report contents. A repository CASE tool may be integrated that can be used to store graphics and other information in a central repository. An SDM CASE tool that provides structures for preparing output descriptions may be integrated with this task.

Task 4. AMPLIFY HARDWARE/SOFTWARE REQUIREMENTS

Amplify Equipment Requirements. The objective of this task is to amplify the equipment requirements defined during the requirements definition phase by providing detailed information regarding types and locations of terminals/workstations, types and locations of printers, additional peripheral equipment required (e.g., scanners, bar code readers, etc.), and the operational characteristics and availability of the equipment. The end-item deliverable is an updated equipment requirements document. A reengineering CASE tool may be integrated with this task to evaluate existing equipment configurations. A repository CASE tool may be integrated that can be used to store the updated equipment requirements document(s) in a central repository. An SDM CASE tool that provides structures for redefining support equipment requirements may be integrated with this task.

Amplify Hardware Architecture Requirements. The objective of this task is to amplify the hardware architecture requirements contained in the requirements definition project file by providing detailed descriptions of processor requirements, including number of each and the size of internal storage; storage media requirements, including number of cartridges, disk units, tape units, etc.; output device requirements; including number of each on-line/off-line; and communications network requirements, including redundancy and line speed requirements. The end-item deliverable is an updated hardware architecture requirements document. A repository CASE tool may be used to store the hardware requirements documents in a central repository. An SDM CASE tool that provides structures for describing the hardware environment may be integrated with this task step.

Amplify Support Software Requirements. The objective of this task is to amplify the support software requirements defined during the requirements definition by providing detailed descriptions of the software with which the programs to be developed must interact. Included in the updated requirements must be references to the languages used, the operating system used; and the nomenclature and documentation of each support software system. The end-item deliverable is an updated support software requirements document. A reengineering CASE tool can be integrated with this task step to create structure charts that describe the support software with which the system will interact. A repository CASE tool may be used to store the updated support software requirements in a central repository. An SDM CASE tool that provides structures for redefining support software requirements may be integrated with this task.

Task 5. AMPLIFY SYSTEM IMPACTS

Amplify Organizational Impacts. The objective of this task is to amplify the organizational impact statements contained in the requirements definition project file. The updated organizational impact statements should include the modifications of responsibilities and the addition or elimination of responsibilities that will be necessary to use the proposed system. The end-item deliverables are (1) a user organization impact document, and (2) an organization chart showing the organizational impacts. A diagraming CASE tool may be integrated with this task step to create updated organization charts. A repository CASE tool may be used to store the organizational impact statements and structure charts in a central repository. An SDM CASE tool that provides structures for describing organizational impacts may also be integrated with this task step.

Amplify Operational Impacts. The objective of this task is to amplify the operational impact statements contained in the requirements definition project file. The updated operational impact statements should consider the proposed procedural changes for entering and accessing data; the impacts on the user to change from the current operational procedures; new data sources; quantity, type, and timeliness of data to be used in the system; data retention requirements; and modes of user operation. The end-item deliverable is an updated operational impact statement. A diagraming CASE tool may be integrated with this task step to create flow diagrams illustrating changes in work processes. A repository CASE tool may be used to store the operational impact statements and structure charts in a central repository. An SDM CASE tool that provides structures for describing operational impacts may also be integrated with this task step.

Task 6. DEVELOP SECURITY, PRIVACY, AND CONTROL APPROACH

Amplify Security and Privacy Requirements. The objective of this task is to amplify the security and privacy requirements contained in the requirements definition project file. The updated security and privacy requirements should consider the degree of sensitivity of the data, data files, inputs, and outputs in the system; proprietary and management constraints; and the levels of availability, integrity, and confidentiality of the system. The end-item deliverable is a data security requirements document. A diagraming CASE tool may be integrated with this task step to create flow diagrams illustrating security procedures. A repository CASE tool may be used to store the security and privacy requirements documentation in a central repository. An SDM CASE tool that provides structures for defining security and privacy requirements may also be integrated with this task step.

Amplify Control Requirements. The objective of this task is to amplify the control requirements contained in the requirements definition project file. The updated control requirements should consider requirements for data completeness and accuracy, file recovery and reconstruction, and audit trails; preprocessing, input/output processing, and postprocessing times; and identification, access, surveillance, and balancing control. The end-item deliverable is a data control requirements document. A diagraming CASE tool may be integrated with this task step to create flow diagrams that illustrate the control requirements. A repository CASE tool may be used to store the control requirements documentation in a central repository. An SDM CASE tool that provides structures for defining control requirements may also be integrated with this task step.

Task 7. PREPARE EXTERNAL DESIGN PHASE END-DOCUMENT

Prepare the External Design Phase End-Document. The objective of this task step is to prepare an external design phase end-document that communicates the results of the external design phase to the end-user. The end-item deliverable is an external design phase document. An SDM CASE tool that provides a structure for preparing an external design phase document may be integrated with this task step.

Process External Design Document for Review. The objective of this task step is to pass the external design phase document through review points for concurrence and sign-off. The end-item deliverable is a concurrence and sign-off sheet. A project management CASE tool that provides a structure for concurrence and sign-off of phase documents may be integrated with this task step.

Prepare Work Plan for Internal Design Phases. The objective of this task step is to prepare a work plan for performing the internal design tasks. The plan should consider the work breakdown structure and the cost and schedule projections for the phase work. The end-item deliverables are (1) an internal design task planning checklist, (2) a committed cost estimate document, (3) a target schedule document, and (4) milestone charts. A diagraming CASE tool may be used to create project structure charts. A project management CASE tool may be integrated with this task step to prepare the internal design project plan. An SDM CASE tool that provides structures for defining the tasks and task steps to be performed may be integrated to define the work breakdown structure. A repository CASE tool may be used to store the internal design work plan documentation in a central repository.

8.2.3 Internal Design CASE Integration

The internal design phase breaks down into 10 major tasks. Each task produces one or more end-items that can be prepared using specified CASE tools. Table 8-5 shows the internal design task end-item correlation and identifies the types of CASE tools that may be integrated to accomplish a particular internal design task result.

Table 8-5. Internal Design Task/CASE Tool Correlation

Task/Task Step	End-Item	Applicable Tool(s)
1. Review external design documentation.		Repository Configuration Management
2. Finalize function allocations.	Detailed System Structure Diagram Data Flow Diagram	Diagraming Repository Syntax Verifier SDM
3. Develop detail transaction structure.	Hierarchical Menu Structure Diagram Top-Level Structure Diagram Detailed Structure Diagram Transaction Logic Diagram Transaction Logic Narrative	Diagraming Repository Syntax Verifier SDM
4. Prepare data base specifications.	List of Entities Entity-Relationship Diagram Logical Data Base Design Specification Physical Data Base Design Specification	Diagraming Repository Syntax Verifier ReEngineering SDM

Table 8-5. Internal Design Task/CASE Tool Correlation *(continued)*

Task/Task Step	End-Item	Applicable Tool(s)
5. Prepare on-line program specifications. Specifications	Screen Layouts Functional Routine Logic Diagrams Logic Narratives	Prototyping Repository Diagraming Syntax Verifier Configuration Management SDM
6. Prepare batch program specifications.	Report Layouts Security Interface Specifications Batch Routine Logic Diagrams Logic Narratives Job Flow Diagrams Job Description Narratives	Prototyping Repository Diagraming Syntax Verifier SDM Configuration Management
7. Finalize special design specifications.	Data Control Specification Data Access Specifications Application Access Specifications Procedural Control Specifications Audit Trail Flow Diagrams Application Security Specifications Security Transaction Definitions Backup, Recovery, and Restart Procedures Statement of Constraints	Diagraming Repository Configuration Management SDM
8. Finalize program development procedures.	Program Development Standards Statement of QA Responsibility and Authority QA Technical Review Plan	Repository Configuration Management SDM
9. Prepare test, conversion and implementation plans	Test Plan Conversion Plan Implementation Plan Configuration Management Plan	Repository Project Management Reengineering Configuration Management SDM
10. Prepare and review internal design document	Internal Design Phase Document Sign-off Sheet	SDM

In summary, the general tasks involved in the systems design process are concerned with

- Segmenting the system into modules
- Designing the data base
- Specifying the programs necessary to achieve the system's objectives
- Designing input/output documents and screen formats
- Designing the system's controls
- Obtaining the required hardware and supporting software

The CASE environment may consist of a variety of tools that can be used to support the design process. Diagraming CASE tools can provide automated support for drawing data flow diagrams, structure charts, and other graphics. Syntax verifier CASE tools can be used to support diagraming techniques. They can perform consistency checks, level balancing of data, and other error-checking processes. Central repository CASE tools can provide the link between graphics, data definition, and screen and report definitions. Prototyping CASE tools can be used to define interface specifications prior to programming. SDM and project management CASE tools can provide methods guidelines and define procedures for tracking progress and managing resources. Reengineering CASE tools may be utilized to integrate structure charts, data dictionaries, etc., of the existing system with the design of a new system.

The tasks performed during the internal design phase establish the design baseline for configuration management. During this phase, the specifications for each system element are finalized. The specifications for the data bases are generated, and the plans for testing, implementation, and configuration management are prepared. All of the specifications necessary for a programmer to code the programs are included. The internal design phase breaks down into 10 major tasks:

1. *Review External Design Documentation.* The internal design process gets under way by reviewing the document items delivered to the project file during the external design phase and/or contained in the external design phase document.

2. *Finalize Function Allocations.* The objective of this task is to finalize the structural composition of the system. Functional decomposition diagrams are created so that every functional element can be identified with one or more program modules. The relationships among the program modules are also defined.

3. *Develop Detail Transaction structure.* This task translates the structural design charts and data flow diagrams into a physical model of the system. Menu structures and global facilities are defined and exploded down to the individual transaction level.

4. *Prepare Data Base Specifications.* The data structures underlying the program functions are developed using either a normalization or entity-relationship approach. The specifications created should enable program specifications to be written that include identification of where each data element is to be stored or accessed.

5. *Prepare On-Line Program Specifications.* The purpose of this task is to create detailed specifications for each of the on-line functions identified in the detailed functional allocation. Program logic, screens, and transaction formats are specified in a manner that en-

ables a programmer to develop executable program code, without ambiguity as to what logic or error detection is required.

6. *Prepare Batch Program Specifications.* This task results in report and program specifications for the batch processes identified in the functional allocation process.

7. *Finalize Special Design Specifications.* The objective of this task is to define the control, security, backup, file retention, and restart procedures to meet the requirements definition document and expanded upon during the external design. Incorporate any design constraints imposed on the system by the operating time window, hardware, software, and communications environments.

8. *Finalize Program Development Procedures.* This task specifies the applicable programming guidelines and quality assurance procedures that will guide the program generation activities.

9. *Prepare Test, Conversion, and Implementation Plans.* The documents produced as a result of this task outline the steps necessary for program testing, file conversion, and implementation of the system.

10. *Prepare and Review Internal Design Document.* When all of the internal design tasks have been performed and documented, the internal design phase end-document is produced to establish the design baseline for configuration management.

Each task is further broken down into a series of task steps, and a definable end-item is identified for each task step. The integration of CASE tools to serve the end-item orientation of the internal design process is explained and illustrated below and on the following pages.

Task 1. REVIEW EXTERNAL DESIGN DOCUMENTATION

Review System/Subsystem Specifications. The objective of this task step is to conduct a paper review of all document items delivered to the project file during the external design phase of project development that define the system/subsystem specifications of the system being designed. In an on-line environment, a repository CASE tool may be integrated with this task step to retrieve data stored in the project file. In either an on-line or an off-line environment, a configuration management CASE tool may be used to identify and retrieve system/subsystem specifications from the project file.

Review Security and Control Requirements. The objective of this task step is to conduct a paper review of all document items delivered to the project file during the external design phase of project development that define the security and control requirements of the system being designed. In an on-line environment, a repository CASE tool may be integrated with this task step to retrieve data stored in the project file. In either an on-line or an off-line environment, a configuration management CASE tool may be used to identify and retrieve security and control specifications from the project file.

Review Technical Environment Requirements. The objective of this task step is to conduct a paper review of all document items delivered to the project file during the external design phase of project development that define the technical requirements of the system being designed. In an on-line environment, a repository CASE tool may be integrated with this task step to retrieve data stored in the project file. In either an on-line or an off-line environment, a configuration management CASE tool may be used to identify and retrieve technical environment specifications from the project file.

Review Interfacing Requirements. The objective of this task step is to conduct a paper review of all document items delivered to the project file during the external design phase of project development that define the interfacing requirements of the system being designed. In an on-line environment, a repository CASE tool may be integrated with this task step to retrieve data stored in the project file. In either an on-line or an off-line environment, a configuration management CASE tool may be used to identify and retrieve interface specifications from the project file.

Task 2. FINALIZE FUNCTION ALLOCATIONS

Prepare Structural Design Chart. The objective of this task step is to prepare a diagram illustrating the structure of the system. The diagram should indicate the functional requirement(s) associated with each program module. Every function defined in the requirements definition document and expanded upon in the external design document should be correlated to one or more program modules. The end-item deliverable is a detailed system structure diagram that graphically illustrates the logical structure of the system. A diagraming CASE tool may be integrated with this task step to create the detailed structure diagram. A repository CASE tool may be used to store the completed diagram and to retrieve the functional requirements and specifications. A syntax verifier CASE tool may be used to validate the structure of the diagram. An SDM CASE tool that provides structures for presenting the structure diagram may also be integrated with this task step.

Prepare Detailed Data Flow Diagrams. The objective of this task step is to graphically illustrate the flow of data into, through, and out of each program module. An overall data flow diagram may be developed showing the classes of data associated with each of the subsystems. Each subsystem is, in turn, diagramed until individual program modules and data elements are represented. The end-item deliverable is a detailed data flow diagram for each program. A diagraming CASE tool may be integrated with this task step to create the data flow diagrams. A repository CASE tool may be used to retrieve related information and to store the final diagrams. A syntax verifier CASE tool may be used to ensure completeness and correctness of the diagrams. An SDM CASE tool that provides structures for presenting the data flow diagrams may also be integrated with this task step.

Task 3. DEVELOP DETAIL TRANSACTION STRUCTURE

Create Menu Structure. The objective of this task step is to translate the structure diagrams and data flow diagrams created in the previous task into a hierarchical menu structure, starting with the application entry point, down through the programs that perform the actual functions. The end-item deliverable is a detailed hierarchical menu structure diagram for the system. A diagraming CASE tool may be integrated with this task step to create the structure diagrams. A repository CASE tool may be used to retrieve related information and to store the final diagrams. A syntax verifier CASE tool may be used to ensure completeness and correctness of the diagrams. An SDM CASE tool that provides structures for presenting the menu structure diagrams may also be integrated with this task step.

Specify Global Facilities. The objective of this task step is to create specifications for the facilities which will be globally available in the system (i.e., accessible from any screen). Examples of such facilities include help information, application exits, transaction exits, exit to next higher menu, exit to main menu, and screen prints. The output of this process is combined with the menu hierarchy of the previous task step to generate a top-level structure diagram. A diagraming CASE tool may be integrated with this task step to create the structure diagram. A repository CASE tool may be used to retrieve menu hierarchy information and to store the final structure diagram. A syntax verifier CASE tool may be used to ensure completeness and correctness of the diagrams. An SDM CASE tool that provides structures for presenting the menu flow diagrams may also be integrated with this task step.

Explode Down to Individual Transactions. The objective of this task step is to finalize the logical structure of the application. The process involves adding the individual transaction definitions to the top-level structure diagram created in the previous task step. At each submenu level, the locally global transactions are defined (transactions applicable to all options under the menu). The process continues until all individual transaction definitions have been specified. The output of this process is combined with the top-level structure diagram of the previous task step to create a detailed structure diagram. A diagraming CASE tool may be integrated with this task step to create the structure diagram. A repository CASE tool may be used to retrieve top-level structure information and to store the final structure diagram. A syntax verifier CASE tool may be used to ensure completeness and correctness of the diagrams. An SDM CASE tool that provides structures for presenting the structure diagrams may also be integrated with this task step.

Create Transaction Logic Definitions. The objective of this task step is to define the logic options within each transaction. This process includes creating detailed logic diagrams for each of the transactions defined in the detailed structure diagram. Each transaction definition should include a narrative description of the processing logic. Include optional routines which may be executed, such as error-handling routines. The end-item deliverables of this task are (1) transaction logic diagrams and (2) transaction logic narratives. A diagraming CASE tool may be integrated with this task step to create the transaction logic diagrams. A repository CASE tool may be used to retrieve detailed transaction information and to store the final logic diagrams. A syntax verifier CASE tool may be used to ensure completeness and correctness of the diagrams. An SDM CASE tool that provides structures for presenting the transaction logic diagrams and narratives may also be integrated with this task step.

Task 4. PREPARE DATA BASE SPECIFICATIONS

Perform Detailed Data Analysis. The objective of this task step is to define the relationships between the data elements identified in the detailed data flow and structure diagrams of the previous tasks. The end-item deliverables of this task are (1) a list of entity types and (2) an entity-relationship diagram that shows the entities, their attributes, and their relationships. A diagraming CASE tool may be integrated with this task step to create the entity-relationship diagrams. A syntax verifier CASE tool may be used to ensure uniqueness of entities and the logical consistency of the diagram. A repository CASE tool may be used to record entity definitions, attributes, and relationships. A reengineering CASE tool may be used to chart entities and attributes of existing systems with which the new system will interface. An SDM CASE tool that provides structures for presenting the entity-relationship diagrams may also be integrated with this task step.

Develop Logical Data Base Design. The objective of this task step is to translate the data relationships into logical data base structures. These structures represent the view of the data as seen by the application under development. The end-item deliverable of this task is a logical data base design specification. A repository CASE tool that provides data modeling and normalization functions may be integrated with this step to produce the logical data base design. An SDM CASE tool that provides structures for presenting the data base design may also be used.

Develop Physical Data Base Design. The objective of this task step is to translate the logical data base design into the physical design applicable to the data base management system in use. Performance considerations may prevent direct translation of the normalized logical design. The end-item deliverable of this task is a physical data base design specification. A repository CASE tool that provides conversion of the logical data base to a physical design may be integrated with this step. An SDM CASE tool that provides structures for presenting the data base design may also be used. Some CASE vendors provide performance prediction tools which may also aid in determining the optimal physical implementation of the data base design.

Task 5. PREPARE ON-LINE PROGRAM SPECIFICATIONS

Prepare Input Screen Layouts. The objective of this task step is to prepare screen layouts for all input screens. The layouts should include the data elements to be entered, the display attributes of each element, the text and location for all display fields, the paths to and from the screen, and the transaction ID for processing the data upon entry. The end-item deliverable is a screen layout for each input screen. A prototyping CASE tool that provides screen painting capability may be integrated with this task step to generate the screen layouts. A repository CASE tool may be used to retrieve data element definitions and field length information. A configuration management CASE tool may be used to track requirements against screen content. An SDM CASE tool that provides structures for presenting screen layouts may also be integrated with this task step.

Prepare Inquiry/Output Screen Layouts. The objective of this task step is to prepare screen layouts for all inquiry and output screens. The layouts should include the data elements to be displayed; the display attributes of each element; the header text, location, and attributes; and the processing paths to and from the screen. The end-item deliverable is a screen layout for each inquiry and output screen. A prototyping CASE tool that provides screen painting capability may be integrated with this task step to generate the screen layouts. A repository CASE tool may be used to retrieve data element definitions and field length information. A configuration management CASE tool may be used to track requirements against screen content. An SDM CASE tool that provides structures for presenting screen layouts may also be integrated with this task step.

Define Detailed Application Logic. The objective of this task step is to prepare logic diagrams for each of the functional application routines executed in the on-line environment. The diagrams should be accompanied by narratives explaining the logic. The end-item deliverables are (1) a functional routine logic diagram and (2) a logic narrative for each on-line program routine. A diagraming CASE tool may be integrated with this task step to create the logic diagrams. A syntax verifier CASE tool may be used to ensure consistency and completeness of the diagrams. A repository CASE tool may be used to retrieve functional requirement and transaction definition data and to store the completed logic diagrams and descriptions. A configuration management CASE tool may be used to track requirements against the resultant logic. An SDM CASE tool that provides structures for presenting logic diagrams and logic narratives may also be integrated with this task step.

Task 6. PREPARE BATCH PROGRAM SPECIFICATIONS

Prepare Report Layouts. The objective of this task step is to prepare report layouts for all batch output functions. The layouts should include the data elements to be printed; the print attributes of each element; the header text, location, and attributes; and the initiation process for report generation. The end-item deliverable is a report layout for each batch report. A prototyping CASE tool that provides report generation capability may be integrated with this task step to generate the report layouts. A repository CASE tool may be used to retrieve data element definitions and field length information. A configuration management CASE tool may be used to track requirements against report content. An SDM CASE tool that provides structures for presenting report layouts may also be integrated with this task step.

Define Batch Processing Logic. The objective of this task step is to prepare logic diagrams for each of the functional application routines executed in the batch environment. The diagrams should be accompanied by narratives explaining the program logic and the initiation parameter requirements. The end-item deliverables are (1) a functional batch routine logic diagram and (2) a logic narrative for each batch program routine. A diagraming CASE tool may be integrated with this task step to create the logic diagrams. A syntax verifier CASE tool may be used to ensure consistency and completeness of the diagrams. A repository CASE tool may be used to retrieve functional requirement and data element definition data and to store the completed logic diagrams and descriptions. A configuration management CASE tool may be used to track requirements against the resultant logic. An SDM CASE tool that provides structures for presenting logic diagrams and logic narratives may also be integrated with this task step.

Develop Job Streams. The objective of this task step is to prepare job flow diagrams and narratives that define the frequency, sequences, and dependencies for running the batch jobs. Jobs requiring intervention by computer operations staff should be identified. The end-item deliverables are (1) a job flow diagram and (2) a job description narrative. A diagraming CASE tool may be integrated with this task step to create the flow diagrams. A syntax verifier CASE tool may be used to ensure consistency and completeness of the diagrams. A repository CASE tool may be used to retrieve structure diagrams and functional requirement data and to store the completed logic diagrams and descriptions. A configuration management CASE tool may be used to track requirements against the resultant logic. An SDM CASE tool that provides structures for presenting logic diagrams and narratives may also be integrated with this task step.

Task 7. FINALIZE SPECIAL DESIGN SPECIFICATIONS

Prepare Data Control and Audit Trail Specifications. The objective of this task step is to finalize the specification documents that define requirements for data control and auditability. The documentation should specify controls for data entry and access, submitting and receiving information from data processing operations, ensuring that file integrity is maintained, logging onto on-line processing systems, ensuring that maintenance transactions are properly handled, and audit trail processing controls for tracing input transactions. The end-item deliverables are (1) a data control specification, (2) an access control specification, (3) a procedural control specification, and (4) an audit trail flow diagram. A diagraming CASE tool may be integrated with this task step to prepare flow diagrams illustrating the control and audit processes. A repository CASE tool may be used to retrieve requirements specification relative to security and control requirements and to store the completed specifications. A configuration management CASE tool may be used to track requirements against the specifications. An SDM CASE tool that provides structures for presenting the flow diagrams and narrative specifications may also be integrated with this task step.

Prepare Security Specifications. The objective of this task step is to finalize the specification documents that define how security functions will be implemented. The transaction definitions created earlier should incorporate the security requirements specified during the external design and requirements definition phases. These definitions are reviewed and, if necessary, updated to meet the requirements. If security software is installed, or if the DBMS in use provides data-level security, the method of interfacing the application to the existing software should be specified. If application-specific security is required, the transaction definitions and logic prepared in previous tasks should be reviewed to ensure that all security requirements have been addressed. The end-item deliverables are (1) a security interface specification, (2) an application security specification, and (3) updated/verified security transaction definitions. A diagraming CASE tool may be integrated with this task step to retrieve the transaction diagrams prepared in task 3 for review and/or update. A repository CASE tool may be used to retrieve and store the specifications and diagrams. An SDM CASE tool that provides structures for presenting the security specifications may also be integrated with this task step.

Finalize Recovery and Restart Procedures. The objective of this task is to define recovery and restart procedures. The documentation should include frequency of backup, retention duration, procedure for accomplishing recovery, and requirements for restart. The end-item deliverables are procedural instructions for backup, recovery, and restart. A repository CASE tool may be integrated with this task step to retrieve requirements specifications relative to backup and recovery and to store the finished procedures. An SDM CASE tool that provides structures for presenting the defined procedures may also be integrated with this task step.

Define Developmental Constraints. The objective of this task is to define the constraints imposed on the system by the operating time window, communications networks, and system and support software. The end-item deliverable is a detailed statement of constraints imposed on the development and operation of the application by the equipment, operational, and software environment in which it will operate. A repository CASE tool may be integrated with this task step to store the final statement of constraints. An SDM CASE tool that provides structures for presenting the statement of constraints may be integrated with this task step.

Task 8. FINALIZE PROGRAM DEVELOPMENT PROCEDURES

Specify Programming Guidelines. The objective of this task is to specify the programming guidelines to be observed by the programmer when producing the program. The documentation should specify the programming language, the supporting systems (e.g., CASE tools, monitor, loader, librarian, debug, utilities, etc.), and the mnemonic labeling conventions to be observed in development of the computer program. The end-item deliverable is a program development standards document. A repository CASE tool may be integrated with this task step to retrieve existing development standards. A configuration management CASE tool may be used to track specific requirements or deviations from standard programming procedures. An SDM CASE tool that provides structures for presenting development specifications may be integrated with this task step.

Define Quality Assurance Procedures. The objective of this task is to define the review procedures for verification of the computer program design. The documentation should specify QA responsibility and authority and the technical review requirements. The end-item deliverables are (1) statements of QA responsibility and authority, and (2) a QA technical review plan. A repository CASE tool may be integrated with this task step to retrieve and store QA procedures. A configuration management CASE tool may be used to track QA requirements against the QA plan. An SDM CASE tool that provides structures for presenting a quality assurance plan may be integrated with this task step.

Task 9. PREPARE TEST, CONVERSION, AND IMPLEMENTATION PLANS

Prepare Test Plan. The objective of this task is to prepare a plan that defines the scope of testing to be conducted. The documentation should specify test requirements for each level of testing to be performed, test management responsibilities for conducting and coordinating test activities, personnel required to perform the tests, test hardware requirements, support software requirements, test schedules to be followed, and the procedures for reviewing and evaluating the final outcome of the test results. The end-item deliverable is a test plan. A project management CASE tool may be integrated with this task step to prepare test schedules. A configuration management CASE tool may be used to track functional requirements against test plans. An SDM CASE tool that provides structures for presenting a test plan may also be integrated with this task step.

Prepare Conversion Plan. The objective of this task is to prepare a plan that defines the conversion requirements. The documentation should address computer processing workloads, data conversion requirements, data loading requirements, manual support requirements, special forms and procedures, file verification and control considerations, interim maintenance requirements, and special training programs. The end-item deliverable is a conversion plan. A repository CASE tool may be integrated with this task step to retrieve file definitions and data input specifications and to store conversion plan data. A reengineering CASE tool may be used to create structure charts of existing files requiring conversion. A project management CASE tool may be used to generate conversion schedules and track progress. An SDM CASE tool that provides structures for presenting conversion plans may also be integrated with this task step.

Prepare Implementation Plan. The objective of this task is to prepare a plan that defines the implementation requirements. The documentation should provide implementation schedules; plans for deactivating existing systems; configuration identification of all files, libraries, etc., that must be activated for production operation; standards for preparing and maintaining user documentation and operator manuals; and procedures for conducting implementation reviews. The end-item deliverable is a detailed implementation plan. A repository CASE tool may be integrated with this task step to retrieve previous implementation plans for review and to store the plan when complete. A reengineering CASE tool may be used to create structure charts of existing systems to identify requirements for deactivating them. A project management CASE tool may be used to generate the implementation schedules. An SDM CASE tool that provides structures for presenting the implementation plan may also be integrated with this task step.

Prepare Configuration Management Plan. The objective of this task is to prepare a plan that defines the requirements for managing changes to the system. The documentation should specify procedures for identifying software configuration items, controlling changes to baseline items, configuration accounting and reporting, and procedures for verifying and validating the software configuration. The end-item deliverables are (1) configuration identification procedures, (2) change control procedures, (3) configuration accounting procedures, and (4) configuration auditing procedures. A repository CASE tool may be integrated with this task step to retrieve configuration item definitions. A configuration management CASE tool may be used to track configuration items. An SDM CASE tool that provides structures for presenting a configuration management plan may also be integrated with this task step.

Task 10. PREPARE AND REVIEW INTERNAL DESIGN DOCUMENT

Prepare the Internal Design Phase End-Document. The objective of this task step is to prepare an internal design phase end-document that communicates the results of the internal design phase to management and the program development staff. The end-item deliverable is an internal design phase end-document. An SDM CASE tool that provides a structure for preparing an Internal Design Phase End-Document may be integrated with this task step.

Process Internal Design Document for Review. The objective of this task step is to pass the internal design phase end-document through review points for concurrence and sign-off. The end-item deliverable is a concurrence and sign-off sheet. A project management or SDM CASE tool that provides a structure for concurrence and sign-off of phase documents may be integrated with this task step.

8.3 CASE TOOL PRODUCTS AND VENDORS

This section provides a listing of CASE products that are applicable to analysis and design functions. The list is by no means all-inclusive. It was derived from a data base developed and maintained by ISPAS Enterprises, a California research organization that conducts surveys of available software. Other published works that identify available CASE software include the *CASE Product Guide* published by Software Magazine and the software edition of *Data Sources* which profiles CASE products.

$Name. This CASE package provides a set of routines that are used to enforce naming standards. It runs on IBM MVS, VM/CMS. **GLOBAL SOFTWARE, P.O. Box 2813, Duxbury, MA 02331; Telephone – 617/934-0949; FAX – 617/934-0697**

ACPVision. This is a diagraming and syntax verifier CASE tool that supports creation and presentation of Mascot ACP diagrams. It performs diagram entry and editing functions, annotates and documents design objects, and provides ACP design rule checks. The software runs on Apple Macintosh compatible computers. The minimum memory requirement is 512 kilobytes. The source code is written in C. **ANDYNE COMPUTING, LTD., 544 Prince St., Suite 202, Kingston, ON, CD, K7L 167; Telephone – 800/267-0665, 613/548-4355; FAX – 548-7801**

AdaFlow (Version 3.0). This is a diagraming CASE tool that serves as an add-on to Iconix's Power Tools CASE workbench. The package supports Buhr diagraming techniques. It groups objects of a similar nature according to the operations to be performed. The software runs on Apple Macintosh compatible computers. **ICONIX SOFTWARE, 2800 28th St., Suite 320, Santa Monica, CA 94045; Telephone – 213/458-0092; FAX – 213/396-3454**

Adminis/32. This is an application tool set with repository. It runs on DEC VAX/VMS. **ADMINIS INC, 432 Columbia St., Cambridge, MA 02141; Telephone – 617/494-5100; FAX – 617/494-8645**

Analyst/RT. This is an SDM CASE tool. It tracks requirements related to the preparation of design documents that conform to DOD-STD-2167/A. The package provides for traceability of documentation that defines specifications and requirements and other document items contained in a software design document (SDD). The software runs on DEC VAX/VMS and ULTRIX compatible computers. **MENTOR GRAPHICS CORP., 8500 S.W. Creekside Place, Beaverton, OR 97005; Telephone – 800/547-7390, 503/626-7000; FAX – 503/626-1212**

AnaTool Workbench. This workbench provides CASE tools that can be used to perform structured analysis, data modeling, and structured design tasks. The software runs on Apple Macintosh Plus, 512, SE, and II compatible computers. The package supports the Presentation Manager graphical interface. The minimum memory requirement is 512 kilobytes. The source code is written in C. **ADVANCED LOGICAL SOFTWARE, INC., 9903 Santa Monica Blvd., Suite 108, Beverly Hills, CA 90212; Telephone – 213/653-5786; FAX – 213/655-2711**

Application Development Workbench. This workbench provides CASE tools for diagraming, code generation, repository, and SDM applications. It supports IBM's Application Development/Cycle (AD/Cycle) and complies with SAA and CUA standards. The package includes planning, analysis, design, and construction workstation modules. It stores information about a given application in a repository called *Encyclopedia* which is compatible with IBM's repository product. Access to Encyclopedia and access to the services are provided through a common interface. The software runs on OS/2 compatible computers. It supports the Presentation Manager graphical interface. The minimum memory requirement is 8192 kilobytes.

KNOWLEDGEWARE, INC., 3340 Peachtree Road, N.E., Atlanta, GA 30026; Telephone – 800/338-4130, 404/231-8575; FAX – 404/364-0883

APS Development Center. This is a data dictionary/repository CASE tool with a full lifecycle applications generator dictionary reporting capability. It runs on IBM PC, OS/2. **INTERSOLV, 3200 Tower Oaks Blvd., Rockville, MD** 20852; **Telephone – 301/230-3200; FAX – 301/231-7813**

Auditor. This is a diagraming CASE tool that creates and evaluates structured analysis documents for real-time systems. The package supports Hatley and Ward/Mellor real-time extensions to the Yourdon/DeMarco structured analysis methodology. It stores graphics in ASCII format and creates child data flow diagrams that balance with parent diagrams. The software runs on DEC VAX and MicroVAX/VMS compatible computers. **MENTOR GRAPHICS CORP, 8500 S.W. Creekside Place, Beaverton, OR 97005; Telephone – 800/547-7390, 503/626-7000; FAX – 503/626-1212**

Auto-Mate Plus. This is a front-end CASE tool that provides for prototyping, document production, record layout, data sharing, data base generation, and normalization. It includes encyclopedia capabilities. The package supports Yourdon, Chen diagram, and IEM methodologies. It also supports Telon and APS development interfaces. The software runs on PC-MS/DOS compatible computers. The minimum memory requirement is 640 kilobytes. **LBMS, INC., 2900 North Loop West, Suite 800, Houston, TX 77092; Telephone – 800/231-7515, 713/682-8530; FAX – 713/956-1829**

Blue/60. This is a diagraming CASE tool that creates and maintains data models in software development. It produces standard entity-relation diagrams using the Boyce-Codd method. The software runs on Apple Macintosh compatible computers. The minimum memory requirement is 1024 kilobytes. **ADVANCED LOGICAL SOFTWARE, INC., 9903 Santa Monica Blvd., Suite 108, Beverly Hills, CA 90212; Telephone – 213/653-5786; FAX – 213/655-2711**

CA-Advisor. This is a project management and systems development CASE tool. It is a strategic planning advice system with an expert knowledge data base of application development methodologies. It enables users to plan and manage application development projects. The software runs on PC-MS/DOS compatible computers. The minimum memory requirement is 320 kilobytes. The source code is written in C. **COMPUTER ASSOCIATES INTERNATIONAL, INC., 1814 S. Main St., South Bend, IN 46613; Telephone – 800/727-3169, 219/232-7921**

CA-Estimacs. This is an expert system for business application estimating. It provides support to MIS management in making decisions based on financial data and risk analysis. It groups estimated projects into portfolios for horizon planning. It can be used for budget preparation, project staffing, and audit reviews. The software runs on PC-MS/DOS compatible computers. The minimum memory requirement is 256 kilobytes. The source code is written in compiled BASIC and C.

COMPUTER ASSOCIATES INTERNATIONAL, INC., 1814 S. Main St., South Bend, IN 46613; Telephone – 800/727-3169, 219/232-7921

CA-PlanMacs (Rel. 2.0). This is a project management package that allows a project manager to graphically edit project plans at any level. It can be used to adjust relationships between individual phases, tasks, and activities. The package builds detailed phase, task, and activity definitions that comprise the methodology. Entire phases can be added, deleted, lengthened, or shortened for a specific project before detail activities are generated. The software runs on PC-MS/DOS compatible computers. The minimum memory requirement is 256 kilobytes The source code is written in BASIC and C. **COMPUTER ASSOCIATES INTERNATIONAL, INC., 1814 S. Main St., South Bend, IN 46613; Telephone – 800/727-3169, 219/232-7921**

CADMAC. This is a computer-aided document management and control system. It provides on-line management of product definition data including drawings, source code and object code libraries, and specifications. Modules include EM*MACS Engineering Manufacturing Management and Control System, SD*MACS Software Development Management and Control System, and MACS*Net Management and Control System Network. The software runs on PC-MS/DOS, DEC VAX, Micro VAX, and Data General MV compatible computers. The minimum memory requirement is 640 kilobytes. **Infodetics, 1341 S. Claudina St., Anaheim, CA 92805; Telephone – 714/491-6100; FAX – 714/635-4270**

CasePac (Rel. 3.0). This is a diagraming and repository CASE tool that can be used to store information collected in various phases of the program development cycle. The software allows programmers to share information by using the DB2 data dictionary. The software runs on IBM/MVS/XA compatible computers. The minimum memory requirement is 88 kilobytes. The source code is written in COBOL. **On-Line Software, International, 2 Executive Drive, Ft. Lee Executive Park, Fort Lee NJ 07024; Telephone: – 800/642-0177, 201/592-0009.**

Case Bench. This is a diagraming CASE tool that helps users create and document specifications and designs. It performs analysis and design functions for real-time systems. Applications include defense/aerospace and industrial engineering projects. The package can be adapted to meet unique project needs. The software runs on DEC VAX, MicroVAX/VMS, and ULTRIX compatible computers. **MENTOR GRAPHICS CORP., 8500 S.W. Creekside Place, Beaverton, OR 97005; Telephone – 800/547-7390, 503/626-7000; FAX – 503/626-1212**

Case Project. This is a project management and systems development CASE tool that tracks requirements from initial user requirements to finished code. It generates document structures based on DOD-STD-2167/A. Capabilities include the maintenance of document versions and controlled access to these documents. The package produces traceability reports which show relationships between the documents. The software runs on DEC VAX, MicroVAX/VMS compatible computers. **MENTOR GRAPHICS CORP., 8500 S.W. Creekside Place, Beaverton, OR 97005; Telephone – 800/547-7390, 503/626-7000; FAX – 503/626-1212**

Case Station. This is a diagraming and reengineering CASE tool for integrated analysis and design. It provides an interactive graphics editor and window interface and handles reverse engineering for verifying source code or documenting existing code. The package supports Hatley/Pirbhai and Ward/Mellor real-time extensions to Yourdon/DeMarco structured analysis and Page-Jones structured design methodologies. The software runs on Apollo DOMAIN 3000 and 4000 compatible computers. **MENTOR GRAPHICS CORP., 8500 S.W. Creekside Place, Beaverton, OR 97005; Telephone – 800/547-7390, 503/626-7000; FAX – 503/626-1212**

CASE Tools. This is a workbench that provides tools for diagraming, code generation, and repository functions. It includes an X-Window based CASE*Designer user interface, CASE*Dictionary, and CASE*Generator interface with Oracle's SQL*Forms. The software runs on DEC VAX/VMS, IBM mainframe, SUN/UNIX, and PC-MS/DOS compatible computers. **ORACLE CORP., 20 Davis Drive, Belmont, CA 94002; Telephone - 800/345-3267, 415/598-8000; FAX - 415/595-0630**

CASE Toolset. This is a workbench that providess tools for diagraming and systems development. Modules include PSL/PSA* for requirements and analysis, RSI* for custom reporting and bridging to other tools, VSI for data modeling, Structured Architect* on PC for graphical analysis, Structured Architect-Integrator* for integrating multiple Structured Architects, and Quick Spec* on PC for data entry and manipulation. The software runs on IBM/VM/CMS, MVS/TSO, UNIX, DEC/VAX, Gould 3287, Apollo, and Unisys compatible computers. The minimum memory requirement is 1024 kilobytes. The source code is written in FORTRAN. **META SYSTEMS, LTD., 315 E. Eisenhower Parkway, Suite 200, Ann Arbor, MI 48108; Telephone – 313/663-6027; FAX – 313/663-6119**

Checkpoint. This is a project measurement tool. The package provides functions for estimating, planning, and controlling. It also monitors progress of programming activities and factors affecting them and analyzes quality and productivity. The package offers cost estimates within 5 percent of accuracy levels. The software runs on PC-MS/DOS compatible computers. The minimum memory requirement is 512 kilobytes. It utilizes EMS. The source code is written in C. **SOFTWARE PRODUCTIVITY RESEARCH, 1972 Massachusetts Ave., Cambridge, MA 02140; Telephone – 617/495-0120; FAX – 617/495-0012**

CoCoPro. This is a project-management-oriented CASE tool for estimating resources needed to complete software development projects. It is a module of the ICONIX Power-Tools CASE workbench. The package uses exponential functions and attributes to calculate development costs. It covers personnel experience and capabilities, project complexity, product factors, and hardware limitations. The software runs on Apple Macintosh Plus, XL, SE, and II compatible computers. The minimum memory requirement is 1024 kilobytes. **ICONIX SOFTWARE, 2800 28th St., Suite 320, Santa Monica, CA 94045; Telephone – 213/458-0092; FAX – 213/396-3454**

CorVision. This is an integrated CASE tool that automates the system lifecycle phases from system design through implementation and enhancement. It provides diagraming and painting facilities on a PC workstation linked to an application generator on the VAX. It supports prototyping and provides automated document generation capability. The software runs on DEC VAX, VAXStation 2000, and MicroVAX II/VMS compatible computers. The minimum memory requirement is 4096 kilobytes. The source code is written in MACRO and C. **CORTEX CORP., 138 Technology Drive, Waltham, MA 02154; Telephone – 617/894-7000; FAX – 617/894-4729**

Cradle. This is a diagraming CASE tool combined with tools for configuration management. The package supports multiple users and multiple projects across networks. The software runs on Apollo/UNIX compatible computers. **YOURDON INC., 1501 Broadway, New York, NY 10036; Telephone – 212/391-2828**

CQS-DMT. This is a repository tool for the migration of data definitions from existing data dictionaries to the IBM Repository Manager/MVS. **CARLETON CORP, 8 New England Executive Park, Burlington, MA 01803; Telephone – 617/272-4310; FAX – 617/272-2910**

Customizer. This is a diagraming CASE tool that customizes Intersolv's Excelerator products. It includes a system dictionary, shape editor, screen design, and SLD interface. The software runs on PC-MS/DOS and DEC/VMS compatible computers. The minimum memory requirement is 640 kilobytes. It requires high-resolution graphics and a mouse. **INTERSOLV, 1 Main St., 9th Floor, Cambridge, MA 02142; Telephone – 800/777-8858; FAX – 617/577-8945**

Data Analyst. This is a diagraming CASE tool and expert system to aid in information modeling and data analysis. It assists analysts in creating DBMS-independent information models through the use of graphical tools and expert assistance in developing, consolidating, editing, validating, and reengineering information models. The software runs on PC-MS/DOS compatible computers. **BACHMAN INFORMATION SYSTEMS, 4 Cambridge Center, Cambridge, MA 02142-1401; Telephone – 617/354-1414; FAX – 617/354-0971**

Database & Development System. This is a data base and application development CASE tool that uses a common data dictionary. It runs on DEC VAX/VMS and IBM PC/MS-DOS. **BROWNSTONE SOLUTIONS, INC., 521 5th Ave., New York, NY 10175; Telephone – 212/370-7160; FAX – 212/667-2520**

Data Dictionary/Solution. This is a DB2-based repository CASE tool. It runs on IBM MVS, DB2 platforms. **BROWNSTONE SOLUTIONS, INC., 521 5th Ave., New York, NY 10175; Telephone – 212/370-7160; FAX – 212/667-2520**

Data-Station. This is a CASE tool that bridges Oracle RDBMS with AutoCAD to provide a drawing generator and optimizes object placement and routing of relationships and data flows. It includes 80 tables with 600 columns of information, 30 screens, and 60 reports. Adhoc SQL queries and reporting are supported in an open architecture. The package supports a math coprocessor. The software runs on PC-MS/DOS, Apollo, Sun, and DEC MicroVAX compatible computers. The minimum memory requirement is 640 kilobytes. The source code is written in C. A mouse is required. **CHARLES RIVER DEVELOPMENT, 483 Beacon St., Boston, MA 02115; Telephone – 617/424-1820; FAX – 617/267-2742**

Design/1. This is an integrated front-end CASE tool that includes either a data dictionary or an encyclopedia. It provides prototyping, report layout, document production, desktop publishing, record layout descriptions, diagram organization, and printing and data sharing capabilities. The package supports Yourdon, Chen diagraming, and Warnier-Orr methodologies. The software runs on PC-MS/DOS compatible computers. The minimum memory requirement is 640 kilobytes. Novell, 3Com, and NetBIOS network versions are available. A mouse is required. **ANDERSON CONSULTING, 69 W. Washington, Chicago, IL 60602; Telephone – 312/580-0069; FAX – 312/507-2548**

Design4Applications. This is a diagraming CASE tool that provides a framework for developing a detailed design of an application system. It provides a comprehensive and structured approach to modeling. The software runs on PC-MS/DOS compatible computers. The minimum memory requirement is 640 kilobytes. **HOLLAND SYSTEMS CORP., 3131 S. State St., Suite 303, Ann Arbor, MI 48104; Telephone – 313/995-9595**

Design/IDEF. This is a diagraming and SDM support CASE tool for planning, modeling, and development of systems requirements utilizing IDEF systems design methods. It provides both graphics and text capabilities. The package includes a data dictionary to import/export data to a word processing, data base, or desktop publishing program. The software runs on Apple Macintosh Plus, SE, and II compatible computers. The minimum memory requirement is 512 kilobytes. The source code is written in C. **META SOFTWARE CORP., 363 Seventh Ave., New York, NY 10001; Telephone – 212/695-5870**

Design/ML. This is a graphics interface CASE tool that can be used for diagraming and building prototypes. It creates diagrams and flowcharts that display boxes and graphics representing different program functions. The package interfaces with Meta Software's MetaDesign and Design/OA. It supports standard ML symbolic programming language. The software runs on Apple Macintosh Plus, SE, and Mac II compatible computers. **META SOFTWARE CORP., 363 Seventh Ave., New York, NY 10001; Telephone – 212/695-5870**

Design/Simulator. This is a diagraming CASE tool that allows users to draw objects and their interrelationships and to map information flow through these objects. The package allows analysts to build a Colored Petri Net information model. It provides a systematic way for evaluating dynamics of possible changes to the model. The software runs on Apple Macintosh compatible computers. **META SOFTWARE CORP., 363 Seventh Ave., New York, NY 10001; Telephone – 212/695-5870**

DesignAid. This is diagraming and repository CASE tool that can be used for structured analysis and design. It supports word processing and graphics requirements, validates and balances data flow diagrams, and extracts key information and loads it into a design dictionary. The software runs on PC-MS/DOS and DEC VAX compatible computers. The minimum memory requirement is 640 kilobytes. The source code is written in Pascal. **NASTEC CORP., 24681 Northwestern Hwy., Southfield, MI 48075; Telephone − 800/872-8296, 313/353-3300; FAX − 313/353-0707**

Designer. This is a diagraming and reengineering CASE tool that can be used to create and verify a structured design model of the system. It generates the initial design from the system specifications made with MGC's Analyst/RD and creates a design model from source code. Graphics are stored in ASCII format. The software runs on DEC VAX/VMS and ULTRIX compatible computers. **MENTOR GRAPHICS CORP., 8500 S.W. Creekside Place, Beaverton, OR 97005; Telephone − 800/547-7390, 503/626-7000; FAX − 503/626-1212**

DesignMachine. This is a repository CASE tool that supports both project management and systems development concepts. It automates the steps required by the requirements definition phase of Optima's Data Structured System Methodology. Capabilities include maintenance of an integrated design data base and generation of DSSM graphics, forms, and logical data base descriptions or DB2 table definitions from the applications requirements. The software supports and enforces quality assurance and change control. The software runs on PC-MS/DOS compatible computers. The minimum memory requirement is 640 kilobytes. The source code is written in Pascal. **OPTIMA, INC., 1300 Woodfield Road, Suite 400, Schaumburg, IL 60173; Telephone − 800/633-6303, 312/240-1888; FAX − 312/240-9073**

Designmanager. This is a diagraming CASE tool that provides a top-down/bottom-up approach for dictionary-driven modeling and design. It generates third-normal form conceptual schema and logical and physical data base designs for relational, hierarchical, or network data bases. The package is supplied only in conjunction with MSP's Controlmanager. The software runs on IBM 370, 30XX, 4300, 9370/MV, MVS/XA, VSE, VM, and VSI compatible computers. The minimum memory requirement is 2500 kilobytes. The source code is written in FORTRAN IV and Assembly. **MANAGER SOFTWARE PRODUCTS, INC., 131 Hartwell Ave., Lexington, MA 02173-3126; Telephone − 617/863-5800; FAX − 617/861-6130**

DesignVision. This is a diagraming and code generator CASE tool for design, analysis and documentation. It allows the system developers to select a standard modeling technique or create a custom diagraming model. Capabilities include maintenance of an object-oriented data base with a data dictionary. The software allows definition of custom diagram models and supports project operations diagram hierarchies and repository export through SQL. The software runs on PC-MS/DOS compatible computers. The minimum memory requirement is 640 kilobytes. The source code is written in C. **OPTIMA, INC., 1300 Woodfield Road,**

Suite 400, Schaumburg, IL 60173; Telephone – 800/633-6303, 312/240-1888; FAX – 312/240-9073

DesignVision ELS. This is a diagraming tool that includes predefined models for 10 diagraming methods including Warnier/Orr, Yourdon, Gaine and Sarson, and Chen/Entity relationship. It is an entry-level version of Optima's Design Vision. A user interface and optional full-color high-resolution graphics of Microsoft Windows are included to provide a software engineering environment. The software runs on PC-MS/DOS compatible computers. The minimum memory requirement is 640 kilobytes. **OPTIMA, INC., 1300 Woodfield Road, Suite 400, Schaumburg, IL 60173; Telephone – 800/633-6303, 312/240-1888; FAX – 312/240-9073**

Developer. This is a diagraming and prototyping management support CASE tool. It provides for graphics, text, matrices, data and referential integrity, customization, ad hoc query, prototyping, documentation generation, and project management support. The software runs on PC-MS/DOS compatible computers. The minimum memory requirement is 640 kilobytes. **ASYST TECHNOLOGIES, INC., 1 Napierville Plaza, Napierville, IL 60563; Telephone – 800/359-1101, 312/416-2990; FAX – 312/416-2374**

DFDP (Diagraphics for Data Processing). This is a diagraming, syntax verifier, and repository CASE tool that uses 3270-type terminals to produce data flow diagrams, structure charts, job step diagrams, and related graphics. It validates data names, I/O balance, and procedure leveling and creates formatted entries for data dictionaries. Capabilities include graphics created for major design methodologies. The software runs on IBM 360, 370, 30XX, 40XX, MVS, and MVS/XA compatible computers. The minimum memory requirement is 512 kilobytes. The source code is written in Assembly. **ADPAC CORP., P.O. Box 3337, San Francisco, CA 94119; Telephone – 415/974-6699; FAX – 415/546-7130**

DFDdraw. This is a diagraming CASE tool with a graphics symbols template for preparing data flow diagrams. It positions, connects, and annotates the symbols and performs scale, size, pan, zoom, and restore functions. The package integrates with Stradis/Draw and Prokit*Analyst. The software runs on PC-MS/DOS compatible computers. The minimum memory requirement is 320 kilobytes. The source code is written in Assembly. **MCDONNELL DOUGLAS INFORMATION SYSTEMS CO., 325 McDonnell Blvd., St. Louis, MO 63042; Telephone – 800/325-1551, 314/234-4117**

DSIMS Data Dictionary. This is a VAS Common Dictionary CASE tool. It supports IMS, DB2, SQL and CICS. **DSIMS, 510 Water St., Waxachachie, TX 75165; Telephone – 214/923-2087**

Easyspec. This is a repository and reengineering CASE tool that automates the design of data base table structure in third normal form. It provides a data base design interface to Rdb, INGRES, ORACLE, DB2, SQL, NOMAD2, IDMS, and other DBMSs. Capabilities include creation of a centralized user requirements data base for applications/projects data dictionary. The package provides for reverse engineering. The software runs on OS/2 and PC-MS/DOS compatible computers. The minimum memory requirement is 512 kilobytes. The source code is written in C. **EASYSPEC, INC., 17629 El Camino Real, Suite 202, Houston, TX 77058; Telephone – 713/480-3233**

EPOS. This is an integrated CASE tool that supports the full life cycle from requirements definition through design, coding, and maintenance of a software development project. Capabilities include documentation, analysis, and code generation for FORTRAN, Pascal, and Ada. The package provides requirements traceability. The software runs on PC-MS/DOS, DEC VAX, IBM mainframe, UNIX, DG/AOS/VS, Concurrent Computer/OP 32, Apollo, Sun, and HP Workstations and computers. The minimum memory requirement is 640 kilobytes. The source code is written in C. **SPS SOFTWARE PRODUCTS & SERVICES, 14 East 38th St. - 14th Floor, New York, N.Y. 10016; Telephone – 216/686-3790; FAX – 212/481-7464**

ER-Designer. This is a CASE design tool with an integrated data dictionary. It runs on IBM PC-MS DOS. **CHEN & ASSOCIATES, 4884 Constitution Ave., Baton Rouge, LA 70808; Telephone – 504/928-5765; FAX – 504/928-9371**

ERVision. This is a diagraming and syntax verifier CASE tool for data base design. It supports the entity-relationship (ER) approach and provides a graphical method of describing relationships within data base designs. Capabilities include diagram creation and editing, information zoom, and design rule checks and annotations. The software runs on Apple Macintosh compatible computers. The minimum memory requirement is 512 kilobytes. The source code is written in C. **ANDYNE COMPUTING LTD., 544 Princess St., Suite 202, Kingston, ON, CD K7L 1C7; Telephone - 800/267-0665, 613/548-4355**

Estimator. This is a project management support CASE tool that enables simulation of time and resource requirements based on what-if conditions and the development of detailed project plans. The software runs on IBM mainframe computers. The minimum memory requirement is 2048 kilobytes. **SPECTRUM INTERNATIONAL, INC., 5839 Green Valley Circle, Suite 205, Culver City, CA 90230; Telephone – 213/417-5150**

Excelerator. This is a diagraming CASE tool for systems analysis. It supports facilities for creating and modifying systems diagrams, charts, and screen and report specifications. It provides a project dictionary that stores entries and tracks relationship between them. The package includes a block security device. Versions are available for real-time and embedded systems. The software runs on PC-MS/DOS, and DEC/VAX/VMS compatible computers. The minimum memory requirement is 640 kilobytes. The source code is written in C. **INTERSOLV, 1 Main St., 9th Floor, Cambridge, MA 02142; Telephone – 800/777-8858; FAX – 617/577-8945**

Excelerator/CSP. This is a diagraming CASE tool that supports graphical design of cross system product/application development (CSP/AD) systems. It provides an integrated dictionary customized to support information required by CSP/AD, including 11 dictionary items and 3 design-related diagraming techniques. The software runs on PC-MS/DOS compatible computers. **INTERSOLV, 1 Main St., 9th Floor, Cambridge, MA 02142; Telephone – 800/777-8858; FAX – 617/577-8945**

Excelerator/RTS. This is a diagraming CASE tool for real-time systems analysis and design. It offers capabilities needed to design and document complex or embedded systems, including avionics process control and communications. The package supports Ward/Mellor and Hatley techniques. The software runs on PC-MS/DOS and DEC VAX/VMS compatible computers. The minimum memory requirement is 640 kilobytes. **INTERSOLV, 1 Main St., 9th Floor, Cambridge, MA 02142; Telephone – 800/777-8858; FAX – 617/577-8945**

4FrontDesigner. This is a diagraming and methods CASE tool that supports logical modeling of a data base system based on automatic normalization and multiple projects. Users' views of data usage are synthesized and normalized to produce nonredundant data models for projects. The software runs on IBM/MVS compatible computers. The minimum memory requirement is 4096 kilobytes. **HOLLAND SYSTEMS CORP., 3131 S. State St., Suite 303, Ann Arbor, MI 48104; Telephone – 313/995-9595**

FACT. This is a diagraming and code generator CASE tool that supports Focus application creation to streamline a large-scale application development project. It provides an icon-driven user interface. A graphics and text editor is included, supplemented by Focus-based rules. Capabilities include generation of standard Focus code, including master file description, I/O screens, procedures, and reports for designing large-scale applications that are portable to all Focus operating environments. The software runs on OS/2 compatible computers. **INFORMATION BUILDERS, INC., 1250 Broadway, New York, NY 10001; Telephone – 212/736-4433; FAX – 212/967-6406**

FastTask. This is a diagraming CASE tool that provides real-time support for the Iconix Power Tools CASE workbench. It supports Ward/Mellor and Hatley methods for illustrating relations between tasks in a real-time system. It works with a graphics editor to map state transition diagrams and then translate the data into corresponding matrices and tables. The software runs on Apple Macintosh Plus, XL, SE, and Mac II compatible computers. The minimum memory requirement is 1024 kilobytes. **ICONIX SOFTWARE, 2800 28th St., Suite 320, Santa Monica, CA 94045; Telephone – 213/458-0092; FAX – 213/396-3454**

Focus. This is a 4GL/DBMS CASE tool with an integrated data dictionary. It runs on IBM VM/CMS, DOS/VSE, MVS, PC-MS-DOS. **INFORMATION BUILDERS, INC., 1250 Broadway, New York, NY 10001; Telephone – 212/736-4433; FAX – 212/967-6406**

Foresight. This is a prototyping CASE tool that performs animated simulation of embedded real-time systems. It enables developers to uncover design errors before hardware and software implementation. The package includes a graphics editor to create specifications diagrams, executable library real-time functions and I/O devices, a consistency analyzer, and a discrete event simulator. The software runs on DEC VAX station compatible computers. **ATHENA SYSTEMS, INC., 139 Kifer Court, Sunnyvale, CA 94086; Telephone – 408/730-2100**

Foundation. This is a repository and SDM support CASE tool that can be used to automate the life cycle of applications software development. It includes a central design repository, DB2-based development dictionary with a layered processing architecture, and Method/1, Design/1, and Install/1 modules. The software runs on PC-MS/DOS and IBM 370/MVS compatible computers. The minimum memory requirement is 512 kilobytes. The source code is written in COBOL and COBOL II. **ANDERSEN CONSULTING, 69 W. Washington, Chicago, IL 60602; Telephone – 312/580-0069; FAX – 312/507-2548**

Foundation Basys. This is a prototyping, code generator, and SDM support CASE tool for full life cycle on-line transaction processing applications. It contains reusable components, providing a complete application shell. The package supports all standard Pathway terminals. An IDS option supports advanced workstation and special device interfaces. The software runs on Tandem compatible computers. **MENLO BUSINESS SYSTEMS, INC., 201 Main St., Los Altos, CA 94022; Telephone – 415/948-7920; FAX – 415/949-6655**

Foundation SQL. This is a code generator and SDM support CASE tool for nonStop SQL on-line transaction processing applications development. It provides an optimized interface, system architecture, and a data base design methodology. The software runs on Tandem nonStop compatible computers. **MENLO BUSINESS SYSTEMS, INC., 201 Main St., Los Altos, CA 94022; Telephone – 415/948-7920; FAX – 415/949-6655**

Foundation Translator. This is a code generator CASE tool that provides design translation to generate Tandem software components. It includes interfaces for compiling Vista designs in a Tandem environment and for generating Pathway screen definitions and DDL components for both data base definitions and interprocess messages. Capabilities include creation of Pathway components compatible with Basys and non-Basys environments. It runs on Apple Macintosh and Tandem compatible computers. **MENLO BUSINESS SYSTEMS, INC., 201 Main St., Los Altos, CA 94022; Telephone – 415/948-7920; FAX – 415/949-6655**

Foundation Vista. This is a diagraming and repository CASE tool for on-line transaction processing applications development. It provides a graphics-oriented design workbench to build data base designs and screen forms as the application is configured. The package includes a data dictionary and design compiler which checks logical design and consistency. The software runs on Apple Macintosh compatible computers. The minimum memory requirement is 250 kilobytes. The source code is written in C. **MENLO BUSINESS SYSTEMS, INC., 201 Main St., Los Altos, CA 94022; Telephone – 415/948-7920; FAX – 415/949-6655**

FreeFlow (Version 3.0). This is a module of the Iconix Power Tools CASE workbench. It is a diagraming and repository CASE tool for structured analysis that includes multiple-window architecture and hierarchical editing. Capabilities include creation of leveled sets of data, control flow diagrams, process specifications, and data dictionary. The software runs on Apple Macintosh Plus, XL, SE, and Mac II compatible computers. The minimum memory requirement is 1024 kilobytes. **ICONIX SOFTWARE, 2800 28th St., Suite 320, Santa Monica, CA 94045; Telephone – 213/458-0092; FAX – 213/396-3454**

Hugo/ISPF. This is an ISPF application that provides controlled access to MSP's data dictionary. It runs on IBM MVS, VM, ISPF. **GLOBAL SOFTWARE, P.O. Box 2813, Duxbury, MA 02331; Telephone – 617/934-0949; FAX – 617/934-0697**

IDEF/Leverage. This is a diagraming CASE tool that supports industrial strength activity and data modeling for large models from logical design to physical SQL prototype. It uses an IDEF syntax. Capabilities include generation of graphic placement, English language business rules, reports, and quality assurance tests beyond normalization. It merges business views and supports application development for Cincom's Supra SQL DBMS. The software runs on IBM 30XX, 43XX/MVS, and DEC VAX/VMS compatible computers. The minimum memory requirement is 2048 kilobytes. The source code is written in C. **D. APPLETON CO., 1334 Parkview Ave., Suite 220, Manhattan Beach, CA 90266; Telephone – 800/322-6614, 213/546-7575; FAX – 213/545-5486**

IDMS/Architect. This is a code generator and reengineering CASE tool that supports systems analysis, design, and physical implementation of data bases and applications. It can be integrated in Culinet's mainframe environment. Capabilities include generation of physical data bases from logical models. It offloads application design to a PC. The package supports reverse engineering of data bases. The software runs on PC-MS/DOS compatible computers. The minimum memory requirement is 640 kilobytes. The source code is written in C. **COMPUTER ASSOCIATES INTERNATIONAL, INC., 1814 S. Main St., South Bend, IN 46613; Telephone – 800/727-3169, 219/232-7921**

IE Admin/Solutions. This is a bidirectional bridge between KnowledgeWare's IEW Analysis and Design tool and Brownstone's Data Dictionary Solution CASE tool. It runs on IBM MVS, DB2. **BROWNSTONE SOLUTIONS, 521 5th Ave., New York, NY 10175; Telephone – 212/370-7160; FAX – 212/667-2520**

Information Engineering Workbench/Analysis Workstation (Rel. 5.0). This is a diagraming CASE tool that supports the analysis phase of systems development. It captures and analyzes system requirements using integrated diagrams, including decomposition, data flow, entity relationship, and action diagrams. The software maintains level consistency in data flow diagrams. It supports the consolidation of information from different encyclopedias and provides for real-time error checking. It shares captured data with KnowledgeWare's planning, design, and construction workstations. The software runs on PC-MS/DOS compatible computers. The minimum memory requirement is 640 kilobytes. The source code is written in C,

Prolog, GEM, and Btrieve. **KNOWLEDGEWARE, INC., 3340 Peachtree Road, N.E., Atlanta, GA 30026; Telephone – 800/338-4130, 404/231-8575; FAX – 404/364-0883**

Information Engineering Workbench/Design Workstation (Rel. 5.0). This is a diagraming CASE tool that supports the design phase of system development. It captures knowledge about screen layouts, program structures, procedural logic, and data base and file structures. The package helps users move from a logical representation of what a system should do into the physical specifications for how the system will actually be implemented. Capabilities include composition of integrated design diagrams, including structure charts, data structure diagrams, presentation diagrams for screen design, and action diagrams for modules and a data base diagramer. The package shares data with KnowledgeWare's planning, analysis, and construction workstations. The software runs on PC-MS/DOS compatible computers. The minimum memory requirement is 640 kilobytes. The source code is written in C, Prolog, GEM, and Btrieve. **KNOWLEDGEWARE, INC., 3340 Peachtree Road, N.E., Atlanta, GA 30026; Telephone – 800/338-4130, 404/231-8575; FAX – 404/364-0883**

Information Engineering Facility (IEF). This is a data dictionary/repository CASE tool with full life cycle CASE capabilities. **TEXAS INSTRUMENTS, Piano, TX 75265; Telephone – 214/995-2011; FAX – 214/995-4360**

Information Engineering Workbench/Mainframe Encyclopedia and Knowledge Coordinator (Rel. 5.0). This is a repository CASE tool that allows users of Workstation tools to use the security and capacity of a mainframe to manage information collected on PCs. It creates, maintains, and stores encyclopedias of virtually unlimited size. The software provides for multiple user shared access of a common encyclopedia, either at a single site or at several sites. Project control can be divided among team members or combined and reconciled to handle large projects. The software runs on IBM 370, 30XX, 43XX/MVS/SP, TSO/E, OS/MVS, and MVS/XA compatible computers. The minimum memory requirement is 4096 kilobytes. The source code is written in Prolog and C. **KNOWLEDGEWARE, INC., 3340 Peachtree Road, N.E., Atlanta, GA 30026; Telephone – 800/338-4130, 404/231-8575; FAX – 404/364-0883**

Integrater. This is a diagraming, repository, and project management CASE tool that provides for multiple views of information (e.g., text, graphics, forms and matrices, version and release control, data and referential integrity, project management, security, and import/export). It is compatible to on-line, multiuser, and multiproject environments. The package provides user definition of objects and validation rules. The software runs on IBM/MVS and DEC VAX/VMS compatible computers. **ASYST TECHNOLOGIES, INC., 1 Napierville Plaza, Napierville, IL 60563; Telephone – 800/359-1101, 312/416-2990; FAX – 312/416-2374**

Integrated Workstation. This is a project management CASE tool that provides a direct interface between Asystis Developer, desktop publishers, graphics packages, word processors, text editors, spreadsheets, and project management packages. The software runs on PC-MS/DOS compatible computers. **ASYST TECHNOLOGIES, INC., 1 Napierville Plaza, Napierville, IL 60563; Telephone – 800/359-1101, 312/416-2990; FAX – 312/416-2374**

Intergrator. This is a data dictionary/repository CASE tool that stores and validates development specifications. **STERLING SOFTWARE, INC, 21050 Vanowen St., Canoga Park, CA 91304; Telephone – 818/716-1616; FAX – 818/716-5998**

KangaTool. This is a diagraming, code generator, and project management CASE tool that supports the systems development life cycle. It analyzes, designs, codes, tests, and maintains various phases. Capabilities include generation of flow diagrams and structure charts, testing, and the overall management of software projects. The software runs on Sun Workstation compatible computers. **U.S. SERTEK, INC., 1012 Stewart, Sunnyvale, CA 94086; Telephone – 408/733-3174**

LifeCycle Manager. This is a project management and systems development CASE tool that supports project managers in planning and estimating systems development projects. The software runs on PC-MS/DOS compatible computers. The minimum memory requirement is 640 kilobytes. The source code is written in Pascal. **NASTEC CORP., 24681 Northwestern Hwy., Southfield, MI 48075; Telephone – 800/872-8296, 313/353-3300; FAX – 313/353-0707**

Life-Cycle Productivity System. This is a diagraming, code generator, and project management CASE tool. It automates production work while planning, designing, developing, and supporting information systems. Modules include Strategic Systems Planner, System Designer, System Implementer, CORE Foundation Software, and Life-Cycle Project Manager. The software runs on PC-MS/DOS compatible computers. The minimum memory requirement is 640 kilobytes. A mouse is required. The source code is written in COBOL. **AMERICAN MANAGEMENT SYSTEMS, INC., 1777 N. Kent St., Arlington, VA 22209; Telephone – 703/841-6000; FAX – 703/841-6146**

Lyddia. This is a diagraming and code generator CASE tool that uses interactive graphics to build associative data models of logical requirements. It automatically draws entity-relationship (E-R) diagrams and prints a data specifications document. Capabilities include code generation for data bases in standard languages, including SQL, dBase, and Focus. The software runs on PC MS/DOS compatible computers. **CASCADE SOFTWARE SYSTEMS, INC., 33 Bedford St., Lexington, MA 02173; Telephone – 617/862-6246**

MacBubbles. This is a diagraming and repository multiwindow CASE tool that provides support for Yourdon's modern structured analysis methodology. It creates data flow and entity-relationship diagrams and includes a data dictionary and mini-specifications editor. The package supports real-time DFD symbols defined by Boeing/Hatley, Ward and Mellor, and ESML. The software runs on Apple Macintosh Plus and SE compatible computers. **STARSYS, INC., 1113 Norlee Drive, Silver Spring, MD 20902; Telephone – 301/946-0522**

Maestro. This is a reengineering and project management CASE tool that provides an integrated environment for the software development life cycle. It establishes an environment for structured design and analysis, file management, document processing, procedural language, coding, testing and maintenance, and reengineering with real-time project management. The package includes communications utilities and terminal emulation capabilities. It supports Bisynch, SNA, X.25, and other protocols. The software runs on PC-MS/DOS, IBM mainframe, Honeywell, Unisys, and OS/2 compatible computers. The source code is written in Assembly. **SOFTLAB, INC., 188 The Embarcadero, Bayside Plaza, 7th Floor, San Francisco, CA; Telephone – 415/957-9175; FAX – 415/957-9879**

ManagerView. This is a diagraming and repository CASE tool. It provides a workstation-based graphical information engineering tool that is driven by a mainframe corporate dictionary/repository. The package supports Windows 286/386. When integrated with Microsoft Windows, Presentation Manager, and Host Manager products, it provides a full CASE environment for the systems development process. The software runs on PC MS/DOS compatible computers. The minimum memory requirement is 640 kilobytes. A mouse is required. The source code is written in C. **MANAGER SOFTWARE PRODUCTS, INC., 131 Hartwell Ave., Lexington, MA 02173-3126; Telephone – 617/863-5800; FAX – 617/861-6130**

Mast-ER. This is a diagraming CASE tool for an interactive system. It supports analysis, design, and documentation of data base applications. The software runs on PC-MS/DOS compatible computers. **INFODYNE INTERNATIONAL, 24 W. Erie, Chicago, IL 60610; Telephone – 312/664-1166**

Meta Design, Meta Design/Plus. This is a diagraming CASE tool set used to design and track diagrams and system models. It utilizes a hierarchical structure that speeds design of systems flowcharts, information networks, computer programs, organizational charts, production line diagrams, technical documentation, and presentation graphics. The software runs on Apple Macintosh Plus, SE, II, and PC-MS/DOS compatible computers. The minimum memory requirement is 2048 kilobytes. The package supports Windows 286/386. The source code is written in C. A mouse is required. **META SOFTWARE CORP., 363 Seventh Ave., New York, NY 10001; Telephone – 212/695-5870**

Method/1. This is a prototyping, repository, and SDM CASE tool. It performs data dictionary or encyclopedia, prototyping, report layout, document production, desktop publishing, record layout descriptions, diagram organization, and printing and data sharing functions. It provides support for information engineering, iterative and package systems design, and production support methodologies. The software runs on PC-MS/DOS compatible computers. The minimum memory requirement is 640 kilobytes. Novell, 3Com, and NetBIOS network versions are available. A mouse and VGA graphics are required. **ANDERSEN CONSULTING, 69 W. Washington, Chicago, IL 60602; Telephone – 312/580-0069; FAX – 312/507-2548**

Methodmanager. This is a diagraming and SDM CASE tool that provides a dictionary-driven information engineering methodology and support environment for specification, development, installation, maintenance, and enhancement of information systems. Capabilities include affinity analysis, functional decomposition, entity modeling, and data normalization. It runs on IBM 4300, 30XX, 370, 9370/MVS, MVS/XA, VS1, VSE, and VM compatible computers. The minimum memory requirement is 3072 kilobytes. **MANAGER SOFTWARE PRODUCTS, INC., 131 Hartwell Ave., Lexington, MA 02173-3126; Telephone – 617/863-5800; FAX – 617/861-6130**

MicroStep. This is a diagraming and code generator CASE tool that provides a graphic development environment for data processing applications. It generates C source code and produces executable programs from graphics specifications. The package includes graphical editors for screen and report formatting. It produces and maintains documentation. The software runs on PC MS/DOS compatible computers. The minimum memory requirement is 640 kilobytes. It utilizes EMS. A Microsoft-compatible mouse is required. The source code is written in C. **SYSCORP INTERNATIONAL, INC., 9420 Research Blvd., Suite 200, Austin, TX 78759; Telephone – 800/727-7837, 512/388-0591; FAX – 512/338-9713**

Model-S. This is a prototyping and repository CASE tool that performs data dictionary or encyclopedia, prototyping, report layout, diagram organization and printing, record layout descriptions, data sharing, and documentation functions. It generates dBase applications. It runs on PC MS/DOS compatible computers. The minimum memory requirement is 256 kilobytes. **PC-SYSTEMS, 307 Barwynne Lane, Wynnewood, PA 19151; Telephone – 215/649-8981**

Multi/CAM. This is an SDM CASE tool for a micro-mainframe system that develops, maintains, and enhances information systems. It integrates software development tools, software design and production models, project management, and any other user-selected CASE tools into a unified, automated work environment. The package supports electronic mail management and LAN printing. The software runs on PC MS/DOS, IBM/MVS/TSO, and VM/CMS compatible computers. The minimum memory requirement is 640 kilobytes. It utilizes EMS. Novell, NetBIOS, and IBM Token Ring Network versions are available. The source code is written in Assembly and C. **AGS MANAGEMENT SYSTEMS, INC., 880 First Ave., King of Prussia, PA 19406; Telephone – 800/678-8484, 215/265-1550; FAX – 215/265-1230**

Natural Construct. This is a prototype and code generator CASE tool for building customized Natural applications. User-specified parameter values in the fill-in-the-blank panels are used to generate full-function applications from predefined program models. The package supports rapid prototyping and provides a help text facility. The software runs on DEC VAX, MicroVAX, VAXstation, Wang, VS, IBM/MVS/XA, MVS/ESA, DOS/VSE, DOS/VSE/SP2, OS/VSI, OS/MVS, and VM/CMS compatible computers. **SOFTWARE AG OF NORTH AMERICA, INC.,**

11190 Sunrise Valley Drive, Reston, VA 22091; Telephone – 800/843-9534, 703/860-5050; FAX – 703/391-6975

NETRON/CAP. This is a diagraming, prototyping, and reengineering CASE tool used for development of COBOL applications. It is based on Bassett Frame Technology software architecture for reusing code. The package enables rapid prototyping and application portability across hardware lines and operating systems. The software runs on Wang VS; PC-MS/DOS; IBM 308X, 309X, 43XX, 93XX/VMS/TSO, MVS/IMS, MVS/CICS, DOS/CICS, DOS/IMS, VM/CMS; DEC VAX, MicroVax, MicroVAX/VMS and MicroVMS compatible computers. The minimum memory requirement is 512 kilobytes. The source code is written in COBOL. **NETRON, INC., 99 St. Regis Crescent N., Downsview, ON, CD M3J 1Y9; Telephone – 416/636-8333; FAX – 416/636-4847**

Network Software Environment (NSE). This is a project management CASE tool that provides for control of large-scale software development projects. The package supports various development objects used during each phase of software development. The software runs on UNIX compatible computers. **SUN MICROSYSTEMS, 2550 Garcia Ave., Mountain View, CA 94043; Telephone – 800/821-4643, 800/821-4642 (CA), 415/960-1300; FAX – 415/969-9131**

NRUNOFF. This is a diagraming CASE tool. It provides a series of text and graphics utilities that can be integrated into a CASE 2000 DesignAid environment. The package has the text benefits of Digital Standard Runoff with the ability to integrate CASE graphics from Nastec's DesignAid software. The software runs on DEC VAX compatible computers. The source code is written in C. **NASTEC CORP., 24681 Northwestern Hwy., Southfield, MI 48075; Telephone – 800/872-8296, 313/353-3300; FAX – 313/353-0707**

Olga. This is a batch population tool for MVS JCL. It runs on IBM MVS and VM/CMS. **GLOBAL SOFTWARE, INC, P.O. Box 2813, Duxbury, MA 02331; Telephone – 617/934-0949; FAX – 617/934-0697**

Pac Base. This is a full life cycle CASE tool with a centralized enterprise-wide dictionary. It runs on IBM-PC/MS DOS, MVS, DOS/VSE; Honeywell GCOS-7 and GCOS-8, and Unisys 1100. **CGI SYSTEMS, Pearl River, NY**

ParaView. This is a repository and project management CASE tool that can be used for software development on a distributed network comprised of UNIX-based workstations and file servers of various brands. It enables project team members to control the programming, debugging, and release environments while working either separately or collectively. Capabilities include problem reporting and tracking, network-wide builds of libraries and executables, file dependency resolution, milestone marking, and audit trails. The package supports NFS, X-Window, and Sun View. The software runs on UNIX compatible computers. **Athena Systems, Inc., 139 Kifer Ct., Sunnyvale, CA 94086; Telephone – 408/730-1210**

PC-Proto II. This is a diagraming and prototyping CASE tool for application design and modeling. It enables the prototyping of applications without programming.

The package includes a design encyclopedia, a notepad, field notes, screen and report painter, and DOS file utilities that are used to build working systems models. The software runs on PC MS/DOS compatible computers. The minimum memory requirement is 640 kilobytes. **KARTECH DATA SERVICES, INC., 165 Pinewood Ave., Toronto, ON, CD M6C 2V6; Telephone – 416/656-2032**

Personal IDEF/Leverage. This is a diagraming CASE tool that creates data model diagrams in IDEF syntax. The models can be communicated to IDEF/Leverage on the host system for further processing. The software runs on PC-MS/DOS and DEC VAX/VMS compatible computers. The minimum memory requirement is 640 kilobytes. The source code is written in C. A mouse is required. **D. APPLETON CO., 1334 Parkview Ave., Suite 220, Manhattan Beach, CA 90266; Telephone – 800/322-6614, 213/546-7575; FAX – 213/545-5486**

PLANCODE (Planning Control and Decision Evaluation). This is a project management CASE tool that uses a modular English-like calculation system for creating planning models. Software capabilities include workforce planning, plant site selection, union contract negotiations, capacity planning, production scheduling, and cash flow analysis. It includes standard graphics report formats and provides a method for defining new reports. The software runs on IBM/CICS/IMS, VM, TSO, DOS/VS, OS, and VS compatible computers. The source code is written in PL/1. **IBM, Old Orchard Road, Armonk, NY 10504; Telephone – 914/765-1900**

POSE (Picture Oriented Software Engineering). Ths is a diagraming, prototyping, and reengineering CASE workbench. It includes the following modules: Data Model Diagrammer, Data Model Normalizer, Logical Database Designer, Data Base Aid, Screen Report Prototyper, Action Chart Diagrammer, Decomposition Diagrammer, Structure Chart Diagrammer, and Data Flow Diagrammer. The modules are integrated through an interactive graphics interface. The software runs on PC-MS/DOS compatible computers. Mouse support is provided. *Approximate purchase price* - $885 (four-module tool kit), $494 per module. **COMPUTER SYSTEMS ADVISERS, INC., 50 Tice Blvd., Woodcliff Lake, NJ 07675; Telephone – 800/537-4262; 201/391-6500; FAX – 201/391-2210**

PowerPDL. This is a reengineering CASE tool that generates formatted documentation from PDL files. It is a module of Iconix PowerTools CASE workbench. Listings include a table of contents, design body, data and subprogram cross-reference lists, and a subprogram nesting tree. The package provides call structures that the Iconix SmartChart module can use to generate structured charts. The software runs on Apple Macintosh Plus, XL, SE, II; PC-MS/DOS, and DEC VAX/VMS compatible computers. The minimum memory requirement is 1024 kilobytes. **ICONIX SOFTWARE, 2800 28th St., Suite 320, Santa Monica, CA 94045; Telephone – 213/458-0092; FAX – 213/396-3454**

PowerTools (Version 2.0). This is a diagraming CASE workbench designed to support the systems development process from analysis through design, coding, implementation, and maintenance. The software provides for the creation of data and control flow diagrams, the preparation of process specifications, and a data dictionary. The package modules include FreeFlow, AdaFlow, SmartChart, PowerPDL, FastTask, ASCII Bridge, and AdaFlow. The software runs on Apple MacIntosh Plus, XL, SE, and II compatible computers. The minimum memory requirement is 1024 kilobytes. **ICONIX SOFTWARE, 2800 28th St., Suite 320, Santa Monica, CA 94045; Telephone – 213/458-0092; FAX – 213/396-3454**

Power Tools. This is a prototyping and SDM support CASE tool set for a 4GL environment. It includes user help, documentation, and development support and reporting tools for building and modifying prototypes or full systems. The software runs on UNIX, XENIX, PC-MS/DOS, DEC VAX/ULTRIX, IBM RT/AIX, Convergent Technologies/CTOS/BTOS, and OS/2 compatible computers. A Novell network version is available. **CASE Tools/Workbenches, 1800 Australian Ave. S., West Palm Beach, FL 33409; Telephone – 800/858-8963, 407/697-3400; FAX – 407/697-3411**

Pride-DBEM. This is a diagraming CASE tool that can be used to design and develop corporate data bases. It includes four data models: application logical, enterprise logical, enterprise physical, and application physical. The package provides a universal approach to data base design. It interfaces to DBMSs, including DB2 and IMS. The software runs on IBM 370, 30XX/OS, MVS, MVS/XA, and DEC VAX/VMS compatible computers. The minimum memory requirement is 256 kilobytes. **M. BRYCE & ASSOCIATES, INC., 777 Alderman Road, Palm Harbor, FL 34683; Telephone – 813/786-4567; FAX – 813/786-4765**

Pride-EEM. This is an SDM support CASE tool for designing and developing enterprise resources and enterprise information strategies. It provides an optional Computer-Aided Planning tool for modeling corporate priorities and performing organization analysis. The software runs on DEC VAX/VMS; IBM 370, 30XX/OS, 43XX/OS, MVS, MVS/XA; Unisys 1100; and NEC compatible computers. **M. BRYCE & ASSOCIATES, INC., 777 Alderman Road, Palm Harbor, FL 34683; Telephone – 813/786-4567; FAX – 813/786-4765**

Pride-ISEM. This is an information system design and development methodology that combines disciplines of information systems engineering, information resource management, and project management. It uses a phased approach to generate system and data base designs and documentation. The package interfaces with MBA's Pride-PMS, Pride-IRM, Pride-DBEM, and Pride EEM. The software runs on IBM 370, 30XX/OS, MVS/XA, MVS, and DEC VAX/VMS compatible computers. The minimum memory requirement is 256 kilobytes. The source code is written in ANS COBOL. **M. BRYCE & ASSOCIATES, INC., 777 Alderman Road, Palm Harbor, FL 34683; Telephone – 813/786-4567; FAX – 813/786-4765**

Projectmanager. This is a project management tool for project resource and budget management. It generates summary and detailed reports of activities. The projects are divided into component tasks, resources, and activities required for completion. The software runs on IBM 4300, 30XX, 370, 9370/MVS, MVS/XA, VS1, and VSE compatible computers. The minimum memory requirement is 100 kilobytes. The source code is written in COBOL. **MANAGER SOFTWARE PRODUCTS, INC., 131 Hartwell Ave., Lexington, MA 02173-3126; Telephone – 617/863-5800**

Project SoftBoard. This is a project management support tool that allows users to initiate action requests, query current status of project, respond to action requests, and monitor project schedules. When integrated into Atherton Technology's BackPlane package, it provides electronic mail system functions such as creating and tracking project work orders. The software runs on UNIX, DEC VAX, MicroVAX/VMS, and MicroVMS compatible computers. **ATHERTON TECHNOLOGY, 1333 Bordeaux Dr., Sunnyvale, CA 94089; Telephone – 408/734-9822; FAX – 408/744-1607**

ProKit*Analyst. This is a diagraming and repository CASE tool for application analysts. It can assist in the preparation of flow diagrams and the transfer of documentation to a data dictionary. The package provides for status information and analysis with 46 reports and for horizontal/vertical balancing. The software runs on PC-MS/DOS compatible computers. The minimum memory requirement is 640 kilobytes. The source code is written in COBOL, FORTRAN, and C. **MCDONNELL DOUGLAS INFORMATION CO., 325 McDonnell Blvd., St. Louis, MO 63042; Telephone – 800/325-1551, 314/234-4117**

ProKit*Workbench. This is a CASE system workbench that contains four modules: Data Modeler, Analyzer, Prototyper, and Designer. It provides support for use of structured techniques, external diagram print/plot functions, and multiuser environments.   The package interfaces with IBM's Cross System Product/Application Development system. The software runs on PC-MS/DOS compatible computers. The minimum memory requirement is 640 kilobytes. **MCDONNELL DOUGLAS INFORMATION CO., 325 McDonnell Blvd., St. Louis, MO 63042; Telephone – 800/325-1551, 314/234-4117**

Prolifio. This is a CASE system that provides for diagraming, code generation, and repository maintenance. It contains a specification dictionary and a PC graphics tool kit, including batch processing, test file generation, testing, and simulation tools. Prolifio supports conventional and CODASYL file organization. It generates file and table management routines and on-line or batch documentation. The software runs on PC-MS/DOS, and Bull DPS 6, 7, 8, and up compatible computers. **INFORMATION SYSTEMS CONSULTANTS, INC. 7816 N. 19th Ave., Phoenix, AZ 85021; Telephone – 602/864-0014**

ProMod (Version 7.1). This is a CASE tool set for systems development. It provides graphics support and options for preparing DoD-compliant 2167A reports. It runs DEC windows. The software runs on DEC VAX/VMS and PC-MS/DOS compatible computers. **PROMOD, INC., 23685 Birtcher Dr., El Toro, CA 92630; Telephone – 800/255-2689, 800/255-4310 (CA), 714/855-3046; FAX – 714/855-8663**

ProMod/CM. This is a configuration management CASE tool. It extends version control of the data that were collected using the ProMod/SART and ProMod/MD modules of Promod's CASE tool set. It compares the current development data base against selected baselines and identifies all changes, additions, and deletions in a series of reports. The software runs on DEC VAX/VMS compatible computers. **PROMOD, INC., 23685 Birtcher Dr., El Toro, CA 92630; Telephone – 800/255-2689, 800/255-4310 (CA), 714/855-3046; FAX – 714/855-8663**

ProMod/MD. This is a syntax verifier CASE tool that provides for the transformation of analysis data to design. Parameters associated with function calls follow data typing concepts. Functions are checked for consistency against the modular design. The package provides for system-level documentation, including graphics. The software runs on DEC VAX/VMS and PC-MS/DOS compatible computers. The minimum memory requirement is 640 kilobytes. The source code is written in Pascal. **PROMOD, INC., 23685 Birtcher Dr., El Toro, CA 92630; Telephone – 800/255-2689, 800/255-4310 (CA), 714/855-3046; FAX – 714/855-8663**

ProMod/SART. This is a diagraming CASE tool that supports structured analysis with real-time extensions. Capabilities include the preparation of data flow and control flow diagrams and control specifications. It can generate multiple reports for both graphical and textural documentation. The software runs on DEC VAX/VMS and PC-MS/DOS compatible computers. The minimum memory requirement is 640 kilobytes. The source code is written in Pascal. **PROMOD, INC., 23685 Birtcher Dr., El Toro, CA 92630; Telephone – 800/255-2689, 800/255-4310 (CA), 714/855-3046; FAX – 714/855-8663**

ProMod/TMS. This is an SDM and project management support tool that provides traceability throughout the analysis and design process. It has the ability to trace requirements from external documents into analysis models, from analysis models into design models. The software runs on DEC VAX/VMS and PC-MS/DOS compatible computers. The minimum memory requirement is 640 kilobytes. The source code is written in Pascal. **PROMOD, INC., 23685 Birtcher Dr., El Toro, CA 92630; Telephone – 800/255-2689, 800/255-4310 (CA), 714/855-3046; FAX – 714/855-8663**

QuickSpec. This is a repository and reengineering CASE tool that provides data entry and data base review for PSL/PSA*. It has its own local repository with which analysts and designers can interact. The package uses Microsoft Windows. The software runs on PC-MS/DOS compatible computers. The minimum memory requirement is 640 kilobytes. The source code is written in C. **META SYSTEMS, LTD., 315 East Eisenhower Pkwy., Suite 200, Ann Arbor, MI 48108; Telephone – 313/663-6027**

R.A.P. (Rapid Automatic Programmaker). This is a prototyping and repository back-end CASE tool that supports a structured programming methodology. It includes data dictionary/encyclopedia, prototyping, document production, record layout descriptions, and data sharing capabilities. The software runs on PC-MS/DOS compatible computers. **SYNOPTIC CONSULTING, INC., 10 East 39th St., New York, NY 10016; Telephone – 212/779-1588**

RAPID/USE. This is a diagraming and prototyping CASE tool that supports application development. It provides for prototyping user interfaces/interface analysis and interactive information systems development. The package consists of a Transition Diagram Interpreter module and an Action Linker module. The software runs on UNIX compatible computers. The minimum memory requirement is 128 kilobytes. **INTERACTIVE DEVELOPMENT ENVIRONMENTS INC., 595 Market St., San Francisco, CA 94105; Telephone – 800/888-4331, 415/543-0900; FAX – 415/543-3716**

Repository Explorer. This is a repository learning CASE tool. It runs on IBM PC, OS/2.. **INTERSOLV, 3200 Tower Oaks Blvd., Rockville, MD 20852; Telephone – 301/230-3200; FAX – 301/231-7813**

Repository Manager. This is a stand-alone repository CASE tool. It runs on IBM MVS. **IBM, Old Orchard Road, Armonk, NY 10504. Telephone – 914/765-1900**

Re-engineering Product Set (Version 2.1). This is an integrated reengineering CASE tool that provides for data modeling and enhancing existing mainframe data base designs. It can also be used to generate DB2 SQL code. The package modules include Database Administrator, Database Administrator (DB2), Catalog Extract, Data Analyst, Data Analyst Capture (IMS), and Data Analysis Capture (Files). The software runs on IBM/MVS, PC-MS/DOS, and OS/2 compatible computers. **BACHMAN INFORMATION SYSTEMS, INC., 4 Cambridge Center, Cambridge, MA 02142-1401; Telephone – 617/354-1414; FAX – 617/354-0971**

RMS/PC. This is a project management and configuration management support tool that can be used for requirements management and tracing. The package provides capabilities for capturing, editing, and updating requirements; and defining attributes and hierarchical structures of components. It allocates requirements to components and uses powerful requirements subset select features. Standard report formats are used to document results. The software runs on PC-MS/DOS compatible computers. The minimum memory requirement is 640 kilobytes. The source code is written in Pascal. **NASTEC CORP., 24681 Northwestern Hwy., Southfield, MI 48075; Telephone – 800/872-8296, 313/353-3300; FAX – 313/353-0707**

RTrace. This is an SDM support tool that organizes requirements, builds system architecture, allocates requirements, and generates reports. It is compatible to DOD 2167 and can be applied to any life cycle methodology. The software runs on DEC VAX/VMS compatible computers. The minimum memory requirement is 4096 kilobytes. The source code is written in C. **NASTEC CORP., 24681 Northwestern Hwy., Southfield, MI 48075; Telephone – 800/872-8296, 313/353-3300; FAX – 313/353-0707**

SAIC-SDDL (Software Design and Documentation Language). This is an SDM support tool for software design and documentation. It includes a table of contents, module cross-reference listings, and invocation trees. User-defined keywords and structured design constructs support a top-down approach to software design. The software runs on PC-MS/DOS, IBM 308X/MVS, DEC VAX/VMS, TOPS, Prime/PRIMOS, Unisys/EXEC 8, Gould/UTX, Sun/UNIX, and DG/AOS/VS compatible computers. **SCIENCE APPLICATIONS INTERNATIONAL CORP., Systems Integration Operation, P.O. Box 1661, Santa Ynez, CA 93460; Telephone – 805/688-1731; FAX – 805/688-4193**

SCdraw. This is a diagraming CASE tool that uses structure chart graphics symbols. The package includes group/individual moves and deletes. It changes colors and symbol label/positions and rescales chart with zoom/pan. It allows 800 symbols. The software runs on PC-MS/DOS compatible computers. The minimum memory requirement is 320 kilobytes. The source code is written in FORTRAN and Assembly. **MCDONNELL DOUGLAS INFORMATION SYSTEMS CO., 325 McDonnell Blvd., St. Louis, MO 63042; Telephone – 800/325-1551, 314/234-4117**

Schooner. This is a data-driven, object-oriented code generator CASE tool that allows users to design, document, and run applications without generating code. It also allows Clipper, C, and ASM routines to be lined in and called from anywhere in the system. The software runs on PC-MS/DOS. **QUICKTEK CORP., 224 Whiteside Place, Thousand Oaks, CA 91362; Telephone – 805/498-5853**

SDL (Software Design Language). This is an SDM support tool that can be used for software design at any level: process level, module level, and algorithm level. The formatted output contains a title page; table of contents; text, data definition, and logic flow segment bodies; and data item cross-reference, flow segment cross-reference, and flow segment cross-reference trees. The software runs on PC-MS/DOS compatible computers. The minimum memory requirement is 128 kilobytes. **COMPUTER SCIENCE INNOVATIONS, INC., 1280 Clearmont St., N.E., Palm Bay, FL 32905; Telephone – 407/676-2923; FAX – 407/676-2355**

SDM/Structured. This is an information system methodology that uses structured documentation and generic techniques. The methodology conforms to a single set of development standards. It includes quality assurance guidelines. The software runs on IBM/DOS, OS, and DEC compatible computers. **AGS MANAGEMENT SYSTEMS, INC., 880 First Ave., King of Prussia, PA 129406; Telephone – 800/678-8484, 215/265-1550; FAX – 215/265-1230**

SEAS (Software Engineering Assessment Service). This is a project management CASE tool that utilizes a combination of numeric measures, environmental analysis, and graphical industry comparisons for software productivity evaluation. The software runs on PC-MS/DOS compatible computers. **QUANTITATIVE SOFTWARE MANAGEMENT, 1057 Waverly Way, McLean, VA 22101; Telephone – 703/790-0055; FAX – 703/749-3795**

Silas. This is a CASE workbench for developing DB2 or SQL/DS data bases in a data dictionary. It runs on IBM MVS, VM/CMS. **GLOBAL SOFTWARE, INC., P.O. Box 2813, Duxbury, MA 02331; Telephone – 617/934-0949; FAX – 617/934-0697**

Silverun. This is a diagraming CASE tool that generates high-level, entity-relationship data models, detailed logical data models, documented data flow diagrams, and screen and report layouts. The software runs on Apple MacIntosh and PC-MS/DOS compatible computers. **SYSTEMS CORP., 983 University Ave., Los Gatos, CA 95030; Telephone – 800/344-9223, 408/395-1800; FAX – 408/395-3608**

SimCaSe. This is a diagraming CASE tool that creates software prototypes without any target hardware. It debugs C programs at source level and locates bottlenecks in code. The package consists of a Simulator Engine, C and A Assembler Source Debugger, Performance Analysis Tool, and an Input Stimulus Generator. The software runs on PC-MS/DOS compatible computers. The minimum memory requirement is 640 kilobytes. **ARCHIMEDES SOFTWARE, INC., 2159 Union St., San Francisco, CA 94123; Telephone – 800/338-1453, 415/567-4010; FAX – 415/567-1318**

Size Planner. This is a project management CASE tool that enables the user to evaluate size-reduction possibilities of different languages and estimate function points and lines of source code. The package encompasses sixteen different methods and four general techniques for estimating the size of a software development project. The software runs on PC-MS/DOS compatible computers. The minimum memory requirement is 256 kilobytes. **QUANTITATIVE SOFTWARE MANAGEMENT, 1057 Waverly Way, McLean, VA 22101; Telephone – 703/790-0055; FAX – 703/749-3795**

SLIM (Software Lifecycle Model). This is a project management CASE tool that can be used for software cost scheduling and reliability estimation. It discloses the minimum time to develop a system and imposes management constraints on project cost, workforce, and schedule. The software runs on PC-MS/DOS compatible computers. The minimum memory requirement is 256 kilobytes. The source code is written in BASIC. **QUANTITATIVE SOFTWARE MANAGEMENT, 1057 Waverly Way, McLean, VA 22101; Telephone – 703/790-0055; FAX – 703/749-3795**

SmartChart. This is a syntax verifier CASE tool that provides structure charts from files compiled by Iconix's PowerPDL processor. It integrates software design and implementation by combining a language-sensitive editor with a structure chart generator. The software runs on Apple MacIntosh Plus, XL, SE, and II. **ICONIX SOFTWARE, 2800 28th St., Suite 320, Santa Monica, CA 94045; Telephone – 213/458-0092; FAX – 213/396-3454**

Software BackPlane. This is a configuration management CASE tool that provides a framework on which to build a CASE environment. It handles tool integration, configuration management, work flow control, and tool portability. The package can be used to manage large-scale software development projects. The software runs on DEC VAX/VMS, ULTRIX, and UNIX compatible computers. **ATHERTON TECHNOLOGY, 1333 Bordeaux Dr., Sunnyvale, CA 94089; Telephone – 408/734-9822; FAX – 408/744-1607**

Software Through Pictures. This is a CASE workbench that includes tools for diagraming, prototyping, and SDM support. It provides for traceability and the preparation of systems software. The software runs on Sun/UNIX, DEC VAX/ULTRIX, VMS, and HP compatible computers. A mouse is required. The minimum memory requirement is 2048 kilobytes. **INTERACTIVE DEVELOPMENT ENVIRONMENTS INC., 595 Market St., San Francisco, CA 94105; Telephone – 800/888-4331, 415/543-0900; FAX – 415/543-3716**

Sourcemanager. This is a CASE workbench that includes tools for diagraming, prototyping, and repository. It provides for functional decomposition, iterative design, and prototyping with full screen painting for BMS/MFS generation. The software runs on IBM 4300, 30XX, 370/MVS, MVS/XA, VSI, VSE, and VM compatible computers. The minimum memory requirement is 2048 kilobytes. The source code is written in COBOL and Assembly. **MANAGER SOFTWARE PRODUCTS, INC., 131 Hartwell Ave., Lexington, MA 02173-3126; Telephone – 617/863-5800; FAX – 617/861-6130**

SPQR/20 (Software Productivity, Quality and Reliability). This is a project management CASE tool for software development maintenance. It predicts schedules, resources, staff, effort, sizes, costs, defect rates, reliability, and maintenance enhancement levels of software projects. It also estimates the number of code lines and function points required by a project for 30 major software languages. The software runs on PC-MS/DOS compatible computers. The minimum memory requirement is 256 kilobytes. The source code is written in BASIC. **SOFTWARE PRODUCTIVITY RESEARCH, 1972 Massachusetts Ave., Cambridge, MA 02140; Telephone – 617/495-0120; FAX – 617/495-0012**

SPQR Sizer/FP. This is a project management CASE tool that uses a function point method to predict source code size for new or existing software projects. It enables the user to retrofit function points to existing software written in any of 30 major programming languages. The software runs on PC-MS/DOS compatible computers. The minimum memory requirement is 256 kilobytes. The source code is written in BASIC. **SOFTWARE PRODUCTIVITY RESEARCH, 1972 Massachusetts Ave., Cambridge, MA 02140; Telephone – 617/495-0120; FAX – 617/495-0012**

Statemate. This is a prototyping and code generator CASE tool that allows the user to simulate and observe performance of many interactive program modules. It supports multiple chart simulations and generates Ada code, allowing the user to create and test system prototypes. The package consists of the following modules: Kernel, Analyzer, Prototype and Documentor. The software runs on DEC VAX, MicroVAX, Sun, and Apollo compatible computers. **I-LOGIX, INC., 22 Third Ave., Burlington, MA, 01803; Telephone – 617/272-8090**

Stradis/Draw. This is a diagraming CASE system that features interactive construction of data flow diagrams, system structure charts, and data immediate-access diagrams. The package includes all graphics symbols used. It provides for interactive construction of free-form diagrams and text that can be used in the preparation of documentation. The software runs on IBM 360 and up, MVS/TSO, VM/CMS, and CMS/TSO compatible computers. The minimum memory requirement is 900 kilobytes. The source code is written in FORTRAN. **MCDONNELL DOUGLAS INFORMATION SYSTEMS CO., 325 McDonnell Blvd., St. Louis, MO 63042; Telephone – 800/325-1551, 314/234-4117**

Structured Architect. This is a diagraming and repository CASE tool with integrated graphics, analysis, and documentation capabilities. It is based on Meta Systems integrated Encyclopedia, a unified DBMS of processes, data, and relationships. Capabilities include drawing and editing data flow diagrams with zoom and pan across a virtual drawing surface. The software runs on PC-MS/DOS compatible computers. The minimum memory requirement is 256 kilobytes. The source code is written in BASIC. **META SYSTEMS, LTD., 315 East Eisenhower Pkwy., Suite 200, Ann Arbor, MI 48108; Telephone – 313/663-6027**

Structured Architect-Integrator. This is a repository CASE tool that integrates Structured Architect data bases and identifies and protects shared information. It tracks sources of information and generates specification documents. The software runs on IBM MVS/TSO and VM/CMS; UNIX; DEC VAX, MicroVAX/VMS, and MicroVMS compatible computers. The minimum memory requirement is 2048 kilobytes. **META SYSTEMS, LTD., 315 East Eisenhower Pkwy., Suite 200, Ann Arbor, MI 48108; Telephone – 313/663-6027**

Sybase. This is a data dictionary/repository CASE tool with a relational DBMS integrated dictionary. It runs on DEC VAS/VMS, Sun/Unix. **SYBASE, INC., 6475 Christie Ave., Emeryville, CA 94608; Telephone – 415/596-3500**

SYLVA Foundry. This is a workbench that enablers users to structure CASE tools, methodology techniques, and environments. It contains tools for methodology guidance and control, technique creation, technique modification, open architecture interface with other tools, and diagram generation from external data bases. The package embeds invisible text and integrates trigger programs. The software runs on PC-MS/DOS compatible computers. A mouse is required. The minimum memory requirement is 640 kilobytes. The source code is written in C. **CADWARE INC., 50 Fitch St., New Haven, CT 06515; Telephone – 800/223-9273, 203/387-1853, 203/397-2908; FAX – 203/387-0114.**

SYLVA System Developer. This is a CASE workbench that contains tools for technique creation, technique modification, open architecture interface with other tools, and diagram generation via reverse engineering. Capabilities include screen prototyping and code generation. The software runs on PC-MS/DOS compatible computers. The minimum memory requirement is 1024 kilobytes. The source code is written in C. **CADWARE INC., 50 Fitch St., New Haven, CT 06515; Telephone – 800/223-9273, 203/387-1853, 203/397-2908; FAX – 203/387-0114**

System Architect. This is a diagraming and repository CASE tool that includes data dictionary/encyclopedia and diagraming capabilities. It provides multiple-methodology support. It can be used for tracking, leveling, on-line reporting, preparing project style sheets, audit trails, and import/export functions. It supports CAD-like graphics and desktop publishing techniques. The package is Microsoft Windows Interface Network compatible. The software runs on PC-MS/DOS compatible computers. The minimum memory requirement is 640 kilobytes. **POPKIN SOFTWARE SYSTEMS, INC., 111 Prospect St., Suite 505, Stamford, CT 06901; Telephone – 203/323-3434**

System Control. This is a configuration management CASE tool for system design structuring. It provides for print spooling, file table maintenance, and batch execution. It includes a menu driver and performs security functions. It runs on Honeywell Level 6, DPS 6+, DPS 6/GCOS, 6 MOD 400, and HVS-6 compatible computers. The minimum memory requirement is 28 kilobytes. **ICS SOFTWARE GROUP, LTD., 10410 North 31st Ave., Suite 401, Phoenix, AZ 85051; Telephone – 602/866-2600**

Tagus. This CASE tool provides an interface between the corporate repository and other CASE tools. It runs on IBM MVS, VM/CMS. **GLOBAL SOFTWARE, INC, P.O. Box 2813, Duxbury, MA 02331; Telephone – 617/934-0949; FAX – 617/934-0697**

Teamwork/Access. This is a repository CASE tool that provides for data base access and integration. It supports document preparation systems including Interleaf, VAXDocument, and Scribe. The software runs on UNIX, IBM RT, DEC VAX, Apollo, Sun, HP, and OS/2 compatible computers. A mouse is required. **CADRE TECHNOLOGIES, INC., 222 Richmond St., Suite 301, Providence, RI 02903; Telephone – 401/351-5959; FAX – 401/351-7380**

Teamwork/Ada (Ada Design Automation). This is a diagraming CASE tool that builds, revises, stores, and reviews and maintains complex system design. It serves as a design capture navigation and documentation tool. The package supports object-oriented design (OOD) techniques and Ada structure graph (ASG) notations. The software runs on DEC VAX, HP, Sun, and Apollo compatible computers. The minimum memory requirement is 2048 kilobytes. **CADRE TECHNOLOGIES, INC., 222 Richmond St., Suite 301, Providence, RI, 02903; Telephone – 401/351-5959; FAX – 401/351-7380**

Teamwork/IM (Information Modeling). This is a diagraming CASE tool that generates data definitions that associate entities and relationships. It includes an integrated information modeling module and a graphics-based entity-relationship diagram editor based on industry standard Chen notation. The software runs on DEC VAX,UNIX, HP, Sun, Apollo, and OS/2 compatible computers. The minimum memory requirement is 2048 kilobytes. **CADRE TECHNOLOGIES, INC., 222 Richmond St., Suite 301, Providence, RI, 02903; Telephone – 401/351-5959; FAX – 401/351-7380**

Teamwork/PCSA. This is a CASE workbench that includes a diagraming, syntax verifier, and repository tool. It creates and maintains leveled data flow diagrams and a project data dictionary. The package includes bit-block transfer operations and object-oriented pop-up menus on a bit-mapped high-resolution display with a mouse. Capabilities include dragging, rubber banding, smooth curve generation, consistency checking for diagram balancing, and global name replacement. The software runs on PC-MS/DOS compatible computers. The source code is written in C. A mouse is required. The minimum memory requirement is 572 kilobytes. **CADRE TECHNOLOGIES, INC., 222 Richmond St., Suite 301, Providence, RI, 02903; Telephone – 401/351-5959; FAX – 401/351-7380**

Teamwork/RT (Real-time). This is a diagraming CASE tool that provides real-time extensions to Teamwork/SA for real-time structured analysis. It includes a unified control/data flow diagram, state transition diagram, state event matrix, decision table, and a process activation table. Capabilities include displaying data/control flows alone or simultaneously. The package supports a multiuser environment. The software runs on UNIX, IBM RT, DEC VAX, Apollo, HP, and Sun compatible computers. The minimum memory requirement is 2048 kilobytes. The source code is written in C. **CADRE TECHNOLOGIES, INC., 222 Richmond St., Suite 301, Providence, RI 02903; Telephone – 401/351-5959; FAX – 401/351-7380**

Teamwork/SA (Systems Analysis). This is a CASE workbench for a multiuser environment. It integrates system development methodologies, distributed processing, and CAD/CAM/CAE and interactive graphics. It formulates the system requirements, organizes them into modules, and evaluates and maintains the models. Capabilities include examining requirements from multiple viewpoints and checking for errors and consistency. The software runs on UNIX, IBM RT, DEC VAX/VMS, Ultrix, Apollo, HP, Sun, and OS/2 compatible computers. A mouse is required. The minimum memory requirement is 2048 kilobytes. The source code is written in C. **CADRE TECHNOLOGIES, INC., 222 Richmond St., Suite 301, Providence, RI 02903; Telephone – 401/351-5959; FAX – 401/351-7380**

Teamwork for OS/2. Ths is a diagraming and syntax verifier CASE tool for integrated analysis and data modeling in the design environment. Capabilities include syntactical checking and balancing. The package supports work groups. It includes multiwindows, multitasking, and an intuitive graphics user interface. The software runs on OS/2 compatible computers. **CADRE TECHNOLOGIES, INC., 222 Richmond St., Suite 301, Providence, RI 02903; Telephone – 401/351-5959; FAX – 401/351-7380**

TeleArcs. This is a diagraming and SDM support tool for a CASE programming environment that utilizes TeleSoft's TeleGen2 Ada compilation system. It integrates Ada-sensitive tools required for design, development, and testing of software projects. It runs on top of the TeleGen2 Ada program library, includes an EMACS-style Ada language-sensitive editor, and provides for browsing, interactive cross-referencing, and graphical display. The package incorporates macros, command history, window management, symbolic references, system customization variables, and on-line help. The software runs on DEC VAX/VMS and Sun-3 compatible computers. **TELESOFT, 5959 Cornerstone Court, W., San Diego, CA 92121-9891; Telephone – 619/457-2700; FAX – 619/452-1334**

Telon Interface. This is a prototyping CASE tool. It provides a bridge between Nastec's Design Aid and Pansophic's Telon application generation system to facilitate direct conversion from design to prototype. The software runs on PC-MS/DOS and IBM mainframe compatible computers. The minimum memory requirement is 640 kilobytes. **NASTEC CORP., 24681 Northwestern Hwy., Southfield, MI 48075; Telephone – 800/872-8296, 313/353-3300; FAX – 313/353-0707**

Telon/Teamwork (Version 1.0). This is a front-end CASE tool to Pansophic's Telon application development system. It provides an interface between Telon and Cadre Technologies' Teamwork structured analysis and design tools for an OS/2 environment. The software runs on OS/2 compatible computers. A mouse is required. The minimum memory requirement is 6144 kilobytes. **PANSOPHIC SYSTEMS, INC., 709 Enterprise Dr., Oakbrook, IL 60521; Telephone – 800/323-7335, 312/572-6000**

Tip Plan/Define. This is a diagraming and project management CASE tool that can be used in developing strategic plans for an information system. It provides support for modeling, information and data usage, strategic plan analysis, and applications and data base development. The software runs on IBM/VM/CMS and MVS/XA compatible computers. The source code is written in PL/1. **NASTEC CORP., 24681 Northwestern Hwy., Southfield, MI 48075; Telephone – 800/872-8296, 313/353-3300; FAX - 313/353-0707**

Turbo Trace. This is a systems development and configuration management support tool that provides a methodology for verifying and tracing customer requirements. The package provides capabilities for requirements management, configuration management, and updating of configuration baselines on approval. The software runs on DEC VAX/VMS compatible computers. The source code is written in FORTRAN. *Year first installed* - 1986; *approximate number of installations - three; purchase price range* - $4000 to $12,500; *maintenance fees* - $2000 per year. **COMPUTER SCIENCE INNOVATIONS, INC., 1280 Clearmont St. NE, Palm Bay, FL 32905; Telephone – 407/676-2923; FAX – 407/676-2355**

Urma. This is a program information management CASE tool. It reads both language source code and data dictionary. It runs on IBM MVS. **GLOBAL SOFTWARE, INC, P.O. Box 2813, Duxbury, MA 02331; Telephone – 617/934-0949; FAX – 617/934-0697**

User Expert Systems. This is a prototyping, code generator, and SDM tool that supports the information systems development life cycle. It produces logical data models and information systems plans in the task priority sequences. The package defines the goals and objectives of the information system design process. Capabilities include painting forms and reports and generating data bases and applications systems in various formats and languages. The software runs on PC-MS/DOS compatible computers. The minimum memory requirement is 640 kilobytes. **INFORMATION ENGINEERING SYSTEMS CORP., 1235 Jefferson**

Davis Highway, Suite 1405, Crystal Gateway One, Arlington, VA, 22202; Telephone – 703/553-9222; FAX – 703/553-0157

VIS (View Integration System). This CASE package produces third-normal form and conceptual schema for data modeling. It supports Meta's RSI (Report Specification Interface) and PSL/PSA packages. The software runs on IBM MVS/TSO and VM/CMS; UNIX; DEC VAX and MicroVAX/VMS; and Ultrix compatible computers. **META SYSTEMS, LTD., 315 E. Eisenhower Parkway, Suite 200, Ann Arbor, MI 48108; Telephone – 313/663-6027; FAX – 313/663-6119**

Visible Analyst. This is a diagraming CASE tool that provides a selection of standard symbols. Capabilities include custom system creation, scrolling and zooming for large diagrams, dynamic symbol sizing, true point-to-point line drawing, and hierarchical decomposition. The software runs on PC-MS/DOS compatible computers. The minimum memory requirement is 640 kilobytes. The source code is written in compiled GW-BASIC and Macro-Assembler. **VISIBLE SYSTEMS CORP, 950 Winter St., Bay Colony Corporate Center, Waltham, MA 02154; Telephone – 617/890-2273; FAX – 617/890-8909**

Visible Analyst Workbench. This is an integrated workbench that provides for diagraming, error checking, and prototyping. It provides support for the implementation of the Yourdon and Gaine and Sarson methodologies. The package modules are Analyst, Prototyper, and Rules and Dictionaries. The software runs on PC-MS/DOS compatible computers. The minimum memory requirement is 640 kilobytes. The source code is written in compiled GW-BASIC and Macro-Assembler. **VISIBLE SYSTEMS CORP, 950 Winter St., Bay Colony Corporate Center, Waltham, MA 02154; Telephone – 617/890-2273; FAX – 617/890-8909**

Visible Analyst Workbench-Personal Edition. This is a diagraming CASE tool that allows users to work on one design project at a time. It provides for the creation of 25 flowcharts and diagrams. The software runs on PC-MS/DOS compatible computers. The minimum memory requirement is 640 kilobytes. **VISIBLE SYSTEMS CORP, 950 Winter St., Bay Colony Corporate Center, Waltham, MA 02154; Telephone – 617/890-2273; FAX – 617/890-8909**

Visible Dictionary. This is a repository CASE tool that is used with Visible Systems' Visible Analyst and Visible Rules packages. It maintains multiple record types, providing 132 lines of text entry per record. DMBS capabilities include wild card/search/find, next-prior searches, and indexing by entry type. The software runs on PC-MS/DOS compatible computers. The minimum memory requirement is 640 kilobytes. **VISIBLE SYSTEMS CORP., 950 Winter St., Bay Colony Corporate Center, Waltham, MA 02154; Telephone – 617/890-2273; FAX – 617/890-8909**

Visible Prototyper. This is a prototyping CASE tool that simulates any system, including mainframe and PC-based target systems. Capabilities include screen design, panel linking and branching, field masking, and use of data base for simulation, branching, and data modification. The software runs on PC-MS/DOS compatible computers. The minimum memory requirement is 640 kilobytes.

VISIBLE SYSTEMS CORP., 950 Winter St., Bay Colony Corporate Center, Waltham, MA 02154; Telephone – 617/890-2273; FAX – 617/890-8909

Visible Rules. This is a syntax verifier CASE tool that validates structured design models. It is used with Visible Systems' Visible Analyst software. Capabilities include data balancing and tracking of data flow splits. The rules work with both numbers and symbols. It interfaces with Visible Systems' Visible Dictionary to ensure consistency of diagrams. Error reports are provided in either screen or hard-copy form. The software runs on PC-MS/DOS compatible computers. The minimum memory requirement is 640 kilobytes. **VISIBLE SYSTEMS CORP., 950 Winter St., Bay Colony Corporate Center, Waltham, MA 02154; Telephone – 617/890-2273; FAX – 617/890-8909**

VM/IS and VM/IS BASE. These CASE tools provide an integrated software solution for intermediate to low-end 370 environments. The package consists of VM/IS BASE licensed program and eight optional application packages containing 28 licensed programs. The software runs on IBM 370 compatible computers. **IBM, Old Orchard Road, Armonk, NY 10504; Telephone – 914/765-1900**

vsDesigner. This is a CASE diagraming workbench that is used to create symbolic and textual diagrams of a program's data structure, data flow diagrams, and relationships with other programs. The package consists of drawing editor, integral word processor, attribute system, symbol editor, report generator, and virtual display CASE tools. The software runs on PC-MS/DOS compatible computers. The minimum memory requirement is 640 kilobytes. **INTERSOLV, 3200 TowerOaks Blvd., Rockville, MD 20852; Telephone – 800/638-8703, 301/230-3200; FAX – 301/231-7813**

vsObject Maker. This is a diagraming CASE tool that is used to modify or create new design techniques for use with Visual Software's vsDesigner CASE design package. The package provides color graphics capabilities for drawing objects. It defines data dictionary entries and specifies design rules. A bidirectional interface to other CASE tools is provided. The software runs on PC-MS/DOS compatible computers. A mouse is required. The minimum memory requirement is 640 kilobytes. **INTERSOLV, 3200 TowerOaks Blvd., Rockville, MD 20852; Telephone – 800/638-8703, 301/230-3200; FAX – 301/231-7813**

vsReporter. This is a repository and project management CASE tool that provides relational SQL capability. It is used to access design requirements, specifications, documentation, code, and project management information for advanced analyses and management report generation. The package supports ad hoc, interactive, and batch queries. A bidirectional interface to other CASE tools is provided. The software runs on PC-MS/DOS compatible computers. The minimum memory requirement is 640 kilobytes. **INTERSOLV, 3200 TowerOaks Blvd., Rockville, MD 20852; Telephone – 800/638-8703, 301/230-3200; FAX – 301/231-7813**

Workstation Aided Software Engineering. This is an SDM tool that supports the application development life cycle process by providing definitions, workstation panels, host connectivity activities, and documentation. The software runs on PC-MS/DOS compatible computers. The minimum memory requirement is 640 kilobytes. **IBM, Old Orchard Road, Armonk, NY 10504; Telephone – 914/765-1900**

XL/Interface for DB2. This is a repository CASE tool that transforms logical design data produced in Excelerator into physical design data, including SQL which can be used to implement a DB2 data base. The package provides access to Excelerator's analysis and ad hoc reporting capabilities. The software runs on PC-MS/DOS compatible computers. The minimum memory requirement is 640 kilobytes. **INTERSOLV, 3200 Tower Oaks Blvd., Rockville, MD 20852; Telephone – 301/230-3200; FAX – 301/231-7813**

XL/Interface Project Workbench. This is a project management CASE tool that links ITC's Excelerator systems analysis and design program with ABT's Project Workbench project management system. It provides for data transfer between project plan and project deliverables. Capabilities include creation of work breakdown structure (WBS) graphs that model relationships among various end products or deliverables. The software runs on PC-MS/DOS compatible computers. **INTERSOLV, 1 Main St., 9th Floor, Cambridge, MA 02142; Telephone – 800/777-8858; FAX – 617/577-8945**

XL/Quick Start. This is a diagraming CASE tool that contains standards and guidelines for all Excelerator entities and functions. It includes sample project and naming conventions, instructions for using graph commands, and standards for XLDictionary entries. The software runs on PC-MS/DOS, DEC VAX/VMS, and UNIX compatible computers. **INTERSOLV, 1 Main St., 9th Floor, Cambridge, MA 02142; Telephone – 800/777-8858; FAX – 617/577-8945**

XL/Recover. This is a reverse engineering CASE tool for the design recovery of COBOL systems. It runs on IBM PC/MS-DOS. **INTERSOLV, 1 Main St., 9th Floor, Cambridge, MA 02142; Telephone – 800/777-8858; FAX – 617/577-8945**

Index

ABOUT THE AUTHORS

STEVE AYER and FRANK PATRINOSTRO are founders of
Technical Communications Associates, located in
Sunnyvale, California. **Frank Patrinostro** is an
internationally-recognized documentation specialist. He
has served as a consultant to government and industry for
more than 20 years. **Steve Ayer** has worked as a
documentation specialist and methods analyst for several
leading companies, including ITT, Fairchild, and
Westinghouse. He also conducts seminars on how to
document a computer system. Together, they have
authored numerous publications on documentation
development and management.